PUTIN'S WARS

OSPREY
PUBLISHING

*Dedicated to all the many thousands of Russians who,
deriding Kremlin propaganda and defying Kremlin repression,
protested against the invasion of Ukraine.*

MARK GALEOTTI

PUTIN'S WARS

From
Chechnya
to
Ukraine

OSPREY PUBLISHING
Bloomsbury Publishing Plc
Kemp House, Chawley Park, Cumnor Hill, Oxford OX2 9PH, UK
29 Earlsfort Terrace, Dublin 2, Ireland
1385 Broadway, 5th Floor, New York, NY 10018, USA
E-mail: info@ospreypublishing.com
www.ospreypublishing.com

OSPREY is a trademark of Osprey Publishing Ltd

First published in Great Britain in 2022

A catalogue record for this book is available from the British Library.

ISBN: HB 978 1 4728 4754 6; PB 978 1 4728 4755 3; eBook 978 1 4728 4753 9;
ePDF 978 1 4728 4751 5; XML 978 1 4728 4752 2

22 23 24 25 26   10 9 8 7 6 5 4 3 2 1

Plate section image credits are given in full in the List of Illustrations (pp. 8–10).

Images from the Russian Ministry of Defence and Kremlin.ru are available under CC BY 4.0,
https://creativecommons.org/licenses/by/4.0/.
Maps by www.bounford.com
Index by Zoe Ross

Typeset by Deanta Global Publishing Services, Chennai, India
Printed and bound in Great Britain by CPI (Group) UK Ltd, Croydon CR0 4YY

Contents

Author's Note

Translating out of Cyrillic always poses challenges. I have chosen to transliterate names as they are pronounced, and have also ignored the diacritical 'soft' and 'hard' signs found in the original. The only exceptions are names that have acquired common forms in English – for example, I use the spelling 'Gorbachev' rather than the phonetically correct 'Gorbachov'. I also accept local practice, so what used to be called Kiev is rendered as Kyiv, but the names of Russian-speaking Ukrainians in the rebel Donbas region are given Russian-style.

In addition, the maps show Crimea as part of Russia purely to illustrate Russian military placements, not in any way to imply an acknowledgement of Moscow's claims to the region.

List of Illustrations

List of Maps and Diagrams

MAPS

DIAGRAMS

Abbreviations

APC	Armoured Personnel Carrier
AV-MF	*Aviatsiya Voyenno-Morskovo Flota*, Naval Aviation
BF	*Baltiisky Flot*, Baltic Fleet
BMP	*Boyevaya Mashina Pyekhoty*, Infantry Combat Vehicle
BTG	Battalion Tactical Group, self-contained and modular manoeuvre force of 700–900 soldiers generated by a brigade
CFE	Conventional Forces in Europe Treaty (1990)
ChF	*Chyornomorsky Flot*, Black Sea Fleet
CIS	Commonwealth of Independent States
DA	*Dalnaya Aviatsiya*, Long-Range Aviation
FA	*Frontovaya Aviatsiya*, Frontal Aviation
FSB	*Federalnaya Sluzhba Bezopasnosti*, Federal Security Service, main domestic security and counter-intelligence agency
FSK	*Federalnaya Sluzhba Kontrrazvedki*, Federal Counter-Intelligence Service, predecessor to the FSB, which it became in 1995
GBU	*Gruppa Boyevovo Upravleniya*, Combat Management Group, within the National Defence Management Centre

GOU	*Glavnoye Operativnoye Upravleniye*, Main Operational Directorate (of the General Staff)
GOZ	*Gosudarstvenny Oboronny Zakaz*, State Defence Order
GPV	*Gosudarstvennaya Programma Vooruzheniya*, State Armament Plan
GRU	*Glavnoye Razvedyvatelnyoe Upravlenie*, Main Intelligence Directorate (of the General Staff), military intelligence (later officially known as GU)
GU	*Glavnoye Upravleniye*, Main Directorate (of the General Staff), military intelligence (from 2010, though still widely called GRU)
GVS	*Gruppirovka Voisk v Sirii*, Group of Forces in Syria
ICBM	Inter-Continental Ballistic Missile
IFV	Infantry Fighting Vehicle
INF	Intermediate-Range Nuclear Forces Treaty (1987)
KF	*Kaspiiskaya Flotilya*, Caspian Flotilla
KGB	*Komitet Gosudarstvennoi Bezopasnosti*, Committee for State Security, Soviet intelligence and security service
KSSO	*Komandovaniye Sil Spetsialnalnykh Operatsii*, Special Operations Forces Command
KV	*Kosmicheskiye Voiska*, Space Forces
MChS	*Ministerstvo po Chrezvychainym Situatsiyam*, Ministry for Emergency Situations
MLRS	Multiple-Launch Rocket System
MP	*Morskaya Pyekhota*, Naval Infantry
MRAU	*Massirovanny Raketno-Aviatsionny Udar*, Massed Missile-Aviation Strike
MRL	Multiple Rocket Launch system
MVD	*Ministerstvo Vnutrennykh Del*, Ministry of Internal Affairs

NTsUO — *Natsionalny Tsentr Upravleniya Oboronoi*, National Defence Management Centre

OGFV — *Obedinennaya Gruppa Federalnykh Voisk*, Joint Group of Federal Forces (in Chechnya)

OMON — *Otryad Militsii Osobennovo Naznacheniya*, Special Designation Police Unit, later renamed *Otryad Mobilny Osobennovo Naznacheniya*, Special Designation Mobile Unit, riot police

OMRPSN — *Otdelny Morskoy Razvedyvatelny Punkt Spetsialnovo Naznacheniya*, Independent Special Designation Naval Reconnaissance Point

OOSN — *Otdelny Otryad Spetsialnovo Naznacheniya*, Independent Special Designation Detachment (*Spetsnaz*)

OSCE — Organization for Security Cooperation in Europe

OSK — *Operativnoye Strategicheskoye Komandavaniye*, Operational-Strategic Command

OSKVKO — *Obedinyonnoye Strategicheskoye Komandovaniye Vozdushno-Kosmicheskoi Oborony*, Operational-Strategic Aerospace Defence Command

OSpN PDSS — *Otryad Spetsialnovo Naznacheniya Borby s Podvodnymi Diversionnymi Silami i Sredstvami*, Independent Special Designation Detachments to Combat Submarine Subversive Forces and Means

PVO-PRO — *Voiska Protivovozdushnoy i Protivoraketnoy Oborony*, Air and Missile Defence Forces

RPG — Rocket-Propelled Grenade

RVSN — *Raketniye Voiska Strategicheskovo Naznacheniya*, Strategic Rocket Forces

SAM — Surface-to-Air Missile

SF — *Severny Flot*, Northern Fleet

SKVO	*Severo-Kavkazsky Voyenny Okrug*, North Caucasus Military District
SPG	Self-Propelled Guns
SV	*Sukhoputnye Voiska*, Ground Forces
SVR	*Sluzhba Vneshnei Razvedky*, Foreign Intelligence Service
TF	*Tikhoökeansky Flot*, Pacific Fleet
TsVO	*Tsentralny Voyenny Okrug*, Central Military District
VDV	*Vozdushno-Desantniye Voiska*, Air Assault Troops
VKS	*Vozdushno-Kosmicheskiye Sily*, Aerospace Forces
VO	*Voyenny Okrug*, Military District
VP	*Voyennaya Politsiya*, Military Police
VTA	*Voyenno-Transportnaya Aviatsiya*, Military Transport Aviation
VV	*Vnutrenniye Voiska*, Interior Troops
VVKO	*Voiska Vozdushno-Kosmicheskoye Oborony*, Military Aerospace Forces
VVO	*Vostochny Voyenny Okrug*, Eastern Military District
YuVO	*Yuzhny Voyenny Okrug*, Southern Military District
ZATO	*Zakrytoye Administrativno-Territorialnoye Obrazovaniye*, Closed Administrative-Territorial Entity
ZVO	*Zapadny Voyenny Okrug* – Western Military District

Ranks: Lt. (Lieutenant), Maj. (Major), Lt. Col. (Lieutenant Colonel), Col. (Colonel), Maj. Gen. (Major General), Lt. Gen. (Lieutenant General), Col. Gen. (Colonel General), Gen. (General), R. Adm. (Rear Admiral), Adm. (Admiral)

Cast of Characters

Bortnikov, Alexander: Director of the Federal Security Service since 2008, a loyal supporter of Putin's and acolyte of Patrushev's.

Dudayev, Dzhokar: The Soviet air force general who became the first president of Chechnya when it proclaimed independence (1981–86), presiding over first a virtual gangster take-over of the republic, and then a bloody war with Moscow, before being killed by Russian missiles.

Gerasimov, Gen. Valery: Chief of the General Staff from 2012, the longest-serving incumbent in that role since the Soviet era. A tough tank officer and effective uniformed strong right arm to Minister Shoigu.

Girkin, Igor: Known by his nom de guerre 'Strelkov', 'Shooter', a nationalist ex-FSB officer and military re-enactor who played a crucial role in triggering the Donbas conflict in 2014.

Gorbachev, Mikhail: Last General Secretary of the Communist Party of the Soviet Union (1985–91), first and last elected President of the Soviet Union (1988–91), the man who hoped to reform the USSR and instead ended up dissolving it.

Grachyov, Gen. Pavel: An undeniably brave paratrooper and Afghan War veteran, out of his depth as Yeltsin's first defence minister (1992–96), facing particular criticism for his inept handling of the First Chechen War.

Ivanov, Sergei: The urbane but hawkish KGB foreign intelligence officer who became Putin's defence minister, deputy prime minister, chief of staff and then apparent heir, until the death of his elder son in 2014 seems to have made him reassess his priorities. (He became the Special Presidential Representative for the Environment, Ecology and Transport, and of all his achievements is reportedly proudest of saving the Siberian Tiger from extinction.)

Kadyrov, Ramzan: The erratic and authoritarian warlord who rules the Chechen Republic as a personal fiefdom, even while swearing his undying loyalty to Putin.

Kryuchkov, Viktor: Sinister but smart final head of the KGB, who turned against Gorbachev when he opted for reforming rather than preserving the old USSR and the Communist one-party state, but who didn't prove smart enough to carry off a coup.

Lavrov, Sergei: Russia's long-serving (2004–) foreign minister, once a legend in diplomatic circles, yet from 2014 increasingly side-lined and relegated to the miserable task of defending the indefensible and clearing up the diplomatic messes created by others.

Lebed, Gen. Alexander: Gravel-voiced paratrooper commander who became Yeltsin's security chief, but who soon fell out with him as he never knew when to keep quiet.

Makarov, Gen. Nikolai: Highly competent Chief of the General Staff 2007– 12, the architect of the subsequent military reforms that were introduced by Shoigu and Gerasimov.

Maskhadov, Aslan: A brilliant Chechen rebel commander and a failed civilian leader, a decent man squeezed between a revanchist Russia and jihadists at home.

Medvedev, Dmitry: Part of the team of former members of St Petersburg mayor Sobchak's team that Putin brought into government; Medvedev was his chief of staff, then presidential stand-in 2008–12 while Putin effectively ruled from the prime minister's chair, then prime minister under Putin until 2020 when he was given something of a make-work position as deputy chair of the Security Council. Generally regarded as at once liberal and lightweight.

Mishustin, Mikhail: Medvedev's successor as prime minister, a technocratic manager who believes that centralization, automation and big data can make administering Russia efficiently possible – at last.

Patrushev, Nikolai: Ascetic KGB veteran and perhaps the leading hawk in Putin's inner circle. Secretary of the Security Council since 2008, Patrushev is in effect the national security adviser, and has played a key role in every major foreign policy decision since before 2014.

Pugo, Boriss: Latvian-born hard-line Minister of Internal Affairs who played a key role in the 1991 August Coup, and shot himself when it failed.

Putin, Vladimir: 'The Body' in Presidential Administration slang: the ultimate decider but also a man happy to let his subordinates come up with ideas for him to approve or reject, as he prosecutes his campaign to both stay in office (he can theoretically remain until 2036) and make Russia a great power again.

Rutskoi, Alexander: A pilot and decorated Afghan war hero, who for a while was Yeltsin's vice-president until breaking with him spectacularly in 1993.

Serdyukov, Anatoly: 'The Furniture Salesman', the tax official who became Defence Minister 2007–12 and became monumentally unpopular with the High Command for forcing necessary but difficult reform on this most conservative of institutions.

Sergeyev, Marshal Igor: The former commander of the Strategic Rocket Forces and then Defence Minister 1997–2001, whose time in office is frankly unmemorable.

Shoigu, Sergei: One of the most popular and powerful figures in Russian politics, the former Minister for Emergency Situations and Governor of Moscow Region, who became Defence Minister in 2012 and has presided over a period of both continued military modernization and also unprecedented activity, but whose inexorable rise may be at an end with the 2022 invasion of Ukraine.

Yazov, Marshal Dmitry: Soviet Defence Minister (1987–91) who presided over the draw-down of Soviet forces from Afghanistan and Central Europe, but balked at the reform of the USSR and joined the 1991 August Coup, after which he was dismissed and imprisoned.

Yeltsin, Boris: A Communist Party official turned anti-Party radical, who in many ways forced Gorbachev's hand in making him dissolve the USSR. Much more effective as a political insurgent than a nation-builder, he presided over a decade of near-anarchy in a haze of alcohol, until handing power to Putin in 1999.

Zolotov, Gen. Viktor: 'Putin's Doberman', the former KGB bodyguard who became head of the Presidential Security Service (2000–13) and then first head of the National Guard (2016–); regarded as a man who puts loyalty to the boss above petty constraints of legality.

Chronology

1991	December	Dissolution of the USSR: formal independence of Russia under Boris Yeltsin
1992	March	Russian Defence Ministry established
	March–July	Transnistrian War
1993	January	USA and Russia sign START II arms control treaty
	October	'October Coup' as Yeltsin forces dissolution of Congress of People's Deputies
	November	New Military Doctrine adopted
1994	October	Abortive Russian-backed attack on Grozny
	November	Start of First Chechen War
	December	Budapest Memorandum sees Belarus, Ukraine and Kazakhstan agree to transfer nuclear weapons to Russia
1995	January	Grozny falls to federal forces
	June	Chechen rebels seize hospital in Budyonnovsk
1996	April	Chechen leader Dudayev killed
	July	Grachyov replaced as Defence Minister by Rodionov
	August	Yeltsin re-elected in elections suspected of irregularities
		Rebels retake Grozny
		Khasavyurt Accord ends First Chechen War
1997	May	Rodionov replaced as Defence Minister by Sergeyev
		Agreement on division of the Black Sea Fleet

1998	July	Putin appointed director of the Federal Security Service
1999	June	'Pristina Dash' in Kosovo
	August	Chechen radicals invade Dagestan
		Putin appointed Prime Minister
	September	Apartment bombings across Russia
	October	Start of Second Chechen War
	December	Yeltsin resigns in favour of Putin
2000	February	Grozny falls to federal forces
	March	Putin wins presidential election
	August	*Kursk* nuclear submarine sinks, with all hands; Putin faces criticism for his tardy response
2001	March	Sergeyev replaced as Defence Minister by Ivanov
2002	July	USA withdraws from 1972 Anti-Ballistic Missile (ABM) treaty
	October	Chechen terrorists seize Moscow Dubrovka theatre
2003	June	USA and Russia sign Strategic Offensive Reductions Treaty (SORT)
2004	March	Putin wins second presidential term by landslide
	September	Chechen terrorists seize school in Beslan
2005	March	Chechen rebel leader Aslan Maskhadov killed
2006	July	Chechen warlord Shamil Basayev killed
	November	Former FSB officer Alexander Litvinenko dies in London of radioactive polonium poisoning blamed on Moscow
2007	February	Putin delivers belligerent speech at Munich Security Conference
		Ivanov replaced as Defence Minister by Serdyukov
		Ramzan Kadyrov becomes head of Chechnya
	June	Baluyevsky replaced as Chief of the General Staff by Makarov
	November	Russia suspends participation in the 1990 Conventional Armed Forces in Europe (CFE) treaty

2008	March	Dmitry Medvedev wins presidential elections as Putin's proxy; Putin to become Prime Minister
	August	Russo-Georgian War
	October	Serdyukov announces 'New Look' military reforms
2009	April	Moscow formally announces end of military operation in Chechnya
2010	April	USA and Russia sign New START strategic arms treaty
	May	*MV Moscow University* incident off Somalia
2012	March	Putin wins presidential elections, followed by widespread protests
	November	Serdyukov replaced as Defence Minister by Shoigu
		Makarov replaced as Chief of the General Staff by Gerasimov
2014	February	'Euromaidan' revolution: President Yanukovych flees Ukraine
		Russian forces seize Crimea
	April	Strelkov leads incursion into the Donbas
	July	Malaysian Airlines airliner MH17 shot down by rebels over the Donbas
	August	Battle for Ilovaisk sees first substantial deployment of Russian troops into the Donbas
	September	Minsk Protocol signed
	October	Sabotage of Vrbětice arms depot, Czech Republic
2015	February	Minsk Package of Measures (Minsk II) signed
	August	Creation of combined Aerospace Forces (VKS)
	September	Russia deploys forces to Syria
	November	Turkey shoots down Russian bomber operating over Syria
2016	March	Battle for Palmyra
	April	Formation of National Guard
	July–December	Battle for Aleppo
2017	January	Battle for Avdiivka
	April	Terrorist suicide attack on the St Petersburg metro system

2018	February	Wagner Group decimated at Deir ez-Zor
	March	Attempted poisoning of former spy Sergei Skripal in Salisbury blamed on Russia by UK government
		Putin wins fourth presidential election
		In his 'state of the federation' speech, Putin announces six new strategic weapons systems
2020	September	Armenia–Azerbaijan War
2021	March	Russia begins troop build-up on Ukrainian border
	April	Kerch Straits incident
	December	Moscow issues demands for 'security guarantees' over Ukraine
2022	January	CSTO deployment to Kazakhstan
	February	Launch of full-scale invasion of Ukraine

I

Introduction

The annual Victory Day parade through Red Square says so much about how war and the military are seen by the Kremlin and the Russian people alike. Although there is also room for solemnity and reflection in the overall commemoration of the perhaps 27 million Soviets who died (14 million of them Russian) in what they call the Great Patriotic War – the Second World War – the parade itself is an unapologetic celebration of triumph and military power. Thousands of soldiers arrayed in their ranks delivering the traditional *Ura!* cheer, the latest military hardware rumbling over the cobbles, the 'Victory Banner' (or at least a faithful copy of the original red flag hoisted in Berlin by the 150th Rifle Division) carried the length of Red Square by a goose-stepping honour guard of the Moscow Commandant's Regiment Honour and Colours Guards to the strains of 'Sacred War':

Arise, you mighty motherland,
Arise for Sacred War
To crush the evil fascist hordes,
Unite and drive them back.

Foreign dignitaries and ambassadors will be invited to join the watching crowd, from wartime allies to present geopolitical fellow travellers. Nonetheless, they are there not to participate, but to witness, because for the best part of two decades, this has been Vladimir Putin's show. He only went through minimal reserve training at university, then had his national service obligation waived by joining the Soviet security and intelligence service (KGB: *Komitet Gosudarstvennoi Bezopasnosti*), but nonetheless he has done everything he can to associate himself with his country's martial glories. The photo opportunity of Putin in a jet's cockpit, hefting a new gun, or driving a tank has become a cliché (and also the subject of many a cringingly sycophantic calendar). So too, presiding over *Dyen Pobedy*, Victory Day, is an unmissable chance to connect himself not just with triumph, but also a specifically Russian one.

The Russian Great Patriotic War ran 1941–45, beginning with the Nazi invasion of the Soviet Union, not the invasion of Poland in 1939 (after all, Stalin also bit himself off a piece of this traditional enemy at the same time), nor even the occupation of France. It is also celebrated on 9 May, not 8 May as elsewhere. This is not, as some conclude, a bloody-minded statement of independence, simply a product of differing time zones: by the time the final peace treaty had been concluded, it was next morning in Moscow.

But there is also something more specific about Victory Day, and that is the degree to which it is still genuinely a national event. The skies are almost always blue (not least thanks to the Russian air force seeding potential rain clouds with dry ice to make them precipitate before the day), and loudspeakers around the city are blaring patriotic tunes. Couples walk the streets wearing matching *pilotkas*, the distinctive khaki sidecap of the Red Army, and children hand flowers to veterans, whose chests rattle and glitter with their old medals. Of course, the Kremlin does everything it can to stir up and encourage this expression of nostalgic patriotism, from the huge murals extolling past generals, to its take-over and then relaunch of the 'Immortal Regiment' movement in which people march holding the black-and-white picture of a fallen family member. This is not just some empty, state-mandated ritual, though. People tie the black-and-orange St George's ribbon, symbol of Russian military success, to their car rear mirrors not because Putin tells them to, but because they want to.

Much the same is true of the militaristic and patriotic t-shirts you can pick up in kiosks around the city or, if you want to go up-market, the over-priced Army Stores like the one sited – in what I cannot help but suspect is an act of retail trolling – right in front of the American embassy on Novinsky Boulevard. (My favourite has a picture of Foreign

Minister Sergei Lavrov on the front, and Defence Minister Sergei Shoigu on the back, with the caption 'If you don't want to talk to Lavrov … You'll have to deal with Shoigu.') It is precisely the way in which cynical state propaganda and genuine popular enthusiasm converge on the nation's military and its wars that is striking, distinctive and, at times, disturbing.

ARMY GAMES

Like many, I never really lost the inner nine-year-old who rejoices at the sight of armed soldiers marching in lockstep, or the rumbling, squealing, slab-sided lumps of metal that are modern war machines. To a large extent, it is probably because we have never had to face them in war. One of the best ways to get a sneak preview of the latter is to bag a place along Tverskaya, one of Moscow's great radial boulevards, during a *repetitsiya*, one of the rehearsals in the week before the actual parade. The brand-new T-14 Armata tank, with its unmanned gun turret; BMPT Terminator tank support fighting vehicles, bristling with missile pods and autocannon; blocky Ural Typhoon troop carriers in pale grey National Guard livery; there's more than enough hardware on display. Yet equally on display is the equal-opportunities nature of the crowd. Young women dressed up for a night on the town snap selfies in front of self-propelled guns before heading off to the bar. Pensioners lean on the metal barricades set up along the road by the police and benignly watch BMP-2 infantry fighting vehicles line up in order. Pre-teen girls in pink jackets jostle as eagerly as their male counterparts to watch the hardware. Fun for all the family?

I had a similar reminder of the way war and warriors were still closer to the hearts of the Russian people when, courtesy of no less than HBO Sports, I attended the finals of the Tank Biathlon at the 2018 International Army Games. Billed as the 'military Olympics', Russia set up these games in 2015 and they have grown to include over 30 countries participating in more than 30 air, land and sea competitions, from drone-flying to dog-handling. As I wrote at the time, 'Russia's successful blending of sport, warfare, soft power, and spectacle is a high-octane form of public entertainment.'[1] The biathlon finals, for example, saw teams from Russia, China, Belarus and Kazakhstan racing T-72B3 tanks (except for the Chinese, who had brought their equivalent, the Type 96) around a course, fording water obstacles and blowing up targets with their 125mm guns. An excitable commentator provided the voice-over and the crowd could watch close-up pictures of the more distant action on great screens facing the bleachers. Like any sponsored race car, the Russian tank was even emblazoned with the logo of Uralvagonzavod, its manufacturer.

From the state's point of view, this is an exercise in military soft power, bringing together once and potential future allies, from India to Israel. It's also something of a showroom in advance of the serious arms dealing. It is a huge exercise in military public relations, though. Away from the deafening roar of the tank engines, the Alabino testing ground is converted for the duration of the event into something of a military theme park. It is not just that there are tanks to be clambered over, and displays to be watched. Kids queue up for a chance to shoot an AK-74 assault rifle, while their proud parents take pictures to send to granddad. There are souvenirs for sale in the Voentorg PX service booths, and then the family can head to the big olive drab mess tents – surely one of the rare times people pay good money for the privilege of tucking into Russian army *kasha* (buckwheat porridge) and stew.

RUSSIA AND WAR

All nations have to some extent been shaped by wars, after all – not just fighting them, but building the tax system to pay for them – but this is especially true for Russia, a country with no natural borders, located at the crossroads of Europe and Asia. The very origins of what would eventually become Russia lie in invasion, with the advent of Viking – 'Varangian' – conquerors in the ninth century, and since then, its people have been the targets of whomever is the rising military power of the age, whether the Mongols in the 13th century, the Teutonic Knights, Poles or Swedes in the 13th, 17th or 18th centuries respectively, Napoleon in the 19th or Hitler in the 20th. The Russians have not simply been on the defence, though. The very boundaries of their nation in its various incarnations – Muscovy, Tsarist Russia, the Soviet Union and now the Russian Federation – have to a large degree been drawn by wars, products of the balance between Russia's capacity and desire to expand, and the will and strength of neighbours to resist.

Wars have also shaped Russia's myths, its stories about itself. When Prince Dmitry of Moscow defeated the Tatar-Mongol Golden Horde at Kulikovo in 1380, it was an impressive feat of generalship, but by no means such a turning point as would later be claimed. After all, two years later, a Golden Horde army would take and sack Moscow and force Dmitry to swear renewed fealty to the Khans, and it would be another century before the Russians were free of the so-called 'Mongol Yoke'. Yet Dmitry was able to spin it as a triumph and it was subsequently mythologized as proof of a fundamental message that Vladimir Putin would later embrace: that when the Russians were divided, they were prey, but when they were united, they were unbeatable.[2]

The success of the 'People's Militias' driving Polish-Lithuanian Commonwealth forces out of Russia in 1612 was hijacked by the new Romanov dynasty to burnish their patriotic credentials (even though they had done their fair share of collaboration with the invaders). Defeat of the French in 1812 – in what the Russians call not the Napoleonic but the 'Patriotic War' – was not only a case study in the value of defensive depth, but became an excuse to avoid reform at home for the next 50 years.[3] Defeat in the Crimea forced the beginnings of reform on the regime,[4] but then another in the 1904–05 Russo-Japanese War rocked tsarism,[5] being seen as a symbol of a wider malaise of backwardness and incompetence in the empire. The disaster that the First World War brought to Russia finally brought down a dynasty that had endured for three centuries. Conversely, the epic story of endurance and then victory during the Great Patriotic War consolidated the Soviet Union's status as a superpower, and conveyed on the brutal Stalinist police state a legitimacy at home that had hitherto escaped it.

There was nowhere to go but down, and in hindsight, that's exactly the trajectory the Soviet Union took. To be sure, it was able to crush peaceful expressions of protest in its new imperial possessions: East Germany in 1953, Hungary in 1956, Czechoslovakia in 1968. However fearsome it seemed in the nose-to-nose confrontation in Cold War Europe, though, until 1979, the closest the Red Army came to fighting a war was a seven-month undeclared border conflict with China in 1969, much of which was actually fought by Border Troops. In 1979, however, the Soviet Union, already in what proved terminal decline, followed in the footsteps of Alexander the Great and the British Empire and headed into Afghanistan (admittedly, as the United States would later demonstrate, this seems an imperial temptation as irresistible as it is injudicious). A textbook commando operation to seize the capital, Kabul, and depose the erratic Afghan dictator Hafizullah Amin,[6] was the start of what would prove a painful and difficult war. The Soviets never lost on the battlefield, but they could not win against the rebels, either.[7] Ten years later a new Soviet leader, Mikhail Gorbachev, admitted defeat and brought the boys home.

Defeat in Afghanistan – a relatively limited war, for all its brutality, whose toll of some 15,000 Soviet lives lost in a decade was dwarfed even by deaths on the country's roads[*] – was not in itself a cause of the Soviet collapse, but instead it was almost a metaphor for the reasons behind its fall. A nation with an economy that was falling increasingly behind the West's; ruled by old men out of touch with what was going on in their own country, let alone outside its own borders; being hollowed out by corruption, cynicism, alcoholism and apathy. I remember once talking to a Ukrainian *afganets* – one of the veterans of the war – who had only been back less than a year. He recounted tales of officers who launched raids on Afghan villages purely as excuses to loot, of soldiers selling guns for hashish, of political officers who by day would lecture them that they were there to help the legitimate government against US-backed mercenaries, and by night pass round a bottle and curse out the Kremlin leadership as bitterly as any of the men. Then, when that *afganets* came home, he returned to food queues, empty promises of a new flat, and triumphalist news that Soviet victories were being fêted by a happy Afghan people on TV. No wonder he went from disillusion to nationalism, getting involved in the anti-Soviet activism that would soon help midwife an independent Ukraine.

Then, at the very end of 1991, after miners' strikes and inter-ethnic unrest, an abortive hard-line coup and declarations of independence from many of the constituent states of the Union of Soviet Socialist Republics, President Gorbachev signed his last decree, dissolving the Union. Russia was its own master, but in a crumbling house and a rough neighbourhood. The 1990s, as will be discussed in Part One, were to a great extent a time of chaos and crisis. Post-Soviet Eurasia faced border disputes, communal violence and economic freefall. The Russian military, gripped by indiscipline, criminality and demoralization, could

---

[*] Some 40,000 Soviets died directly or indirectly from road accidents every year in the 1980s.

not even quell a rebellion in the North Caucasus region of Chechnya, whose population accounted for only around one-hundredth of the Russian Federation's.[8] Internationally, the former great power was regarded as a great problem, an irrelevance except when it came to its under-secured nuclear arsenal or the erratic foreign policy of its first president, Boris Yeltsin.

PUTIN

When Yeltsin was replaced by Putin, it is perhaps unsurprising that he was so determined to do something about all this, and as Part Two shows, he quickly moved to begin to rebuild the military, throwing it into a second Chechen war that saw the rebels finally subdued with a mix of extravagant firepower and the deployment of loyal Chechens. Hopes of a pragmatically positive relationship with the West – he even floated the idea of Russia joining NATO – soon soured, though (see Part Three). Increasingly, Putin would see Russia's military strength as not just a guarantee of its security but also what would make the country a credible international power again. He stepped up his campaign to revive Russia's military capabilities, thanks to bountiful oil and gas revenues (see Part Four).

Nonetheless, the Kremlin was well aware that even rearmed, Russia's military strength was not NATO's match, and that in any case open conflict would be disastrous and self-destructive. Hence, as Part Five discusses, the rise of new forms of warfare, often covert and indirect, fought by cyber-attack, disinformation, assassination and mercenaries. These have been deployed to greater or lesser extents in the range of conflicts in which Russia has engaged since, from the five-day war in Georgia in 2008, through the annexation of Crimea in 2014, to interventions in Syria and beyond, culminating in the 2022 invasion of Ukraine.

Nonetheless, Russia under Putin – and his successor, whoever and whenever that will be – still faces serious challenges. As Chapter 28 considers, these range from the near-inevitability of renewed conflict in the North Caucasus to growing rivalries within the countries it considers to be its 'Near Abroad', its sphere of influence. Above all, will a rising China, so far publicly hailed as a great ally, become a threat? Or maybe the real question is *when* it will do so. Either way, Putin – a man clearly thinking of his place in history – has, like many a prince or tsar before him, turned to military might and warfighting as a crucial instrument not just in re-asserting his country's place in the world, but also in rebuilding a national myth of pride, glory and success. He is actively recreating a narrative of Russia's evolution through the centuries that emphasizes the lessons that suit his interests: that the world is a dangerous place, that Russians need to stay united and disciplined, that to look weak is to invite attack, and that, as Tsar Alexander III memorably asserted, 'Russia has just two allies: its army and its navy.'

And yet opinion polls show that Russians themselves seem unconvinced. They may have celebrated the return of Crimea to Russian control but they were sceptical about the undeclared war in the Ukrainian Donbas that ensued and led to the 2022 invasion,[9] just as they are lukewarm about the deployment to Syria, however much the state media hypes it as a successful modern 'techno-war'. Most simply do not see Russia as being under a military threat, even while the Kremlin's propaganda machine pumps out all kinds of toxic claims of Western plots and looming dangers. For all that, the armed forces are a symbol of national pride and power, and while not all Putin's wars can be considered victories, there seems no likelihood of any pacifist turn under Putin – or, quite possibly, under his eventual successor, whoever that may be.

This was made starkly clear in February 2022 when Putin unleashed a full-scale invasion of Ukraine. By that stage, this book's manuscript had been completed, but it was impossible to ignore this extraordinary escalation in his belligerence and audacity. The main body of the text has been lightly edited in light of this and a new chapter added to reflect the situation as in June 2022.

PART ONE
Before Putin

2

Born in Chaos

I was sitting in the lieutenant's pokey little kitchen in an overcrowded flat half-way up a tower block in Moscow's impoverished southern Chertanovo neighbourhood. It was 1990, and he had just made it back home from a year spent in Tajikistan after his unit was withdrawn from Afghanistan at the end of that nasty war. He was not in a good shape; apparently he still had nightmares replaying the time he almost didn't get out of a burning BTR personnel carrier when it hit a mine, he obsessively fiddled with a red star cap badge, and he drank vodka like, well, a cliché Russian. He was angry and haunted, but certainly no fool, and he was sure tough times were coming. 'It's all going to fall apart, you know, and when it does, everyone is going to prey on us. They always do. When we're weak, they come, they always do.' He took another swig from the bottle. 'And before you know it, we'll need another *vozhd*', a 'boss'.

He wasn't alone in such assumptions, and considering Russia's deep-seated historical fears about its security, it is easy to understand why the events of the late 1980s and early 1990s created such concerns in Moscow, and contributed to a consensus within the elite that their country needed a strongman to replace Boris Yeltsin and reassert regional hegemony over a Eurasia riven with border disputes, inter-ethnic rivalries, historical grudges and potential foreign interference.[1]

THE SOVIET DISUNION

After all, the collapse of the USSR was in some ways extraordinary in its bloodlessness and orderliness, compared with the break-up of so many other multi-ethnic states, such as the Austro-Hungarian Empire before it or Yugoslavia in the 1990s. The three Baltic States – Estonia, Latvia and Lithuania – had only been annexed in 1940, and were likewise the first to declare themselves independent, in 1990, although this was only really achieved the next year. While there were growing nationalist movements opposed to the Soviet Communist Party in the other 12 constituent republics that made up the USSR, it is questionable whether they really expected or, in some cases, wanted a rapid dissolution of the Union. Rather, the 1980s had seen the country grind to a halt: the economy was in chaos, the shops were empty, and attempts by Mikhail Gorbachev to try to reform the system actually seemed to be making things worse. The campaign of *glasnost*, of 'openness' or 'speaking out', had unearthed all kinds of dark episodes from the recent past, from Stalin's murderous purges to the incompetence behind the 1986 Chernobyl nuclear disaster, when an accident at a power plant in Ukraine blew a plume of radiation across Russia and Europe.

As Gorbachev increasingly saw the Communist Party and its iron grip on the political system as the key problem blocking reform, he began a limited democratization of the system. This encouraged and empowered a whole new generation of political leaders to emerge, who supported neither Gorbachev nor the Party, but instead advocated more freedoms – and ultimately independence – for their own republic. In some cases, this took an ugly turn. Turkic Azerbaijan and Christian Armenia had a long history of mutual rivalry and intolerance, and there had already been local cases in which Armenians living in cities in Azerbaijan were attacked, driven out, or even lynched. In January 1990, though, in what was the harbinger of later violence, Azerbaijan's capital Baku experienced a seven-day orgy of violence that left around 50 ethnic Armenians dead and thousands driven out, before Moscow declared martial law and sent in troops bloodily to impose order, at the cost of some 150 more lives.

Desperately, Gorbachev looked for some way to contain the looming chaos. In the winter of 1990–91, he even began to lean towards the hard-liners who felt that there needed to be a reassertion of political order – by force if need be – to allow economic reform. In January 1991, they used this to try to break a stand-off between Moscow and the nationalist leaderships of the Baltic States with violent clashes in both Lithuania (where 14 civilians died when KGB special forces and paratroopers of the 76th Guards Air Assault Division seized the main TV tower) and Latvia, where hundreds of thousands of people gathered in the capital Riga, vowing to defend it.

In fact, Gorbachev was already regretting his flirtation with reaction, realizing that it would just push more republics into secession. In March 1991, the government held a referendum on whether people 'consider necessary the preservation of the Union of Soviet Socialist Republics as a renewed federation of equal sovereign republics'. A resounding 77.85% voted yes, but in part because the more radical republics – Armenia, Estonia, Georgia, Latvia, Lithuania and Moldova – boycotted it. A majority of Soviet citizens still wanted some kind of Union to be preserved, but arguably it was already too late. Gorbachev took this as an opportunity to open negotiations with the leaders of the constituent republics, and by summer had hammered out an agreement that would have transformed the USSR from being in effect an empire, into a genuine federation. Republics would be free to leave this new 'Union of Soviet Sovereign Republics' if they wanted, most powers would devolve to the republics, and the central government would just be responsible for key roles such as foreign affairs, defence and communications. The age of the Communist Party's dominance would have been over, the massive Red Army would be slimmed down, and the much-feared KGB, that united political control, domestic security and foreign intelligence, would be broken into more manageable services. Defence Minister Marshal Dmitry Yazov, Interior Minister Boriss Pugo and KGB chair Viktor Kryuchkov, hard-liners all, would have to be retired.

Unfortunately for Gorbachev, since he had backed away from his alliance with them, Kryuchkov had had him under constant observation. His every move was watched, every conversation recorded. Indeed, this was taken to ludicrous extremes, with one surveillance logbook entry reading '18:30. 111 is in the bath.'[2] Gorbachev was 'Subject 110', his wife Raisa 111. No wonder, then, that Kryuchkov and the rest knew what was in store for them, and decided to act first.

THE AUGUST COUP

By the beginning of August, the final draft of the new Union Treaty had been hammered out through lengthy negotiations in Novo-Ogaryovo, a government estate outside Moscow. It was to be signed by Gorbachev and the heads of the republics choosing to remain in this reformed state on 20 August. The process had been gruelling, and on 4 August, an exhausted Gorbachev headed for his summer home at Foros in Crimea for a fortnight's rest before returning to Moscow for the official signing. It was not to happen.

The hard-liners realized that this was their last chance to avert what for them was little short of treason. Kryuchkov quietly began to prepare for a coup. Trusted KGB officers had their summer leaves cancelled, an order was placed for 250,000 extra pairs of handcuffs, and he even had papers drawn up to relieve Gorbachev of his duties on supposed mental health grounds. On 17 August, he convened a gathering of likeminded hawks in a KGB safe house on Tyoplostansky Passage, in Moscow's south-western suburbs. There, a final decision was made to act. A delegation flew down to Crimea to present Gorbachev with an ultimatum to shelve the new Union Treaty and declare a state of emergency and let them 'restore order' their own way, or else stand down and let his deputy, Gennady Yanayev, take over as Acting President.

They seem genuinely to have believed that Gorbachev would bow to the inevitable and bless their venture. When he damned them and threw them out, they were visibly shaken, but the die had been cast. The KGB controlled all communications to and from the Foros mansion, and promptly cut him off. His personal security team was also made up of KGB officers, but they remained loyal to Gorbachev. Other KGB armed officers blockaded the mansion, though.

On the morning of 19 August, Soviets awoke to the news that Gorbachev had 'temporarily stepped down for reasons of ill health', and a 'State Committee on the State of Emergency' was in charge. As regular TV and radio programming was replaced by broadcasts of the ballet *Swan Lake*, paratroopers from the 106th Guards Airborne Division and troops from the 2nd Guards Tamanskaya Motor Rifle and 4th Guards Kantemirovskaya Tank Divisions – elite 'palace guard' forces – rolled into Moscow, some 4,000 soldiers in all. It was a coup, but a singularly inept one. The eight men of the State Committee

– including Kryuchkov, Yazov and Pugo, along with Yanayev as their lightweight figurehead – seemed not to realize how Gorbachev's reforms had kindled a new spirit of resistance, and truly believed that a stern press conference and the sight of tanks on the streets would be enough to cow the population and wind the clock back to the early 1980s.

They were wrong. Out of over-confidence or under-planning, they failed to arrest Boris Yeltsin, the elected president of the Russian republic. From the White House, Russia's parliament building on the banks of the Moskva River, he announced his opposition to the coup, and called for a general strike. Crowds began to gather around the White House, but on that first day, everyone was waiting to see what would happen. Had the so-called 'Gang of Eight' been willing and able to strike quickly and ruthlessly, then they might have carried the day. The police, for example, experienced record levels of absenteeism, as officers called in sick to avoid having to commit one way or the other.

It soon became clear that the plotters lacked a real strategy, though. On TV, Yanayev was hesitant, trembling, drunk. Soldiers in Moscow began openly siding with the crowds, including the crews of ten tanks from the Kantemir division, albeit without ammunition. Boris Yeltsin, in a moment that defined his image for years to come, clambered onto an armoured vehicle in front of the White House to address his supporters. While Soviet TV and radio did not cover it, the international media did, and across the USSR, people gathered around radios to listen in.

The next day, tensions rose. Col. Gen. Nikolai Kalinin, commander of the Moscow Military District, announced a curfew that night, while the head of the KGB's *Alfa* Group anti-terrorist commandos, along with Gen. Alexander Lebed, a hard-nosed veteran of Afghanistan and the deputy commander of the Airborne Troops, mingled with the defenders to consider how best to take the parliament building. Their conclusion was that it would be a bloody affair, as the crowds were getting bigger and more determined.

Nonetheless, the 'Gang of Eight' decided to go ahead with what was called Operation *Grom* ('Thunder'), involving *Alfa* and the parallel *Vympel* commando group, as well as three companies of tanks, paratroopers, Special Designation Police Unit (OMON: *Otryad Militsii Osobennovo Naznacheniya*) riot police and the paramilitary security forces of the Ministry of Internal Affairs (MVD: *Ministerstvo Vnutrennykh Del*) Interior Troops. The expectation was that there would be at least 500 civilian deaths, maybe more. Although figures such as Kryuchkov were comfortable with that, many more were not. Lebed and the head of the Air Assault Forces (VDV: *Vozdushno-Desantniye Voiska*), Gen. Pavel Grachyov, remonstrated with Yazov; even members of *Alfa* and *Vympel* were making it clear they would refuse to attack the White House.

Just after midnight on the 21st, a platoon from the Taman Division clashed with defenders who were moving busses and street cleaning trucks to form a barricade: three civilians were killed when panicked troops opened fire. This seems to have shocked Yazov into refusing to sanction military action, although it may simply have been that he did not want to risk giving orders that might not be obeyed. Either way, the troops began to be pulled back, and the coup began to fall apart.

A delegation of plotters flew to Foros, apparently to try to rebuild bridges with Gorbachev: he refused to see them. He flew back to Moscow, but the triumph was not his, but Yeltsin's. The Russian president had a deep grudge against his Soviet counterpart, who had first promoted him to Party First Secretary for Moscow in 1985 then ditched him in 1987 when he made too many enemies. Yeltsin had agreed to the new Union Treaty primarily for fear of what the hard-liners would do. But they had made their move and failed, so Yeltsin had no reason to continue to back Gorbachev.

Symbolically, the statue of Felix Dzerzhinsky, founder of the Bolshevik secret police, was toppled from its place in front of the KGB headquarters. The old institutions of state power and control were now in ruins. Yeltsin ruthlessly expanded his powers and publicly humiliated Gorbachev, suspending the Russian Communist Party and making it clear he no longer was willing to sign the Union Treaty. After some months of fruitless wrangling, Gorbachev bowed to the inevitable, especially after the leaders of Belarus and Ukraine joined Yeltsin. On 25 December 1991, as his last act as Soviet president, he signed a decree resigning his position – and dissolving the Soviet Union.

The manner of the passing of the USSR would have significant impacts on the future security situation in Russia and the rest of post-Soviet Eurasia. It precipitated a peaceful, but unexpected partition, which left all kinds of challenges still to be resolved. A once-unitary military structure was fragmented, leaving troops, arsenals and, above all, nuclear weapons scattered across the region. Defence-industrial supply chains were broken. Communities of ethnic minorities were left outside 'their' nations, creating the basis for future conflicts. It also catapulted Boris Yeltsin, a man who until then had been defined essentially by domestic politics and opposition, into power over a nuclear-armed and crisis-gripped remnant of a superpower at a time in which old assumptions and power relationships alike were being re-examined.

BORIS YELTSIN: THE MAN WITHOUT THE PLAN

The tragic irony is that Boris Yeltsin, post-Soviet Russia's first president, was ruthless and focused when he had an enemy to defeat, but had almost no real vision for the kind of country he wanted to build after he had won. Politically, he believed in democracy – but only when it suited him. In 1993, he was locked in a stalemate with the Supreme Soviet, the parliament he inherited from when it was elected in 1990, and which was packed with Communists and nationalists. He resolved it by sending in the same forces that had hung back in 1991, to shell and capture the White House. This was a breach of the constitution, but he simply held a referendum that retrospectively revised it to clear him. Likewise, when the Russian Communist Party looked likely to win the 1996 presidential elections, on the back of widespread public dissatisfaction at massive levels of poverty and unemployment, Yeltsin struck a deal with the so-called 'Seven Bankers', a collection of oligarchs, financiers and media moguls. They threw their money and their weight behind a campaign of bribery, scaremongering and outright vote rigging that swung his re-election.

They were, after all, personally invested in maintaining the status quo. The Russian economy was in a terrible state, and the crash privatization campaigns which took place in the period 1992–96 may have been necessary both to move assets out of state hands and to allow some inefficient industries to fold, but they concentrated massive amounts of wealth into relatively few hands. Banks, corrupt officials, and well-connected entrepreneurs were able to pick up assets at bargain basement prices.

To a large extent, the West was happy to turn a blind eye to all this. They too did not want to see Russia falling into the hands of Communists or ultra-nationalists. After all, in the 1993 elections to

the new parliament, the State Duma, the Liberal Democratic Party of
Russia (LDPR) – which was and is neither liberal nor democratic, but
rabidly nationalist – received the largest share of the vote. It was also
because the greatest Western concern related to how the post-Soviet
space could be stabilized, especially in regard to the approximately
45,000 nuclear weapons the USSR had amassed, as well as the materials
and expertise which could be used by states or even non-state actors to
develop their own weapons of mass destruction.

What made this even more problematic was the state of not just
the Russian military, but its command structure. Many within the
Soviet High Command had been in broad sympathy with the August
Coup. Defence Minister Yazov had been one of the State Committee.
The acerbic and able Deputy Defence Minister and Commander of
the Army Gen. Valentin Varennikov had been one of his main allies.
Former Chief of the General Staff Marshal Sergei Akhromeyev, another
of the giants of his generation, committed suicide after the failure of
the August Coup, leaving a suicide note reading 'I cannot live when my
Fatherland is dying and everything that I have always considered to be
the meaning of my life is destroyed.'[3] Not feeling – with, in fairness,
some reason – that he could trust the High Command, at first Yeltsin
declared himself Russia's defence minister, more than anything else
because he did not know to whom he felt he could entrust the job.
In May 1992, though, he opted for Pavel Grachyov, the paratrooper
commander who had crucially refused to support the August Coup,
who had been acting as Yeltsin's deputy.

As will be discussed in Chapter 4, this was a decision which made
sense in political terms, but was a disaster for the military. Grachyov was
a brave and energetic officer, who had served two tours in Afghanistan
and been made a Hero of the Soviet Union – the USSR's highest award
– for his performance there. On being made minister, he was also
elevated to the rank of full army general – making him, at age 44, the
youngest in the country. It soon became painfully clear that he was out
of his depth, especially in a time of crisis and retrenchment. He lacked
authority with his peers; he lacked a wider sense of the strategic needs
of the time. I remember being out drinking with some paratroopers
at the time of his elevation, some of whom had served in the 103rd
Guards Airborne Division in Afghanistan when he had commanded it.
I asked them what they thought of his becoming a minister. There was

a brief embarrassed silence, then one almost apologetically said he was *molodets*, which in context means a 'good lad'. It's how you might describe a promising recruit, not the minister of defence. When even his own 'blue berets' had their misgivings, this was not a good omen.

Indeed, this was to be evident in the politically inevitable but logistically nightmarish task of withdrawing from empire and bringing Russian forces back from their far-flung bases. This pre-dated the end of the USSR, but became all the more complex as new nations began not only to look to their own security interests, but to turn to their scavenged portions of the Red Army to resolve old and new disputes, and settle domestic scores. Freed from the enforced and skin-deep fraternalism of Soviet rule, geopolitics were to return to the former Soviet Union with a vengeance and like it or not, Russia – as both the largest successor state and also the one that had in effect broken the USSR – could not but find itself involved.

It is understandable that little thought had been given to the formation of post-Soviet armies when, until those crowded final months, few had seriously anticipated the collapse of the USSR. Ironically, the only people who had given this some consideration were the Soviet General Staff which, since 1990, had been quietly moving tactical nuclear weapons and some of the infrastructure of the strategic forces out of the rest of the republics and back to Russia. Beyond that, though, there was little planning and no consensus, even though according to the 1991 Belavezha Accords between the leaders of Russia, Ukraine and Belarus, a loose new union, the Commonwealth of Independent States (CIS), was formed, which initially included Armenia, Belarus, Kazakhstan, Kyrgyzstan, Russia and Uzbekistan. It had its own supreme military commander – Marshal of Aviation Yevgeny Shaposhnikov, one of the senior Soviet commanders who had hung back from supporting the August Coup – and provisional control over joint forces. In practice, though, in the immediate aftermath of the end of the Soviet Union, control of its forces and assets de facto devolved to whichever newly created republic in which they found themselves.

Gorbachev had passed on to Yeltsin the *Cheget*, the 'nuclear suitcase' that provided command access for missile launches, as well as the relevant codes, but the Russian state initially had no army as such. At first, Yeltsin announced that Russia would simply have its own 100,000-strong National Guard, with security depending on joint CIS forces, under Shaposhnikov as their commander-in-chief. In March 1992, though, the old Soviet Defence Ministry was rechristened the Russian Federation Defence Ministry, and the writing was on the wall for Shaposhnikov's command. After all, it had always been really only a stopgap measure. Actually having joint forces would depend on agreement about their role and their size, who would pay for them, and who would serve. It is not so much that no common ground was reached on these thorny issues, so much as that none of the member states really even tried, recognizing a lost cause when they saw one. Soon enough, even the pretence was shed, and in September 1993, the CIS heads of state abolished Shaposhnikov's job. Henceforth, the CIS's only real security role would be supporting cooperation between members. Instead, a majority of the old Soviet military, over 2 million soldiers, ended up under Moscow's control. It had an army – of sorts. But was this an asset or a liability?

3

A Military in Crisis

In 1994, investigative journalist Dmitry Kholodov wrote, 'our Russian army is sliding down into a world of organized crime'.[1] Amongst other stories, he was digging into claims that commandos from the elite 16th *Spetsnaz* Brigade were working as hitmen for the mafia, or even running training programmes for their gunmen. Mainly, though, he was on the track of claims that Defence Minister Grachyov had been involved in massive embezzlement of army funds. Shortly thereafter, he was contacted by someone claiming to have information for him, directing him to a briefcase in the left-luggage at a Moscow train station. He was told it was full of documents, and hurriedly took them to the offices of his newspaper, *Moskovsky Komsomolets*. When he opened it, a bomb exploded, killing him instantly.

The newspaper openly accused Grachyov of being behind the murder. He denied any responsibility, but years later, when six men – four of them still serving military officers – were on trial for the murder, Grachyov admitted that he had called Kholodov an 'enemy at home' and tasked Col. Pavel Popovskikh, head of Airborne Forces intelligence, with 'dealing with' him. He disingenuously added that he had meant only 'broken legs' but that 'some of my subordinates misunderstood my words'.[2] It was a sign of the times that this somehow in itself was not grounds for Grachyov himself to be prosecuted. In any case, in the face of considerable public uproar and the anger of the Prosecutor General's Office, the six were acquitted in two separate trials, and the case remains unsolved to this day.

AN ARMY GONE BAD

In the 1990s, it was easy to see Russia's military less as a security asset and more as a threat. Soldiers were hungry, under-trained and undisciplined. In part, this was for historic reasons. The Soviet military had been especially afflicted by an institutionalized culture of hazing known as *dedovshchina* or 'grandfatherism'. No army is immune to bullying and abuse, but this was exacerbated by a combination of the lack of any professional corps of non-commissioned officers (NCOs) and the way the cycle of spring and autumn call-ups meant that conscripts were divided into four six-monthly cohorts during their two years in service. They progressed through a series of informal but universally recognized stages of military life. The rookie *molodoy* ('youngster') could expect to be lorded over by the *dedy* ('grandfathers') who were more than half-way through their service and the *dembely* (from 'demobilizing') in the last hundred days of theirs. This could mean anything from crude pranks to being forced to hand over food (especially that sent from home) or perform senior soldiers' chores. Most would end up being 'assigned' to a *dembel* and have to go through the ritual of the 'hundred days': putting a cigarette under his pillow every night until the end of his service.

To challenge *dedovshchina* was to invite brutal retribution, and several hundred draftees would die each year, whether from beatings or the effects of other punishments, such as being forced to work in winter outdoors without coats. The system persisted because, although officially banned, in practice it was widely seen as a crude but efficient way of enforcing discipline due to the lack of veteran NCOs – a key weakness of the Russian military. A sergeant and even a *starshina*, roughly equivalent to a master sergeant in Western terms, would simply be a particularly promising conscript given advanced training. Although in 1971 the rank of *praporshchik*, warrant officer (*michman* in the navy), was re-introduced for volunteers who had already served their national service, they were too few in number (and often too indifferent in quality) to make a real difference.

How could a newly minted lieutenant, probably scarcely older than many of the conscripts under his command, make his authority felt? For too many of them, the answer was in effect to lean on the *dedy* to keep the rest in line, in return for indulgence towards their bullying. In peacetime, it worked in its own thuggish way, after a fashion. It often proved a serious problem in combat, when squads must stick together. Indeed, veterans of the Soviet war in Afghanistan often commented that *dedovshchina* tended to disappear there, not least as bullies could too easily meet their end in unexpected ways on the battlefield. However, it also made military service extremely unappealing, contributing to high levels of draft dodging: 'life is a book' went the Russian saying, 'and military service two pages torn out of it'. Those who could, used bribery and the distinctive Soviet practice of *blat*, the exchange of favours, to stay out of the armed forces; those who couldn't, served.

As the Soviet Union collapsed, all kinds of other problems which had long afflicted the military became chronic: pay arrears, a shortage of accommodation, poor rations. In the 1990s, the chronic became crisis. Officers' families were being forced to live in unheated tank sheds, soldiers were being fed rotten food, pay was often up to five months in arrears. No wonder officers and men alike often turned to crime, whether moonlighting as everything from taxi drivers to contract killers, or simply stealing whatever they could find. Most of this was small-scale and opportunistic. This was a time when, for example, it was routine for soldiers to steal light bulbs from barracks and parts from cars to sell on the black market. Often, though, it had fatal implications. In Chechnya, starving soldiers would swap weapons for food, even though they knew those guns would later be turned against them or their comrades. In other cases, whole criminal business empires were formed, officers doing everything from illegally hiring out soldiers as labourers to using military flights and convoys (which were exempt from police and customs checks) to smuggle heroin from Central Asia and stolen cars from Europe.

National service became harder and harder to police, and although Yeltsin tried to make it more palatable in 1993 by reducing conscription from two years to 18 months, this did little to help its image but much to reduce the combat effectiveness of the soldiers. Units had to resort to turning training grounds into fields to raise their own crops or foraging for mushrooms and berries in local woods to supplement their diet, or hiring out their men to local councils and enterprises as cheap labour. Some of the proceeds were pocketed by the officers, the rest spent keeping the lights and heating on. In 1994, Grachyov warned the

Duma that 'no army in the world is in as wretched a state as Russia's', and he had a point.[3] (Of course, part of the reason for the unexpectedly lacklustre performance of the Russian military in Ukraine in 2022 suggests that 28 years later, too little had changed.)

NUKES FOR SALE?

All that was bad enough, but the state of the Strategic Rocket Forces (RVSN: *Raketniye Voiska Strategicheskovo Naznacheniya*) was a constant concern. Their capacity to detect and respond to nuclear attack was questionable, but fortunately there appeared no imminent threats from abroad. The real dangers were from within, with fears for the security of the 40,000-plus nuclear weapons and roughly 1.5 million kilograms of plutonium and highly enriched uranium held in the dilapidated and under-protected stockpiles across the former USSR, which were now being consolidated inside Russia as Ukraine, Belarus and Kazakhstan in particular agreed to hand over weapons that they could not, in any case, use. The fears were not wholly unfounded. In 1993, just to take one example of the kind of low-level thefts which were taking place at the time, two disgruntled naval officers stole three uranium fuel rods used in submarines' nuclear reactors from the Sevmorput naval shipyard outside Murmansk by the hardly sophisticated means of walking past the two sentries at the gate, squeezing through a hole in the perimeter fence and sawing their way through the rusty padlock on the bunker door. The irony was that they had no idea what to do with the fuel rods, and were caught six months later as they tried to find a buyer.

The real nightmare, of course, was that gangsters, rogue states or terrorists might be able to steal or buy warheads. In 1993, there was even a panic when it appeared that a number had actually disappeared from a stockpile in the Russian Far East. It turned out that this was simply an accounting error, but nonetheless the fear did encourage the West to provide resources to secure sites, accelerate warhead decommissioning programmes and provide nuclear scientists and technicians who otherwise would have been out of work with some support for them and their families.

Only the threat of so-called 'suitcase nukes' continued to worry Western security services into the late 1990s, although that appears to have been largely mythical. In 1997, Yeltsin's former security chief Alexander Lebed claimed that 84 suitcase-sized nuclear bombs, built by the Soviets as a doomsday weapon to be planted secretly in the West, had gone missing, and Yeltsin had sacked him to try to keep him quiet. Then, in September, he upped his claim to more than a hundred of the 250 such devices which had been in the Soviet arsenal. Not surprisingly, this caused an uproar, especially in the United States, given that Lebed claimed that each could kill upwards of 100,000 people. Moscow did not help itself by claiming first that no such weapons had ever existed. This stretched credibility, especially as experts came forward who had worked on a range of such weapons, from nuclear mines to the RYa-6 'nuclear satchel', which weighed just 25 kilograms and had a 1-kiloton yield. GRU defector Stanislav Lunev also claimed that RA-115 nuclear mines were hidden in the United States, although no traces were found in any of the locations he cited. In any case, in mid-1998, Moscow acknowledged that there had been such a programme but said that a special commission had inventoried all remaining examples and found none were missing. The consensus among Western experts was that they were right and Lebed was wrong. Fortunately.

As it was, outside the movies, no weapons went missing, but this was at least as much because they were weapons so dreadful that even the hint of any trades would likely have brought the ruthless attention of the world's intelligence services – such as Mossad, ever-vigilant to potential threats to Israel.

BRINGING THE BOYS BACK HOME

Even before the end of the Soviet Union, the Red Army was in retreat. The strong right arm of the Communist Party, which had crushed risings in East Berlin in 1953 and Hungary in 1956, smothered hopes of 'socialism with a human face' in Czechoslovakia in 1968 and backed Polish martial law in 1981–83, was based throughout the satellite nations of the Warsaw Pact. This 'alliance' was really just a thin veil of legitimacy over a Soviet empire in Central Europe, but this was an empire which demanded military, political and above all economic support from Moscow to survive. During Gorbachev's tenure, the decision was made to bow to the inevitable: the USSR could no longer afford to keep these increasingly restive nations under its control. On 7 December 1988, in a momentous speech to the United Nations, Gorbachev announced that the Red Army would start withdrawing. Without Soviet economic subsidies and military support, puppet regimes were swept away by popular risings or simply collapsed in a period of dramatic change between 1989 and 1991. On 25 February 1991, the Warsaw Pact was formally disbanded.

Where would the returning soldiers – some 600,000 officers and men and more than 150,000 dependants – go? None of the former subject nations wanted Soviet troops there any longer than necessary, but Moscow wanted a slow withdrawal to give it time to build the new bases, barracks and apartments this would require. Even then, where would the money to pay for this come from? West Germany, as was, helped pay to get the Soviets off German soil, but this would still take until 1994. Other new nations lacked the resources to help or, often, the inclination. New governments in Central Europe, their own economies in chaos, had other priorities. As of mid-1990, 280,000 military families were reportedly without housing.

EMPTY DREAMS

In November 1993, Russia adopted a new Military Doctrine. In Soviet and then Russian practice, this is a tremendously important, foundational document, describing when and how Russia believes it might go to war, how it would fight, and what it needs for the job. The Doctrine drives almost everything else, from procurement of new kit to the size of the military. This turned out, though, to be an exercise in fantasy planning. It acknowledged that Russia ought to consider itself a regional rather than global power, and to that end, it envisaged modernizing and professionalizing the army. These were fine words, but they came at a time when the treasury was bare and the political will to act was equally absent.

Meaningful reform of the military had stalled. Yeltsin's army was to a large extent the Soviet army in organization, culture and role, just smaller and poorer. As of 1996 it numbered 670,000 officers and enlisted personnel, divided between eight Military Districts (VO:

Voyenny Okrug) and the separate Air Assault Forces (VDV: *Vozdushno-Desantniye Voiska*). There were 85 divisions, but given the lack of personnel and the very officer-heavy distribution of these forces – more than one in three, 290,000, were commissioned officers – the majority existed largely on paper. At best, they were structures ready to accept reservists in case of national mobilization, but at worst they were ghost units kept on simply to find something for professional soldiers to do.

There was talk of creating a Rapid Deployment Force, of creating a smaller, all-professional army, but these dreams came to nothing. After all, for most of the 1990s, the army was consumed by a desperate struggle simply to survive, in a decade of social turmoil, economic crisis and political unrest. In 1995, a Defence Ministry spokesman warned that 'if no radical decision is made shortly, the Russian army may well find itself on the verge of starvation'.[4] Reports were coming in that in parts of Siberia, recruits were being given animal feed, and even soldiers in the Moscow VO were having to beg to survive. These concerns were given a human face in 1996, when the press seized on the story of Misha Kubarsky, a conscript from Yaroslavl. He died from starvation three months into his national service. When he complained of fatigue, he was weighed and found to be 12 kilograms underweight and he was sent to a military hospital, but died on the way. A medical commission then ran a spot check on his unit and found fully half the regiment to be body-mass deficient, but this was hardly a surprise given the lack of proper food that it had been able to find. Indeed, for the past week, its commissariat had not been able to find anything to feed them but cabbage.

Of course, there were still some pockets of professionalism, and a few capable units, especially within the more elite services such as the paratroopers, Naval Infantry and *Spetsnaz* special forces. They were too few in number, though, to match Russia's apparent aspirations. In particular, Defence Minister Grachyov, paratrooper to the core, clung to the fond hope that they could form the kernel of an effective Mobile Force, a 100,000-strong rapid-deployment formation ready for anything from foreign actions to domestic security. This dream was as grandiose as it was unattainable, but the amount of time and energy wasted trying to achieve it, at a time when soldiers were living in barracks without heating because the ministry couldn't pay their electricity bills, speaks volumes about the degree to which the senior military leadership could not – would not – come to terms with the realities of the situation.

'PASHA MERCEDES'

Grachyov's tragedy was that he was the quintessential fighting general – personally brave, an officer most at home on the offense – in an era when his job was really about managing decline, one which demanded not élan but adroit political skills, personal honesty and a comprehensive attention to detail. Sadly, he had none of these characteristics.

Born in a provincial village in 1948, he joined the army on leaving school. He was physically tough, hard working, and, as one officer who knew him for much of his career put it, 'smart enough, but not too smart'. He was snapped up as a promising candidate by the VDV – different arms of service had different priorities, and the paratroopers, while not as exalted as the eggheads of the RVSN or the political zealots of the KGB's forces, picked before the ordinary Ground Forces – and sent to the Higher Airborne Command School in Ryazan. He did well, graduating with a gold medal in two distinct specialties, as a 'Platoon Commander of the Airborne Troops' and as an 'Assistant-Translator from German'. The latter put him on track for the VDV's reconnaissance troops, something of an elite within an elite, generally regarded as just a step down from the *Spetsnaz*. He rose to command a scout company in the 7th Guards Airborne Division and then a paratrooper training battalion. As was usual for officers heading up the ranks, he then went to the MV Frunze Military Academy, graduating in 1981. By this time, the Afghan War was in full swing, and the VDV was shouldering much of the heavy lifting. He served first (1981–83) as deputy commander and then commander of the 345th Guards Independent Parachute Regiment, then later (1985–88) as major general and commander of the 103rd Guards Airborne Division. In between, he returned to the 7th Guards Airborne Division as chief of staff. Grachyov had a good war and in 1988 he was made a Hero of the Soviet Union, and sent to the Military Academy of the General Staff. On graduating in 1990, he became First Deputy Commander of the Airborne Forces, then their commander.

During the August Coup, Grachyov initially appeared to be loyal to the State Emergency Committee, leading the 106th Guards Airborne Division into Moscow, and deploying them to secure key locations in the city. However, he quickly joined officers such as Marshal Shaposhnikov in backing away from the coup, opposing any plans to take the White House by force. His reward was to be promoted to colonel general and First Deputy Minister of Defence by Gorbachev – in part because of the need to purge the top command – but then he was, in effect, poached by Yeltsin for his new State Committee for Defence Issues. Later he became First Deputy Commander-in-Chief of the Joint Armed Forces of the CIS, and then Russia's First Deputy Minister of Defence under Yeltsin. In short order, though, Yeltsin made him minister – according to Grachyov's own account, he learned about this in a short phone conversation, in which Yeltsin said, 'I'm so tired of being the minister! Therefore, I signed a decree on your appointment.'[5]

He proved to be a political lightweight. He tried to resist the accelerated withdrawal of Russian troops from abroad, to no avail. In 1992, he formally handed over half the armaments stored in the unruly region of Chechnya, because he did not know how to prevent this – weapons that would later be used against the Russians. He tried to avoid the politicization of the military, but when Yeltsin was embroiled in a bitter constitutional struggle with his own parliament in 1993, he was forced off the fence. After all, Yeltsin had inherited a parliament – the Congress of People's Deputies, from which the smaller working Supreme Soviet was elected – from the Soviet era, the product of a voting system that guaranteed it was packed with Communists. Unsurprisingly, president and parliament were increasingly at odds, and on 21 September 1993, Yeltsin decided to dissolve both bodies. This was a clear breach of the constitution, but Yeltsin felt he had public opinion on his side. He certainly had the Moscow security forces. The Supreme Soviet impeached Yeltsin, declared Afghan war hero Alexander Rutskoi Acting President, and called on volunteers to help defend the parliamentary seat, the building known as the White House. On 3 October, a pro-parliament crowd seized the offices of the mayor and tried to take the TV tower. This was a massive political mistake, as it gave Yeltsin the excuse he was looking for to call in the army, and allowed him to present himself as the defender of public order. Grachyov duly complied, and by dawn the next day, five tanks of the elite 2nd Guards Tamanskaya Motor Rifle Division were drawn up on the Novoarbatsky Bridge by the White House and five more in a playground on the other side of it. They started shelling the parliament, high-explosive anti-tank rounds punching easily through the building's façade and starting fires that would gut the building. Troops and commandos from the *Alfa* and *Vympel* anti-terrorist forces then moved in, and by the afternoon the conflict was over. All told, 25 soldiers and police and 122 civilians would die in what would be the deadliest street fighting in Moscow since the 1917 Revolution. As for the constitution, Yeltsin retrospectively rewrote it, to make what he did legal, after all – an act that was clearly morally and legally dubious, but he had shown he had the power.

Part of the problem was that Grachyov did not know how to say no to Yeltsin – he knew that his own high command regarded him as an over-promoted upstart and so without full presidential backing, he was no one. This would prove disastrous in 1994 when, out of a combination of hubris and a desire to please, he airily reassured Yeltsin that the rebellion in Chechnya could easily be quelled, and that the Chechen capital Grozny could be taken 'by a single parachute regiment, in two hours'.[6]

The subsequent bloody war, which can only be interpreted as a defeat for Russia (see Chapter 4), effectively spelled the end of his career. He was sacked in 1996 as part of a political deal between Yeltsin and one of Grachyov's former subordinates, Alexander Lebed. Nonetheless, he did not suffer too badly. He reportedly had in any case made sure he personally benefited from his position. Indeed, he acquired the nickname 'Pasha Mercedes' because of the way he acquired luxury German cars with money earmarked to cover the withdrawal of forces from Germany. Yeltsin also ensured that Grachyov's loyalty did not go unrewarded. After he was sacked, he was given a comfortable sinecure as an adviser to Rosvooruzheniye, the state arms export company.

He was undoubtedly a brave man and an inspiring tactical commander. He made 647 parachute jumps in his career, was wounded in battle, and led from the front. However, he was the wrong man for the times. Igor Rodionov, a former commander of the 40th Army in

Afghanistan, who briefly served as defence minister 1996–97, was not a man to suffer fools or rogues lightly. His acerbic judgement was that 'Grachyov in my 40th Army was a good commander for an airborne division. He never rose above this level. He became a minister only because he defected to Yeltsin's side in time.'[7] That is probably the most fitting epitaph.

4

The First Chechen War

The true depths to which the Russian military had sunk – and Pavel
Grachyov's failings as both politician and commander – were best
and bloodily demonstrated in the debacle that was the 1994–96 First
Chechen War. Pitted against rebels in the habitually mutinous southern
republic of Chechnya, with a population of maybe 1.2 million, or
a seventh of the size just of Moscow, all Grachyov's forces could do
was essentially secure a draw. It was a humiliation, and contributed
not only to the further demoralization of the military but also to the
backlash against the decay of the Russian state that led to the rise of
Vladimir Putin.[1]

RESISTANCE AND RESENTMENT

Fiercely independent and proverbially tough, the Chechens – who
proudly compared themselves to wolves – had long been a thorn
in Russia's side. In the 19th century, as the empire tightened its
grip on the North Caucasus, not least to secure its southern flank,
it conquered the Chechens but never subdued them. As rebels or
bandits, the Chechens and their Ingush cousins continued to challenge
their notional masters, such that in 1944, Stalin launched Operation
Chechevitsa ('Lentil'), the mass deportation of the entire Chechen
and Ingush population to Central Asia, on the pretext that they were
planning to help the Nazis. Some half a million men, women and
children were forced from their homes at gunpoint, and at least a

quarter died in the process or in the early years of exile. It would be 13 years before they were allowed to return, after Stalin's death, although even then they would often find Russian migrants occupying their old homes, and the gravestones of their ancestors used to build walls and pavements. No wonder a fierce resentment against Moscow continued to burn in the hearts of the Chechens.

In 1990, when still campaigning against Soviet power, Boris Yeltsin had urged regional leaders to 'Take as much sovereignty as you can swallow!' The Chechens took him at his word. In the immediate aftermath of the 1991 August Coup, they threw out the Communist Party administration and under former air force general Dzhokar Dudayev, declared independence. Yeltsin actually flew security troops to the Chechen capital Grozny to arrest him, but when they were blockaded in the airport, he backed away from confrontation and stood them down. Nonetheless, this was no more than a pause. Yeltsin had been happy to champion local autonomy when he was in opposition, but had no intention of actually allowing the Chechens to secede from the Russian Federation the way Russia had effectively seceded from the USSR.

Dudayev's rule was marked by a mix of enthusiasm, amateurishness and criminality. Warlords, gangsters and corrupt officials became rich, but not a single new school or hospital was built. In March 1992, Dudayev's rivals tried to unseat him, but they were forcibly suppressed. When the Chechen parliament looked ready to hold a vote of no confidence in him the next year, he dissolved it and maintained direct presidential rule.

To a considerable extent, though, it didn't matter whether Dudayev's regime was legitimate and effective or not. For Yeltsin, this self-declared independent state could not be allowed to survive, let alone thrive, lest other regions decide that they could also secede. Although Yeltsin claimed in August that 'intervention by force is impermissible and must not be done … there would be such blood that nobody would ever forgive us', nonetheless he launched what today might be called a 'hybrid war' operation.[2] Moscow organized and armed a few hundred Chechens and Ingushetians opposed to Dudayev – or simply willing to fight him for pay. In October 1994, they launched an attack on Grozny, backed by Russian tanks and airpower. This was repelled by Dudayev's loyalists, as was a second, larger assault in November. All the more embarrassing for Moscow, 20 Russian soldiers were captured, and it became clear that they were not even obeying the military chain of command, but were instead under orders from the Federal Counter-Intelligence Service (FSK: *Federalnaya Sluzhba Kontrrazvedki*) security service, the successor to the Soviet KGB. What had been meant to be a quick, quiet and deniable proxy coup was turning into a public humiliation. True to form, an embarrassed Yeltsin doubled down. He ordered the Chechens to surrender. When they refused, he formally turned to the Russian military to 'restore constitutional order'. After all, Grachyov and most of his other advisers were reassuring him that this would be an easy win: reportedly, he told the Security Council at a secret session on 28 November that it would be a 'bloodless blitzkrieg'. Likewise, Minister for Nationalities Affairs Nikolai Yegorov affirmed that 70% of the population would welcome Russian troops, and the remaining 30% stay neutral.[3] If only.

HIGH HOPES, QUICK DEFEATS

That day, the Russian air force began the campaign, bombing Chechnya's small air force on the ground (although there are reasons to believe its small stock of training aircraft could not fly) and closing its two airfields at Kalinovskaya and Khankala by cratering their runways. On 6 December, Dudayev and Grachyov agreed to 'avoid the further use of force'. It was an empty pledge, of course: the Chechens were trying to shame Moscow into standing down, the Russians were trying to lull the rebels. Neither was successful. Even as they were exchanging platitudes, Chechens were digging trenches outside Grozny and an invasion force was being mustered under Col. Gen. Alexei Mityukhin, commander of the North Caucasus Military District (SKVO: *Severo-Kavkazsky Voyenny Okrug*).

Together with other forces, including the air assets committed to the operation, the Joint Grouping of Federal Forces (OGFV: *Obedinennaya Gruppa Federalnykh Voisk*) numbered around 23,700 men, including 80 tanks, but was very much a scratch-built force. Right up to the eve of the invasion, the General Staff was hunting for units that were close enough to their establishment strength to be deployed, and whose vehicles were (mainly) ready to move and their supplies (mainly) adequate. As one officer who had been in the attack later reminisced, 'honestly, it was a wonder we could even move, we ended up having to cannibalize about a third of our trucks to get the rest on the road.'

This reflected a much wider failure on the part of the Russian military, from junior officers who lacked the confidence and training to lead their men in messy, dangerous close-quarters battle, up to a High Command that had trained for one kind of war and seemed unable to come to terms with another. The level of understanding shown by the most senior commanders about the proper use of airpower was, for example, apparently pitiful. In his memoirs, Yevgeny Fedosov, head of GosNIIAS, the State Scientific Research Institute of Aviation Systems, recalled being summoned to a council of war with the five men essentially in charge of the operation. These were Deputy Prime Minister Oleg Soskovets, Defence Minister Grachyov, FSK chief Sergei Stepashin, Interior Minister Viktor Yerin and Border Troops commander Andrei Nikolayev. They wanted to know how to deliver a pinpoint strike on Dudayev's bunker under the presidential palace in Grozny. Fedosov explained that the latest Su-24M and Su-25T ground attack aircraft could launch high-precision strikes with weapons that could blast through into an underground bunker. However, it turned out that the 4th Air Army, which was deployed to the war, largely lacked aircraft fitted with 'smart' bombs, and while it did have Su-24Ms, their pilots had no experience using 'smart' weapons in combat. At this point, according to Fedosov, Grachyov's lack of understanding became clear:

> Leaning imposingly in his armchair, he declared: 'Let me tell you how our air force is fighting. During an air strike on the aerodrome at Khankala, a regiment of Tu-22M bombers completely destroyed all of Chechnya's aviation, and one bomb destroyed Dudayev's personal helicopter with a direct hit.'[4]

When Fedosov tried to explain that sending 20 bombers, each carrying 20 tonnes of ordnance, to carpet bomb an essentially undefended airfield was actually wasteful overkill – a single squadron would have been enough – and was a wholly different kind of mission, this was met with disgruntlement. Eventually, the decision was to set up a special force of Su-24Ms with experienced pilots drawn from across the entire country. By the time it was ready, though, a flight of Su-25 attack aircraft had already blasted the presidential palace to rubble with conventional bombs – and in any case, Dudayev hadn't been there.

THE PLAN

The attack on Chechnya would come along three axes. The largest force, commanded by Lt. Gen. Vladimir Chilindin, would move from Mozdok in North Ossetia, north-west of Chechnya. Its 6,500 men were drawn from the 131st Independent Motor Rifle Brigade, nine separate Ministry of Internal Affairs (MVD: *Ministerstvo Vnutrennykh Del*) Interior Troop security battalions, and the 22nd Independent *Spetsnaz* Brigade. The second force, striking from Vladikavkaz, west of Grozny, comprised 4,000 troops under Lt. Gen. Alexander Chindarov, the deputy head of the Airborne Forces. As well as a regiment of paratroopers from the 76th Air Assault Division and a battalion from the 21st Independent Air Assault Brigade, it included mechanized infantry of the 19th Motor Rifle Division and five Interior Troop battalions. The third, under Lt. Gen. Lev Rokhlin, assembled at Kizlyar, in Dagestan, north-east of Chechnya. Rokhlin, a decorated veteran of the Afghan War who would become an outspoken critic of the conduct of the Chechen operation, commanded more than 4,000 troops, largely from the 20th Motor Rifle Division, along with six Interior Troop battalions.

The presence of the Interior Troops (VV: *Vnutrenniye Voiska*) reflected the operational plan, which was to focus on seizing Grozny, with the assumption that once their capital was taken, Chechen resistance would soon dissolve. Rokhlin and other *afgantsy* quietly grumbled that a similar strategy had been tried in the 1979 invasion of Afghanistan, and that had not worked out quite so well, but Grachyov was adamant that this had to be a quick triumph. He had, after all, promised Yeltsin that the operation would not last beyond 20 December. The three contingents would advance on the city along six axes and besiege it. While the VV sealed Chechnya off and prevented any reinforcements from reaching Grozny, the army would enclose and then, if need be, seize the city. The plan was doomed from the start, but the inclusion of MVD forces introduced a further weakness given just what a mixed bag they were. Their best were very good indeed, especially the elite Moscow-based 'Dzerzhinsky Division' (formally the 1st Independent Operational Designation Division). Most, though, were units made up of conscripts chosen for their willingness to do the Kremlin's dirty work as much as anything else. Many would be implicated in brutal abuses of the civilian population in Chechnya, sometimes out of a misplaced sense that it was the only way to force the rebels to submit, but more often because of the simple fear experienced by poorly trained troops more used to guarding facilities and escorting prisoner convoys than counter-insurgency operations against a tough and committed enemy.

The plan had been to invade on 7 December, but the troops simply were not yet ready. Only on 11 December did they cross the border and head for Grozny. Everything went more slowly than intended. Although the north Chechen plains are relatively forgiving compared with the mountains of the south, nonetheless bad weather often grounded the helicopters on which cautious commanders had hoped to depend for reconnaissance and close air support, vehicles broke down with embarrassing regularity, and small groups of Chechen fighters sniped at advance patrols and staged ambushes that slowed the pace of the advance to a relative crawl.

They did not close their 'ring of steel' around Grozny until 26 December, which gave the rebels ample time to evacuate some civilians, but above all to bring in their reinforcements and supplies from the south and step up their preparations to greet the Russians warmly. They had two hundred years of oppression and near-genocide to make up for, after all.

TAKING GROZNY …

So the Chechens were ready. Dudayev's nation had in many ways become a bandit kingdom, and its 3,000-strong 'armed forces' – comprising the army, National Guard and Interior Ministry units – were rather less extensive than they might appear on paper. The army's sole motor rifle brigade was actually little more than a 200-strong company, the same size as its Shali Tank Regiment, which had only 15 working tanks, largely T-72s. The light motorized Commando Brigade was a little larger, albeit mainly equipped with trucks and jeeps, and the artillery regiment had just 30 light and medium guns and a few BM-21 multiple rocket launchers. The Ministry of Internal Affairs Regiment was another light motorized force of 200 men. The National Guard accounted for the bulk of the Chechen military, a random assortment of units, everything from leaders' personal retinues to local clan militias. While their grandiose and picturesque names such as the Abkhaz Battalion and the Muslim Hunter Regiment – neither of which was more than company-strength – might suggest ineffectiveness, though, there is a reason why the Chechens have long loomed as a larger-than-life menace in Russian literature and history.

A young Chechen would often be expected to start learning to shoot as a teenager, and their fabled toughness also meant that a disproportionate number ended up serving in the Soviet special forces and paratroopers. Indeed, Chechnya may be landlocked, but Chechens were twice as likely to end up in the Naval Infantry marines than any other nationality. They were often experienced; they knew how the Soviet and thus 1990s Russian army fought; and they were defending their homeland. They had also been able to concentrate their forces in Grozny – with volunteers, the defenders amounted to some 9,000 fighters – and were gifted with an unusually able operational commander in Chief of Staff Aslan Maskhadov. He was born in Kazakhstan in 1951 after his family had been forcibly resettled. Like so many Chechens, he nonetheless joined the army, serving as an artillery officer and retiring with the rank of colonel in 1992. Returning home, he joined the 'independent' Chechen forces, quickly being made chief of staff. He would prove an unexpected asset for the rebels, a meticulous planner who also had an instinct for when it was time for a daring gamble.

The urban environment is an unforgiving one for the attacker, and under the best circumstances, an initial assault force of some 6,000 Russian troops was outmatched by 9,000 prepared and dug-in defenders. Nonetheless, Moscow was working to a political timetable, and the High Command was unwilling to accept that a ragtag collection of rebel irregulars posed enough of a challenge to demand a change of plans. Those plans called for a pincer movement following the traditional preparatory air and artillery bombardment. Batteries of 122mm and 152mm howitzers hammered the city – heedless of the risk to civilian life – and Su-24 and Tu-22M bombers hit the city from the air.

Then the assault began, on New Year's Eve. From the north, Maj. Gen. Konstantin Pulikovsky led a mechanized force drawn from the 81st and 276th Motor Rifle Regiments and a battalion of the 131st Independent Motor Rifle Brigade. From the west, Maj. Gen. Valery Petruk led elements of the 19th Motor Rifle Division supported by two regiments and two battalions of paratroopers along the railway tracks to seize the central station and then advance on the presidential palace. From the east, the 129th Motor Rifle Regiment and a battalion each of the 98th and 104th Airborne Divisions under Lt. Gen. Nikolai Staskov would make a similar thrust along the railway line to Lenin Square in the heart of the city and from there take the bridges across the Sunzha River. From the north-east, Rokhlin himself would lead elements of the 255th and 33rd Motor Rifle Regiments and the 66th Reconnaissance Battalion of the 20th Motor Rifle Division to take the Central Hospital complex, while units of the 76th and 106th Airborne Divisions would secure the Lenin and Sheripov oil processing factories and chemical works, to prevent the rebels from destroying these crucial economic assets.

On paper, this looked like a clear and decisive plan in the best traditions of the Red Army. Maskhadov, though, had other ideas. He had organized three concentric defensive rings around the city, while the centre had become a nest of ad hoc fortifications. Buildings were sandbagged and reinforced to provide firing positions, sniper nests established on rooftops, and what tanks and artillery pieces the Chechens retained were emplaced to command the bridges across the Sunzha River and those roads wide enough for an armoured assault. Petruk's advance was soon bogged down. Staskov's was first attacked while crossing the Sunzha, then detoured into a maze of minefields and strongpoints, where panic and confusion led to friendly fire incidents often as lethal as anything the Chechens did. Despite several times being snarled in traffic jams of its own making, the result of cobbling together a command from units which had not had the chance to train together, Pulikovsky's force did manage to reach the presidential palace.

There it found itself dangerously isolated, though, in a crossfire of machine gun and rocket fire. A battalion of the 131st Independent Motor Rifle Brigade had been detached to take the main railway station instead of Petruk's deadlocked command, but there it was ambushed by well-positioned Chechen forces in buildings all around the square. Their BMP-1 and BTR-80 personnel carriers were being riddled with heavy machine-gun fire and brewed up by RPG-7 rockets, and when the survivors fled into the station building, it was set on fire. When they tried to withdraw, they found themselves trapped in narrow streets with no room to turn, as Chechens dropped grenades and petrol bombs on them from high buildings. As Rokhlin recounted: 'First, the vehicles at the head and tail of the column were burned ... and then the blow fell on the middle. The armoured vehicles had no chance to manoeuvre. And they burned like candles.'[5]

The battalion lost more than half its men and almost all its vehicles; in effect, it ceased to exist as a viable unit. Although the 66th Reconnaissance Battalion did get mauled trying to relieve the 131st Independent Motor Rifle Brigade, only Rokhlin's command was largely in good order. In part, this was because his mission had been less ambitious, and in part because he was canny enough to realize that Grozny was going to be a hard nut to crack. His forces had taken the Central Hospital, and dug in. Even so, by 3 January, the Russian attack had effectively been beaten back.

The assault had also claimed another victim: the reputation of the T-80B and T-80BV tank. First fielded in 1976, the T-80 only received its baptism of fire in Chechnya. Its gas turbine made it nimble, but also terribly thirsty, and it was not unusual for inexperienced crews to empty its fuel reservoirs by thoughtlessly allowing the engine to idle. At first, it had seemed to live up to its billing as a deadly tank-hunter: T-80s destroyed at least six rebel tanks, and one would withstand three hits from 125mm guns and still keep fighting. Once the T-80s of the 3rd and 133rd Tank Battalions were incautiously deployed into Grozny, though, they were prey to the inherent vulnerabilities of tanks in built-up environments, a specific design flaw (which meant it was vulnerable to attacks from above) and the lack of proper preparation (many were fielded without the explosive inserts in their reactive armour, which should have protected them from rocket-propelled grenades [RPGs]). The infantry who should have been providing the tanks with cover were often staying buttoned-up inside their armoured vehicles, and even when they were on the street, the Chechens – who knew their enemies' weaknesses well – used sniper and machine-gun fire to disperse them before hitting the T-80s with RPGs, recoilless rifles and grenades from cellars below and rooftops above. The result was a bloodbath. Eighteen of the 80 T-80s deployed were lost, and while the tank's defenders point to similar attrition of the older T-72, nonetheless the T-80 would never shake off the stigma of Grozny.

Moscow would not be denied, though. The air and artillery campaign was redoubled, and Mityukhin and the High Command abandoned hopes of a quick victory and instead adopted a much more cautious campaign. Reinforcements were rushed to Grozny, and the Russians methodically ground their way through the city, all but destroying it on their way. On 19 January, they finally seized the presidential palace – or what was left of it after it had been cracked open by BETAB-500 bunker-busting bombs, each half a tonne in weight. The Russian flag flew again over central Grozny, but the city was a ruin. Mopping up operations would continue for weeks, largely at the hands of the VV, while it would take months to collect and dispose of the bodies of civilians caught in the crossfire. Possibly up to 35,000 died in the bloodbath that the Organization for Security and Cooperation in Europe (OSCE) described as an 'unimaginable catastrophe'. This would not, however, be the last battle for this ill-fated city.

... AND LOSING GROZNY AGAIN

While federal forces moved on to take the battle to the rest of the country, in the face of continuing armed opposition, Yeltsin gave Deputy Interior Minister Gen. Anatoly Kulikov, head of the Interior Troops, overall command, in what was meant at once to be a rebuke to the military and an attempt to portray the operation as shifting to a mere policing one. As if this were the case; instead, there was a desperate search for more, better troops to throw into the war. The OGFV was expanded to 55,000 troops by March, including more *Spetsnaz* and the MVD's *Vityaz* anti-terrorist commando unit (often being pressed into service as glorified light infantry), the army's elite 506th Motor Rifle Regiment and even Naval Infantry.

In March, the cities of Gudermes and Argun fell, but even by May, Grozny was still under curfew and the acting field commander of the OGFV, Col. Gen. Mikhail Yegorov, was admitting that at least a fifth of the country was still in rebel hands. Day by day, Moscow seemed to be winning, but this quick and easy blitzkrieg was proving a frustratingly slow grind. In particular, the Russians fell foul of the same misunderstanding that had dogged their Afghan war, the assumption that controlling the towns and cities brought mastery of the countryside. If anything, the opposite was true. By day, army and MVD patrols on the plain and Mi-24 helicopter gunships in the air preserved the illusion of control, but in the mountains and in the night, the rebellion still burned.

The war was shifting to a new phase, a terrorist one. One rebel commander, Shamil Basayev, accompanied by 195 fighters, bribed and bluffed his way 110 kilometres into Russia and seized first the mayor's office and police station and then a local hospital in the town of Budyonnovsk. There he took 1,800 hostages, mostly civilians and including some 150 children. Demanding that Moscow withdraw from Chechnya, eventually Basayev negotiated a deal directly with Prime Minister Viktor Chernomyrdin that allowed him and his men safe passage back home. The government did not pull out of Chechnya, but its airy claims that it was on the verge of winning took a beating.

FSK director Sergei Stepashin and Interior Minister Viktor Yerin were forced to resign because of the mismanagement of the crisis, but this became the new model of war. The Chechens could not beat the federal forces on the battlefield but could determine the place, time and terms of any engagement. In December 1995, for example, 600 rebels under Salman Raduyev seized much of Gudermes, Chechnya's second largest city. They held it against massed federal assaults for two weeks, then agreed a ceasefire that likewise allowed them to leave unhindered. Then, on 9 January 1996, Raduyev launched an attack on Kizlyar airbase in neighbouring Dagestan, and when federal forces responded, took the hospital and over a thousand hostages, which he again traded for safe passage (although this time the Russians broke their agreement, and attacked the rebels as they left, regardless of the 150 human shields they had retained). Terrorist warfare could not break the federal forces, but nor could the Russians find and destroy the rebels.

The stalemate would be broken, ironically, by a Russian intelligence success. Dudayev could be a charismatic leader, but he was no strategist. Three government assassination attempts against him had failed, but on 21 April 1996 he was speaking on a satellite phone when Russian electronic warfare officers in a specially modified A-50 'Mainstay' surveillance aircraft were able to triangulate his location. Two Su-24 bombers were scrambled and hit his location, mortally wounding him. He was succeeded by his vice-president, Zelimkhan Yandarbiyev, but real power devolved to Maskhadov. He knew something dramatic would be needed to force Moscow to negotiate seriously: not just a terrorist operation, but something to change the whole political calculus. He needed to take back Grozny.

The tempo of guerrilla attacks began to slacken, and Moscow allowed itself to believe that it was winning, that Dudayev's death had somehow changed the game. At the end of May, Yeltsin visited Grozny and told the assembled troops that 'the war is over, you have won'. To reflect this, conscript-heavy units were sent home, and the OGFV shrank from its peak of 55,000 to just over 41,000: 19,000 regular troops and 22,000 police and VV. Yeltsin also sacked Grachyov, whose reputation for corruption and incompetence had come to outweigh his political utility, as part of a pre-election deal with Alexander Lebed, the tough ex-paratrooper and Afghan War veteran, whom he wanted as his running mate. Grachyov was no great loss to the Defence Ministry, but it meant that at a crucial time, it was first headed by an interim, acting minister (Chief of the General Staff Gen. Mikhail Kolesnikov) and then by a new minister, Gen. Igor Rodionov, in transition. It contributed to a lack of attention being paid to the situation on the ground. Instead, policy was being shaped by politics and Yeltsin's need to tell the Russian people that the war was all but over. The plan was that by the end of the year, only a single VV brigade and the army's 205th Motor Rifle Brigade would be left in Chechnya. Of the forces remaining, more were sent south in what was seen as a last push to take the remaining rebel strongholds.

Maskhadov had a plan of his own, though. On the night of 5/6 August, before the day Yeltsin was going to be inaugurated after his re-election to the presidency in a poll widely regarded as rigged, 1,500 rebels were quietly infiltrating Grozny in 25-man squads, easily bypassing the checkpoints and guard stations from which Russian troops rarely ventured after dark. At 0550 hours, they launched a surprise offensive, and within three hours, most of the city was in their hands. Federal forces were holding out in the centre and at Khankala airbase, but most of the 7,000 army and MVD garrison fled or hunkered down in their garrisons, around which the rebels hurriedly placed mines and firing positions.

Volunteers and reinforcements swelled Maskhadov's forces to around 6,000 men over the coming days, but even so this was a stunning blow to the Russians. Desperate to retake it, Pulikovsky sent columns into the city piecemeal, and so they were defeated in detail. On 11 August, a battalion from the 276th Motor Rifle Regiment did manage to break through to the defenders still holding the centre but this did not change the reality on the ground, that the rebels were holding Grozny and blockading around 3,000–4,000 federal troops. Infuriated, on 19 August Pulikovsky demanded that the rebels surrender, and even before his ultimatum had expired, launched mass air and artillery bombardments. An already battered city began to be flattened further, and by 21 August, an estimated 220,000 people had fled Grozny, leaving no more than 70,000 civilians in a city which before the war had been home to 400,000.

Ultimately, there was no doubt that the federal forces could win militarily, but Maskhadov was rightly counting on the fact that all wars are ultimately political acts. The spectacle of the Russian army losing a city to rebels who had publicly been discounted as all but beaten, and their capacity also to steal Yeltsin's day of glory, all led to a massive political backlash. Lebed, now the secretary of Yeltsin's Security Council, had long been sceptical about the war. He flew to Chechnya and ordered Pulikovsky to stand his forces down. Yeltsin just wanted the problem to go away, and so he authorized Lebed to hold direct talks with Maskhadov.

On 30 August, the two veterans of the Red Army concluded the Khasavyurt Accord. It was hardly the basis for a lasting peace. It shelved the fundamental question of Chechnya's constitutional status but instead recognized Chechen autonomy, while leaving all kinds of thorny issues as to its limits unresolved. In effect, so long as Chechnya pretended to be part of Russia, Moscow would not try to actually assert any control over it. It would prove no more than a temporary pause, and in 1999, war would return to Chechnya. As so often the case, a brilliant guerrilla commander does not always turn out to be so lucky or capable as a national leader and he would prove unable to prevent the slide into a second conflict. But for now, federal forces were withdrawn, the Chechens could start to rebuild their devastated country, and Yeltsin had one fewer pending crisis in his in-box: the First Chechen War was over.

5

The Wars of Russian Assertion

The First Chechen War was a disaster for the Russian army. It had been outsmarted and outfought, even losing cities to a ramshackle guerrilla army. It had been clumsy and brutal. All the inefficiencies, brutality and corruption of the army had been put on public display, not least thanks to a critical media that chronicled its failings. It also contributed to a massive public backlash against the military and a further spike in draft dodging. The Russian military was left at the very lowest ebb of its fortunes and credibility. And morale: Gen. Rokhlin, one of the few commanders who had genuinely distinguished himself in Chechnya, refused to accept the Hero of Russia, saying: 'The war in Chechnya is not Russia's glory, but its misfortune.'[1]

Yeltsin, never a man to pass up on a good scapegoat, had sacked Grachyov and also forced the resignation of FSK security service chief Sergei Stepashin and Interior Minister Viktor Yerin. Grachyov's successor, the acerbic Rodionov, did not last long in the position: his frustration with what he saw as the government's refusal to fund the military properly ('what kind of "@*/?!" reforms are you talking about? We are starving!' he exploded at a reception in 1997 to military journalist Pavel Felgenhauer[2]) combined with a resistance to subordinating the military to a new – and short-lived – Defence Council and its secretary, Yuri Baturin, who he felt was wilfully short-changing them. In May 1997, less than a year after taking office, Rodionov was sacked and replaced by Gen. Igor Sergeyev, head of the Strategic Rocket Forces. As the price for his elevation, Sergeyev was

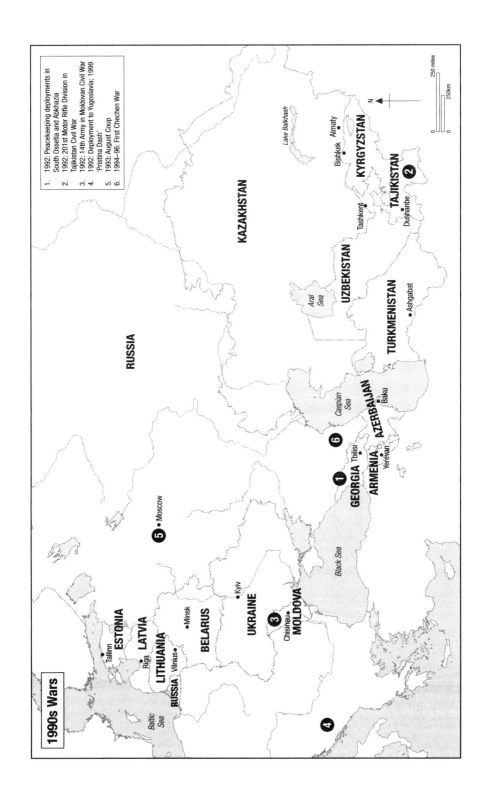

1990s Wars

1. 1992: Peacekeeping deployments in South Ossetia and Abkhazia
2. 1992: 201st Motor Rifle Division in Tajikistan Civil War
3. 1992: 14th Army in Moldovan Civil War
4. 1992: Deployment to Yugoslavia; 1999 'Pristina Dash'
5. 1993: August Coup
6. 1994–96: First Chechen War

much less outspoken, and devoted more of his efforts to protecting his old service than the armed forces as a whole. What this meant was that for most of the 1990s, the Russian military was led by political appointees more concerned with protecting their positions and appeasing Yeltsin than articulating some coherent vision for the country's armed forces. They ended the decade scarcely any more reformed – just smaller – than when they had started.

Yet at the same time, they were being called on to protect the Motherland's interests in a growing number of theatres. Beyond the Chechen war, they would be deployed in neighbouring post-Soviet states, as both peacekeepers and imperial enforcers, and even deployed into Yugoslavia during the civil war that tore it apart, prompting a military stand-off with US forces. This was a decade of living dangerously, in which Moscow tried to play the role of a great power, or at least a regional one, while its soldiers were underpaid, underfed, undervalued and undertrained. In many ways, what is striking is that they did as well as they did.

MOLDOVA'S POST-SOVIET HANGOVER

Why is there still a slice of the territory legally part of the Republic of Moldova, in which Russian is still the official language, and statues of Lenin still loom over the main squares? There was still an assumption in the Kremlin that Russia was the regional hegemon of what it called the 'Near Abroad' – the other post-Soviet states. I remember back in 1995, a Russian diplomat earnestly telling me that 'we have no dispute with the sovereignty and independence of foreign nations; but these countries, they are hardly foreign, we feel they are still part of our family.' Russia, he implied, was very much head of the household, and these countries' freedom was only insofar as they did not challenge Moscow's authority. It would exploit territorial disputes, historical grievances and inter-ethnic rivalries to force neighbours into line, especially by backing local minorities, often ethnic Russians, in their disputes with their governments. Encouraging or downright forcing Russian colonists to move to conquered territories was a measure applied first by the tsars and then, even more deliberately, by the Soviets. When the USSR was dissolved, there were more than 20 million ethnic Russians living outside the boundaries of the Russian Federation, something Putin would later call 'a major geopolitical disaster of the century'.[3] While many adapted, and simply acclimatized to their new nationalities, others felt marginalized or discriminated against, and these became allies or pretexts for Moscow's meddling.

This was especially evident in Moldova, one of the smaller republics, sandwiched between Ukraine and Romania. Around three-quarters of the population are of Romanian heritage, and speak a language which is essentially Romanian. Just under 15% were ethnic Russians and other Slavs, disproportionately concentrated on a sliver of land on the east bank of the Dneistr River. As Party rule declined, in Moldova as elsewhere, nationalism rose in response. In 1989, the local authorities made Moldovan the main state language, relegating Russian to a secondary status, and abandoned the use of the Cyrillic alphabet. The Russians of what would become Transnistria, formally the Pridnestrovian Moldavian Republic (PMR), became increasingly alarmed. Many did not want the USSR disbanded, seeing it as their protection against the Moldovans. In August 1990 they had actually declared independence even if, to be blunt, neither Moscow nor the Moldovan authorities in Chisinau paid much attention.

By winter 1991–92, Transnistrian militants were clashing sporadically with Moldovan police. In response, the government began forming a National Guard and then established a proper ministry of defence, and armed forces. These were based on elements of the Soviet 14th Guards Army that had been based in western Moldova, as well as an array of volunteers, reservists and conscripts.

The irony is that the 14th Army, which was headquartered in Tiraspol, east of the Dneistr, also became the key protector of the PMR. Although Moscow was officially neutral, many of the army's officers and men either came from the region or sympathized with the rebels. Indeed, its commander, Lt. Gen. Gennady Yakovlev, made no secret of his support for them, and in December also accepted the role of chair of the PMR's de facto defence minister. The Kremlin's position was ambiguous. Shaposhnikov decided Yakovlev could not be both a PMR minister and a Russian commander and replaced him at the head of the 14th Army with the rather more neutral Lt. Gen. Yuri Netkachev. Still, though, weapons continued to flow out of the armouries of the 14th, and on 5 April 1992, Vice-President Rutskoi visited Tiraspol and encouraged the Transnistrians to seek their independence.

March and April had seen sporadic skirmishes along the eastern bank of the Dneistr, but the most serious fighting was to take place in the strategic city of Bender. Although largely populated by Russian-speakers, Bender is actually on the western bank, and on the main road from Chisinau to Tiraspol. Notionally controlled by the government, it was a constant source of instability, and when police arrested a Russian major from the 14th Army on suspicion of helping insurgents, it triggered a violent confrontation. Both sides sent forces into Bender, and the PMR's Republican Guards were supported by T-64 tanks from the 14th Army. At least two were knocked out by Moldovan T-12 anti-tank guns, and left stranded in the street, their tell-tale Russian markings belying Moscow's claims that its forces were keeping out of this fraternal spat.

As Moldovan troops pushed forward and looked about to take the bridge over the Dneistr, Tiraspol threw all the forces it could muster into Bender, including armed Cossack volunteers from Russia and eastern Ukraine. Slowly, they pushed back into Bender amidst vicious house-to-house fighting. The 14th Army seems to have played no more than a supporting role in this fighting, but Chisinau was convinced that the only reason why its forces were not in retreat was because the Russian military was directly involved. Believing that the 14th Army was preparing to invade, it dispatched two of Moldova's handful of flightworthy MiG-29 fighters (inherited from the Soviet 86th Guards Fighter Aviation Regiment) to try to destroy the Bender Bridge: six OFAB-250 bombs were dropped, but none hit. Nonetheless, this was enough for the 14th Army to activate its air defences. The conflict was escalating.

Fearing that an internal struggle was going to turn into a war between Russia and Moldova, Yeltsin dispatched his national security adviser, the ex-paratrooper Alexander Lebed, to Tiraspol. His orders were to stop the fighting by whatever means necessary, and he adopted a characteristically ferocious approach. On arriving at the 14th Army headquarters, he relieved Netkachev and took personal command. Early in the morning of 3 July, massed fire from the army's 4th Artillery Regiment – unguided 220mm rockets from BM-27 Uragans, 122mm shells from D-30 howitzers and 152mm rounds from several batteries of 2A36 Giatsint field guns – shattered Moldovan encampments around Bender.

Lebed had no real sympathy for either side. Possibly apocryphally, he is meant afterwards to have said, 'I told the hooligans in Tiraspol and the fascists in Chisinau – either you stop killing each other, or else I'll shoot the whole lot of you.'⁴ But he was there to make peace and, true to form, he was going to do so through superior firepower. The 14th Army was, by this stage, scarcely much larger than a division in strength, with around 14,000 effectives. Nonetheless, they were well armed, and not only did the bombardment effectively end the government's push on Bender, but it raised the prospect that they would have to take on a combined force of PMR militia, volunteers and Russian troops that outnumbered Moldova's still-forming army. At the same time, Lebed made it clear to the PMR leadership that the price for Russian protection was a peace deal, and on 21 July, Yeltsin signed a ceasefire agreement with his Moldovan counterpart, Mircea Snegur. This would be secured by a peacekeeping force of three battalions of Moldovan troops, two of PMR soldiers – and five from the 14th Army.

There would be sporadic clashes thereafter, but under the shadow of the 14th Army, the deal held, as it has to this day. Perhaps a thousand died all told, both civilians and combatants, and Moldova in effect lost the east bank of the Dneistr. In 1995, the 14th Army became the Operational Group of Russian Forces in Transnistria, and as of 2022, it is made up of maybe 1,500 men in two Independent Peacekeeping Motor Rifle battalions. But they are there as much as anything else as a token of Moscow's continued commitment to maintaining the PMR, now a heavily criminalized and almost Soviet pseudo-state. It is not that the Kremlin really cares about the PMR and its people – rather, it is a symbol of its willingness to defend the interests of ethnic Russians in the 'Near Abroad' (when it suits) and a convenient base for political mischief in the region. The precedent Lebed set, the use of force to support convenient insurgents and create a 'frozen conflict' that permits Moscow to retain a foothold in post-Soviet neighbours, would be used repeatedly in the future, and helps demonstrate how the Russian military became and remains a key instrument of its foreign policy, too.

CENTRAL ASIA: THE TAJIKISTAN CONTINGENT

Likewise, another military unit became an instrument of Russian power in Central Asia. The 201st Gatchina Twice Red Banner Motor Rifle

Division, which had taken part in the Soviet invasion of Afghanistan in 1979, had then been based in Tajikistan, with its headquarters in the country's capital, Dushanbe. It was slated for withdrawal back to Russia, provisionally in September 1992, when civil war broke out in Tajikistan. Rebels would several times try to raid its bases for weapons and supplies, and many of the unit's soldiers, who were conscripts drafted locally, simply deserted. The predominantly Russian officers held the unit together, though, and were reinforced with *Spetsnaz* in a bid by Moscow to maintain its operational status and use it to prop up what was admittedly an authoritarian Soviet-era government against rebels from minority ethnic groups and Islamic extremists, including radicals from Afghanistan.

Although officially just part of a CIS peacekeeping force, in practice the 201st became Moscow's main agent in Tajikistan. When Dushanbe fell briefly to the rebels in late 1992, it played a crucial role in its recapture in December, providing heavy fire support for the pro-government security forces and militias from the Kulob region, from whence new Tajik leader Emomali Rahmon drew his main support. In 1993, the 201st was reinforced with the 41st Separate Helicopter Squadron equipped with Mi-24s, the 2nd Separate Rocket Artillery Battalion with Uragan MLRS and an aviation group based as Dushanbe airport. This reflected the broadening of its duties: as well as combating insurgents directly and interdicting attempts to cross the Tajik–Afghan border, it was now escorting vital convoys bringing food, medicines and military materiel to outlying cities. One officer of the 201st, who had served in Afghanistan, described it in 1992 as 'eerily like *Afgan*, just without the rebels – so far'. His caution was justified, as the 201st became increasingly embroiled in fighting. In July 1993, as many as 250 Tajik and Afghan fighters tried to storm the 12th Outpost of the Border Troops assigned to Tajikistan. There were 47 Border Troops and one civilian at the outpost, but they held off the militants for 11 hours. The arrival of elements of the 201st Motor Rifle Division's 149th Guards Motor Rifle Regiment ended the attack, which left 25 Russians and up to 70 militants dead.

The civil war would rage until 1997, and in that time the 201st would be brought up to full divisional strength – albeit largely by again recruiting Tajiks to serve under Russian officers – and would be embroiled in numerous raids and skirmishes. Peace was eventually achieved through a mediation process brokered by both Washington and Moscow, but when the guns fell silent it was nonetheless Russia that retained a crucial role in the country. Rahmon was in power, and remains so as of writing, atop a corrupt and heavy-handed regime maintained by a series of dubious elections.

Although in 1994 it was renamed the 201st Military Base, the division continues to prop up the government in Dushanbe and, by extension, maintain Moscow's authority in Central Asia. In 2012, the base's lease was extended to 2042, and at present its main combat elements are the 92nd and 149th Guards Motor Rifle Regiments, the 2nd Separate Rocket Artillery Battalion, a reconnaissance battalion in Dushanbe and the 191st Motor Rifle Regiment in Kurgan-Tyube. There is also a helicopter squadron and air group at Dushanbe. Considering that the 201st Base now consists of some 7,000 largely professional soldiers, equipped increasingly to the highest Russian standards, while the total Tajik armed forces number a reported 9,500, Moscow has a considerable role in regional security. Again, military deployments abroad are converted into influence, in this case in support of a friendly regime – or at least one that knows it pays to keep on Russia's good side.

BALKAN DASH

Yugoslavia had been a long-term thorn in Moscow's side during the Cold War: a notionally socialist state, yet one which had refused to bow to Soviet hegemony. This multi-ethnic state essentially disintegrated at the same time as the USSR, though, especially as opportunist Communist Party official Slobodan Milosevic reinvented himself as a Serbian nationalist leader. Amidst protests, strikes and inter-ethnic clashes, nationalists rose across the country and civil war exploded in 1991–92.

On one level, it could be argued that this was none of Moscow's business. Russia has deep historical and cultural connections to the region, especially to the Orthodox Christian Serbs, but nonetheless at first it paid little attention to the Balkans. It had, after all, enough to occupy it at home. However, by 1993, this was changing. Extreme nationalist politicians like Vladimir Zhirinovsky, head of the Liberal Democratic Party (which, as has already been noted, is neither liberal nor democratic), were using the situation to paint the Yeltsin government as weak and willing to betray traditional allies to curry favour with the West. Furthermore, the Kremlin was beginning to feel taken for granted by that same West, and this gave it an opportunity to try to show that it was not a spent force.

Russia would play a role within UNPROFOR, the UN Protection Force which sought in 1992–95 to make a tenuous peace in Bosnia and Herzegovina and Croatia, amidst ethnic cleansing and vicious conflicts that pitted neighbour against neighbour. An initial force of 900 soldiers would in due course be scaled up to an airborne brigade of 1,500 paratroopers in the Implementation Force (IFOR) and Stabilization Force (SFOR) that replaced it in 1996. The largest non-NATO contingent in these forces, Russia's peacekeepers played a useful role not just on the ground but also in making the case that, for all its troubles, Russia ought still to be considered a serious global player. When IFOR and SFOR were formed, a Russian general was invited to become a Special Deputy to the NATO Supreme Allied Commander, Europe (SACEUR) in the hope that this would resolve command and control issues – and also symbolize a closer NATO–Russia relationship.

The 1990s, though, saw Russia increasingly dissatisfied with how it was being treated and becoming worried that the West was coming to see itself as the global hegemon, banker and policeman, all in one. The expansion of NATO, seen as still an essentially anti-Russian alliance, was a particular bone of contention. When US president Bill Clinton visited Moscow in May 1995, Yeltsin said this was 'nothing but a humiliation' for Russia, and he flatly rejected the idea: 'for me to agree to the borders of NATO expanding towards those of Russia – that would constitute a betrayal on my part of the Russian people.'[5] Yet NATO still expanded, taking in Poland, Hungary, and the Czech Republic in 1999, and nine more countries were offered Membership Action Plans detailing their path to joining the alliance. However, Russian suspicions truly came to the fore during the 1998–99 Kosovo War. This ethnically Albanian region of what was left of Yugoslavia – then just Serbia and Montenegro – was increasingly restive, and terrorist attacks by the Kosovo Liberation Army prompted a heavy-handed Serbian response that was crossing the line between legitimate counter-insurgency, and outright ethnic cleansing.

When peace talks failed, NATO launched a massive aerial bombing campaign in March and June 1999, with the stated aim of getting 'Serbs out, peacekeepers in, refugees back'. Almost a thousand aircraft flew over 38,000 combat missions, and 218 Tomahawk cruise missiles were launched. First they targeted Yugoslav air defence and high-value military targets, then military units and command hubs. Inevitably, there were civilian casualties and targeting errors – not least, the bombing of the Chinese embassy in Belgrade – but eventually Milosevic had to accept NATO's terms, which included the withdrawal of his forces from Kosovo and the deployment of a multi-national peacekeeping force.

The Russians had been instrumental in persuading Milosevic to stand down, and insisted on being involved in this force. They presumed that they, like other major participants, would be assigned their own peacekeeping sector. NATO, fearing this would essentially create a Serb-controlled region, refused, and so Moscow decided it would make its own facts on the ground. On the first day of the peace, 11 June 1999, 250 Russian paratroopers under Col. Gen. Viktor Zavarzin rushed from their SFOR base in Bosnia to seize Pristina International Airport in Kosovo's capital first. By the time substantial numbers of troops from KFOR, the NATO-led Kosovo Force, had reached Pristina, the Russians were emplaced.

There followed a tense standoff, only partly eased when KFOR's commander, Britain's Lt. Gen. Mike Jackson, met Zavarzin in the ruins of the airport terminal, and the two men shared a flask of whisky. Jackson, who had read Russian Studies at Birmingham University, did not accept SACEUR Gen. Wesley Clark's belief that this was just a bridgehead and the start of a Russian occupation. Clark wanted Jackson to defy the Russians and occupy and block the airport runways, and Jackson reportedly eventually retorted, 'I'm not going to start the Third World War for you.'[6]

Jackson was right, in that while there were other Russian forces on alert, there was no wider plan for invasion. The three remaining VDV battalions would only have been deployed had NATO tried to dislodge the Russians by force. Instead, Clark was overruled by Gen. Hugh Shelton, Chair of the US Joint Chiefs of Staff, and a deal was struck allowing both sides to save face, with Russian peacekeepers deploying throughout Kosovo, but without their own sector and outside NATO's command structure. This was, after all, more about Moscow's use of the military to make a wider political point, both at home and abroad. The 'Pristina Dash' heartened a Russian public and military which had been starved of good news. It also set the tone for future Russian interventions, relying on élan, surprise and a willingness to bluff. These were exactly the kind of characteristics that appealed to the man who, in 1999, had just been appointed Prime Minister, Vladimir Putin.

PART TWO
Enter Putin

6

Putin's Priorities

On 7 May 2000, a rather grey, slightly stooped man passed between two files of Honour Guards of the Presidential Regiment, his dark suit contrasting sharply with the bright blue tunics and red facings of their ceremonial uniforms. This was the inauguration of newly elected President Vladimir Putin, a man who had been virtually unknown to most Russians a couple of years before, yet who had been elected in a convincing first-round victory with 53.4% of the vote, leagues ahead of his nearest rival, the Communist Party's Gennady Zyuganov, with 29.5%.[1]

His speech seemed to offer something for everybody. He celebrated that, for the first time in Russia's history, there had been a peaceful change in leadership through the ballot box (which would prove ironic in light of his future efforts to cling to power). He promised to protect and extend democracy (also ironic). Yet at the same time, he warned his listeners that:

> We must not forget anything, we need to know our history, know it for what it is, draw lessons from it, and always remember those who created the Russian state, defending its dignity, made it a great, powerful, mighty state.[2]

At the time, this may have sounded like so much political rhetoric, even if 22 years later, the full meaning of these lines would be visited on a Ukraine that he felt challenged Russia's 'dignity'. After all, no one seemed to know who Putin really was, and everyone wanted to claim him. Liberal politicians in his home city of St Petersburg declared with satisfaction that 'their man' had ascended to the highest position in the land. Others pointed to his past career in the KGB and suggested that this was a statist first, a democrat second. It would turn out that the latter were right.

WHO IS VLADIMIR PUTIN?

By the later 1990s, Boris Yeltsin's incapacity to rule was becoming increasingly obvious. When he had an enemy, he could be focused and effective, but it was clear he had little real vision for Russia. He had risen to power as the candidate of the opposition: to the Communist Party, to Gorbachev, to the Soviet state. Quite what he was *for* never really became clear – except that all too often he was for ample supplies of alcohol, sometimes washing down prescription medications. In 1994, during a state visit to Washington DC, he had memorably been discovered by Secret Service agents drunk and in his underwear on Pennsylvania Avenue, looking for pizza. Visiting Stockholm in 1997, with a pronounced slur, he suddenly announced that Swedish meatballs reminded him of the face of tennis star Björn Borg. He also suffered numerous heart attacks – he had an emergency quintuple heart bypass in November 1996 – so perhaps it was unsurprising that his closest allies and backers – known as 'the Family' – had by then begun looking for a safe and loyal successor.

They found him in Vladimir Putin, a man who, until his elevation to the presidency, had seemed to be everybody's loyal aide. It is well known that he had from a young age wanted to join the KGB, the Soviet intelligence and security agency. Notoriously, even as a child he had visited the KGB's headquarters in St Petersburg – then still known as Leningrad – for all that the so-called *Bolshoi Dom*, the 'Big House', had an infamous reputation from the days of the old Stalin-era secret police in the 1930s. There, he asked a bemused officer how to join and was told to run along and come back when he had graduated from university. This he duly did, joining in 1975.

He was a scrappy kid from a poor family, whose childhood had been lived in the ruins of post-war Leningrad, a city which was hammered and starved by the Nazis during its 872-day siege in

1941–44. There is no evidence he joined the KGB to be 'sword and shield of the Communist Party', as it described itself, but rather because it offered a chance to rise in the system and emulate the heroes of Soviet spy films and TV series. He was enthusiastic, to be sure, but never a high-flier. He began his career in the Second Chief Directorate of the KGB, counter-intelligence, and although his fluent German allowed him to transfer to the elite foreign espionage service, the First Chief Directorate, he was not destined for a career as a case officer working undercover in some embassy around the world. Instead, he was posted to Dresden, where he was essentially a liaison officer with the Stasi, East Germany's counterpart to the KGB. Claims that he was involved in nefarious covert operations, such as running terrorists in the West, appear wholly unfounded. Instead, his days were largely spent filing reports to Moscow, routing documents to his Stasi contacts, and generally handling the day-to-day bureaucracy of secret police work.

The closest thing he saw to action was the admittedly tense moment when, as the East German regime collapsed in 1989, he had to face down a crowd of protesters who would otherwise have mobbed the KGB's offices, while indoors his colleagues were desperately trying to contact the local Soviet garrison. Nonetheless, the KGB officers in Germany were forced to return home, and he soon left KGB service, although it is unclear whether he was kept on their books as a reservist. In a country in collapse, he scrabbled around for work, first getting a job at Leningrad State University – probably thanks to his KGB connections – and then as an adviser to newly elected city mayor Anatoly Sobchak.

This is when he discovered his talent as fixer. He became Sobchak's head of international affairs and then deputy. He wheeled and dealed, reaching accommodations with everyone from foreign companies to the mafia. He prospered, but he also made sure he had Sobchak's back: when the major failed to win re-election in 1996, Putin moved on to Moscow, but when investigators started looking into Sobchak's financial affairs in 1997, it was Putin who arranged for him to fly to France ahead of any arrest warrants. In Moscow, he became deputy to the head of the Presidential Property Management Department – one of the most infamously corrupt branches of the Presidential Administration – and then deputy head of the Presidential Administration. He was discreet, efficient, loyal and sober, all characteristics that endeared him to the Family.

Up to then, he had always been a figure modestly standing behind his patron of the moment, but in 1998, he would come out of the shadows, when Yeltsin appointed him director of the Federal Security Service (FSB: *Federalnaya Sluzhba Bezopasnosti*). For the eager KGB middle-achiever, it was a career milestone, although he did not stay long at the offices in the Lubyanka building in central Moscow. After only a year, he was made one of three First Deputy Prime Ministers – and later that same day, Prime Minister. By this stage, it was clear that the Family had made its choice.

In the Russian system, the prime minister is more the administrator-in-chief than anything else: real executive power sits with the president. However, the constitution does give him one particular role: if the president is ever incapacitated or stands down, he becomes Acting President. On 31 December 1999, less than five months into Putin's premiership, Yeltsin duly resigned. The first presidential decree the new acting president signed explicitly gave Yeltsin and his relatives immunity from any future corruption charges – Putin knew how to look after his patrons. Yeltsin's resignation triggered early presidential elections, catching Putin's rivals off guard. With effective incumbency, and the full power of the Kremlin machine behind him, Putin easily won the March poll. At last he was no one's understudy or fixer, but the boss. Now he had power, what would he do with it?

PUTIN IN CHARGE

It quickly became clear that Putin intended to restore the power of the state at home and Russia abroad, by whatever means necessary. The billionaire oligarchs who had run much of the country behind the scenes under Yeltsin were brought to heel, not least when the richest of them all, Mikhail Khodorkovsky, was arrested and imprisoned when he seemed not to realize that the days when they could involve themselves with politics were over. Putin was not going to be anyone's catspaw or instrument.

However, his immediate focus would be Chechnya, and this became something of a test case for the new order. In September 1999, explosions had rocked four apartment buildings in Moscow, Buynaksk in the North Caucasus region of Dagestan and Volgodonsk in the southern Rostov region. More than 300 civilians were killed and more than a thousand injured. Jihadists from Chechnya were immediately blamed. The public response was a predictable mix of fear and anger, and this helped confirm a national consensus that the country needed a strong, tough hand. There is continued controversy around these bombings, with good reasons to suspect they were actually organized by Putin's backers within the security community – with or without his knowledge – but either way, a public which for a long time had shied away from the thought of any renewed war in Chechnya began to waver. After all, a month earlier the Chechen warlord Shamil Basayev, along with Saudi-born jihadist Samir Saleh Abdullah, known as Khattab, had launched a military incursion into Dagestan. It had been repelled in a month of sporadic fighting, but this seemed further evidence that Maskhadov either could not or would not control the extremists in Chechnya.

In October, as will be discussed in the next chapter, the Russians launched the Second Chechen War, and it was soon clear that they had been preparing for it. Compared with the shambolic and often half-hearted way the Kremlin had fought the first war, it had not only assembled a suitable and powerful military force, it also made sure it controlled the narrative at home. The invasion of Dagestan and the apartment bombings provided a powerful rationale for action, and the consequent invasion, launched while Putin was prime minister but fought during his presidency, set the tone for his rule. The Russian state was back: it would brook no challenges at home, or on its borders, and it would assert its security interests no matter what the outside world might think.

Putin was never anything less than a convinced Russian nationalist. Even before he was president, he had made it clear that, in his opinion, 'Russia has been a great power for centuries, and remains so. It has always had and still has legitimate zones of interest ... We should not drop our guard in this respect, neither should we allow our opinion to be ignored.'[3] However, at first he seemed genuinely to believe this could be achieved in some kind of partnership with the West – indeed, in 2000 he even seemed to think someday Russia could join NATO.[4] Putin was the first world leader to call President George W. Bush after the 2001 9/11 terrorist attacks, and he seemed very willing to cooperate

in the 'Global War on Terror'. According to then-defence minister Sergei
Ivanov, as US and NATO forces were invading Afghanistan later that
year, officials from the Islamist Taliban movement actually approached
Russian border guards on the Tajik–Afghan border. They had a message
for Moscow, which they were offering an anti-American alliance. As
Ivanov put it, 'we rejected it with the world famous English-speaking
gesture: "F... off."'[5]

The trouble is that from the first, there was a clear disconnect
between how Putin and the West saw the relationship. He saw
Russia's Chechen war as its own front in that global struggle, and
was outraged when human rights abuses on the ground were
criticized in the West. Meanwhile, he believed that Russia had an
absolute right to hegemony over the post-Soviet successor states and
a promise – which the West denied – that NATO would not expand
eastward. When, in 2004, seven nations were allowed into what he
considered an anti-Russian club – including the three Baltic States,
which had been part of not simply the Warsaw Pact, but actually
the USSR – he was furious. By 2006, he was feeling that Russia had
been exploited, conned and marginalized, and at a keynote speech in
Munich, in February 2007, he suggested that the United States was
trying to create a 'unipolar' world, one in which 'there is one master,
one sovereign' through the 'almost uncontained hyper use of force –
military force – in international relations, force that is plunging the
world into an abyss of permanent conflict.' Concluding that 'Russia
is a country with a history that spans more than a thousand years
and [which] has practically always used the privilege to carry out an
independent foreign policy', he made it clear that Moscow was once
again considering itself a great power, and would assert that without
worrying if it pleased the West.[6]

PUTIN'S MINISTERS

Putin could not and did not do it all himself. Later chapters will detail
the specific arms of service and the character and reforms associated with
each of his defence ministers. Nonetheless, there is a clear trajectory
that mirrors his own evolving perception of Russia's needs and also the
challenges associated with bringing change to a large, proud and often
self-interested organization.

PUTIN'S DEFENCE MINISTERS

Period	Defence Minister	Background
1997–2001	Marshal Igor Sergeyev	Military
2001–07	Sergei Ivanov	KGB/FSB
2007–12	Anatoly Serdyukov	Head, Federal Tax Service
2012–	Sergei Shoigu	Minister for Emergency Situations, Governor of Moscow Region

He inherited Marshal Igor Sergeyev, the former Strategic Rocket Forces commander, who had tried to introduce some reorganization and modernization, much of which meant closing down various military educational establishments and joining together the Siberian and Trans-Baikal Military Districts in the interests of efficiency. Some divisions were formally assigned 'constant readiness' status, which was meant to mean that they were fully equipped and kept at not less than 80% of their establishment strength, but it is questionable how often this was really achieved.

It was a mark of Putin's interest in rebuilding Russian military strength from the first that he soon replaced Sergeyev with one of his closest allies, Sergei Ivanov. A contemporary of Putin's, he also came from Leningrad and joined the KGB, where the two men got to know each other. Whereas Putin's KGB career was lacklustre, though, Ivanov was on the fast-track, joining the elite First Chief Directorate, its foreign espionage arm, and later transferring to the post-Soviet FSB. In the early years, there were limited extra resources available for the military, and those were to a large degree swallowed up by the Second Chechen War. Although essentially a victory, this was more because the Russians managed to avoid the mistakes of the first war rather than demonstrating any particularly greater capability.

This was to be Ivanov's task, although from the first he was hindered by his limited military expertise and also the resistance of the generals. It was also a gargantuan task, after years of neglect and mismanagement. He did make some progress, to be sure, especially in pushing for a reduced dependence on conscripts. National service was reduced to 12 months. Many within the High Command resisted this: they felt Russia had to have a millions' strong reserve pool of ex-draftees in case of a major war, and that 18 months, let alone 12, was not long enough for the men to be properly trained and deployable for longer than a few months. Regardless, Ivanov was committed to a slightly smaller army, but one made up of a greater proportion of *kontraktniki* volunteers serving on longer-term contracts, and Putin was won over both by the argument that such a military would be more effective, and also by the fact that this was politically popular in the country.

One of Ivanov's biggest problems was that he was indispensable, though. He was one of Putin's key advisers on security and foreign affairs, and in 2005 was also made Deputy Prime Minister responsible for the defence industries. The other was that he was neither a military man nor a money man. He was dependent on the advice from the generals – who often were simply arguing for more of everything – and although more and more money was being spent, without any clear blueprint for change and buy-in from the High Command, much was being wasted on contradictory or redundant boondoggles.

In 2007, Ivanov was promoted to the position of First Deputy Prime Minister. This time, Putin went for a money man, someone with a track record of institutional reform and no particular problems with alienating the High Command: Anatoly Serdyukov. His detractors – of whom there were many – called him the 'furniture salesman' because he had once worked for a homewares company, but his previous career had been heading and modernizing Russia's dysfunctional tax service. Serdyukov would prove an unexpectedly successful reformer of the military because of three great strengths: his Chief of the General Staff, Nikolai Makarov; the 2008 Georgian War; and the fact that he really didn't care what his generals thought of him. Gen. Makarov was a serious and well-respected officer, who had a good sense of what was needed. The underwhelming performance of the military in Georgia gave Serdyukov and Makarov grounds to force the conservative High Command to accept serious reforms. And Serdyukov's willingness to court the generals' disfavour – so long as he had Putin's support, that was all he needed – allowed him, an outsider with no ties to military traditions or arm of service loyalties, and everything to prove, to embark on a systematic and brutal series of reforms.

In October 2008, he unveiled a plan for what he described as the most radical changes since the end of the Second World War, intended to create modern, flexible forces ready at any time for anything from a full-scale war to out-of-area interventions. The total establishment strength of the military was to be reduced by 200,000 in the next four years, with a further increase in the proportion of professionals. The Ground Forces would move from being built around the division to the smaller and more flexible brigade, all – not just the precious 20% – in permanent readiness. These brigades would also go through a sustained modernization, such that by 2020, 70% of all their weapons systems would be of the latest generation.

Meanwhile, he trained his sights on the officer corps, which Serdyukov said was 'reminiscent of an egg which is swollen in the middle. There are more colonels and lieutenant-colonels than there are junior officers.'[7] Some 205,000 officers' positions were cut, and the higher ranks were pruned especially dramatically, with 200 generals dismissed. At the other end of the scale, new programmes were launched to recruit, train and retain professional NCOs, whose lack had been a serious and traditional weakness of the Russian military.

No wonder Serdyukov was so roundly despised within the so-called 'Arbat Military District' – the senior officers working within the Defence Ministry and General Staff buildings near that famous Moscow street – but it was actually a sex scandal with political overtones that led to his downfall. By that stage, the reform programme was underway, but the anger and resentment of the generals obvious. Putin needed someone who not only knew how to knit communities back together, but also had a track record of successful institutional reform, and the best candidate was Sergei Shoigu. Russian politics are notoriously vicious and factional, but despite being one of the longest-serving figures on the national stage – pre-dating Putin – Shoigu has the singular distinction of rising far without seeming to make blood enemies. In the 1990s, he took a series of corrupt and inefficient services and brought them together as the Ministry for Emergency Situations (MChS: *Ministerstvo po Chrezvychainym Situatsiyam*), which emerged as one of the country's more efficient and better-run agencies. He had just taken up the position as Governor of the Moscow Region when Putin suddenly needed a new defence minister, but took on the new job without complaint.

Shoigu will not be minister for ever. There has been talk of his becoming Governor of Siberia, Prime Minister, even President some day, if the position ever falls vacant, although the 2022 invasion of Ukraine and the poor performance of Russia's troops mean that his reputation is now getting distinctly tarnished. However, he and his hard-nosed Chief of the General Staff Valery Gerasimov had presided over the creation of an instrument which granted Putin considerable authority at home and abroad, at least until truly put to the test. These have been years of war, in Chechnya, in Crimea and the Donbas, in Syria, and then in all of Ukraine. Some of these wars proved invaluable learning opportunities for the military as a whole, but the 2022 invasion of Ukraine also demonstrated that there was much still to reform, and also that Putin himself may have become over-confident precisely as a result of the military's apparent progress.

7

The Second Chechen War

Chechen rebel commander Aslan Maskhadov went on to become Chechnya's prime minister before winning the presidency in 1997 by a landslide victory, but it proved easier to defeat the Russians than control his own people and make a success of the uneasy peace that followed the 1996 Khasavyurt Accord.[1] Ultimately, he could win a war, but not the peace. Chechnya was in ruins, and the warlords who had emerged in the first war were unwilling to stand down. Worse yet was the rise of jihadists. While most Chechens were, like Maskhadov, Muslims, they held to a relatively moderate form of their faith. During the first war, though, local extremists had found common cause with foreign jihadists, including some linked to the Al-Qaeda terrorist movement.

The most notorious was Saudi-born Thamir Saleh Abdullah Al-Suwailem, who assumed the nom de guerre of Emir Khattab. He had fought against the Soviets in Afghanistan, where he met Osama Bin Laden and became an Al-Qaeda troubleshooter, seeing action in Tajikistan, Azerbaijan and the former Yugoslavia. In 1995, he had entered Chechnya under the guise of a journalist and began training Chechens as well as distributing funds and weapons provided by Al-Qaeda. He built up a network of local allies, including perhaps the most famous of the Chechen field commanders, Shamil Basayev. Khattab was not committed to Chechen independence as such, but to raising a general jihad across the North Caucasus to drive out Christian Russia and create an Islamic caliphate. As such,

Maskhadov's moderation, his willingness to try to make a success of the peace rather than commit to a renewed struggle, made him Khattab's enemy. He was likely behind several of the assassination attempts made on Maskhadov's life, but his real influence was to encourage cross-border raids into neighbouring Russian regions. In August 1999, Khattab and Basayev led a mixed force of some 1,500 Chechen, Dagestani and Arab fighters across the border into Dagestan. Calling themselves the 'International Islamic Peacekeeping Brigade', they proclaimed the 'Islamic State of Dagestan', then advanced on Botlikh, the nearest town.

They seem to have expected to be welcomed as liberators; they were wrong. Even before federal forces could respond, heavily armed locals converged on their positions. A combined contingent of the MVD's 102nd Interior Troops Brigade, Dagestani police and Russian *Spetsnaz*, backed by air support, drove them back, and then countered a second attempted incursion in September. This played into the hands of a Russian government that had been waiting for an excuse to avenge itself for its earlier defeat.

Maskhadov disavowed and condemned the attacks, but nonetheless Russian bombers launched punitive missions first on border villages where the International Islamic Peacekeeping Brigade had mustered, then on Grozny. Meanwhile, Putin – then still prime minister, but looking for a chance to demonstrate his resolve and his capacity to turn around Russia's fortunes – instructed his generals to muster for war. They had, after all, prepared contingency plans, and while the North Caucasus Military District (SKVO: *Severo-Kavkazsky Voyenny Okrug*) had, like every field command, suffered cuts as a result of budget crises and draft-dodging, its commander, Lt. Gen. Viktor Kazantsev, had clearly been given a mandate to strengthen its combat capability. His friend, patron and predecessor in charge of the SKVO, Gen. Anatoly Kvashnin, had been responsible for the initial and disastrous attack on Grozny in 1994 and was determined to atone for his earlier failure. In 1997, he had become Chief of the General Staff, and he made sure that what resources he could divert to the district, he would. By the beginning of 1998, for example, volunteer soldiers, *kontraktniki*, made up 20–30% of the SKVO's complement, a relatively high figure for such a command. In addition, the Daryal mountain warfare training centre in nearby North Ossetia, abandoned in 1992, was reopened. They were training for a renewed conflict, and in July 1998 even mounted a major exercise across the North Caucasus in which 15,000 army and MVD troops practised fighting 'terrorists'.

ROUND TWO

The September apartment bombings discussed in the previous chapter and the Dagestan incursion left the Russian people anxious and angry, and this gave Putin the opportunity to strike. After all, he had made it clear what his priorities were when he told journalists, using the criminal slang 'soaked' for wiped out, that:

> We will hunt the terrorists everywhere ... If you'll excuse me, if we catch them in the toilet, we'll soak them in the toilet, if that's what it takes. It will all be finally sorted.[2]

On 1 October, he formally declared Maskhadov and the Chechen government illegitimate and reasserted the authority of the Russian Federation over its wayward subject, as the newly formed Joint Group of Federal Forces (OGFV: *Obedinennaya Gruppa Federalnykh Voisk*) was completing its muster, comprising *Spetsnaz* and a regiment each of the 2nd, 3rd, 20th, 27th and 34th Motor Rifle Divisions and the 4th Guards Tank Division, the 205th Independent Motor Rifle Brigade, and also three Independent Operational Designation Brigades of the MVD Interior Troops (21st, 22nd and 33rd), the '*Rosich*' 7th VV Special Forces Detachment and OMON riot police.

Overall command was under Lt. Gen. Kazantsev, and instead of the foolhardy direct assault of the first war, his plan was a staged and brutally methodical one. The first phase was as far as possible to seal Chechnya's borders, while forces were assembled. All told, these numbered some 50,000 regular military troops and another 40,000 MVD VV and OMON riot police, some three times as many men as had taken part in the 1994 invasion. While Maskhadov was trying and failing to persuade Moscow to talk peace, the OGFV first occupied a cordon sanitaire along Chechnya's northern border, then advanced to the Terek River, occupying the northern third of the country, with the regular army leading the advance, the MVD forces securing their rear.

The presence of the specialist riot police of the OMON, which originally stood for the Special Designation Police Unit (*Otryad Militsii Osobennovo Naznacheniya*), has been a distinctive feature of Russian military operations, even in Ukraine. Formed in 1989, they acquired something of a reputation as the heavy-handed stormtroopers of the state in the decaying years of the USSR. They were also used in high-risk policing missions, such as raids on organized crime hideouts, but in the desperate search for combat-ready forces in the First Chechen War, OMON in their distinctive blue tiger-striped urban camouflage and black berets were increasingly widely used. They were treated as light infantry, especially in the kind of operation known as a *zachistka*, a 'clean up', in which a village or neighbourhood would be surrounded and then subjected to a house-by-house search. They would again be deployed in the Second Chechen War, especially for rear-area security and urban operations. Because these units were locally raised across Russia, their training, skill and discipline varied widely, with some being accused of especially serious human rights violations. It also meant that they often had trouble cooperating. This led to some serious friendly fire incidents, the worst of which took place in Grozny, in March 2000. OMON from Podolsk ambushed a convoy of OMON from Sergiyev Posad coming to relieve them, believing them to be insurgents. In the ensuing firefight, 24 OMON were killed. Incorporated into the new National Guard in 2016 (still called OMON, now standing for *Otryad Mobilnyy Osobovo Naznacheniya*, 'Special Designation Mobile Unit'), these approximately 30,000 officers, all professionals and most army veterans, are still routinely deployed for security sweeps across the North Caucasus, as well as their usual public security missions.

Resistance was sporadic and localized, in part because many Chechen fighters pulled back to Grozny after it became clear that the Russians were no longer so prone to leaving themselves open to ambush. Scouts and helicopters reconnoitred routes in advance, potential ambush sites were pre-emptively shelled, and tank forces were accompanied by vigilant infantry screens. As towns and villages were taken, they would be searched, and MVD forces left behind as garrisons to ensure the security of the Russian rear. On 12 October, the OGFV pushed across the Terek, advancing towards Grozny along three axes. The Western Group pushed through the Nadterechny district until it reached the western suburbs of Grozny; the Northern Group pushed down across the Terek at Cherevlyonnaya; while the Eastern Group swung past Gudermes and likewise moved to flank Grozny from the east.

While Maskhadov declared martial law and prepared his forces, the Russians slowly encircled the city. While it came under sporadic but heavy bombardment, including strikes by OTR-21 Tochka short-range ballistic missiles with conventional warheads, Kazantsev was in no hurry to send his mechanized forces into Grozny's streets. Instead, he slowly expanded their area under his control, and his forces began to be augmented with local allies. After all, years of in-fighting in Chechnya, and the rise of the jihadists, had eroded their unity. A number of powerful figures and clans that had lost out were willing to throw in their lot with Moscow. The city of Gudermes, for example, fell largely thanks to the defection of the Yamadayevs, the dominant local family of the Benoi clan. The GRU (*Glavnoye Razvedyvatelnyoe Upravlenie*, the Main Intelligence Directorate) took them under its wing, and their private army would become the basis of the *Vostok* (East) Battalion. Likewise Ahmad Kadyrov, who had been a supporter of Dudayev's in the first war, switched sides, along with his followers, who numbered several hundred but had grown to 3,000 by 2003.

RETAKING GROZNY

Towns that did not surrender faced siege and bombardment, amidst the bitter North Caucasus winter. Argun fell in early December, followed by Urus-Martan. Of course, this strategy gave the rebels time to prepare. They fortified Grozny, digging trenches, laying mines, building fortified positions inside some buildings and booby-trapping others, drawing on the lessons of the first war. However, the Russians had also learnt their lessons. First of all, they launched high-altitude reconnaissance flights over the city, and where they were identified, rebel strongpoints were pounded by aircraft, artillery or more long-range Scud and OTR-21 missiles. At peak, they were firing up to 4,000 shells and rockets a day into the city. Thermobaric rockets fired by the TOS-1 '*Buratino*', which release and then ignite an aerosolized cloud of explosive, were especially feared, as one could bring down a whole apartment building – however few might still have been standing.

By early December, only some 40,000 civilians were left in the ruins of a city that back in 1989 had been home to ten times as many. There were also around 2,500 rebels, against whom Kazantsev planned to launch 5,000 federal troops, along with around 2,000 MVD troops and OMON as well as about as many pro-Moscow (or at least anti-rebel) Chechen fighters in a militia commanded by Beslan Gantemirov. A convicted embezzler who had been pardoned in return for his service, he had recruited a force of volunteers, patriots, mercenaries, opportunists and criminals whom Moscow trusted little – the MVD only issued them out-dated AKM-47s from reserve stocks – but who nonetheless knew the city and were as fierce and flexible as Maskhadov's men.

On 12 December, Kazantsev began his assault. First, reconnaissance and *Spetsnaz* patrols went in to spot for airstrikes and artillery, then his main force – the 506th Motor Rifle Regiment and two MVD VV brigades – swept in. First they took Khankala airbase, then began probing the centre. It was impossible to avoid Chechen ambushes such as the one which killed Maj. Gen. Mikhail Malofeyev, commander of the Northern Group. However, the OGFV was much more cautious, and the new T-90 tank proved much more resistant to RPGs than the old T-80, one even surviving seven hits. Troops moved forward methodically, checking for rebels hiding in cellars and rooftops and making sure no units advanced too far from their support. Soldiers wore identification armbands to reduce the risk of friendly fire, and better communications were established between army, OMON and VV troops. The fighting was fierce, but Kazantsev had the luxury of being able to cycle in fresh troops. After a week's close-quarters fighting, about a quarter of the soldiers of the 506th had been killed or wounded, so he withdrew it and threw the fresh troops of the 423rd Guards Motor Rifle Regiment into their place.

By the end of January, running low on men, ground to retreat and ammunition, the rebel commanders opted to abandon the city, regroup at the village of Alkhan-Kala south-west of Grozny and make for the highlands in the hope of following the same trajectory as in the first war. Many never made it, trapped by OMON on the outskirts of Grozny, chased by *Spetsnaz*, or caught in minefields outside Alkhan-Kala.

By 6 February, the Russians formally declared Grozny 'liberated'. Nonetheless, the city was in ruins and it would take a month for

OMON and Gantemirov's militia to mop up a few remaining hold-outs in the city and a year for all the bodies from the battle to be found and buried. Unlike during the first war, now the Russians had taken Grozny, they would not let it go. The city was swamped both with federal forces and allied Chechens, while roving patrols on land and in the air watched the outskirts to prevent another infiltration. To mark Yeltsin's inauguration as re-elected president in 1996, the rebels had retaken Grozny. While Putin was being inaugurated on 7 May 2000, the main phase of the war had been won.

OPERATION *WOLF HUNT*

While Grozny was under siege, the federal forces had been consolidating their hold on the northern and central regions of the country under the rubric of Operation *Wolf Hunt*, going after the rebels who fled Grozny and then remaining hold-outs. The MVD was establishing not just its own network of strongpoints and Interior Troop and OMON garrisons, but also launching aggressive patrols and search operations to locate rebels, arms caches and safe houses. When some rebels tried to flee north from Grozny, they were met with patrols able to block, intercept and eliminate them.

However, the next priority was to take the unruly southern highlands, which in the past had been havens for the rebel forces. In April 2000, Col. Gen. Gennady Troshev was appointed head of the OGFV. A hard-fighting and tough-talking tank commander, who had commanded during the first war, he would become notorious for his public pronouncements, proposing that Grozny should be left in ruins as a warning to others, and that rebels ought to face public execution: 'This is how I'd do it: I would gather everyone in the square, then I would have hoisted the bandit, and let him hang, let everyone see!'[3] Nonetheless, from his experiences in the first war, he appreciated that conquering Chechnya was not the same as pacifying it, and that this would be a long haul.

The Russians' best estimate was that there were still some 2,000–2,500 rebels on the loose, but any easy assumption that they were too scattered to pose any serious challenge was mistaken. The rebels could still cohere in units numbering several hundred and engage in operations which could cause serious Russian casualties. For example, one of the last major pitched engagements of the war took place in March, at Komsomolskoye, a village south of Grozny and the home village of warlord Ruslan Gelayev. An OMON unit from Russia's Yaroslavl Region first encountered Gelayev and his men there, as they prepared to break through to the cover of the Argun Gorge. Once their numbers became clear – estimates ranged from 500 to 1,000, but the real figure was closer to 600 – the OMON settled for trapping them in the city and calling for support. They were promptly reinforced by a VV regiment and more OMON and special police units. After four days of almost constant bombardment, including attacks by Su-25 ground-attack jets and salvoes from TOS-1 launchers, they stormed the village. Nonetheless, it took another week and a further bombardment before Komsomolskoye was pacified, and a wounded Gelayev still managed to slip out of the village. For its size, this was one of the bloodiest battles of the war, with the official butcher's bill being 552 Chechens and more than 50 Russians. The village itself was all but levelled; journalist Anna Politkovskaya called it 'a monstrous conglomerate of burnt houses, ruins, and new graves at the cemetery'.[4]

More often, though, the rebels would simply mount ambushes and hit-and-run attacks. With 80,000 soldiers and security police deployed across the country, the environment became increasingly hostile for them. There would inevitably be successes. On 19 August 2002, for example, a small group of rebels with one of their few remaining Igla (SA-16) shoulder-fired surface-to-air missiles (SAMs) managed to bring down one of the Russians' Mi-26 transport helicopters as it approached Khankala airbase. The Mi-26 is a mammoth of the air, usually capable of carrying 90 soldiers and five crew, but this was overladen, with 142 soldiers being brought in as part of a troop rotation. In tragic irony, it crashed inside a minefield around a Russian command post, and between the impact, the fire when aviation fuel leaked into the crew compartment, and the mines, 127 died in what was up to then the Russian military's most deadly aviation disaster.

More often, though, the successes were minor and the retaliation devastating, and meanwhile, the rebel commanders were one by one being, as the Russians put it, 'neutralized', as often by covert operations as direct military action. Khattab, who had survived being blown up by a landmine and shot in the stomach, was killed in March 2002 when an

FSB undercover agent passed him a letter steeped in poison. Self-styled Chechen president in exile Zelimkhan Yandarbiyev had fled to Qatar, but in February 2004, GRU agents killed him by placing a bomb under his car. In 2005, Maskhadov died during a commando attack by FSB forces on a hideout in Tolstoy-Yurt, probably at the hand of his nephew and bodyguard, who had orders to shoot him rather than let him be captured. Basayev was blown up in July 2006 when a mine exploded as he inspected it.

THE CREATION OF 'KADYROVSTAN'

As the remnants of the rebels became increasingly leaderless, hopeless and marked for capture or elimination, Moscow was looking to its own Chechen allies to stabilize the country. In June 2000, Putin had appointed a former rebel, Ahmad Kadyrov, as the interim head of the Chechen government. He had been the Chief Mufti of Chechnya in the inter-war era, but had fallen foul of the extremist Wahhabist strain of Islam that had become increasingly dominant, so he and his son Ramzan defected to the government's side in 1999. His personal militia, the so-called *Kadyrovtsy* ('Kadyrovites'), were originally just one of several such loyalist forces, but as the Kadyrovs became increasingly dominant, the others were forced to join or be disbanded.

Ahmad Kadyrov was formally sworn in as Chechen President in 2003, but he was killed the next year, when rebels detonated a bomb under the podium at the Dinamo football stadium, during the annual Victory Day parade. While Ramzan was too young formally to succeed, this was clearly on the cards. Things had become personal, and he and the *Kadyrovtsy* energetically set to wiping out the remnants of the rebels – and any political rivals – in the process. In 2007, after his 30th birthday, he was officially declared President, and since then he has held Chechnya in his ruthless, if capricious grip.

On 16 April 2009, Russia's National Anti-Terrorism Committee formally declared the 'counter-terrorist operation' in Chechnya over, in effect declaring victory. Admittedly, just as during the First Chechen War, the rebels tried to use terrorism outside Chechnya's borders as a way of bringing the war to Russia. Most notoriously, in October 2002, 40 terrorists seized the Dubrovka theatre in Moscow, taking some 850 hostages. After two days of failed negotiations, a narcotic gas was pumped into the building, which was then stormed by the *Alfa* counter-terrorist team. The terrorists were killed, but 179 hostages died, almost all because of miscommunication, the medical first responders not having been told which gas was used and thus not giving the right treatment. In September 2004, 32 terrorists seized School Number One in the North Ossetian town of Beslan on the first day of the new school year. Of the 1,100 hostages taken, most were children. On the third day of the ensuing siege, when one of the terrorists' bombs exploded, the building was stormed: 334 hostages died, including 186 children. However, while during the first war the authorities had been willing to compromise, under Putin the Kremlin took a tough line and continued its campaign in Chechnya. Since then, there have been isolated attacks connected with the war, often suicide bombings, such as the 2009 derailing of the Nevsky Express high-speed train from Moscow to St Petersburg, which killed 27, or the 2011 suicide bombing at Moscow's Domodedovo airport, which left 37 dead. Taking their lead from Putin – who, after Beslan, said that in the past 'We showed ourselves to be weak. And the weak get beaten' – the authorities have refused to compromise with terrorists, and such attacks remain rare.[5]

In Chechnya itself, the insurgency had indeed been broken. Those few who remained tended to be jihadist extremists – in 2007 they had declared a 'Caucasus Emirate' – and the centre of insurgent gravity shifted to other republics of the North Caucasus. Russian forces in Chechnya were steadily reduced to around 10,000 soldiers, in the 46th Brigade of what was the MVD Interior Troops and is now the National Guard, and the regular military's 42nd Motor Rifle Brigade. Most forces in Chechnya, while technically police or Interior Troops units, are really *Kadyrovtsy*: the 141st 'Ahmad Kadyrov' Special Purpose Police Regiment in Grozny, the 249th Independent Special Motorized Battalion '*Yug*' (South) in Vedeno, the 424th IOD Brigade and 359th Independent Special Police Motorized Battalion in Grozny and several independent battalions: the 360th (Shelkovskaya), 743rd (Vedeno) and 744th (Nozhai-Yurt). These wear regular Interior Troop uniforms and are now formally subordinated to the North Caucasus National Guard District headquarters in Rostov-on-Don, but they swear personal oaths of fealty to Kadyrov and in practice it is widely acknowledged that their primary loyalty is likely to be to him.

However, the irony is that in order to defeat the rebellion, the Kremlin may have granted Chechnya more autonomy in practice than it has had in the past two centuries. Kadyrov never fails loudly to proclaim his loyalty to President Putin, but in reality he rules Chechnya as he sees fit, while receiving generous federal subsidies from Moscow that he ploughs into vanity projects (the Ahmad Kadyrov Mosque in Grozny is one of the largest in Russia), living a high life and rewarding his cronies. From time to time, the government looks as if it is losing patience with its Chechen warlord, such as when his men gunned down opposition figure Boris Nemtsov literally outside the Kremlin in 2015. Each time, though, it has backed down, fearing that attempts to unseat him would force them to wage a third Chechen war.

Of course, they may only be postponing it. Back in 1995, in the midst of the First Chechen War, Gen. Kvashnin certainly seemed to think so:

> We will beat the Chechens to pulp, so that the present generation will be too terrified to fight Russia again. Let Western observers come to Grozny and see what we have done to our own city, so that they shall know what may happen to their towns if they get rough with Russia. But you know, ... in 20–30 years a new generation of Chechens that did not see the Russian army in action will grow up and they will again rebel, so we'll have to smash them down all over again.[6]

LESSONS LEARNED

In the meantime, it is clear that the Russians had learned lessons from the earlier debacle, and from their rematch, as well. Some of these were technical and tactical. New weapons and equipment made an appearance, from body armour to reconnaissance drones. Then, Russian tanks and armoured personnel carriers (APCs) had had trouble engaging targets on upper stories of tower blocks without commanders having to expose themselves to fire by popping their hatches to use top-mounted machine guns. This time, they advanced into cities accompanied by gun trucks mounting ZU-23 23mm anti-aircraft guns able to rake the rooftops. Where tanks had previously been painfully vulnerable to close-range RPG attacks, now they were fitted with reactive armour and accompanied by infantry support. Special 'storm detachments' were established for the specialized experiences of urban warfare, of 30–50 men apiece, typically divided into teams of five, including one sniper and one man with an RPG or an RPO-A Shmel incendiary rocket launcher. Meanwhile, *Spetsnaz* anti-sniper teams used rocket launchers and their own snipers to pick off Chechen marksmen. More broadly, adopting a more methodical approach than the first war's 'dash for Grozny', the federal forces were also much more effectively coordinated.[7]

The lessons were also political. The official butcher's bill for the first war was 5,500 police and soldiers dead, with another 5,200 in the second. Admittedly, these figures have been questioned, not least as they may omit those dying of their wounds later in hospital. These figures were serious enough, but they also led to serious resistance to conscription: in 2000 alone, draft-dodging rose by 50%. However, the political effects were largely managed, to a considerable degree because the Kremlin took much greater care to control the narrative. While there were courageous journalists who risked their lives – and lost them – reporting on the realities on the ground, there was much wider use of censorship, 'housetrained' journalists and carefully framed narratives to present this as a war forced on Russia by Chechen gangsters and jihadists, and fought as expeditiously as possible.

This was helped by the 'Chechenization' of the war. The various Chechen contingents not only took many casualties that otherwise might have fallen to federal forces, but they brought local knowledge and undeniable enthusiasm to the war, seeing this often as a chance to satisfy blood feuds and win political status. The presence of these forces also allowed disaffected or demoralized rebels to switch sides, rather than forcing them to fight to the death. Besides, by elevating the Kadyrovs, the Kremlin's claim to be fighting a war to restore a legitimate Chechen order looked more plausible.

The reason why this mattered was that this war would not only consolidate Putin's status as a tough, even ruthless defender of Russia's interests, but also established certain assumptions about the use of force. Putin's willingness to visit the North Caucasus to be seen with the troops, and his street-slang references to the Chechens, all these did his macho reputation no harm. However, the outrage expressed by the West at the brutal tactics used to subjugate Chechnya also played a role in shaping his views on geopolitics. First of all, he felt this was hypocrisy and bad faith considering, as he saw it, his willingness to let Washington wage its war against Al-Qaeda however it wanted to. He felt Chechnya was his front in the 'Global War on Terror', and seems to have been genuinely offended when Western governments questioned his methods. However, he also noted that the West stuck to stern words and diplomatic expressions of grave concern. He began to believe that, especially when faced with a fait accompli and a tough rebuttal, for all the West's economic and, indeed, military might, it lacked one crucial strategic asset: will. That, he seems to have concluded, was Russia's strategic advantage.

8

Ivanov, the Initiator

The irony is that even though he presided over the rearmament of his country, and for all of his evident love of a photo opportunity in the cockpit of a fighter, driving a tank, or trying out the latest service pistol, Vladimir Putin never really served in the military. He avoided the draft by enrolling at Leningrad State University, and while that meant he was required to train as a reserve officer – he graduated as a reserve lieutenant commanding a howitzer artillery control platoon – memoirs of the time stress just how cursory and minimal this really would have been. It meant a few weeks a year in classroom and fitness training, some basic target practice and participation in a few routine and choreographed wargames, and typically some weeks in the summer bringing in the harvest as a 'volunteer'.

His time in the KGB was first as a political policeman at home, then a low-level intelligence manager in East Germany. He never had much contact with military men, and none of his close friends, allies and patrons were soldiers, either. Although he knew he wanted a powerful Russian military – while he felt the country needed one – he would have to depend on others to build it for him. This was especially because, while Yeltsin had turned to soldiers in the 1990s, the tradition was that the position of Minister of Defence was an essentially political one, filled by trusted civilians who could keep the soldiers in check as much as they argued their case. Men like Grachyov and Rodionov saw themselves as soldiers first, politicians later, and perhaps this helped explain why they had been unsuccessful. Putin needed men he could trust, but also who could handle the challenges of the time.

MY NAME'S IVANOV, SERGEI IVANOV

As discussed in Chapter 6, the three men he chose, then, were in many ways symbolic of what Putin felt was needed: first the spy, then the accountant, and finally the engineer. His first defence minister, Sergei Ivanov, was a high-flying ex-KGB foreign intelligence officer, in many ways the suave yet tough spy, the Slavic James Bond, that Putin himself had always wanted to be. His job was to assert the political realities as the new government saw them, that Russia was under threat and needed to be strong to survive. He was followed by Anatoly Serdyukov, an accountant who had led the Federal Tax Service, who was eventually able to break the resistance of a conservative officer corps and force reform on them. This was a divisive and uncomfortable process, though, and he was followed by Sergei Shoigu, a veteran political operator with a knack for turning around dysfunctional institutions and giving them a real esprit de corps. If Putin is the father of the modern Russian military, these three men were at the very least its midwives.

Sergei Borisovich Ivanov was, like Putin, a KGB recruit from Leningrad, but of a very different stamp. He was quickly inducted into the KGB's First Chief Directorate, its elite foreign intelligence arm, after coming to London in 1974 to learn English at Ealing Technical College. He served in Leningrad alongside Putin before being posted abroad under diplomatic cover, in first Finland, then Kenya, until he was 'outed' by defector Oleg Gordievsky and had to return to Russia. When the Soviet Union collapsed, he transferred seamlessly to the new Russian Foreign Intelligence Service (SVR: *Sluzhba Vneshnei Razvedky*), becoming first deputy director of its European Department.

In 1998, he moved sideways into the FSB, becoming its deputy director and head of its Department of Analysis, Forecast and Strategic Planning. This was around the time Putin was appointed to head the FSB, and although he must have felt some satisfaction that the 'low-flier' was now Ivanov's boss, Putin also respected the other man's talents, especially his quick grasp of complex strategic situations and his cool authority, even when dealing with older, more senior figures. The former made him Putin's choice to be secretary of the Security Council – in many ways Russia's equivalent of the National Security Adviser – in 1999, and in 2001, he replaced Marshal Sergeyev as Defence Minister, a post he would hold through to 2007.

Former US National Security Adviser and then Secretary of State Condoleezza Rice recounted one telling exchange: 'President [George W.] Bush said to Putin, "I have to know whom you trust. Who is the person we should turn to if there are sensitive matters between us?" "Sergei Ivanov, the minister of defence," Putin answered.'[1]

He may have had Putin's confidence, but Ivanov also had an unenviable mission. When appointed, Chechnya was dominating the ministry's agenda, and although the war was being won, it was still an uncomfortable reminder of the weaknesses of the Russian military that it was having to level cities with artillery barrages and arm and empower local militias to subjugate even this small region. Even after the war had been effectively won on the battlefield, there were still huge challenges, including mitigating the danger of terrorism, and addressing the damage done to the image of the military. At a time when Putin was increasingly becoming angered by what he saw as Western hypocrisy and hostility, especially over NATO expansion eastwards – in 2004 Ivanov himself said Russia would take 'adequate measures' if it went ahead[2] – he ended up being the defence minister who was able to ask the key questions, not come up with answers.

THE SPY AND THE GENERALS

Admittedly, Ivanov was a capable and competent foreign affairs professional. Indeed, Condoleezza Rice (who once sneaked out unofficially with Ivanov to go to the ballet in St Petersburg) praised him highly in her memoirs, saying: 'Sergei was tough and somewhat suspicious of the United States, but he was dependable. He never told me that he would do something that he did not do.'[3]

However, he was no more a military insider than Putin. He had more money to spend, that was true, but while the generals were happy to receive pay rises and new toys, they were unwilling to embark on the kind of structural reforms that were needed to translate that into a genuine transformation. Putin had charged Ivanov with creating a military machine that was capable of defending the Motherland from a full-scale military invasion but the trouble was that the generals were torn by two imperatives. On the one hand, ever since Operation *Desert Storm* in 1991, the coalition invasion of Iraq, they had come to appreciate the way new technologies, and especially long-range precision-guided munitions, were revolutionizing warfare. Saddam Hussein's Iraq had fielded a relatively experienced and well-trained army built along essentially Soviet lines and armed with fairly modern Soviet kit. The success of the coalition blitzkrieg – they suffered 379 fatalities, the Iraqis more than 20,000 – was largely explained by Russian analyses as the result of superior Western technologies that gave them a crucial edge. Then Yugoslavia reinforced both the sense that 'non-contact' war fought through long-range precision weapons was the wave of the future – for which they were not prepared – and also that NATO, for all its talk of being a defensive alliance, was perfectly able and willing to intervene and reshape nations when it suited its interests.

So they fully appreciated the need for modernization. At the same time, though, they resolutely clung to Soviet notions of the importance of a mass army, and that meant conscription. The key value of the draft, after all, is that it creates a pool of trained (or semi-trained) reservists who could be called up in time of war to create the kind of millions-strong army they felt the defence of the nation demanded. In other words, they wanted more soldiers and also better kit. The additional funds at Ivanov's disposal would not cover both, and in any case the spy, who seems to have had something of an instinctive disdain for the soldiers under his command, became increasingly exasperated by their desire to have their cake and eat it.

Traditionally, the job of translating political decisions into military policy, and selling them to the High Command, was the job of the top soldier, the Chief of the General Staff. Ivanov, though, initially found himself saddled with one who felt that civilians had no place trying to foist changes on the armed forces. Gen. Anatoly Kvashnin had been Chief of the General Staff since 1997. Perhaps best known for his tough line during both Chechen wars, he had also been a key mover behind the 1999 'Pristina Dash' which had earned him Boris Yeltsin's favour for having, according to one media commentator, 'put a hedgehog into the enemy's trousers'.[4] (A phrase used every now and then since 1962, when Soviet leader Khrushchev, always prone to folksy expressions, asked his defence minister if it was time 'to put a hedgehog in the Americans' trousers' by sending Soviet nuclear missiles to Cuba.[5]) He had wanted the minister's job, and had even appealed to Yeltsin over the head of his chief of staff, Alexander Voloshin, to try to get it. When Sergeyev was appointed instead, Kvashnin made no secret of his anger and did his best to foil many of his intended changes. He encouraged the General Staff apparatus to drag its feet, and when Ivanov replaced Sergeyev, he managed to reverse many of them.[6]

He proved no more comfortable a subordinate for Ivanov. He made it clear that he regarded the minister as his peer, not his superior, an interpretation unfortunately possible thanks to the wording of the Law on Defence. He openly disagreed with official policy, and even ordered the General Staff apparatus not to act on official instructions from the minister unless he had countersigned them. He could get away with this kind of behaviour under Sergeyev and Yeltsin, but not Ivanov and Putin. Although there was a shared agreement between them that it was best to avoid major military shake-ups while the Second Chechen War was at its peak, by 2003 the main combat phase of the war was over, and it was time to push ahead.

IVANOV'S REFORMS

In January 2004, Ivanov signalled that change was in the air when he used his keynote speech at the annual Academy of Military Sciences conference to criticize the General Staff for getting bogged down in day-to-day administration and neglecting the big picture. Shortly thereafter, the Law on Defence was amended to make it clear that the minister was in charge. In July, Kvashnin was replaced by Col. Gen. Yuri Baluyevsky, a man with a reputation as a good strategic planner and, crucially, for being less of a bull in a china shop.

A reform blueprint had already been proposed in 2003 in a paper called *Urgent Tasks for the Development of the Armed Forces of the Russian Federation*, based heavily on the experiences of the Chechen wars and the problems they had illustrated. The key issue was qualitative: modern war required soldiers with the skills and experiences that could not necessarily be imparted in a conscript's induction training, and units which had worked and trained together rather than be subject to the six-monthly churn of the draft cycle. Given that there was no chance of raising an all-professional army large enough to meet Russia's security needs yet which the country could afford, in effect Grachyov's original notion of a force divided between a mass, conscript-heavy army and a smaller contingent of all-professional permanent-readiness units was still the only viable option. The trouble was that the High Command was still ultimately trying to have that same cake and eat it: maintaining the draft and a huge military to continue to generate a large reserve, while also attracting and retaining large numbers of volunteer *kontraktniki*, who would need to be paid a decent wage. Although Russia's official position was that no major wars with NATO or China were at all likely, and that the real threats came from terrorism and smaller-scale local conflicts, the generals – perhaps aware that a smaller military would need far fewer of them – were still determined to prepare for the former.

There was also a challenge of arsenals and depots still packed with increasingly obsolete Soviet-era weaponry. These still had to be inventoried, guarded and maintained, even though their real combat value was deeply questionable. The 5350th Weapons and Equipment Storage Base at Abakan in Khakassia, for example, became something of a public scandal when it became known that it was still storing 1950s-vintage S-60 57mm anti-aircraft guns that had been replaced by modern systems and SAMs back in the 1970s. It was not just institutional inertia that kept them, though: if Russia ever envisaged mobilizing millions of reservists, they needed huge stocks of weapons, however aged.

Squaring this circle demanded tough decisions and tough leadership to force them on the High Command. Ivanov was still too dependent on the generals and too distracted by other duties for this. After all, he was still one of Putin's inner circle, a key adviser on security and foreign policy and, as mentioned, in 2005 would also be appointed Deputy Prime Minister responsible for the defence industries. This meant that he was in the unenviable position of being both in charge of the defence industries – who wanted lots of orders and large profit margins – and their main customer. As a result, reform was slow and piecemeal.

A single regiment of the 76th Guards Airborne Division became a test case for these all-professional forces, and although the experiment had mixed results, it was deemed a success in 2005 and more units began to be converted. Meanwhile, Baluyevsky was working on streamlining the national command structure, folding the existing Military Districts (VO: *Voyenny Okrug*) into three regional groupings. The Western Command would incorporate the Moscow and Leningrad VOs, the

Baltic and Northern Fleets, and a central Special Air Force and Air
Defence Command. The Southern Command would cover the North
Caucasus and part of the Volga-Urals VOs, the Black Sea Fleet and
the Caspian Flotilla. The rest of the country would be covered by the
Eastern Command, subsuming the Far Eastern, Siberian and most of
the Volga-Urals VOs and the Pacific Fleet. Meanwhile, the roles of the
service Main Commands – Ground Forces, Navy and so on – would
be pruned. A series of experiments with a new Operational Strategic
Command (OSK: *Operativnoye Strategicheskoye Komandavaniye*)
structure was held, but inevitably faced resistance from entrenched
interests, especially those Main Commands themselves.

SIZE DOES MATTER

All of this may have made sense, but failed to address the crucial question:
the size of the military. There simply wasn't enough money to rearm,
reorganize and replace conscripts with *kontraktniki*. The volunteers had
largely signed up on 12-month contracts, and not only were conditions
still poor, but there were growing opportunities in the civilian economy
as the Russian economy prospered. Thus, the overwhelming majority
simply chose not to sign up for further tours. For instance, in 2006,
the 382nd Motor Rifle Regiment of the 122th Motor Rifle Division
signed on 2,700 *kontraktniki* – of whom only 400 stayed past their first
year. Nonetheless, the government had committed to this project and
even though by 2005 more than half the entire defence budget was
going on efforts to recruit, house, pay and retain these professionals, it
simply wasn't working. Worse, efforts to modernize the armed forces as
a whole were being stymied by the sheer cost of this quixotic campaign.
Baluyevsky's reforms were shelved, even if in 2008 they would largely
re-emerge as the 'New Look Army' programme.

Eventually, Ivanov brokered something of a half-measure. National
service was vastly unpopular in the country, and Ivanov, like many
within the civilian security establishment, was unconvinced by its
value. The high-profile case of the terrible abuse of one draftee, Private
Andrei Sychyov, gave him the political ammunition to address this. In
2006, Private Sychyov, a conscript working at the Chelyabinsk Tank
School, fell foul of his platoon sergeant, one Alexander Sivyakov. On
New Year's Eve a drunk Sivyakov forced him to sit for three hours in

an uncomfortable half-squat for no other reason than to humiliate him. Whenever Sychyov tried to move, Sivyakov would beat him. The blood clotted in his legs, and sepsis and gangrene set in. By the time anyone realized what was happening and called an ambulance, it was too late. Both Sychyov's legs and his genitals had to be amputated. The local commanders would probably have hushed it up, had not one of the doctors at the hospital tipped off the local Committee of Soldiers' Mothers, a charity established precisely to highlight and combat such abuses. Even so, the military hierarchy did everything they could to minimize the story, until Ivanov found himself fielding a question from a journalist about the case. Ivanov blithely affirmed that 'nothing serious happened', because 'otherwise he would have been told'.[7] It was a public embarrassment for a man who prided himself on the appearance of being in command of his brief. A hurried criminal investigation saw Sivyakov and two accessories charged and convicted for serious abuse of office. The sergeant was sentenced to four years in prison; his accomplices received one-year suspended sentences.

This generated an ugly spat between Ivanov and Main Military Prosecutor Alexander Savenkov. Certain generals had apparently tried to bully prosecution witnesses into withdrawing their testimony, and when Savenkov warned that hazing was actually on the rise, Ivanov tried to pin the blame on the Main Military Procuracy and claimed they were in the pocket of 'forces that have set out to make dubious political capital of the army's current problems'.[8] Ultimately, this was a case study in the personal politics of the Putin regime: Ivanov was one of the president's personal allies and Savenkov was not, so the former stayed and the latter had to step down. Even so, this was an unedifying spectacle that further tarnished the reputation of the military and probably ensured that Ivanov would not become Putin's chosen successor. As for the unfortunate Private Sychyov, after months of medical care, and kidney failure, he was finally discharged. He moved in with his mother in a house ultimately paid for by the Ministry of Defence.

Over the top of the generals' complaints, Ivanov announced that the period of conscription would be reduced to 12 months. This did nothing to address the fundamental problems, including the need to stockpile weapons for a huge reserve that would likely never be mobilized, and it also angered the generals, who felt that this did not allow long enough to train soldiers properly and have them actually deployable for more than a few months. However, it did free up some money – because even if conscripts were only paid a pittance, they still needed to be armed, trained and housed – and allowed him to shrink the size of the armed forces, but not enough.

This was only a small step, though, and although more money was being spent, it is questionable whether it was doing much to strengthen a Russian military that was still 1.1 million strong in 2007. Ultimately, Ivanov had made the intellectual case for reform, but was unable to impose it on a recalcitrant High Command. While Baluyevsky was no Kvashnin, even he began to show signs of siding with his generals over the political leadership. Ivanov had his sights set on higher things – he was at the time regarded as a potential successor for Putin, who was coming to the end of his second term as president – and was disinclined to fight them. He was also too distracted with other responsibilities, and lacked the specific skills to ensure that the money being spent was being spent wisely. He had made a start, no more.

As it was, in February 2007 he exchanged the position of Minister of Defence for an elevation to the position of First Deputy Prime Minister, although he never would rise to the presidency. This was at the time when Putin was increasingly unhappy with Russia's place in the world order. NATO was expanding, with fully seven new members joining in 2004: Bulgaria, Estonia, Latvia, Lithuania, Romania, Slovakia and Slovenia. At his speech in Munich that month, Putin had signalled that Russia would no longer accept what he saw as the West's attempts to deny it its rightful status as a great power. Later that year, Russia would suspend its participation in the Conventional Armed Forces in Europe (CFE) treaty that limited the deployment of heavy military equipment across the continent, claiming that it had 'ceased to respond to modern European realities and to meet our security interests', and accusing NATO member states of anyway breaching its spirit and the letter.[9]

It was clear to the Kremlin that military reform needed to be made a reality. That would take someone willing to tackle the High Command and who understood how to turn the resources Putin was willing to spend on the military – between 2001 and 2007, the defence budget would almost quadruple – into meaningful change. It would also, it turned out, take a botched war in Georgia.

9

Serdyukov, the Enforcer

It was pretty difficult at the time to find a Russian officer with anything good to say about Anatoly Serdyukov, the rather podgy former head of the Federal Tax Service who replaced Ivanov as Defence Minister in February 2007. 'The accountant', they called him, 'the taxman' (because who loves the taxman?) or, more obscurely, 'the furniture salesman', because before moving into the Federal Tax Service in 2000, he had been the general director of a St Petersburg-based furniture company. In 2021, nine years after he had left the ministry, it was still hard to get anyone military to be especially generous about Serdyukov the man, but there was also a grudging recognition that the reforms he forced on an uncooperative military were both necessary and successful.

ENTER THE TAXMAN

Serdyukov had served first as deputy chief and then chief of the St Petersburg Directorate of what was then still called the Tax Ministry, succeeding Viktor Zubkov, his father-in-law. Coming from the president's home city and family patronage are, after all, two well-established routes to success in Putin's Russia. Within four years, he had been appointed head of the whole Federal Tax Service, where he made a name for himself as a stickler for detail and an effective financial manager, and this was why Putin appointed him. As he said, when announcing Serdyukov's promotion: 'for effective management in modern conditions, for rational spending of huge amounts of budget money, you need a person with experience in the field of economics and finance.'[1]

His appointment as Defence Minister did come as a bombshell, though. He had no military experience, or apparent particular interest, and was not even well known in wider security circles, the so-called *siloviki*, or 'men of force'. In fact, this was part of the reason for his selection, precisely because he had no existing ties to any factions within the military and would be dependent on pleasing the president. What the president wanted was results. More and more money was being spent on the armed forces, but there was little sense it was bringing about the kind of fundamental changes required to make Russia both secure within its borders and capable of projecting its will and power beyond them.

From the first, Serdyukov faced resistance. Indeed, Chief of the General Staff Gen. Yuri Baluyevsky hardly endeared himself to his new boss by suggesting publicly that before he gave a single instruction, he should spend a month being 'trained up' so that he would get a sense of the 'job in hand'. Whereas Ivanov had often been too busy with other responsibilities to get too taken up with his personal relationship with the generals – and was sufficiently secure of Putin's support not to take occasional snipes too seriously – Serdyukov was both a rather touchier individual and also well aware that he had to show the boss that he was up to this promotion and would not be cowed by the High Command.

SERDYUKOV'S PURGE

Serdyukov may not have known much about the military, but he did know bureaucracy and accounting very well. He instituted an audit of both ministry finances and also whether senior officers were indeed keeping up with their mandatory physicals. He brought in his own people, civilian specialists from the Federal Tax Service, to run the administrative side of the ministry, including his former deputy, Mikhail Mokretsov, as head of his political office and Tatyana Shevtsova and Vera Chistova as deputy ministers. He initiated something of a purge of the High Command, sacking Gen. Vladimir Mikhailov, head of the Air Forces, and the heads of three services especially notorious for their waste and corruption: Col. Gen. Vladislav Polonsky of the Main Armour Directorate (responsible for storage and maintenance),

Gen. Igor Bykov of the Main Medical Directorate and Gen. Anatoly Grebenyuk of medical facility construction. Most importantly, in June 2007, Gen. Baluyevsky was dismissed, banished to a position in the Security Council Secretariat – which offered public honour but private impotence – and replaced as Chief of the General Staff with Gen. Nikolai Makarov. The taxman meant business, and never forgot a slight.

Despite – or perhaps because – of this bloodletting, the High Command were still not reconciled to the kind of dramatic reform that Serdyukov had been appointed to introduce. Furthermore, Putin was coming to the end of his second consecutive term as president, which meant that, by law, he had to stand down. There was considerable uncertainty as to what would happen, and whether he would simply try to have the constitution rewritten, but in any case the last months of 2007 were overshadowed by this issue, and Putin lacked the time or attention to put more political capital behind Serdyukov. Then, on 10 December 2007, he confirmed that he would stand down, and that his current prime minister, Dmitry Medvedev, was his preferred successor. What followed was essentially a formality, especially after Medvedev made it clear that this would really be a job swap, with Putin becoming his prime minister. It was pretty obvious all along that Putin would continue to be the power behind the throne, with Medvedev's election posters showing the two men side-by-side with the slogan *Vmeste pobedim*, 'Together We Will Win'.

Medvedev was duly elected in March 2008 and inaugurated in May, but at first the status of the security agencies under what became known as the 'tandemocracy' was unclear. Constitutionally, they reported to the president, but it soon became clear that Putin, now ensconced in the (Russian) White House, was still their overseer. Later, for example, Baluyevsky would grumble that getting Medvedev to pull the trigger on the long-planned war against Georgia in 2008 would require Putin – who was on an official visit to Beijing at the time – getting on the phone to give him 'a kick up the arse'.[2] Either way, for some months it meant there was no unequivocal mandate for Serdyukov – some generals even over-optimistically hoped Medvedev might sack him.

As it was, he would remain in office for another four years and was brought down not by political intrigues or military resistance, but a simple sex scandal. There were allegations that he had been involved in a scam, whereby a state-controlled military contractor had sold assets to private firms at far below the market value, losing the government nearly 3 billion roubles (then equivalent to £62.5 million). This alone would not have been enough to bring him down, as the simple truth of the matter is that no senior Russian government figure does not engage in such schemes to supplement his or her salary. More seriously, when investigators staged a dawn raid on a key suspect, property department head Yevgeniya Vasilyeva, in her 13-room Moscow flat they found almost a million pounds' worth of cash, antiques and jewellery – and Serdyukov in a dressing gown. Fraud is one thing; conducting an extra-marital affair when your wife is the daughter of Viktor Zubkov, a former prime minister, the current chair of the board of directors of Gazprom, Russia's largest corporation, and a close ally of the president, is quite another. Zubkov demanded his head, and Serdyukov had to go, being sacked in November 2012. Nonetheless, in his own way, Putin is loyal to his own. Serdyukov had done what he had been charged to do, and so a subsequent conviction in another case, using army engineers to build a road to his son-in-law's holiday home, was amnestied, and he was later found a comfortable sinecure with the Rostec arms corporation. (Vasilyeva had no such protection: she was sentenced to five years in prison.)

AND ENTER MAKAROV

Nonetheless, Serdyukov had already managed to make progress. Medvedev had not been in a position to sack a defence minister Putin had appointed, even had he wanted to. However, nor did he have the political muscle or respect within the High Command to force them to accept the reform programme. So the deadlock had continued, even while those plans were being refined. Although these are associated with Serdyukov, Chief of the General Staff Makarov was really the driving force behind them. Born in 1949, Nikolai Makarov was a career infantry officer, who had served in a wide range of commands, from the Group of Soviet Forces in Germany to being chief of staff of the Russian deployment to Tajikistan in 1993 and, in 2002, command of the massive Siberian VO. His progression up the ranks had consistently been faster than usual, and in 1999 Defence Minister Igor Sergeyev had singled him out for praise: 'this general has a great future.'[3] Nonetheless, in 2005, he had been appointed a deputy minister of defence in his new role as Chief of Armaments. To some, he was being side-lined from the main military command track to an administrative role, and there may be some truth to that, as Makarov had already been expressing his dissatisfaction with the slow pace of reform, and implicitly the efforts of many of his colleagues precisely to keep it slow. That may help explain why Serdyukov chose him as his Chief of the General Staff: he was a well-regarded field officer but also not part of the quiet opposition within the High Command.

Perhaps most disquieting of all for his peers, he was a man with ideas. When commanding the 2nd Guards Tank Army in 1996–98, he acquired a reputation for innovative training methods. Later, as commander of the Siberian VO, he pioneered less formal and bureaucratic processes for recruitment, precisely to try to attract more volunteers. As Chief of Armaments, he queried many of the illogical procurement decisions of the sort that were driven by politics and patronage rather than the needs of the military, reportedly including the ban on buying kit and components not coming from Russia or other post-Soviet states. The decision to buy T-90A tanks with more advanced ESSA thermal imaging systems built around the second-generation Catherine-FC array designed by the French company Thales, for example, was reportedly rammed through with his backing.[4]

This was an initiative with which Serdyukov would then be associated. The Russian military had not been entirely unwilling to adopt foreign-made equipment, but for reasons of pride, politics and security, this was typically avoided whenever possible. To a degree, Russia was still trapped in the frame of the Soviet-era military-industrial complex, which had often tended towards monopoly manufacturers, many of which ended up in other post-Soviet states. The Antonov concern, for example, which builds larger transport aircraft, was originally based in Novosibirsk in Russia, but was moved to Kyiv in 1952. Although some joint-venture work was continued after 1991, with the 2014 seizure of Crimea, all such collaboration ended. Likewise, Zorya-Mashproyekt in the Ukrainian port city of Mykolaiv used to produce gas turbine engines for Russian warships. Generally, though, foreign purchases were limited to specialized equipment for specialized forces (such as Presidential Security Service snipers) and high-tech components such as the Catherine-FC imaging array. To deliver a warning shot to complacent and corrupt Russian corporations, as well as quickly bring some new capabilities to the field, Serdyukov began buying foreign kit, especially from countries Moscow hoped to woo. Thus, he green-lit the purchase of Italian FIAT-Iveco M65 Lince light tactical multi-role vehicles (which came into service as the *Rys*, the Russian for Lynx), most assembled in Voronezh, as well as two French *Mistral*-class amphibious assault ships and Israeli drones. The *Mistral* deal eventually fell foul of the political fall-out from Crimea: in 2015, Paris cancelled the deal and refunded Russia the equivalent of £590 million it had paid up-front. Although some of the specific items of kit were welcome, the policy overall was unsuccessful with the military and defence industries alike and was reversed when Serdyukov was sacked, although – sometimes by getting round sanctions and export controls – the Russians do still buy foreign kit for their special forces, such as Finnish Sako TRG and British Accuracy International AX338 sniper rifles.

Makarov was also not afraid to draw attention to some of the challenges of the training process. Conscripts are drafted in two annual cycles, in spring and autumn, and this leads to two training cycles, the summer and winter. In winter, recruits concentrate on basic individual and unit training, with the larger joint exercises largely scheduled in summer and early autumn, when the weather is rather more conducive. Overall, though, this training was much too dependent on rote learning and often unrealistic or choreographed exercises. While recruits may well have ended up physically fit and have mastered their basic skills, their capacity to work together in larger units and their officers' experience in dealing with unpredictable and realistic situations was – and remains – distinctly limited. Once Chief of the General Staff, his tone would not soften, and he used an annual meeting of the Academy of Military Sciences as a chance to deliver a scathing review of a military in which only 17% of the Ground Forces and five of the Air Forces' 150 regiments were combat-ready and half the navy's ships were standing idle at anchor.[5]

THE GEORGIAN EXCUSE

If the political stalemate within the military was not going to be settled from above, it would end up being broken by the course of events. Moscow had become increasingly exasperated with the neighbouring state of Georgia, whose firebrand president, Mikheil Saakashvili, was eager to see the country oriented more towards the West. As proxies, the Russians had been supporting the separatists of Abkhazia and South Ossetia. Violence between the Georgian security forces and the South Ossetians had been escalating through the summer, likely at Moscow's instigation. Saakashvili was not a man to take provocation lightly, and on 7 August, Georgian troops moved into South Ossetia and attacked its capital, Tskhinvali. In the process, Russian peacekeepers in the city were engaged, and two were killed.

This gave Moscow the pretext it needed to remind the Georgians that they were in what the Russians considered their sphere of influence. Forces that had been moved close to the border in preparedness were unleashed. However, the actual timing was deeply inconvenient for Moscow. Medvedev was on holiday and, as mentioned, Putin in China for the opening ceremony of the Beijing Olympics. Furthermore, the General Staff's Main Operations Directorate, its primary planning and coordination body, was in the middle of an office move. All this may have magnified the blunders that followed, as abandoned airfields were bombed, officers lost to friendly fire, and advances halted by broken-down vehicles.

As will be discussed in Chapter 11, the Russians certainly won this bitter five-day war, but that was essentially inevitable: the Georgian army had no more than 30,000 soldiers in total, of whom some 2,000 of their best were serving in Iraq alongside coalition forces. The Russians threw in more than twice as many troops, backed by thousands of South Ossetian and Abkhazian militia and overwhelming airpower. The point was that the Russians did far less well than they ought – and the self-evident proof of this gave Serdyukov and Makarov the opportunity at last to force their reforms through.

10

Georgia, 2008 (1): Tbilisi's Move …

'What's the point of an empire that can't impose its will on its subjects?' This was the defiant and rhetorical question I heard from Irakli, a young Georgian academic and would-be politician, in the wake of the 2004 Adjara Crisis.* In the so-called 'Rose Revolution' of November 2003, 20 days of protests after disputed parliamentary elections led to the resignation of President Eduard Shevardnadze and the unopposed election of Mikheil Saakashvili, a fiery, US-educated radical who was eager to see Georgia integrated into Western political, economic and even military structures. The local leadership in Adjara, a region in the south-west of Georgia with its own distinctive culture and identity, refused to acknowledge the change in government, and political name-calling threatened to turn violent as both sides mustered their forces. Perhaps most ominously, Moscow – unhappy with developments in the Georgian capital Tbilisi – began to throw its weight behind Adjaran leader Aslan Abashidze. The government put Adjara under economic blockade and held its biggest ever wargames close to its border as a show of strength that proved sufficiently threatening that the Adjarans blew up the two main bridges over the Choloki River, which marked their region's border. As it was, though, Abashidze's defiance was challenged from within, by public protests and the defection of many of his own

---

* Irakli is a pseudonym, as he later took up a position within the Georgian National Security Council staff.

troops. In May 2004, his government collapsed: 'Aslan has fled, Adjara is free,' Saakashvili exulted, as his rival fled to exile in Moscow.[1]

For Irakli, and his friends, this was a turning point. The Kremlin clearly was unhappy with the new, Westward orientation of Georgia and had tried its usual trick of stirring up a minority to create either a bridgehead or a problem that the Russians could claim only they could fix. As it was, it had failed, and Georgia could now chart a new future out of Moscow's shadows. He was tempting fate.

While Moscow had been comfortable with Adjara being a thorn in Tbilisi's side, it had not really invested itself in its fate, and did nothing much to prevent its fall. Nonetheless, Abashidze's fall did begin to alarm a Russian government that was not simply becoming concerned about the new Georgian regime, but also had a much greater commitment to two other, more substantial break-away regions of the country, Abkhazia and South Ossetia. On the one hand, they were useful means to bringing pressure to bear on Tbilisi when necessary. On the other, there was a genuine sense that these were small nations which deserved to be defended, especially when they looked to Moscow for support.

So in August 2008, looking to punish Saakashvili for his outspoken pro-Western positions and to remind the other states in what Medvedev called its 'sphere of privileged interests' that Moscow ought not to be challenged, the Russians provoked Tbilisi into launching an attack on the rebels of its break-away region of South Ossetia, an attack they had been planning for some time. Saakashvili's move provided the pretext for a lightning attack that saw Georgia's forces decimated within five days and Russian troops theatrically march half the way to Tbilisi before turning back, leaving no one in any serious doubt that, had they wished, they could have occupied the capital, and the whole country.[2]

This short war not only demonstrated Russia's willingness to use force abroad, though; it also showed the shortcomings of the military at that time, and as such provided the crucial final push to allow Serdyukov and Makarov to drive forward their reform programme.

HARBINGERS

Ever since 1783, when the Treaty of Georgievsk saw the first formal accord between Georgia and Russia, this has been a complex relationship which led to the annexation of the former by the latter in 1800. During the chaos of the Russian Civil War (1918–21), Georgia briefly was able to declare itself independent, until reconquered by Bolshevik forces under Joseph Stalin. In 1991, Georgia again became independent, but again it found itself under pressure from Moscow, which used both trade pressure and support for separatist regions as levers to try to maintain its authority over the country. With a population of less than 4 million against Russia's 147 million, this was a deeply unequal contest, although Tbilisi often made up in passion what it may have lacked in pretty much everything else.

After all, along with fine wine, amazing cuisine and copper ore, Georgia is also rich in ethnic and territorial feuds. The Abkhaz minority along Georgia's western coast had been agitating against rule from Tbilisi even before the USSR collapsed, and in 1992, when local militants stormed government buildings in the local capital, Sukhumi, Georgian police, National Guard and paramilitaries responded, and a vicious little war erupted which saw atrocities on both sides. Russia was officially neutral, and brokered a series of ceasefires and accords, but it made little secret of its support for Abkhazia, not least turning a blind eye to the influx of Cossacks and other Russian volunteers to support the separatists, as well as providing weapons and humanitarian relief. In 1993, it was also accused of bombing Sukhumi while it was held by Georgian forces – Russian defence minister Grachyov responded with the implausible and widely derided claim that these were Georgian aircraft painted in Russian colours, bombing their own positions as a provocation. By September 1993, with the rebels' recapture of Sukhumi, the war was effectively over and Abkhazia independent in practice if not in law – but this remained an unresolved issue, with Tbilisi refusing to acknowledge its status, and a quarter of a million ethnic Georgians displaced by the fighting and Abkhaz reprisals.

A similar dynamic was evident in Georgian-controlled South Ossetia, a northern region split from the ethnically similar North Ossetian Region of Russia by the Greater Caucasus mountain range. A long tradition of feud and rebellion re-emerged in the turbulent 1980s, with the rise of Ossetian nationalism. In 1990, Tbilisi revoked what autonomy South Ossetia had, but Moscow stepped in and declared a state of emergency. The South Ossetians made it clear that they would rather be reunited with the North under Moscow, and violence against ethnic Georgians in the region escalated. When Georgian police moved into the South Ossetian capital, Tskhinvali, in January 1991, sporadic violence became sustained, and while a Russian-brokered ceasefire led to a Georgian withdrawal from the city, this soon broke down. Georgian forces, again a mix of police, nationalist militias and the new National Guard, launched several assaults on Tskhinvali through 1991. This was again a vicious conflict which saw ethnic cleansing, indiscriminate reprisals and a flow of refugees into North Ossetia.

In June 1992, the Sochi Agreement brought an uneasy peace to the region, with the South Ossetians likewise having won de facto independence, under the auspices of a joint peacekeeping force of Russian, Georgian and Ossetian troops. Over the next decade, a rough and ready entente saw peace kept at the cost of lawlessness in South Ossetia and neighbouring parts of Georgia, without really resolving the issue. Georgian nationalists – which would include Saakashvili – continued to regard the autonomy of South Ossetia, arguably even more than Abkhazia's, as an affront to their nation's sovereignty. That way would lie disaster.

PROVOKING A WAR

Eduard Shevardnadze, who was Georgian president from 1995 to 2003, adopted a conciliatory policy towards Moscow, even taking moves to block the flow of rebels and materiel to Chechnya through the Pankisi Gorge, which was home to a substantial ethnic Chechen population. However, Shevardnadze's decline would coincide with the rise of Vladimir Putin and a more assertive Russian position over what it considered its sphere of influence. When he was replaced in the 'Rose Revolution' by Saakashvili, the Kremlin both suspected (with no real evidence) that the CIA had had a hand in this, and also saw this as an opportunity to crack the whip and prove not just to Georgia but to the other post-Soviet states that Moscow was back.

Where Shevardnadze had been cautious, Saakashvili was bullish, challenging Russia and making it clear that he saw Georgia's future as being with the West and its security demanding membership of NATO. He embarked on a programme of military modernization which saw the defence budget grow to 9.2% of the country's Gross Domestic Product (GDP) (almost five times the recommended NATO minimum). Whereas Shevardnadze had sent a small contingent of 70 medics and commandos to join the post-war Operation *Iraqi Freedom* peacekeeping force, Saakashvili expanded it as an opportunity to curry favour with Washington. By 2008, there were 2,300 soldiers for the 1st Infantry Brigade deployed there, along with a 550-strong battalion in the separate United Nations Assistance Mission. In return, the United States provided training and equipment, which only heightened Moscow's suspicions that Georgia was becoming little more than an American puppet state.

Relations worsened in a vicious circle. The new National Military Strategy listed as threats not just South Ossetian and Abkhaz secessionists but also Russian peacekeepers, and in 2006, Georgian defence minister Irakli Okruashvili said that he would resign if he was not in a position to celebrate the New Year 2007 in Tskhinvali.[3] In response, Moscow stepped up its intelligence operations, and in 2006 Tbilisi publicly expelled four Russians it claimed were working for the GRU. In 2007, it even alleged that it had shot down a Russian aircraft over Abkhazia (Moscow denied this), even while the Russians downed three Georgian Israel-made Elbit Hermes 450 drones. That year, the legislature also approved measures to increase the size of the Georgian military from 28,000 to 32,000 soldiers, then 37,000 in 2008. The populist Saakashvili seemed to relish the confrontation, and certainly sought to use it for political capital, accusing opposition protests of being stirred up by 'high ranking officials in the Russian special services' engaged in 'dirty geo-political escapades'.[4]

Meanwhile, although in 2008 NATO held back from offering Georgia a full Membership Action Plan, Tbilisi's eagerness angered the Russians. Baluyevsky warned that Moscow would 'take steps' to prevent Georgia (or other post-Soviet states) from joining the alliance. Nonetheless, despite all the warnings he was getting from the West, Saakashvili also seems to have believed that his country would ultimately be protected by NATO or the United States, if the worst came to the worst. Condoleezza Rice, then US Secretary of State, recollected that she 'told Georgian President Mikheil Saakashvili – privately – that the Russians would try to provoke him and that, given the circumstances on the ground, he could not count on a military response from NATO'.[5] Such warnings fell on deaf ears.

It was not simply that Saakashvili was personally committed to restoring Tbilisi's control over the rebel republics; it was also that there was a sense that the time to do so might be running out. The West's recognition of Kosovo's unilateral secession from Serbia in February 2008 infuriated the Russians, who regarded it as a dangerous precedent but also a naked bit of favouritism, given that Serbia was a Russian ally. In response, they began making noises to the effect that if the West could treat secessionist regions as real countries, then so could they. There was a sense that a formal recognition of Abkhazia and South Ossetia – and with it, security guarantees – was just a matter of time. It was also the case that Georgia could not afford these levels of defence expenditure long term, and Saakashvili's calculation was presumably that he could take first one, then the other of the break-aways, at which point he could afford to scale it down. Either way, it was clear that the Georgians were planning to act.

At that stage, Putin technically handed over the presidency to his prime minister, Dmitry Medvedev, but the evidence suggests that already, from 2006, the decision had been made that something needed to be done about Saakashvili. From that year on, the North Caucasus Military District began staging increasingly elaborate and sizeable military exercises that it would turn out were both wargaming invasion and also a cover for the eventual troop build-up. Meanwhile, the Russians brought their peacekeeping contingent in Abkhazia to its permitted ceiling of 3,000, including two companies of *Spetsnaz* and paratroopers from the 7th Air Assault Division. On the other hand, it seemed to neglect South Ossetia, because when it did strike, Moscow wanted to have some pretext, and it knew both that Georgia was actively preparing its own offensive to try to retake the region, and that Saakashvili was a hothead.

South Ossetia was propitious, after all. It could be reinforced via the Roki Tunnel cut through the Greater Caucasus range; its leader, Eduard Kokoity, was fiercely anti-Georgian, and a failed attempt by Georgian forces to regain the region in 2004 had left a legacy of bitterness and mutual suspicion. South Ossetian irregulars, egged on and armed by Moscow, began attacking Georgian civilians and government forces across the disputed border. In some cases, Georgians fired back, and on 1 August 2008, South Ossetians began shelling Georgian villages, in defiance of a 1992 ceasefire agreement. The aim was evidently to provoke Saakashvili into some kind of action that the Russians could use as a pretext. It worked. After a week of claim and counter-claim, ceasefire and ambush, on 7 August Georgian forces began bombarding Tskhinvali. Moscow had got its war.

THE GEORGIAN ADVANCE

The Georgian plan was to take advantage of their qualitative edge over the South Ossetians quickly to engage with and destroy their main field forces, seize Tskhinvali and block the Roki Tunnel and Trans-Caucasus Highway to prevent the arrival of reinforcements, because at that stage they were expecting to face motley collections of Russian volunteer militias, not regular soldiers. Within four days they hoped to have seized the main settlements in the region such that they could instal a new, friendly local administration and turn policing and mop-up duties over to a force of reservist soldiers and police.

To this end, the 4th Brigade was to seize the village of Khetagurovi, west of Tskhinvali, while the 3rd took the Prisi Heights to its east, meeting at Gufti to the north and encircling the city. Then, they would race along the S10 highway up to Djava, and then to the Roki Tunnel. Actually taking Tskhinvali would be the responsibility of the Interior Ministry forces, supported by an army tank battalion, Special Operations Group and artillery. Along with the second-echelon reserves and smaller units deployed to seize other towns, in total Tbilisi threw some 12,000 troops and 4,000 Interior Ministry personnel into the attack: the bulk of its operational forces given that the elite 1st Brigade was at the time in Iraq.

This was a perfectly sensible and well-prepared plan, but it had one crucial weakness: the Russians had a plan, too. Tbilisi's assumption was that Moscow would either use diplomacy before military force or at the very least take days to muster any serious contingent to intervene. Beyond the possibility of ad hoc collections of lightly armed volunteers, no serious efforts were made to address this contingency. The attacking force had no real air defence capability, and the expectation was that Moscow would be presented with a fait accompli.

While the Russians did not know precisely when Saakashvili would show his hand, they had a pretty good idea that it would happen. After the latest of their military exercises, Kavkaz-2008, they had left two reinforced battalions of the 19th Motor Rifle Division just 30 kilometres from the border, kept on stand-by. This meant that some 1,500 troops supported by 14 T-72B tanks, 16 2S3 152mm self-propelled guns and an additional battery of nine BM-21 Multiple Rocket Launch systems (MRLs) could deploy into South Ossetia within hours. Other units, including paratroopers, were on 24-hour readiness, while plans for air attacks on Georgian strategic targets had already been made and distributed.

Just before midnight on 7 August, the Georgians started to bombard Tskhinvali with more than 100 mortars and artillery pieces and 30 MRLs. The plan had been for carefully targeted strikes on strategic locations but, as ever, the reality was much messier. The accuracy of the incoming fire was often questionable, and along with civilian neighbourhoods, some shells hit the compound of the Russian peacekeepers under Lt. Col. Konstantin Timerman, something Tbilisi had wanted to avoid. Moscow immediately claimed that this was an illegitimate act of aggression. In any case, their forces were already moving, having been given the orders at around 0100 hours on 8 August. An hour later, a battalion from the 693rd Motor Rifle Regiment crossed the border, soon followed by another from the 135th Motor Rifle Regiment. Their mission was to take and hold the tunnel and the road to Tskhinvali, keeping it open for further Russian troops.

These, in turn, were mobilizing. At about the time the second battalion was crossing the border, a major task force was being activated. Elements of the 42nd and 19th Motor Rifle Divisions were brought to readiness, along with a battalion tactical group from the 76th Air Assault Division's 104th Regiment. Elements of the 10th and 22nd *Spetsnaz* Brigades were also dispatched. Although, as will be discussed in the next chapter, command and control was often not as clear or as smooth as intended, the Russians had planned and wargamed this, and were ready to move.

THE BATTLE FOR TSKHINVALI

By early morning on 8 August, Georgian forces were already on the outskirts of the city. The relatively meagre artillery available to the Ossetians had not slowed them, and although the defenders were joined by the North Ossetians of the Alaniya Peacekeeping Battalion, there was nothing they could do to prevent the encirclement of the city. Meanwhile, the picture elsewhere was mixed. Forces from the

Georgian Interior Ministry's Constitutional Security Department were mauled when they tried to enter the village of Kvaysa in the east of South Ossetia, even though they faced just a platoon of defenders. They withdrew back over the border to lick their wounds. On the other hand, most of the smaller attacks the Georgians made had proven relatively successful; the key issue, though, was taking Tskhinvali.

As the Interior Ministry forces moved towards the city, they came under fire from the Southern Compound of the Russian peacekeeping detachment. Fire was returned, including by three Georgian army T-72 tanks. Five Russians were killed, but one of the tanks was put out of action by an RPG-7 hit and the other two withdrew. Although Georgian forces were able to bypass it and reach the outskirts of the city, the 250 soldiers in the Russian outpost remained a threat. More tank shelling hit and destroyed their medical station, and by mid-morning the vehicle park was on fire and the Russians had been forced to take shelter in bunkers, basements and their boiler house. The compound was encircled by Georgian troops.

Even so, the security forces were struggling to make headway into Tskhinvali. Their Turkish-made Cobra wheeled APCs, armed with 12.7mm machine guns and 40mm grenade launchers, lacked the firepower and presence to clear their way through defenders armed with RPGs, grenades and Molotov cocktails. The 4th Brigade's 41st and 42nd Light Infantry Battalions were thus detached and sent in to support them, while three of Georgia's small fleet of Mi-24 helicopter gunships began to be prepared to provide close air support. A renewed attack managed to push through the lightly armed militias defending the city and reached their headquarters in the centre. Here the best South Ossetian forces had mustered under Gen. Anatoly Barankevich, secretary of their Security Council. They put up a much more determined resistance, with Barankevich himself firing an RPG-7 round that penetrated the thinner armour on the rear of one tank's turret, detonating its magazine and blowing up the vehicle. Two other T-72s were also hit by other militiamen shortly thereafter.

Just as they were reacting to this unexpected reversal, a pair of Russian Su-25s from the 368th Attack Aviation Regiment appeared in the skies over Tskhinvali. The 42nd Battalion had established positions in the Dubovaya Gardens in the west of the city, and the Su-25s raked them with bomb and rocket fire. More than 20 were killed, and the

Fig. 1. The finals of the Tank Biathlon event at the 2018 Army Games; the T-72B3 tank in the foreground shows the logo of manufacturer Uralvagonzavod. (Mark Galeotti)

Fig. 2. Troops loyal to Boris Yeltsin take cover near the White House during the 1993 'October Coup.' (Getty Images)

Fig. 3. One of the last examples of the Soviet A-90 *Orlyonok* ('Eaglet') ekranoplan, an innovative sea-skimmer that would fly just above the waves. (Mark Galeotti)

Fig. 4. On the eve of the First Chechen War, MVD Interior Troops muster in North Ossetia. (Getty Images)

Fig. 5. An Mi-24 firing salvos of unguided rockets. (RMOD)

Fig. 6. Russian paratroopers who have just taken Pristina airport in June 1999 stop a civilian vehicle. (Getty Images)

Fig. 7. A Chechen National Guardsman – one of the so-called '*Kadyrovtsy*' – in an APC decorated with a portrait of former Chechen president Akhmad Kadyrov. (Getty Images)

Fig. 8. An Mi-24P Hind-F gunship armed with rocket pods and side-mounted twin-barrel GSh-20-2K autocannon. (RMOD)

Fig. 9. Russian troops crossing into South Ossetia, 2008. (Getty Images)

Fig. 10. Ski troops being towed by a BMP-2 in Siberia. (RMOD)

Fig. 11. A combat engineer in full bomb disposal kit. (RMOD)

Fig. 12. A 'little green man' – or, for the Russians, 'polite person' – in *Ratnik* kit with a supporter at Simferopol airport. (Ilya Varlamov, CC BY-SA 4.0)

Fig. 13. Pro-Russian rebels in the Donbas with a tank and BM-21 captured from government forces. (Getty Images)

Fig. 14. Defence Minister Sergei Shoigu at Hmeymim, Syria, in early 2022. (RMOD)

Fig. 15. The pilot of a Sukhoi Su-25 stationed in Syria prepares to return home to Russia. (Alamy)

Fig. 16. A T-14 Armata on parade in Moscow, 2019. (Mark Galeotti)

Fig. 17. An *Orlan*-10 drone is ready for launch, while a soldier in the foreground clutches a REX-1 anti-drone rifle that jams their control signals. (Alamy)

Fig. 18. A *Msta* 152mm self-propelled howitzer. (Mark Galeotti)

Fig. 19. Two Mi-28 gunships from the Western Military District. (RMOD)

Fig. 20. Eager for more *kontraktniki*, the military is increasingly recruiting women, such as this VDV lieutenant from the 38th Brigade, setting up communications systems in a GAZ *Tigr* jeep. (Alamy)

Fig. 21. An S-300V SAM system in launch position. (RMOD)

Fig. 22. An Su-34 dropping KAB-500S bombs over Syria. (RMOD)

Fig. 23. The *Admiral Kutuzov* aircraft carrier, on trials. (RMOD)

Fig. 24. The *Slava*-class missile cruiser *Marshal Ustinov*, with the massive launch tubes
for its P-500 *Bazalt* (SS-N-12 Sandbox) anti-ship missiles clearly visible.
(Royal Navy, OGL v1.0)

Fig. 25. *Krivak IV*-class frigates *Admiral Essen* and *Admiral Grigorovich* frigates in the Mediterranean Sea, launching *Kalibr* cruise missiles at Islamic State targets in Syria in 2017. (Alamy)

Fig. 26. The guided missile cruiser *Moskva*, flagship of the Black Sea Fleet, leaving Sevastopol. The ship was later sunk by Ukrainian missiles in April 2022. (Alamy)

Fig. 27. A *Raptor*-class patrol boat moving at speed. (Alamy)

Fig. 28. A Tupolev Tu-95 strategic bomber with fighter escort. (Getty Images)

Fig. 29. An RS-24 *Yars* road-mobile intercontinental ballistic missile of the 54th Guards Missile Division. (Alamy)

Fig. 30. New recruits to the 106th Guards Airborne Division being sworn in. (RMOD)

Fig. 31. A BMD-2 paratrooper IFV being hoisted into an Il-76 before heading to Kazakhstan in 2022. (RMOD)

Fig. 32. The *Zubr*-class hovercraft *Mordoviya* moving onto the beach to land Naval Infantry. (Alamy)

Fig. 33. A *Spetsnaz* with a VSS *Vintorez* silenced sniper rifle. (RMOD)

Fig. 34. Military Police in Hmeymin, showing the new Russian desert uniform. (Kremlin.ru)

Fig. 35. Military police in a *Kamaz* Typhoon-K personnel carrier on joint patrol with Turkish troops near Idlib in Syria. (Getty Images)

Fig. 36. A column of new T-72B3s arriving at the 201st Base in Tajikistan. (RMOD)

Fig. 37. The letter Z became something of a symbol of the Russian invasion of Ukraine, and these tanks heading out of Mariupol are liberally festooned with them. (Alamy)

Fig. 38. Soldiers from the 1st Guards Engineer Brigade in urban warfare training. (RMOD)

Fig. 39. Spiritual power meets nuclear: a priest blesses a *Yars* ICBM in Teikovo, Ivanovo Region. (Alamy)

Fig. 40. Crest of the Armed Forces on the railings around the General Staff building on Znamenka Street in Moscow, adopted in 1997 in conscious homage to the tsarist one from 1800. (Mark Galeotti)

rest of the battalion panicked, fleeing the city and leaving behind their heavy equipment, including three tanks. As word of this spread, the story became more exaggerated, until it was that the entire battalion had been wiped out. Having managed to take almost a third of the city, Georgian forces actually began to withdraw, often in poor order, and by mid-afternoon they had essentially abandoned Tskhinvali.

Extra troops were rushed to the scene – the 2nd Brigade turned back to return to Tskhinvali, and the 5th Brigade's 53rd Light Infantry Battalion was brought up from the reserves. However, it would take time to prepare to deploy them. President Saakashvili announced a three-hour 'humanitarian ceasefire' ostensibly to allow civilians to leave the city and militias to surrender, but also because of the need to take stock and prepare to face this new situation. The appearance of the Russians, after all, had changed everything.

THE RUSSIAN ADVANCE

The Russian advance guard moved at speed to secure the route to Tskhinvali. At around 0700 hours, forces from the 693rd Motor Rifle Regiment were crossing a bridge on the Djava–Tskhinvali road when they came under attack from four Georgian Su-25s. Their 250-kilogram bombs all missed, causing no casualties and failing to damage the bridge, but the pilots were able to report back that there were Russian troops where the Georgian High Command had not expected them. As speed was of the essence, their vanguard did not have anti-air vehicles, and nor did they yet have fighter cover, so there was little they could do to prevent the word getting back to Tbilisi. That air cover was soon in place, though, with fighters from 4th Air Army reaching South Ossetian airspace about an hour later. News of this development was enough to ground all Georgian Su-25s, as they would be easy targets. Instead, they were dispersed and hidden, in order to reduce the risk of their being destroyed on the ground.

Despite a couple of skirmishes with Georgian enclaves or possibly special forces, the force only suffered the loss of one vehicle, a BMP-2 which broke down on the Gufti Bridge and had to be pushed into the river to allow the rest of the force to pass. Meanwhile, Russian airpower was beginning to make its presence felt. The attack on the 42nd Battalion was just one of several launched against government forces around Tskhinvali. At the same time, Su-25s and Su-24Ms were bombing targets in Georgia itself, including bases in Gori, a town on the Variani–Tbilisi road, and Variani base, where reservists were being mustered. Later, the Russians would also start hitting airbases at Marneuli and Bolnisi. They would lose only one aircraft, a Su-25 shot down by friendly fire, in 63 sorties flown that first day.

Just as Saakashvili's 'ceasefire' was meant to be coming into effect, the 122mm and 152mm guns of the 693rd Motor Rifle Regiment and the BM-21s of the 292nd Combined Artillery Regiment were being readied for action. They began bombarding Georgian positions around Tskhinvali, worsening their panic and ensuring that by late afternoon, the only government force still holding on in the city was the blocking force around the peacekeeper compound. Meanwhile, hopes that the 3rd Brigade could turn things around were dashed when it also came under air and artillery attack and regrouped around the village of Eredvi, east of Tskhinvali.

Although there was one last, abortive assault on the city from the south on the evening of the first day of the war, Tbilisi realized that while the initial force of a little over 3,000 Russian troops was only equivalent to one of their brigades, it was no more than the vanguard and was supported by overwhelming airpower. Besides which, the first of the next echelon of reinforcements were beginning to arrive: the 135th Motor Rifle Regiment's reconnaissance company. Government forces began withdrawing from South Ossetia and lifted their blockade of the peacekeepers. Nonetheless, Saakashvili was not yet willing to accept defeat. With pretty close to the entire Georgian army now deployed on or just over the South Ossetian border (except for the 1st Brigade, still in Iraq), plans for a second attack were hurriedly drawn up that night.

11

Georgia, 2008 (2): … Moscow's Counter

Tbilisi had counted on speed to secure South Ossetia before Russia could react. That having failed, but unwilling to admit defeat after just a single day's fighting, on 9 August government forces returned to the fray, cautiously and methodically in contrast to the previous day's headlong rush. After a brief artillery barrage in the middle of the night, dawn saw the 2nd Brigade lead the renewed offensive, retaking the village of Khetagurovi south of Tskhinvali from a small Russian screening force. Having occupied Khetagurovi, they then inched north to Upper Nikozi, a village closer to the city, where they were met by the 41st Battalion and prepared to move on the city at around 1400 hours, as the Georgian artillery renewed its bombardment.

Meanwhile, the Russian advance guard had relieved the peacekeeping contingent. Two companies from the 135th Motor Rifle Regiment, accompanied by Lt. Gen. Anatoly Khrulyov, commander of the 58th Army and senior figure in the field, were moving towards the city, unaware that the Georgians were about to mount an attack. His convoy came under shellfire but pressed on, meaning that – unbeknown to each other – the Russians entered Tskhinvali from the west at the same time as the Georgians from the south. The 2nd Brigade's reconnaissance company and one of Khrulyov's blundered into each other, and although the government forces withdrew, the general was badly wounded. The main forces then engaged each other, and the Georgians' superior numbers and tanks forced the Russians onto the back foot. Encircled and vulnerable to mortar fire, for a time their position looked

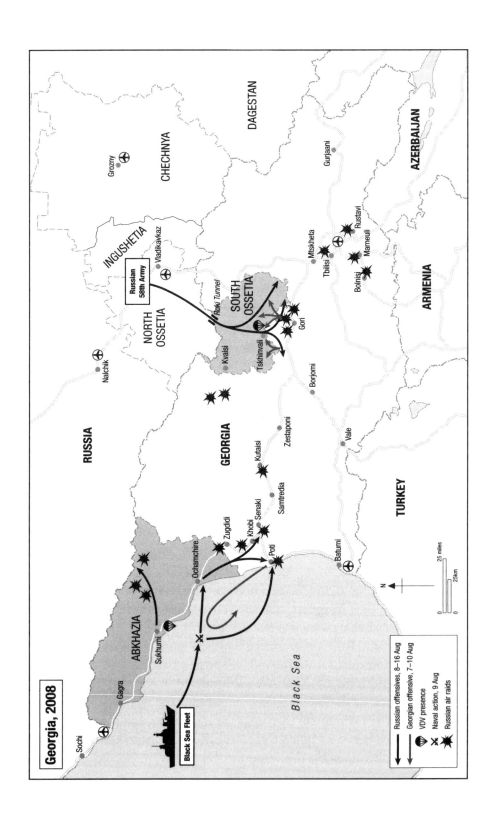

Georgia, 2008

untenable, but reinforcements were on the way. *Spetsnaz* and the GRU's *Vostok* Battalion, a veteran force made up of Chechens who had joined Moscow's side, infiltrated the city to support them, while artillery and airpower was committed to driving the Georgians back. Although the Russian artillery did suffer from counter-battery fire, they could rely on target designation from peacekeepers and *Spetsnaz* on the front line and began a withering barrage that forced back the 41st Battalion, which had been leading the attack.

By late afternoon, the Georgians had again withdrawn from the city. All day, Russian bombers had continued to hit targets both on and behind the front line. This included strikes by heavy Tu-22M bombers from the 52nd Guards Heavy Bomber Regiment, one of which had been shot down by the Georgians, which had closed the Kopitnary airbase at Kutaisi in the west and also hit Gori. Although only 28 sorties were flown that day, and three aircraft lost (the other two to friendly fire again), they proved crucial in preventing the Georgians from exploiting the momentum of their initial assault on Tskhinvali. Along with a strike by a Tochka-U (SS-21) ballistic missile with a conventional cluster bomb warhead, which hit a Georgian force in the west of South Ossetia, they also served a political purpose, reminding Tbilisi of the Russians' reach. While artillery exchanges would continue into the evening, the second full day of war had again seen a Georgian offensive repelled. It was a mark of Tbilisi's desperation that it asked the United States to organize an emergency airlift home of the 2,000 soldiers of the 1st Brigade serving in Iraq.

THE TIDE TURNS

Saakashvili's gamble had failed, and any thought of restoring government control of South Ossetia had been dashed. Instead, the initiative swung to the Russians. The next day saw a major reinforcement as some 4,500 fresh soldiers from the 42nd Motor Rifle Division arrived, along with the 19th Motor Rifle Division's 503rd Motor Rifle Regiment, two battalion tactical groups from the 76th Air Assault Division, elements of the 22nd *Spetsnaz* Brigade and ten Mi-24 gunships and Mi-8 assault transports from the 487th Helicopter Regiment. So numerous were these forces that there were even traffic jams on the road into Tskhinvali. By the end of 10 August, the city was solidly in their hands, with more than 10,000 Russian soldiers in-theatre.

The Georgian forces were in some disarray, but their mission shifted from attack to defence, units digging in along the front line. Tbilisi announced a formal end to its operation, but sporadic artillery duels continued, as did Russian air attacks. These were stepped up during the night of 10–11 August, destroying military and civilian radars to blind its air defences and hammering airbases. This was not simply as harassment but to prepare the ground for a Russian counter-attack, first to secure South Ossetia and then to go further.

To push back government forces so that they could not continue to shell Tskhinvali, the Russians assembled a brigade-strength task force from the 693rd Motor Rifle Regiment, the 70th Motor Rifle Regiment and the 234th Airborne Assault Regiment. On the morning of 11 August, they set out and, despite encountering some resistance, by late afternoon had reached and taken the village of Variani, some 15 kilometres into Georgian territory and the site of a strategically important government supply base. In a move of some desperation, the Georgians lofted all six of their Mi-24s to attack the advancing Russians, but while they made it safely back to base, they only destroyed two trucks and would not again be sent into battle.

The Russians began to dig in around Variani, anticipating a counter-attack, but instead the government forces were in a state of panic and confusion. On a tactical level, the Georgians often fought bravely and well, but a failure to train up a new generation of senior officers capable of coordinating large-scale operations was really beginning to tell. Furthermore, the political leadership failed to get ahead of the crisis. Saakashvili had been visiting Gori, and had been evacuated by his security detail when Russian warplanes were seen overhead. What was good enough for the president was good enough for his men, and shortly thereafter the substantial contingent of government troops in Gori also began to withdraw, most to Tbilisi and a few to Kutaisi. After all, the Russians were still coming, with their strength now reaching around 14,000, and the mood in the capital was sombre: what had started as a surgical campaign to reassert government control over a rebel region now looked like a fight for national survival. The Georgians intensified their efforts to win international support, their efforts compromised by a wave of cyber-attacks presumed to be emanating from Russia, with the Foreign Ministry's website and emails compromised and Saakashvili's own site defaced with images comparing him with Adolf Hitler. Some of these appear to have originated directly from Russian state agencies, but others were from so-called 'patriotic hackers' encouraged or instructed by the Kremlin to launch attacks on their own account.

Next day, the Russians resumed a methodical and essentially unopposed advance towards Gori, taking commanding heights over the city by mid-morning. Two conventionally armed *Iskander* (SS-26) short-range ballistic missiles were launched, one hitting the Marneuli airbase, another Gori's main square. This had previously been a military staging point, but by then all the troops had left, and nine civilians were killed. As they advanced, the Russians found themselves seizing more and more abandoned military materiel, from US-made M16 rifles (which became popular trophies) to artillery pieces. Meanwhile, as the first of the 1st Brigade's troops began to arrive at Tbilisi airport, the Georgian government stepped up its appeals for international support, diplomatic or otherwise, to prevent what it assumed was an imminent attack on the capital. Georgian forces, having rallied, dug in to defend it.

As it was, the Russians felt they had made their point. Just after midday on 12 August, President Medvedev announced that 'the operation has achieved its goal, security for peacekeepers and civilians has been restored. The aggressor has been punished, suffering huge losses.'[1] By 1500 hours, Russian artillery and airstrikes had ceased, and the war was effectively over. The next day, the Russians would occupy Gori, which had already been abandoned by the government forces, but after Saakashvili had signed a peace agreement brokered by French president Nicolas Sarkozy on 15 August, signed by Medvedev the next day, they would be focusing on withdrawal. Of course, they did not go without confiscating all the materiel they could and destroying what they could not. Not only did the Georgian forces suffer some 2,000 casualties – including 182 military dead and 188 civilians – in the fighting, but the losses from this post-war ravaging of their equipment and stores exceeded those from fighting. All told, they lost dozens of tanks, APCs and other vehicles – mainly seized by the Russians. They also lost heavily on what was in many ways a neglected battlefront: Abkhazia.

THE ABKHAZ FRONT

While Tbilisi's focus had been on South Ossetia, the Abkhazians – and the Russians – had spotted an opportunity. Initially, there had been uncertainty in Moscow and the Abkhaz capital of Sukhumi as to whether Saakashvili planned to kill two birds with the same stone. The 2nd and 5th Brigades and Interior Ministry forces west of South Ossetia could, after all, as easily have been ready to drive eastwards into Abkhazia. Hence Russia's reinforcement of its peacekeeping contingent, as well as the Abkhazians' decision to declare a state of emergency on the morning of 8 August, as the Georgians began their operation. Meanwhile, Russia's 7th Airborne Assault Division in Novorossiisk, further north up the Black Sea coast, was ordered to stand up three battalion tactical groups for deployment to Abkhazia. By the end of the day, the first had already embarked on landing ships and was steaming south, escorted by two corvettes, the *Mirazh* and the *Suzdalets*, and two minesweepers. For heavier firepower, the missile cruiser *Moskva*, flagship of the Black Sea Fleet, began urgently to be prepared for action. Four more VDV battalions were later airlifted to Sukhumi, with the rest of the 7th Division transported there by rail, along a line Russian Railway Troops had repaired only that spring.

Although it quickly became clear that Tbilisi was concentrating its efforts on South Ossetia, neither Moscow nor Sukhumi wanted to waste a good opportunity to break Georgia's small navy, hinder the campaign against Ossetia, and drive the Georgians out of the upper reaches of the strategic Kodori Gorge, which Abkhazia had been contesting with the government.

In pursuit of the first goal, first of all the Russians unveiled Tochka-U missiles that had secretly been moved to the coastal town of Ochamchire the year before. Two fitted with cluster warheads were launched against the Georgian naval base of Poti, to the south. Five sailors died, but the main aim seems to have been disruption and to encourage the patrol boats there to head for the relative security of the larger base at Batumi, even further south, rather than pose any risk to the flotilla bringing paratroopers and marines to Ochamchire.

On the afternoon of the 9th, Moscow formally warned that the Abkhaz coastline was now closed to all shipping, as the *Moskva*, escorted by the destroyer *Smetlivy*, set sail from Sevastopol. When four Georgian patrol boats sought to approach Ochamchire and the landing ships that were standing off the coast (it turned out that the harbour had become silted up, so the task force ended up having to disembark on the beach), the *Mirazh* engaged them with P-120

Malakhit (SS-N-9) missiles. Although Tbilisi denied it, the Russians claimed one was sunk, and this was probably the armed Coast Guard cutter *Giorgi Toreli*.

However, the crucial move would come from the land. Russian paratroopers moved south across the Abkhaz–Georgian border on 10 August, initially in connection with the Kodori Gorge operations described below. However, two days later, a special forces team from the 45th Independent Airborne Reconnaissance Regiment – the VDV's own *Spetsnaz* – penetrated the port of Poti, where the bulk of the Georgian navy still lay at anchor. These ships had been abandoned, because their crews were anticipating further air attacks, and so the commandos were able to mine and sink fully six naval and Coast Guard ships, including the fast attack boats *Tbilisi* and *Dioscuria*, their most powerful assets.

There was relatively little that could be done to affect the Ossetian campaign, although an early strike on the 2nd Brigade's base in Senaki did seriously disrupt efforts to muster reservists. Instead, the main additional effort by the Russian forces was put into supporting the Kodori campaign. The Abkhazians deployed the bulk of their forces (which after mobilization numbered some 9,000), supported from the air by helicopters and also their three still-operational L-39 trainer jets, fitted with unguided rockets and bombs. By the afternoon of the 9th, their forces were ready, and after a day of artillery bombardment, on the evening of the 10th they had begun to move into the disputed region of the Gorge. That same day, Russian paratroopers from the 7th Division moved into the Zugdidi region, south of Abkhazia. With a clear military advantage, they negotiated an essentially bloodless occupation of the area, and then took Senaki the next day, where the 2nd Brigade's base had been evacuated. A reinforced company subsequently swung north to close the other mouth of the Gorge. Finding themselves boxed in, the Georgian police and soldiers there largely laid down their weapons and left the Gorge; the Russians let them go. The next day, the Abkhazians swept through the Gorge, flushing out the few remaining pockets of resistance, as Georgian deputy interior minister Eka Zhguladze claimed they were withdrawn as a 'goodwill gesture'.[2] Only two Georgians died, and one Abkhazian (in an accident), but by 12 August, the Gorge was essentially in Sukhumi's hands and this separate little war was over.

THE AUDIT

On 26 August, Moscow formally recognized South Ossetia and Abkhazia as independent states – a decision rejected by the international community – and acquired military protectorates that occupy one-fifth of Georgia's territory, and the constant opportunity to cause more trouble for Tbilisi, should it want to. Both regions' borders are now also monitored by permanent FSB Border Troops posts. There is also a Russian military presence in both regions. In Abkhazia, the 7th Military Base outside Gudauta was formed from the 131st Independent Motor Rifle Brigade, strengthened with new T-90A tanks and S-300PS SAM systems, while the Black Sea Fleet also operates small patrol vessels out of Ochamchire. In North Ossetia, the 693rd Motor Rifle Regiment of the 19th Motor Rifle Division became the basis for the 4th Military Base, along with additional forces including a rocket artillery battery.

In return, the Russians lost no more than 74 dead (figures are contradictory, and some put it in the low 60s), the Georgians more than twice as many, along with large amounts of materiel – including Humvees supplied by the United States – and much of their navy. More to the point, Moscow had demonstrated the will and capacity to use a short, sharp dose of force to punish a neighbour that failed to toe the line.

Saakashvili, predictably enough, would later try to spin defeat as a near-victory, claiming that 'the Russian 58th Army was actually burned by the 4th (Georgian) Brigade'.[3] He was wrong, but nonetheless Moscow was not exulting in its victory. That it had won against a country one-twentieth of its size and when it stuck to limited and achievable objectives was not a surprise. Instead, what quickly became clear to the High Command was that it had not done anywhere near as well as it should.

The whole effort was nowhere near as well coordinated as it should have been. The Russians had known that the Georgians would strike some time, but had not known exactly when. As it was, when it happened, the General Staff's Main Operations Directorate (GOU: *Glavnoye Operativnoye Upravleniye*), its primary organ for planning and organizing operations, was actually in the middle of an office move. Serdyukov had been suspicious of the GOU's former chief, Col. Gen. Alexander Rukshin, whom he felt was too close to dismissed Chief of the General Staff Baluyevsky. By extension, he was wary of the GOU, and after dismissing Rukshin in June, he took his time selecting a successor. Worse yet, he pushed through swingeing 40% cuts to the GOU and, adding insult to injury, forced them to relocate to smaller offices. When Georgian troops started moving, most of the GOU's files were locked away in secure packing crates packed onto a dozen KamAZ trucks, plus the ZAS secure-traffic telephones in their old offices had been cut off, and their new ones had not yet been connected.

Suddenly, military orders of the greatest secrecy were having to be transmitted by civilian cellphone. Chief of Staff Makarov was accused of having forgotten to activate the Air Forces at the same time as he ordered the Ground Forces to move, and only belatedly made good his mistake when prompted, which may explain why the first expeditionary forces were without air cover. Furthermore, command decisions over the Air Force were being made not in the field but by Col. Gen. Alexander Zelin, head of the Air Force Main Staff, by phone from his office. Fortunately for Moscow, the operational plans had already been developed and circulated – ironically enough, by the GOU – and in North Caucasus VO commander Col. Gen. Sergei Makarov (no relation) and 58th Army commander Lt. Gen. Anatoly Khrulyov they had competent, aggressive and experienced men who were willing and able to take the initiative.

It is worth noting, though, that Serdyukov and his Chief of the General Staff did not suffer as a result of this chaos, both because they did win their war and also because there was more than enough blame and inefficiency to go around. Makarov, for example, was scathing about the problem of finding suitable command personnel:

> In order to find one person at the rank of lieutenant colonel, colonel, or general who could ably command troops, it was necessary to search one-by-one through the armed forces, because the full-time commanders who were sitting around leading 'paper regiments and divisions' simply were not in a condition to resolve issues that arose during the five-day war. And when you did send them troops and equipment, they were simply confused, and some even refused to execute their assigned tasks.[4]

This was ungenerous, but not wholly inaccurate. Certainly the forces in this war often made heavy weather of basic inter-unit cooperation, and were thus especially vulnerable to Georgian ambushes and counter-attacks, such as the one that left Khrulyov trapped and seriously wounded. This lack of coordination often reflected patchy and dated communications in the field: at one point Khrulyov even had to borrow a satellite phone from a journalist to give orders. Units on the ground found they could not talk to aircrews above them, contributing to friendly fire incidents such as the very first loss, a Su-25 downed by Russians using shoulder-fired SAMs on the evening of 8 August – because the ground troops had not been told that they were now receiving air cover and they assumed this was a Georgian attack. All told, of the six aircraft Russia lost in the war, three Su-25s, two Su-24Ms and one Tu-22M3, half were casualties of friendly fire. (And two helicopters were lost when a Border Troops Mi-8 hit a M-24 on the ground when coming in for a night landing on 16 August.)

DID ANYTHING WORK WELL?

There were serious problems with breakdowns and malfunctions beyond the Russian communications systems. Many vehicles of the 58th Army never even made it to Ossetia because they would not start or broke down on the way. Although the T-72M tanks deployed were notionally fitted for advanced reactive armour able to defeat man-portable anti-tank weapons, in practice the canisters which would hold the explosive charges meant to disrupt incoming warheads were usually empty. Half the bombs dropped on Kopitnary and Senaki airfields failed to explode. The litany is a long one.

For example, although it had seen limited use over Chechnya, the Georgian War saw the first real operational use of the Yakovlev *Pchela* ('Bumblebee') drone, originally developed in the late Soviet era but only fielded in 1997. Boosted from a launch ramp by rocket, it can loiter for up to two hours, streaming back real-time video footage from a TV and thermal imaging camera in a blister under its nose. Earlier versions used in Chechnya had had some successes, but its two-stroke two-cylinder piston engine was noisy and it could not fly high, leaving it especially vulnerable to high crosswinds in Chechnya's mountain passes. Only eight combat sorties were flown, and two of the drones were shot down by rebel anti-aircraft fire. There were higher hopes of the newer Pchela-1T version, which was specifically intended for the

VDV. However, it signally failed to impress paratrooper Col. Valery Yakhnovets, who was responsible for its field testing in Georgia. In his own words: 'the first drone crashed to the ground, having barely taken off', the second streamed back such unclear footage that the operators couldn't even spot their own column of armoured personnel carriers, while it flew 'so low it seemed you could hit it with a slingshot, and it "growled" like a BTR'. In short, in his opinion, 'its effectiveness is zero and the Airborne Forces do not need it'.[5] Later Russian drones would prove a good deal more effective, and welcomed by their users, but it seems to have taken a disastrous combat debut really to force the military to identify what worked and what did not.

Then there were basic failures of training. Although most of the forces deployed in Georgia were professionals, they often showed little greater skill or aptitude than conscripts. Almost as many Russian casualties were actually sustained in road crashes and other accidents as from Georgian artillery. It is not just that aircraft were downed by friendly fire, but that there was also a number of incidents in which Russian units fired on each other because of poor communications or fire discipline. Indeed, speaking of fire discipline, some units expended their entire basic load of ammunition in just 12 hours, and as resupply was every bit as haphazard as everything else, in some cases they had to be rotated out of harm's way as a result. In the middle of battle, this could have disastrous consequences. The commander of a tank platoon admitted that he lost two of his T-72s in Upper Nikozi because 'we simply ran out of ammunition, and they surrounded us with grenade launchers'.[6]

In short, for a minister who had been looking for a stick long enough and heavy enough to beat his High Command into submission and force them to accept painful reforms, this was just the kind of war Serdyukov needed.

12

'New Look' Army

New York is like London; it's one of those world cities everyone seems to cycle through at some time or another. I had just moved there to take up a position at New York University, and in 2010 there was a gathering of former Western defence attaches who had served in Moscow, in a middling-posh Upper West Side hotel bar to which I had been lucky enough to be invited. It was October 2010, exactly two years after the plans for a 'New Look Army' had been publicly revealed. The details had not been surprising in and of themselves: the essence of the reforms the Russian military needed had been known for years. It had been the will and capacity to push them through that had been lacking.

The size of the military would continue to shrink, with a corresponding increase in the proportion of professional *kontraktniki*. Meanwhile, the bloated and top-heavy officer corps would be slimmed down, not least by shifting the basic army structure from one based around the 10,000-strong division to one in which the 6,000-strong brigade was the basic manoeuvre element. The idea was to create a force that was flexible, geared more for local wars and out-of-area interventions. The brigade of the future would have firepower closer to the old division's, though, thanks to a major modernization programme that would see 70% of all weapons systems brought to modern standards by 2020 and modern command and control to ensure they were used to the maximum effectiveness. There would also be an end to the days of a handful of 'permanent readiness' forces doing the heavy lifting – in theory, 20% of the whole, but in practice more like 12–15% – with all brigades being brought to this standard.

It was an ambitious project, and one in which the pain would come before the gain. Divisions with proud histories dating back to the Great Patriotic War and beyond were divided or shrunk down into brigades. Two hundred generals were sacked, part of a shrinkage of 205,000 officers' positions: from the existing 365,000 in 2008 (one in three of a total military establishment of 1.13 million), there were to be just 142,000 by 2022 (one in six or seven out of just under a million). The 65 military schools were pruned and rationalized into just ten training centres. Ageing stocks of ammunition – including some for Second World War-era T-34 tanks – were decommissioned and destroyed, removing the rationale for thousands of cushy non-jobs inventorying and managing them, however unusable they had become.

Many of those present in that hotel bar were frankly sceptical. They had heard it all before, they had little faith that the High Command would follow through and, perhaps, they also preferred to think that the Russian military would remain an overweight and greying bear. One of the cannier ones there, though, who came from a country with slightly better relations with Russia and who had thus been allowed to spend more time hobnobbing with ordinary Russian officers rather than soldier-diplomats, cautioned his colleagues not to be too complacent. 'This time, the pressure comes from the top, as well as the bottom. The men I got to know, the majors and the colonels, they are sick and tired of 20 years of decay. They're ready – and they are going to surprise us.' He swallowed the last of his drink. 'And we won't like it.'

COMMAND AND CONTROL: UNIFIED
BATTLE MANAGEMENT

At the very top of the system, Makarov would in essence finally introduce the major reforms of the Military District structure that his predecessor Baluyevsky had planned (and that in effect dated back to the 1990s, but like so many other plans from that decade, never really amounted to anything). The old Soviet practice had been that in time of war, a Military District (VO: *Voyenny Okrug*) would in effect split into two elements. The field forces would become a Front, and engage in combat under the VO commander. The rest of the VO's forces would remain under one of his deputies, as the logistical body charged with maintaining security in the rear, generating reserves and essentially supporting the Front. Whereas the peacetime VOs were subordinated to the Ground Forces Main Command, once war started, the Fronts would come directly under the General Staff. On the other hand, the central Naval Main Command largely would continue to control the fleets in war, and the various Air Forces had their own, even more complex subordinations.

It was something of an anachronism. Ivanov and Baluyevsky had sought to end this structure, recognizing both that it was inefficient and that it did not meet the needs of a new era of warfare in which land, air and sea forces had to work together as never before. Nonetheless, declarations of reform had not really led to real changes in practice – a perennial problem in the early 2000s – and there were always other priorities. Under Makarov, though, a modified form of Baluyevsky's plan was adopted, with the existing six VOs and the Kaliningrad Special Region regrouped into four new districts. What may have appeared a rather banal exercise in redrawing the organizational map did, however, have real significance, as these new districts were true joint operational commands, with much greater direct control over air, land and often sea forces, and in time of war would in their entirety become Operational Strategic Commands (OSK: *Operativnoye Strategicheskoye Komandavaniye*), doing away with the old division between Fronts and VOs, and also acquiring control over other militarized forces in their areas of operation, such as the Border and Interior Troops.

The **Western Military District** (ZVO: *Zapadny Voyenny Okrug*) incorporates the former Moscow and Leningrad districts, with the 1st Tank Army, 6th Red Banner Army, 20th Guards Red Banner Army, the Baltic Fleet, and elements of the Northern Fleet. As well as the new Operational-Strategic Aerospace Defence Command, discussed below, this command also includes the 100,000-strong task force in the Russian exclave of Kaliningrad: the 18th Guards Motor Rifle Brigade, 7th Independent Motor Rifle Brigade, and 336th Guards Naval Infantry Brigade.

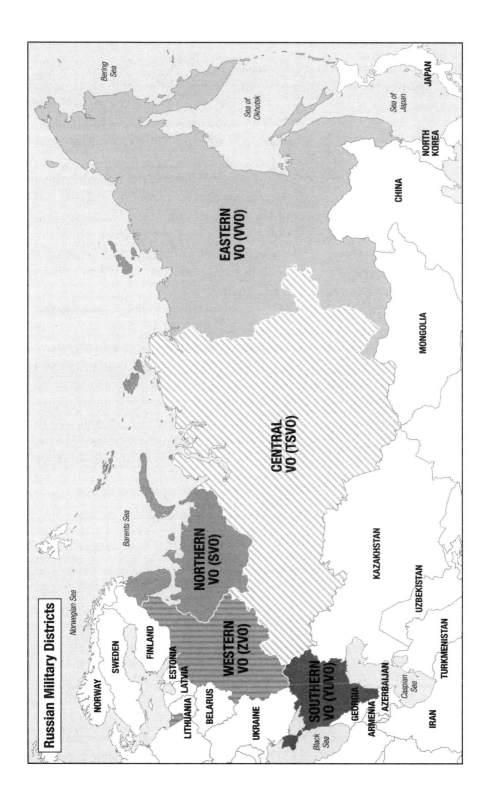

Russian Military Districts

The **Southern Military District** (YuVO: *Yuzhny Voyenny Okrug*), headquartered at Rostov-on-Don, controls the 48th and 49th Armies, the Black Sea Fleet and the Caspian Flotilla; the 102nd Base in Armenia also reports to YuVO, with the twin aims of defending Armenian and Russian airspace and asserting Moscow's authority in the Caucasus.

The **Central District** (TsVO: *Tsentralny Voyenny Okrug*), covering a swathe of the country across the Ural Mountains and western Siberia, has the 2nd Guards Red Banner Army and the 41st Army. Headquartered in Yekaterinburg, it also controls the 201st Base in Tajikistan, a brigade-strength force, whose role is to help defend Tajikistan and its regime in case of insurgency or incursions from Afghanistan, as well as a small contingent at Kant airbase in Kyrgyzstan.

The **Eastern District** (VVO: *Vostochny Voyenny Okrug*) controls not just the Pacific Fleet but also the 5th and 35th Red Banner Armies and the 29th and 36th Armies. Although this sounds like an impressive total, the VVO is regarded as a distant backwater posting, as its main potential enemy is China. Although the General Staff continues to update its contingency plans for a conventional land war on its south-eastern flank, as discussed later, this is increasingly an exercise in futility as the Chinese military continues to modernize. The VVO is headquartered at Khabarovsk on the Chinese border and its units are scattered along an indefensibly long land border, and dependent for supply and reinforcement largely on two railroad lines which could easily be cut. In practice, any such conflict would quickly escalate to the use of at least tactical nuclear weapons.

In 2014 a fifth **North or Arctic Command** was added. Unusually, this is not a Military District; as it is essentially responsible for sea and air space, it was largely built on the basis of the Northern Fleet and attached air units. However, it also fields a small army component, including two specialized Arctic Mechanized Brigades, initially the 200th Independent Motor Rifle Brigade based at Pechenga. The speed with which Moscow can now mobilize forces was evident in 2015 when, shortly after standing up this new command, it mounted a major exercise in the Arctic involving 80,000 troops.

As for the primary service Main Commands – the Navy, Ground Forces and Air Forces – while they had had a distinct role in determining how their forces were used in the past, increasingly these were expected to focus on tactics, equipment and training. In short, the General Staff would provide the grand planning and the Military Districts would operationalize these plans in the field, while the Main Commands made sure they had what they needed to do the job. In contrast, the Strategic Rocket Forces retained their core role, even while shrinking from twelve to eight missile divisions, and the Space Forces were reduced from seven to six units, although in practice this meant no actual cuts to their capacities, just administrative reorganization.

THE MOTOR RIFLE BRIGADE

A typical motor rifle brigade would be made up of 3,800 officers and men in the following organization, although there was and remains considerable variation, especially for brigades with specific missions, such as the 200th Motor Rifle Brigade, which is configured for Arctic warfare, and the 8th Guards Mountain Motor Rifle Brigade. A tank brigade, with three tank battalions and one motor rifle battalion instead, has a smaller establishment strength of 3,000.

1 x brigade HQ and command company
1 x scout company
1 x sniper platoon
1 x electronic warfare company
1 x tank battalion (4 tank companies)
3 x motor rifle battalions (each of 3 companies and a mortar battery)
2 x self-propelled artillery battalions (each of 3 batteries)
1 x rocket battalion (3 multiple-launch rocket batteries)
1 x anti-tank battalion (2 anti-tank missile batteries, 1 anti-tank gun battery)
2 x air defence battalions (one with 3 AA missile batteries, one with 2 AA missile and 1 AA gun battery)
1 x engineer battalion
1 x maintenance battalion
1 x signal battalion
1 x material support battalion
1 x medical company
1 x nuclear, biological & chemical company

THE GROUND FORCES: DIVISIONS TO BRIGADES

Despite the clamour from the military establishment, the reforms went ahead. Before, the Ground Forces had officially fielded 24 divisions (three tank, five machine gun artillery, 16 motor rifle) as well as 12 independent brigades, and two 'bases', as the standing task forces in Armenia and Tajikistan were known. In practice, though, only five motor rifle divisions and perhaps one tank division were really at or close to full strength; the others were essentially just shells awaiting reservists in time of war. Even so, the reserve mobilization system was in chaos, with records lost and most former conscripts not doing their regular refresher training. Even with three months to mobilize, the – quite likely optimistic – official estimate was that nine more divisions could be fielded, still well below the official total.

As a symbolic move, the first division to go was the 2nd Guards Tamanskaya Motor Rifle Division, one of the elite Moscow-based 'palace guard' units, whose colours and battle honours went to the newly formed 5th Guards Independent Motor Rifle Brigade, while other elements went to the new 8th Guards Motor Rifle Brigade. Within a year, only one of the Ground Forces' 24 divisions was still in existence, and this was the 18th Machine Gun Artillery Division, which was a one-off defensive formation guarding the Kuril Islands in the Far East. In their place were 44 manoeuvre brigades: four tank brigades, four air assault brigades, 35 motor rifle brigades and one screening brigade (see Chapter 28). There were also 41 support brigades: 22 missile and artillery brigades, nine air defence, one electronic warfare and nine signal brigades. The transition was not without its challenges. Even by 2012, most of the combat brigades were still 20–30% under-strength, with no more than 17 of the 44 combat brigades fully manned. This would change over time, though. It also provided an opportunity at last to retire much obsolete equipment, including some 20,000 of the more dated tanks.

The 201st Military Base in Tajikistan remained in its current form, not least because it was essentially already at brigade strength (having been the 201st Motor Rifle Division until 2004), based around three regiments, the 92nd Motor Rifle Regiment, 149th Guards Motor Rifle Regiment and 191st Motor Rifle Regiment. Beyond that were two other foreign bases: the 102nd Military Base in Armenia, which had been formed in 2010 on the basis of the 73rd Independent Motor Rifle Brigade, and the former 14th Army, in 1995 renamed the Operational Group of Russian Forces in Transnistria. Since then, this had steadily shrunk to closer to a regiment in size, comprising the 82nd and 113th Independent Motor Rifle Battalions and the 540th Independent Command Battalion with security and support elements, for a total strength of around 1,500 officers and men.

THE AIR FORCES: RATIONALIZED

The reform of the Air Forces essentially related to major reorganization at the top level, and a particular sharp contraction on the ground. The former involved the creation in 2011 of the Aerospace Defence Forces (VVKO: *Voiska Vozdushno-Kosmicheskoi Oborony*) out of the old Space Forces, bringing together early warning and space surveillance assets, Moscow's anti-ballistic missile system built around the Don-2N battle management radar and 68 launchers, the GLONASS global positioning satellites and the Plesetsk cosmodrome, a spaceport in the northern Arkhangelsk Region. In 2015, it would be combined with the air force in the new Aerospace Forces (VKS: *Vozdushno-Kosmicheskiye Sily*).

Meanwhile, a new Operational-Strategic Aerospace Defence Command (OSKVKO: *Obedinyonnoye Strategicheskoye Komandovaniye Vozdushno-Kosmicheskoi Oborony*) was formed from the former Special Purpose Air Force Command. This was really Moscow's air cover, largely made up of the 16th Air Army, which included both front-line combat units and the 237th Guards Air Technology Demonstration Centre headquartered at Kubinka airbase to the west of the capital, along with anti-air defences built around the highly capable S-400 SAM system. Likewise, two specialized Air Armies were redesignated as Commands in their own right: the 37th became Long Range Aviation Command and the 61st, Military Transport Aviation Command.

The other four were directly overlaid onto the new VOs: the old 6th Air Army became the 1st Air and Air Defence Forces Command of the Western VO, the 11th became the 2nd Air and Air Defence Forces Command of the Eastern VO, the 14th the 3rd Air and Air Defence Forces Command of the Central VO and the 4th and 5th Air Armies were merged into the 4th Air and Air Defence Forces Command of the Southern VO. Likewise, the old air defence divisions and corps were reorganized as 13 aerospace defence brigades divided amongst the Military Districts and the OSKVKO.

Overall, the air force went through the same kind of rationalization as the other services, with cuts to airbases that, in practice, were there to service squadrons that didn't exist, could scarcely fly, or were really just notional units awaiting some mythical future mobilization. Of 242 bases, it would be left with just 52, and 340 units on paper would be cut to just 180. Likewise, the divisional structure was abolished in favour of moving field command to the airbases which, in turn, were subordinated to seven new Aviation Commands. A key issue would be greater emphasis on precision-guided munitions and the platforms – and trained pilots – to be able to deploy them. This was one of the particular lessons learned from the two Chechen wars, as well as from observing Western operations in the Middle East and Balkans. At the same time, a concern about a massive Western air campaign – what would become called a Massed Missile-Aviation Strike (MRAU: *Massirovanny Raketno-Aviatsionny Udar*) in Russian thinking – was already evident in both the creation of the VKKO and new thinking about how to survive such an opening aerial blitzkrieg.

THE NAVY: INTEGRATED AT LAST

As for the navy, it was similarly cut dramatically, from 240 to just 123 ships and submarines, but again in the name of modernization and readiness. Many, perhaps even most, of its ships had been under-crewed or simply not seaworthy, but the goal was to ensure that, within the bounds of necessary repair and maintenance, all remaining vessels would be operational. There was an ambitious plan for procuring new ships, with fully 100 meant to be bought (if by no means built, let alone in service) by 2020, especially submarines and more versatile smaller ships. These included 35 corvettes, 15 frigates and 20 submarines.

At the same time, though, with the four Fleets subordinated to the new, larger VOs, there was a fear that this would leave them dominated by the Ground Forces. In practice, however, this was less cause than effect. As is discussed later, the notion that Russia's navy could maintain its status as an arm of service able to conduct truly autonomous operations was long questionable. In reality it had long become little more than a coastal defence force with occasional demonstrative out-of-area operations conducted more for the sake of prestige and diplomacy than anything else. Tighter integration with the Ground Forces arguably made the navy more credible and useful.

The marines of the Naval Infantry went through a rather more restrained contraction, in part reflecting an awareness of the degree to which Russia still needed elite infantry – and had relied on them in both Chechen wars, far from any sea. The Pacific Fleet's 55th Division, which had long been nowhere near at divisional strength, became the 155th Independent Naval Infantry Brigade (whose main manoeuvre elements were the 59th Independent Naval Infantry Battalion and the 47th Independent Naval Infantry Air Assault Battalion), and the Northern Fleet's 61st Independent Naval Infantry Brigade became a regiment (only to return to brigade strength in 2014). However, while the Caspian Flotilla's 77th Brigade, another 'ghost unit', was disbanded, the Black Sea Fleet's 810th Independent Regiment was actually expanded back to brigade strength (having been shrunk down in 1998). In part this reflected its new responsibility of providing marine support for the Caspian Flotilla as and when.

THE AIRBORNE: SURVIVAL

This continued emphasis on elite power projection forces, already disproportionately manned by volunteers, was evident in the treatment of the Airborne Troops. There had been a long-running tussle over whether keeping the VDV as a separate Main Command was an expensive and fragile indulgence and whether the 35,000 paratroopers would be more useful integrated into either the regular Ground Forces or the VOs as a district-level asset. Ultimately, though, the General Staff liked the idea of a separate Airborne arm as its own strategic-level asset, and the paratrooper lobby was powerful enough within both the 'Arbat Military District' and wider political circles to fight its corner well.

Thus, while originally the decision had been to cannibalize the VDV's four existing divisions to form seven to eight air-assault brigades, these moves were not made a priority. In 2009, when the combative and vigorous Lt. Gen. Vladimir Shamanov was appointed their commander, proposed cuts were actually turned into an expansion plan. The decision was made that every VO would have its own independent airmobile brigade as a rapid response force, while the VDV retained its divisions, within which five battalions were to be made up wholly of *kontraktniki* to provide a quick readiness force which could also be deployed abroad. This would, however, prove harder than expected, not least as the paratroopers found themselves competing with the other services for volunteers. According to Shamanov, as of mid-2011, readiness was actually at a lower level than before the reforms began, with only 31% of the force being professional, and even the quick readiness units were only 70% *kontraktnik*. His goal was to ensure that at least half the entire VDV were professional, something that would take years, but which assured that, along with the *Spetsnaz* (who had their own political struggles – see Chapter 24), they would remain Russia's 'tip of the spear' into the future.

The reforms undoubtedly created a much leaner, more effective and responsive military. In 2014, for example, the Russians were able to deploy perhaps 40,000 troops to the Ukrainian border within seven days at the start of their intervention into the south-eastern Donbas region. In 1999, it had taken three times as long to mobilize a similar force for Chechnya. The question was, what was the Kremlin going to do with them? As that veteran defence attaché had predicted, a successfully rearmed Russia would prove an uncomfortable neighbour in the 'Near Abroad' and a tricky policy challenge for the West.

PART THREE

The New Cold War

13

Shoigu, the Rebuilder

The Victory Day parade on 9 May has become one of the Putin regime's holiest of holy days. It is not just the president who benefits from this carefully stage-managed pageant of triumphalism and military might, though. In 2015, as Defence Minister Sergei Shoigu was being driven into Red Square under the Spasskaya – Saviour's – Tower gateway, his car stopped and he deliberately crossed himself. This televised moment was a striking example of his political nous, at once aligning him with the Russian Orthodox Church and also the country's history and traditions. Back in tsarist times, after all, it had been established practice to stop, bare-headed, and show reverence to the icon mounted above the gate. Even tsars would do so, and the legend was that when Napoleon arrogantly rode through the gate in 1812, after his armies had seized the city, a sudden wind blew his hat from his head.

Shoigu is one of the big beasts of the Russian political system, a savvy politician who, despite his origins in the distant Siberian region of Tyva, where the locals still largely practise a form of Buddhism, has won widespread and enthusiastic public support. At least before the 2022 invasion of Ukraine, there was talk of his becoming presidential plenipotentiary to the Siberian Federal District – essentially viceroy of Siberia – but he was also talked about as a future prime minister or, very, very quietly, even president. In part, this was thanks to what appeared to be his capable continuation of the reform process and his capacity to win over even a sceptical and recalcitrant High Command after the Serdyukov era, even if now the question is how far this was just good PR.

WHO IS SERGEI SHOIGU?

Shoigu, after all, has demonstrated his skills at spin and a near-unique ability to rise within this carnivorous and competitive political system without making enemies and by being what in business terms would be a turnaround manager, taking dysfunctional institutions and making them work. Certainly the military needed all his talents after five and a half years of Serdyukov and the dramatic (and, for the generals, unpopular) reforms that had been pushed through after the Georgian War. This was nothing new to him, though. Born in 1955 to an ethnic Tyvan father and a Ukrainian-born Russian mother, Shoigu was an athletic and adventurous boy, whose passion for risky escapades including hopping ice floes across the Yenisei River earned him the nickname *Shaitan* ('Satan'). He was also a good student, though, and graduated as a civil engineer. After a decade working in construction, he became a Communist Party organizer and then got his big break with an appointment in 1990 as deputy chief of the Russian State Architecture and Construction Committee. This meant a move to Moscow, and also responsibility for housing and other building projects at a time when budgets were tiny, the administration was in disarray and the state itself collapsing.

Nonetheless, Shoigu quickly acquired a reputation as a man who could keep his head in a crisis and do his best with what he had. This seemed to prove a mixed blessing when, in 1991, he was then tapped to head the Rescue Corps. The Corps was responsible for everything from search and rescue to civil defence, a grab-bag of agencies and duties characterized by infamous inefficiency, corruption and demoralization. It looked like a career dead-end, especially as it meant, in effect, that Shoigu became responsible for every disaster that befell the country. He made a virtue of a necessity, though. He reorganized the Corps, which became the Ministry for Emergency Situations (MChS: *Ministerstvo po Chrezvychainym Situatsiyam*) in 1994, streamlining the administration, bringing in tough audits to crack down on corruption, and introducing measures such as smart new uniforms to bring an unprecedented esprit de corps.

Meanwhile, Shoigu himself made a point of never shirking attending disasters, from the 1995 earthquake that devastated the oil town of Neftegorsk in Sakhalin, killing more than half its inhabitants, to the crash of 2001 Vladivostok Air Flight 352 while coming in to land at Irkutsk. Instead of becoming the avatar of misery, he became a reassuring presence, comforting the bereaved, coordinating relief operations and briefing the press. He knew how to play the behind-the-scenes bureaucratic games that had seen the Corps made a ministry – and thus, himself a minister – and in 2001 take the State Fire Service from the Interior Ministry. But he also demonstrated that he knew how to run an agency, and by the time he moved on in 2012, he had made the MChS one of the more efficient and even honest state agencies in Russia.

None of this escaped the Kremlin's attention. In 1999, he was made a Hero of Russia, but more to the point, he was appointed point man for Unity, a new political party that was being built to, in effect, provide a power base for the soon-to-be-president Putin. Boris Yeltsin called him 'our greatest star'.[1] It was a naked attempt to cash in on his popularity, but he accepted it, and in 2001 Unity would merge with the Fatherland-All Russia movement to form United Russia, still the basis for Putin's political order.

Nonetheless, Shoigu clearly wasn't especially interested in electoral politics – and realized that there was room only for one 'star' in the firmament. Instead, he set out to build a relationship with Putin, giving the famously dog-loving president a black Labrador, Koni. It was said that Koni was Putin's favourite dog; she also proved a psychological weapon: in 2007, he let her meet the equally famously dog-fearing German chancellor Angela Merkel, who had come for a summit. A keen and aggressive ice hockey player, Shoigu became a fixture on the president's own 'night games' team and also took to inviting Putin on long holiday trips to his native Tyva. Even then, he clearly understood the politics of the situation, diplomatically fading into the background when Putin was being photographed fishing shirtless, hiking the tundra or otherwise demonstrating his macho credentials. In this way, Shoigu has become the only member of Putin's real inner circle who is not an old colleague from KGB or Leningrad/St Petersburg days.

In 2012, he finally left the MChS (although he left it in the hands of a collection of his people), to stand for and win the position of governor of the crucial Moscow Region. Again, it is unclear whether this was Shoigu's initiative or whether he was induced to take the job, but he quickly initiated new infrastructure projects, started to clear out dead wood and dismantled some corrupt circles that were skimming off state funds at a level unacceptable even by the standards of the time. However, after just six months, Putin needed a new defence minister who could continue the reform process but reconcile the High Command to it. It was once more time for Shoigu to step into the breach.

'A SERVANT TO THE TSAR, A FATHER TO THE SOLDIERS'

Appointed on 6 November 2012, he set to with a characteristic mix of charm offensive and administrative drive. On the one hand, he tried to signal to the generals that he was on their side. Whereas Serdyukov always wore a suit, Shoigu adopted a general's uniform (he had a military-style rank from his time at MChS, so this was considered appropriate) as a symbolic gesture. He reversed some of the most resented yet also least consequential of the previous cuts, not least in the cohorts of *Suvorovtsy* and *Nakhimovtsy*, the teenage cadets who attended the Suvorov Military Schools and Nakhimov Naval Schools, respectively, cradles of the next generation officer corps. Where Serdyukov had often dwelt on the military's failings in his public pronouncements, Shoigu talked them up, telling them of the bright future ahead.

Admittedly, Shoigu could afford to be conciliatory, as the most painful aspects of reform, notably the downsizing, had already been accomplished. He made it clear, though, that he did not propose to reverse the process. While the prestigious 'palace guard' Tamanskaya and Kantemirovskaya Divisions were restored, for example, the brigade structure remained the basic element of the army. Instead, he focused on taking the military establishment he had inherited and – as with the MChS – making it work.

The frequency, scale and realism of military exercises began to increase. A comprehensive study by Johan Norberg of the Swedish Defence Research Agency found that 'before 2009, Russia handled armed conflicts and local wars. Military exercises since 2009 display an ambition and capabilities increasingly pertaining to regional wars' – which according to Russian military typology could include a war with NATO.[2] These were serious exercises, too, and the new units would be drilled in wargames that were not, as too many were in the older days, simply staged acts of theatrical competence meant to convey a reassuring message to the political leadership. Instead, they were serious challenges, backed up by snap inspections that could make or break an officer's career. Meanwhile, Serdyukov's efforts to use outsourcing and civilian contractors to improve soldiers' living standards, providing everything from catering to cleaning, were retained and even expanded.

The humble sock became a symbol of a new mood of modernization and common sense. Until 2013, Russian soldiers – like their Soviet and even tsarist forebears – had worn not socks but rectangular cloths called *portyanki* that were wrapped around the foot. Serdyukov had promised to abolish them, but never got round to it. In January 2013, Shoigu was convening a video conference of senior staff across the country, itself an innovation, when he declared that 'we must forget the word "*portyanki*" by the end of this year'.[3] And they did. This may sound like a trivial move, but it was greatly appreciated by long-suffering Russian soldiers, proved that Shoigu could get things done, and demonstrated his concern for the ordinary grunt. It was both necessary and a brilliant bit of public relations, and I remember soldiers talking about how they would ceremonially burn their *portyanki* when their new issue socks arrived. No wonder people began saying of Shoigu, using a line by the 19th-century poet Mikhail Lermontov, that he was 'A servant to the tsar, a father to the soldiers'.[4]

THE CHAIN OF COMMAND

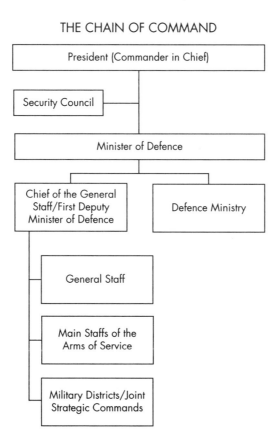

GENERAL GERASIMOV

Chief of the General Staff Makarov was almost as unpopular in the High Command as Serdyukov. What Shoigu needed now was not so much a thinker as a foreman, a hard-driving top soldier able to whip this 'New Look Army' into shape, and so he quickly replaced him with Col. Gen. Valery Gerasimov, a man he rightly described as 'a military man to the roots of his hair'.[5] A former Suvorov cadet, Gerasimov had come from working-class beginnings. He was a tank officer, who had risen through the ranks first in the 90th Guards Tank Division in Warsaw Pact Poland, then in the 29th Motor Rifle Division in the Far Eastern VO, before rising to command the 144th Guards Motor Rifle Division. He led the 58th Combined Arms Army 2001–03, while it was engaged in Chechnya, and later headed the Main Directorate of Combat Training – Makarov's old post. After tours commanding both the Leningrad and then Moscow VOs, in 2010 he had become Deputy Chief of the General Staff, then commander of the newly created Central VO before returning to the General Staff as Shoigu's right hand.

When formally accepting his new position from Putin, he said:

> I believe that all the activities of the General Staff should be directed towards achieving one main goal – maintaining the combat effectiveness of the Armed Forces such as to guarantee that they can accomplish whatever tasks they are set. And I will do everything in my power to achieve this goal.[6]

He meant it. Gerasimov very much drove the campaign to get the newly reorganized forces combat-ready. The exercise cycle cranked up to levels unknown since Soviet times. With Russian ally Syria experiencing growing unrest, the Russians also began maintaining what was in effect a permanent naval task force in the eastern Mediterranean, largely drawn from rotations from the Black Sea Fleet. There were inevitable glitches and blunders, of course. During exercises held in the Central VO in February 2013, for example, coordination between units and ground and air forces continued to be a problem, and failings because of poor maintenance and old kit caused some embarrassing moments, especially when three Mi-24 helicopter gunships simply would not start, and at least two BMD-2 infantry fighting vehicles broke down in the first stage of movement. On the whole, though, the military began to demonstrate the kind of combat readiness which had long been the Kremlin's goal, and even looked modern.

When the 'little green men' – special forces not wearing insignia – were fanning out across the Crimean peninsula in 2014, one detail of their kit assumed a disproportionate significance in much of the media coverage and subsequent online chatter: their kneepads. These are understatedly useful parts of the modern soldier's uniform, but the point was that they had not hitherto been part of the Russians' repertoire, and in many ways they were a metaphor for just how *Western* these invaders looked, from their digital camouflage and modern body armour to the equipment they carried, including earpiece tactical radios and personalized weapons. Putin's suggestion, when asked if these were indeed Russian commandos, that they could simply have been shopping in army surplus stores, was deliberately tongue-in-cheek. This was the first serious outing for the new *Ratnik* ('Warrior') future infantry combat system, a combined suite of uniforms and personal equipment meant to take the country's soldiers firmly into the 21st century.

Over time, the idea is to upgrade *Ratnik* but already an ambitious replacement is in the works. The basis of the futuristic *Sotnik* ('Centurion' for want of a better direct translation) outfit will be a lightweight suit of battle armour, tough enough to resist a heavy machine-gun bullet, yet with a coating that masks the soldier's thermal signature and even has an 'electrochromic' chameleon camouflage that can change colour at the touch of a button. Micro-drones will stream video footage directly to the soldier, while a powered exoskeleton allows him or her to carry heavy loads and move at speed without tiring. All very ambitious, and to be honest *Sotnik* is likely to be a technology concept testing exercise rather than becoming the next standard issue in the next few years.[7] Nonetheless, it is symbolic of Moscow's desire – if probably not ability – to leapfrog into the status of a leading-edge military power.

REARMAMENT AND RECRUITMENT

Meanwhile, Shoigu was taking the lead in rearmament. Serdyukov had tried to crack down on waste, while also negotiating hard with the defence industries. After all, until around 2008, the amount of new, top of the line equipment being bought and fielded was negligible. Serdyukov had forced defence suppliers to increase their quality control and cut their profit margins. He even began to buy foreign systems, in part as a shot across their bows. In fairness, while some of the so-called 'metal-eaters' were complacent, others were frankly struggling to modernize, and so this hard-nosed approach not only made Serdyukov unpopular with the industrialists, but also ironically slowed procurement, as companies had to revamp their procedures.

In 2011, Serdyukov had complained to then-President Medvedev about the industry's failings, blaming it for the incompletion of the 2010 State Defence Order and even arguing that the heads of some companies should be disciplined. (Again, this won him few friends.) Medvedev duly went on to criticize their conduct, grumbling that 'it is an unacceptable situation when decisions are made at the highest level, the money is allocated, and yet the output is not delivered'.[8] He even asked, 'who has been punished for it and how?' and, in a line that evoked the era of Gulag labour camps, added, 'I am sure you realize that in different times half of you present here would already be engaged in hard physical labour in the fresh air'. This sounded like fighting talk, but a few months later, Medvedev announced that he was backing Putin for a return to the Kremlin, and promptly became a lame duck president. His capacity to force change on the powerful defence industrialists – several of whom had ties to Putin – went from limited to non-existent.

Shoigu characteristically mixed carrot and stick. He returned to the old policy of essentially buying kit only from Russian suppliers, except for some traditional exceptions (such as Ukrainian naval engines and particular items needed by the special forces) and adopted a more flexible approach to contract terms. While he had no qualms about calling out companies failing to meet their agreed standards, in the main, he made an alliance with the 'metal-eaters'. Given that he had more money to spend, both thanks to the overall cuts in military manpower and the rising defence budget – in 2010, Putin had announced a 19.4 trillion ruble ($698.4 billion) weapons procurement plan for 2011–20 – he also could dangle sizeable orders as an incentive to get producers to clean up their act.

While only 16% of Russia's equipment was considered 'modern', in 2010 a ten-year State Armament Programme had been adopted that wanted to bring this to 70% by 2020. Admittedly, the notion of 'modern' proved hazy, but essentially it meant either built in the last decade or recently and substantively upgraded. This meant a substantial and sustained procurement campaign, but that figure was reached.

Meanwhile, the armed forces had an establishment strength of a million, but in fact some 220,000 officers, 186,000 *kontraktniki*, and 296,000 conscripts, for a total force of just over 700,000, with almost as many officers as draftees. This was a problem, especially given the rapid churn of conscripts serving just 12-month national service terms and continued problems recruiting and retaining *kontraktniki*. Demographics was also an issue: the 1980s and 1990s had seen the birth-rate fall quite substantially, largely in response to the economic miseries of the time, and this was now working through into the size of the available conscript pool. In 2011, for example, the military had needed some 440,000 conscripts from the spring and autumn draft, but with deferments (largely on educational grounds), medical waivers (many of which were simply bought from corrupt doctors) and the shrinking overall pool, it was getting harder and harder to meet these targets. Since 2009, the *voyenkomaty*, the draft boards, had been having to accept conscripts with criminal records.

In response, Shoigu did what he could to make professional service more attractive, raising pay and improving conditions. In the interim, he reversed another of the Serdyukov/Makarov reforms. The Russian military used to have the rank of *praporshchik*, or warrant officer (*michman* in the navy), the kind of longer-service professional soldiers who might be sergeants in Western armies. In 2009, they began to be phased out, because the expectation was that they would be replaced by *kontraktnik* sergeants. In total, there had been around 142,000 of them, but most lacked the educational background to be promoted into the officer corps but quite understandably did not want to accept the cut in seniority and pay to become sergeants. Some 20,000 did become junior officers, but almost all the rest were lost to a military that was desperate for experienced volunteers. Shoigu promptly reversed this disastrous initiative, and began hiring back 55,000 former *praporshchiki* and *michmany* into the ranks.

READY FOR ACTION

There would inevitably be more changes, not least as Russia's relations with the West worsened. Brigades were all very well for flexible, mobile local wars, but the prospect of major conventional clashes would lead in 2013 to a partial return to divisions, as an altogether more hard-hitting structure able to conduct major mechanized operations, while all-professional battalion tactical groups generated by brigades became modular combat forces, tested out in Ukraine's Donbas conflict. In 2014, the Northern Fleet was detached from Western VO to form the Northern Fleet Joint Strategic Command which, in 2021, became a fully fledged Northern Military District responsible for Russia's Arctic flank. These will be discussed below, but in essence, Shoigu and Gerasimov completed the military machine that Serdyukov and Makarov had set out to build.

This was just as well for the Kremlin. Putin's policies had become increasingly authoritarian and nationalist. Protests against the rigging of the 2011 parliamentary elections and then his return to power in 2012 were perceived as sponsored by the West. Then, a popular rising against the government in neighbouring Ukraine led to the 2014 annexation of Crimea and intervention in the Donbas, triggering Western criticism and sanctions. Facing diplomatic isolation and the potential fall of another of Moscow's client regimes, in 2015, Russian forces deployed into Syria. Each of these conflicts not only exacerbated the worsening relations between Moscow and the West, but they also brought new challenges and new lessons, to which the military would adapt and respond. It also means that the Russian military has a wealth of military experience, hard-learned in a range of combat theatres.

In October 2014, as the new Cold War was brewing, Shoigu's line was that 'Russia's sovereignty, which is secured by its army and navy, will always be the obstacle against which during the 1,152 years of Russia's existence many Western rulers have broken their teeth.'[9] If in 2000 Putin had inherited a country whose military was scarcely functional, in what was actually a strikingly short time Russia had acquired forces that should be capable of waging and winning a whole range of conflicts, from short, sharp interventions to a nasty counter-insurgency fought far from the country's borders. In many ways this will make or break Putin's dreams of a resurgent Russia, but it is also good for his defence minister. Shoigu is a politician, who has carefully curated his image and built alliances with all kinds of constituencies, from the 'fighting generals' with real wartime experience to the Russian Orthodox Church. He knows how to calibrate bombast, talking up Russia without seeming to thrust himself too far into the spotlight so as to risk looking like he is challenging the president. The irony is that the first of the wars of the new era, the one that helped solidify Shoigu's reputation as Russia's new guardian and military figurehead, is one he seems to have been lukewarm about launching: the 2014 seizure of Crimea.

14

Crimea, 2014

I was living in a flat on Valovaya Street, part of the Garden Ring that loops round Moscow's centre. It was an excellent location, if a bit noisy at the best of times, given that's it's an eight-lane highway. Still, on the night of Friday 21 March 2014, I got scarcely any sleep because that was the day Crimea was officially brought back under Moscow's rule, and all night long, cars with blaring horns and equally vocal passengers, flags waving from windows, drove round and round the ring road. It was an extraordinary outburst of patriotic joy that united devoted Putinists and most opposition figures alike. Memes from the quick and decisive seizure of the peninsula abounded, from graffiti proclaiming 'Crimea is ours' to hurriedly printed t-shirts showing one much-circulated picture of a Russian 'polite person' – how they referred to the 'little green men' special forces who played such a crucial role in the operation – presenting a boy with his cat, after a press photo from the time.

The military was equally, if less publicly, exuberant. One retired officer I knew, a veteran of the Soviet invasion of Afghanistan and the First Chechen War, who had left service a couple of years later, thoroughly disillusioned, was vastly proud after the first beer: 'They didn't think we could so something like this, do it so well. We showed them, we showed them all!' A second beer, and he was sentimental, remembering all the good aspects of his time in uniform, forgetting the terrible tales he had told me in the past. But by the third, he was becoming troubled: 'What happens now, though? I fear our leaders may not know where to stop.' Indeed.

The taking of Crimea was, to be sure, an impressive expression of the new capabilities of the Russian military, one conducted with a scalpel rather than the familiar old sledgehammer. When Russian forces, fully armed yet stripped of their insignia, fanned out across the peninsula, they were not just seizing strategically vital territory that Moscow considered historically its own; they were also opening yet another new chapter in a complex relationship rooted in kinship and difference, shared history and divergent politics. They were also kindling a fire that would see the growing Cold War between Russia and the West become increasingly warm and that eventually erupted across Ukraine in 2022.

RUSSIA AND UKRAINE

The very name Ukraine springs from the word for 'border', yet it can rightly call itself the heart and wellspring of the Rus' people, the forebears of the modern Belarusian, Russian and Ukrainian states.[1] Its capital, Kyiv, was politically and culturally dominant amongst their city-states before it was sacked by the invading Mongols in 1240. During the years of Mongol domination, a small town and the ruthlessly opportunistic Rurikid dynasty that controlled it rose to assume Kyiv's place: Moscow. Ukraine would be contested between Orthodox Muscovy and the Catholic Poles and Lithuanians until falling under the rule of Russia in 1654. Part Orthodox and part Catholic, Ukraine would essentially remain part of the Russian Empire for the next three and a half centuries, despite periodic risings and atrocities such as the Holodomor, the enforced mass starvation whereby Soviet dictator Joseph Stalin broke Ukrainian resistance to his rule in the 1930s.

Nationalism re-emerged in Ukraine in the 1980s, as the Soviet Union ground towards its end. On 24 August 1991 the country formally declared itself independent, although in practice this would take months of disengagement. Nonetheless, a referendum ratified this decision, with more than 90% of voters backing independence, even before the Soviet Union itself was formally dissolved at the end of the year.

In common with many other post-Soviet states suddenly thrust into statehood, Ukraine suffered from serious economic, social and political challenges. Inflation skyrocketed, the economy shrank. Despite several dramatic expressions of popular dissatisfaction with corrupt governments and their empty promises – notably the

2004–05 'Orange Revolution' following rigged elections – Ukraine remained torn between its hopes of building a liberal, economically vibrant European democracy, and a reality characterized by systemic corruption, inefficiency and economic decay.

In 2013, President Viktor Yanukovych made a momentous political mistake when he flip-flopped on a proposed treaty with the European Union. Like so many of the so-called 'Donetsk mafia' politicians from the east of the country, Yanukovych looked to Putin's ascendant Russia for patronage and profit. Moscow was determined that Ukraine would remain part of its sphere of influence, but national sentiment, particularly in the west of the country, wanted closer ties to the European Union. Having initially backed an Association Agreement with the EU in 2013, Yanukovych then reversed his policy once Moscow made its hostility clear, especially as it realized that the terms of the deal would prevent Ukraine from also being part of the Eurasian Economic Union, Putin's alternative economic bloc.

Protests began in Kyiv's main Independence Square, and initial attempts to disperse them only galvanized the opposition and brought more to join the rising. The government tried several times to use force to end the so-called 'Euromaidan' demonstrations, but with a mix of brutality and inconsistency that only worsened the situation. On 22 February 2014, facing the threat of impeachment, with his government collapsing around him, Yanukovych fled to Russia, leaving behind 130 deaths and a country rethinking its place in the world. Moscow, alarmed at the prospect of a new Ukrainian government committed to breaking out of its influence, began making its own plans.

'RETURNING CRIMEA TO RUSSIA'

The situation was especially complex in Crimea, a peninsula on the country's southern coast, which was also still home to Russia's Black Sea Fleet. It had been part of the Russian Socialist Federal Soviet Republic until 1954, when Soviet leader Nikita Khrushchev, himself Ukrainian, transferred it to Ukraine. At the time, after all, it didn't seem to matter much, as both the Ukrainian and Russian Soviet Republics were part of the same Soviet Union. Nonetheless, much of its population was culturally Russian, not least because many Black Sea Fleet officers retired there with their families to enjoy its warm climate and relaxed charms.

In 1990, while almost all Ukrainians voted for independence from the USSR, this notion received a much more lukewarm 56% endorsement in Crimea, and since then, Crimeans had often felt neglected by Kyiv.

The Kremlin was alarmed that the collapse of the Yanukovych regime and the emergence of a new government avowedly committed to closer relations with the West – even joining NATO – put its strategic positions on Crimea at risk. Its 1997 agreement with Kyiv on basing the Black Sea Fleet and up to 25,000 military personnel on the peninsula ran through to 2042, but even so, there were many in Moscow who were unwilling to put their faith in what they saw as an illegitimate and nationalistic new regime. NATO's 2008 Bucharest Declaration had affirmed that Georgia and Ukraine 'will become members of NATO', and although realistically this was essentially a political statement rather than the start of a practical process, and few in the West honestly believed that either would join the alliance for at least a decade, for an increasingly paranoid Kremlin, the prospect of its Black Sea Fleet being ejected and replaced with a NATO one seemed entirely possible.

Besides which, President Vladimir Putin, who had enjoyed sky-high approval ratings for so much of his time in office, was watching these figures fall. In the 2000s, Russians had been willing to accept a fake democracy because they were relieved to see an end to the chaos of the 1990s and their standards of living were rising so fast. The Yeltsin era was receding into history, though, and the economy had still only partially recovered from an economic crash in 2009. He knew full well that most Russians believed that Crimea was really part of their own country, unfairly handed to Ukraine. With Putin also apparently coming more and more to believe his own mythology and be looking to establish his place in history as the man who 'made Russia great again', political, military and strategic interests all seemed to converge.

There had, of course, long been contingency plans for a seizure of Crimea. It is, after all, the job of the military planners in the General Staff's Main Operations Directorate to have plans for all kinds of possibilities, just in case. Although I have never been able to get a definite answer, my sense is that they started developing them at least from the mid-1990s. Nonetheless, these did not necessarily demonstrate that this had been considered a serious possibility before 2014, but rather that, given the volatility of Ukrainian politics, it could not be ruled out in the future.

Certainly by 18 February, when some 20,000 protesters clashed with police in the centre of Kyiv, and Yanukovych instituted what was in effect a state of emergency, those plans were already being revisited. Two days later, Vladimir Konstantinov, Speaker of the Supreme Council of Crimea – its local parliament – began publicly speculating about the possible of secession from Ukraine, while he was on a trip to Moscow. According to Putin himself, at an all-night meeting on 22–23 February about how they could exfiltrate Yanukovych, 'when we were parting, I said to my colleagues: we must start working on returning Crimea to Russia.'[2] This is probably disingenuous – the timeline suggests that by then a decision to take the peninsula had been made. Putin had been consulting more widely beforehand, but when it came down to it, the final meeting was one with his closest confidants: Security Council secretary Nikolai Patrushev, FSB director Alexander Bortnikov, Presidential Administration head Sergei Ivanov and Defence Minister Sergei Shoigu. Most were hawks who strongly supported the idea; according to unconfirmed but persistent reports, the only lukewarm voice was that of Shoigu, who apparently was concerned about the long-term consequences. Nonetheless, he is also a politician and a survivor, and he knew better than actively to stand against the decision, confining himself to declaring his willingness to obey orders. Tellingly, Foreign Minister Sergei Lavrov and others who might have also considered the potential downsides, even Prime Minister Medvedev, were not invited.

A decision, perhaps only provisional, seems to have been made by 20 February, two days before Yanukovych fled the country. Accidental corroboration of this was provided, ironically enough, by the very medal stamped by the Defence Ministry to celebrate those who had taken part in the operation. The award For the Return of Crimea, with its distinctive ribbon mixing the Russian tricolour with the black and orange of the St George's ribbon, gives the dates of the operation as 20 February to 18 March. In any case, there was no time to be lost by the planners, because *Vremya Cha* – zero hour – was set for 27 February.

TAKING CRIMEA

On paper, the balance of power on the peninsula looked fairly evenly matched. The Russians had elements of the 510th Naval Infantry

Brigade based at Feodosiya and the 810th Independent Naval Infantry Brigade at Simferopol, along with some Naval *Spetsnaz* from the 431st Naval Reconnaissance Special Designation Point (OMRPSN: *Otdelny Morskoy Razvedyvatelny Punkt Spetsialnovo Naznacheniya*), the Black Sea Fleet's designated special forces unit. The remainder of their military personnel there were sailors. At the same time, more than one-tenth of Ukraine's entire military strength, some 22,000 in all, was based in Crimea. However, most were again naval personnel, and none were kept at a particularly high readiness. Beyond 15,000 in the naval and coastal defence missile forces, as well as an air force brigade and three anti-aircraft missile regiments, the defence of the peninsula was in the hands of the Naval Infantry. There were four units on Crimea: the 36th Independent Mechanized Coastal Defence Brigade at Perevalnoye, the 1st and 501st Independent Naval Infantry Battalions at Feodosiya and Kerch, and the 56th Independent Guards Battalion at Sevastopol. While relatively well trained by the standards of the Ukrainian military, they were all subject to the disruption and demoralization caused by years of under-funding. Beyond that, there were three brigades and two battalions of paramilitary Interior Troops, some 2,500 paramilitaries, subordinated to the Ministry of Internal Security (MVS), and a border guard battalion. While primarily intended for police and security missions, they all had a secondary national defence role. The crucial issue, though, would be the lack of clear orders and, according to some, wilful confusion in the chain of command by officers hostile to the new regime, once the Russians made their move.

Russian forces had been quietly brought to combat readiness the week before the operation, with some elements being sent out from their bases to secure airfields and arms depots. Meanwhile, special forces across Russia were quietly activated under the cover of 'snap inspections', many being airlifted to the Russian airbase at Anapa and naval base at Novorossiisk, both on the Black Sea and close to Crimea. On the night of 22–23 February, the VDV's *Spetsnaz* force, the 45th Independent Regiment, was mobilized and moved from its base at Kubinka, near Moscow. Meanwhile, officers of the military intelligence service (in 2010 technically renamed the GU, the Main Directorate, but still ubiquitously known as the GRU) and the FSB had been brokering deals with local sympathizers, including organized crime groups, as well as volunteers from elsewhere in Russia to ensure that when the operation began, there would be well-armed 'local self-defence groups' on the streets.

Already by 23 February, protests against the new government in Kyiv were attracting tens of thousands. The majority were genuinely outraged by what they saw as a 'coup' and did look to Moscow for some kind of support, chanting 'Putin is our president'. The new government's decision to revoke the law that also made Russian an official language in regions such as Crimea seemed a particularly alarming omen for them. Nonetheless, there is clear evidence also of the presence of Russian agents encouraging them, especially to form 'civil self-defence squads'. Within a day or so, outsiders from Russia – Cossacks, bikers from the nationalist Night Wolves motorcycle organization, Afghan war veterans and others – were also arriving, to add their voices and fists to the anti-Kyiv movement. In part, this was a genuine and spontaneous process, but there was also a clear desire by Moscow to encourage them, sometimes even laying on transport to Crimea.

Meanwhile, Naval Infantry of the Black Sea Fleet had already been taking up positions in Sevastopol and Simferopol airport under the pretext of guarding Russian facilities. This looked mysteriously prescient, as on 26 February violent clashes broke out in the peninsula's capital, Simferopol, between protesters supporting joining Russia and opponents, especially drawn from the Crimean Tatar minority. Some of the pro-Russian partisans were later identified as members of *Salem* and *Bashkaki*, Crimea's most powerful local organized crime gangs, who normally would never cooperate, but who appear to have been recruited by the FSB for this role. There was a sense of imminent chaos, and that same day Putin ordered snap inspections of units across the Western and Central VOs. They turned out to be a crucial smokescreen for the final preparations for the seizure of the peninsula.

At around 0430 hours in the morning of 27 February, armed men in a motley array of camouflage uniforms, but all in modern body armour and hefting a suspiciously modern and extensive range of weapons, seized the local parliament building and hoisted the Russian flag. Calling themselves 'Crimea's armed self-defence force', they represented a mix of forces. The men doing the real heavy-lifting were operators from Russia's newly formed Special Operations Command (KSSO: *Komandovaniye Sil Spetsialnalnykh Operatsii*) supported by more *Spetsnaz* from other detachments, and Naval Infantry. Then there were also other 'volunteers', who would often prove to be little more than thuggish looters, with the exception of a few units such as former Berkut Ukrainian riot police who had joined the anti-Kyiv side or *Rubezh*, a local militia made up of veterans. They often had little operational value, but they gave the Russians political cover as their own well-trained and -armed forces, uniforms bare of any insignia, fanned out to seize the peninsula.

ENTER THE 'LITTLE GREEN MEN'

Over the course of the next few days and weeks, the Russians blockaded the Ukrainian forces in Crimea, closed the neck of the peninsula to reinforcements, and set up a puppet government. The claim that the soldiers were not Russian – remember Vladimir Putin's memorable suggestion that they could have bought their *Ratnik* uniforms and equipment at second-hand shops – sufficed to introduce a note of uncertainty into the situation. In those first few hours, all kinds of wild speculation was doing the rounds in both Kyiv and the West: was this a maverick operation by Black Sea Fleet commanders, were these 'little green men' mercenaries? The truth was, of course, much more simple, but it sufficed to help slow down any meaningful response, giving the Russians the crucial window of opportunity they needed to lock down Crimea.

After all, at the same time, Moscow was also fighting what had been known (somewhat problematically, as will be discussed in Chapter 26) as a 'hybrid war', supporting the deployment of its troops. Cyber-attacks were paralysing Ukrainian communications; Moscow's agents and sympathizers abandoned their positions, sometimes sabotaging equipment as they did so; internet trolls and covert assets alike were spreading wild rumours and challenging the realities of the situation. Meanwhile, Yanukovych held a press conference in Moscow saying that any military action was 'unacceptable' and that, as (in his eyes) legitimate president of Ukraine, he would not request or countenance Russian intervention.[3] It may have been an attempt to retain some credibility but was more likely another mindgame, as by this time he was essentially in the Kremlin's pocket. As the Russians had learned in Georgia, such covert and information operations can be crucial in undermining an enemy's willingness to fight and shattering their cohesion at the crucial moment.

Combined with the speed and professionalism of the operation and the chaos on the government side (Kyiv did not even have a minister of defence until the afternoon of the 27th), this helps explain why, at first, a relative handful of Russian special forces – probably no more than 2,000 in the first few days – along with local allies of often dubious effectiveness managed to bottle up much larger Ukrainian forces. Soon, though, the Russians would send heavier and heavier equipment to the Crimea, including artillery, air defence and mechanized units.

At first, this was done piecemeal. On the afternoon of 27 February, the *Ropucha*-class large landing ship *Azov* docked at Sevastopol and unloaded 300 soldiers from the 382nd Independent Naval Infantry Battalion. The next morning, three Mi-8 transports escorted by fully eight of the latest Mi-35 variant of the Mi-24 gunship – upgraded for full day/night operation – landed *Spetsnaz* at Kacha airport, north of Sevastopol. By that afternoon, though, flights of Il-76 heavy lifters were landing at Simferopol's Gvardeiskoye airport and landing ships with more troops and heavy equipment were converging on the peninsula.

The Ukrainian commanders appear to have been at a loss, and although moves were made to scramble some of their handful of flightworthy Su-27s to interdict more incoming troop flights, the Russians methodically blocked off their avenues for action. On 28 February a Russian missile boat blockaded the harbour at Balaklava. At the same time, marines were seizing Belbek airfield, base of the Ukrainian 204th Tactical Aviation Brigade, neutralizing its 45 MiG-29 fighters. Nonetheless, the Russian forces were still thinly stretched at this point, relying on bluff and confusion (just 20 Naval Infantry were able to bottle up an entire battalion at Kerch), as well as the very fluidity of the situation. It is not as though the Ukrainian forces could not have resisted, nor that Crimea was wholly cut off from the mainland. Indeed, Ukrainian parliamentarian and future president Petro Poroshenko even travelled to Simferopol in a bid to negotiate a settlement, but he was waylaid by protesters.

By 1 March, though, enough extra troops had been sea-lifted in, especially *Spetsnaz* from the 10th Brigade and the 25th Independent Regiment. Alongside volunteers of various stripes, they began to make their presence felt across the peninsula, seizing radar stations and blockading Ukrainian military positions. Some managed to escape: while the entire naval contingent based in Crimea surrendered, defected or was eventually captured, many of the Coast Guard's smaller ships got away by being nimble and moving quickly. On 1 March, witnessing the arrival of a convoy of Russian troops at the gates of their base at Balaklava, the 5th Coast Guard Squadron put straight to sea – by all accounts they had been preparing for just such a situation. In all, 23 Coast Guard vessels were able to evacuate. Likewise, on 3 March, four helicopters and three planes of the 5th Naval Aviation Brigade were able to escape from their blockaded airbase at Novofedorovka; no moves were made to shoot them down.

The opportunities to evacuate were shrinking, though. On 2 March, the commander of the Ukrainian navy and the highest-ranking Ukrainian officer in Crimea, R. Adm. Denis Berezovsky, actually switched sides. Pledging allegiance to 'the people of Crimea', he would later be made deputy commander of the Russian Black Sea Fleet. He began trying to encourage naval vessels to defect with him. While there were at first no takers, the Russians were prepared to give it some time, even replacing their forces around some bases with local militia. After all, the balance of power on the peninsula was shifting. By 6 March, the Russians had managed to bring it almost 2,000 extra soldiers, mainly *Spetsnaz*.

However, that balance of power could swing back. On 2 March, Kyiv had begun moving forces towards the Crimean isthmus, including mechanized units and artillery, which could pose a serious challenge to the lightly armed Russian marines and commandos. In part as a result, Russia began its own build-up on Ukraine's eastern borders, involving some 10,000 soldiers, drawing some of the relatively limited forces Kyiv could deploy away from Crimea.

'CRIMEA IS OURS'

On 6 March, a motion to join with Russia was raised in the Crimean legislature and the date for a referendum on this brought forward to the 16th. The next ten days saw an uneasy calm descend on the peninsula. The Russians continued to blockade remaining Ukrainian forces, but stopped pushing, allowing Ukrainians to come and go from their bases so long as they did so unarmed and out of uniform, and there were even football matches between Ukrainian and Russian marines. The missile cruiser *Moskva*, which had been bottling the 12 elements of the 5th Surface Ships Brigade in Lake Donuzlav, withdrew – only to be replaced with a hulk, which was scuttled in the channel that connected it to the sea. They were still trapped, but in a less overtly confrontational way.

Meanwhile, the heavy equipment that the attackers had been lacking was starting to arrive. The 727th Independent Naval Infantry Battalion and the army's 18th Independent Motor Rifle Brigade, both with their complements of artillery and armour, were brought in by sea from Kerch, with the latter quickly moving to secure the Perekop isthmus. S-300PS SAM systems controlled the airspace, while *Bastion*-P coastal defence missiles kept any potential Ukrainian naval incursions at bay (not that Kyiv had many ships left that it could have used). Any thoughts that Kyiv could reimpose its control over Crimea by force were quickly laid to rest.

After a carefully managed campaign, the referendum duly produced a 97% vote in favour of joining Russia. This was a vote conducted under the shadow of Russian guns, with contrary opinions purged from the media and opposition figures hounded and silenced, ensuring that the international community would reject it, but the irony is that even had it been held wholly fairly, while the result would have been less dramatic, there seems little doubt it would have been squarely in favour of joining Russia. The next day, the Kremlin formally recognized Crimea as an independent state – and the day after welcomed it into the Russian Federation.

What followed was essentially a clean-up. Russian forces began to move into Ukrainian barracks and facilities that had been holding out, generally without violence. Demoralized troops who were now facing much more heavily armed Russian forces and who were being offered safe passage home were generally happy to accept. Many, indeed, chose to join the Russians, who were offering to recognize the existing ranks and seniority of those who signed up as *kontraktniki*. When the 501st Independent Battalion at Kerch surrendered on 20 March, for example, two-thirds of its soldiers took this deal. Ships began running down the Ukrainian flag and hoisting Russian ones, starting with the *Amur*-class command ship *Donbas*.

Where diplomacy and desertion didn't work, force was the option. *Rubezh*, one of the only local militia forces of any real combat effectiveness because it was recruited exclusively from former Naval

Infantry and *Spetsnaz*, stormed the corvettes *Ternopil* and *Khmelnitsky* and the landing ship *Konstantin Olshansky*. Commandos supported by six BTR-82A APCs smashed their way into the compound of the 204th Tactical Aviation Brigade in Belbek and forced them to surrender at gunpoint. The most serious challenge came from the elite 1st Regiment in Feodosia, and so the Russians opted to force them to yield through a show of force. KSSO operators landed in their parade ground from Mi-8 helicopters, with two Mi-35s providing air cover, and proceeded to pepper their barracks with stun and smoke grenades, while firing warning shots into the air. Although there were some brawls, within two hours the Ukrainians had surrendered, with no more than bruises and some broken bones.

In a final coda, the minesweeper *Cherkassy* was boarded by Naval *Spetsnaz* from two Mi-35s on the evening of 25 March, marking the end of Ukrainian resistance. More than 9,000 Ukrainian military personnel opted to join the Russians, and over the coming days and weeks, the rest would be repatriated, along with their equipment. Moscow was perfectly happy to return the tanks, aircraft and artillery, but initially contemplated holding on to all or some of the ships it had captured. Ultimately, though, these proved to be in such poor shape that they returned them all, too.

AN AUDIT OF THE OPERATION

Meanwhile, Crimea was being turned into a militarized bastion. Eventually, the total Russian force on the peninsula would swell to an estimated 31,500 by the start of 2020, including the 22nd Army Corps. The 22nd is technically part of the Black Sea Fleet, in line with the new emphasis on joint commands, and comprises the 127th Independent Reconnaissance Brigade, the 15th Independent Coastal Rocket Artillery Brigade, the 8th Artillery Regiment, the 1096th Independent Anti-Aircraft Missile Regiment, and the marines of the 126th Independent Coastal Defence Brigade. There is also the 810th Naval Infantry Brigade as well as the approximately 900 Naval *Spetsnaz* of the 431st Naval Reconnaissance Special Designation Point and paratroopers of the 171st Independent Air Assault Regiment of the 7th Division. The 39th Helicopter Regiment at Dzhankoy has 38 gunships, a mix of Mi-28s, Mi-35s and Ka-52s.

The troops are protected by an integrated, multi-layer air defence system with new S-400 *Triumf* long-range SAMs supplemented by medium-range *Buk*-M3 (SA-27) missile launchers and *Pantsir*-S1 (SA-22) gun/missile trucks. The 31st Air Defence Division, headquartered at Sevastopol, incorporates two SAM regiments and a radio-technical (EW) regiment. The Black Sea Fleet's Naval Aviation comprises the 43rd Independent Regiment at Saki airbase, with Su-24M bombers and Su-30SM fighters. As for the air force, its 37th Mixed Aviation Regiment is based at Gvardeyskoye, with one squadron of Su-24M bombers and one of Su-25SM ground attack aircraft, and its 38th Fighter Aviation Regiment is at Belbek, comprising a mix of Su-27 and Su-30 aircraft.

For coastal defence, the *Bastion*-Ps were joined by Bal-E (SSC-6) cruise missile launch complexes, able also to dominate the waters around the peninsula. The Black Sea Fleet had also been strengthened, especially with vessels mounting the latest long-range *Kalibr* (SS-N-27) cruise missiles. In this way, the Kremlin not only gained a massive popularity boost – Putin's personal approval ratings shot up from 60% to over 80% – but Russia also strengthened its grip on the Black Sea.

When Putin later asked the question, 'How could we refuse Sevastopol and Crimea to take them under our protection?' he was only partly asking it rhetorically.[4] As with so many of Russia's recent imperial adventures, it was at once driven by Moscow's plans and also the intrigues, interests and interventions of local forces, from ambitious politicians who saw a chance to rise, to ethnic Russians who genuinely feared for their futures under the new government in Kyiv. It is from these complex and often confusing forces that a new kind of conflict was arising.

Crimea was an extraordinary military success. Although two Ukrainian soldiers and one Cossack volunteer died, there were no Russian casualties, and scarcely any fighting. The new KSSO Special Operations Forces Command (see Chapter 24) had its first, and very successful, deployment. Military force, armed proxies, disinformation, deception and disruption in combination with the right mix of careful planning and field improvisation worked beyond Moscow's expectations. Another ex-military contact of mine, a former paratrooper, told me in May 2014 that he was still in disbelief: 'this not the army I remember from Chechnya'. Of course, this was a very different battlefield, and it was an operation largely carried out by elite troops, but nonetheless it did seem to validate the Serdyukov/Makarov reforms, as developed by Shoigu and Gerasimov.

It triggered a wave of Western economic sanctions, which combined with a fall in global oil prices to create a financial crisis for Russia. This proved painful for Moscow, but hardly crippling. Yet the Crimean annexation, which had been envisaged as a one-off move to take advantage of a particular opportunity and also to protect a crucial strategic asset, was to prove just the start of a new round of worsening relations between Moscow and Kyiv, and the West. In part this was because it generated a degree of confidence in some Russian government circles that bordered on hubris. However, it also reflected the downsides in such an operation, fought and justified by self-interested proxies. There was no more room for the enthusiastic volunteers, thugs and mercenaries of the local self-defence units in Crimea, most of whom were either disbanded or encouraged to join the police or military. However, some ended up drifting into the Donbas, driving the next chapter of Moscow's confrontation with Kyiv.

15

Donbas, 2014–

One of the striking aspects of the undeclared and often ill-defined conflict that erupted in south-eastern Ukraine shortly after the Crimean annexation is the degree to which it was at first fought mainly by irregulars, nationalists, patriots and enthusiasts.[1] The man who did the most to, in his own words, 'pull the trigger' on this war, Igor Girkin – more commonly known by his nom de guerre Strelkov, or 'Shooter' – while a former FSB officer, was acting not just *without* orders when he led a rag-tag collection of gunmen across the Ukrainian border in April 2014, but seemingly *against* them. Likewise, in the desperate and confused first weeks and months of the conflict in the Donbas (Donetsk Basin) region, much of the most serious fighting to keep it under Kyiv's control was done not by government soldiers but by volunteers banding together in militias, sometimes under the patronage of local oligarchs. Indeed, some were not even Ukrainian; for example, former Chechen rebel Isa Minayev travelled to Ukraine from exile in Denmark to form the Dzhokhar Dudayev Battalion, largely of former ex-rebels.

Over time, the situation would become more formalized, this messy conflict, half a genuine civil war, half a Russian proxy conflict, being fought between Ukrainian forces on the one hand, and Moscow-supported and -armed rebels often under Russian army commanders and supported by Russian regulars on the other. Nonetheless, in contrast to the Crimean operation, the war in the Donbas was not some long-planned intervention.

In June 2014, when it was already clear that Moscow's follow-on operation in south-eastern Ukraine was not going to plan, a former Russian General Staff officer told me, 'Had the Ukrainians fought for Crimea, we would not now be fighting in the Donbas.' The ease of its seizure, after all, and the disarray in Kyiv encouraged Putin and his advisers to make a fateful over-reach. Crimea had been a unique case: a peninsula where Russia already had a military position, whose population in the main felt unhappy with how Kyiv had treated them for years, and which the majority of Russians rightly felt was theirs. Nonetheless, although not part of the original plan, after Crimea, some within Russia and even within the Kremlin began contemplating a limited and deniable military operation in the more ethnically Russian east of Ukraine. The aim this time was not territorial conquest but political pressure: to convince Kyiv that Moscow could and would punish it for any moves towards closer integration with the West. At the time, the assumption was that this would intimidate Ukraine and force it to accept that it was part of Russia's sphere of influence. It was a fateful miscalculation.

There were genuine protests and concerns in the east, which had been both ousted president Yanukovych's power base and also disproportionately populated by Russian-speakers who were genuinely concerned about the implications of the new government and wanted not so much independence as greater autonomy. This was at once magnified by Moscow's media, which began characterizing the new government as a 'fascist junta'. Meanwhile, there were attempts to start risings in the cities in the east – some purely local efforts, some seemingly backed by figures within Russia acting on their own authority. Most failed, because of either a lack of real support or the timely and effective work of the security forces. In the cities of Donetsk and Lugansk, though, protesters stormed local government buildings and called for referenda on self-determination and even joining Russia, presumably inspired by Crimea's example. Acting Ukrainian president Olexander Turchinov angrily threatened 'counter-terrorism measures'. All that was needed was a spark.

STRELKOV'S SPARK

That spark was provided by 52 volunteers and mercenaries from Crimea commanded by Igor Girkin, better known as Strelkov. An ardent

Russian nationalist with a background in the FSB (although some have claimed he was actually in the GRU), he was a former Russian artillery officer and keen military re-enactor, with two decades of involvements in a variety of often dirty civil wars, supporting pro-Moscow separatists in Moldova in 1992 and Serbs in the 1992–95 Bosnian War, as well as fighting against rebels in Chechnya 1999–2005. In many of these conflicts, he was subsequently accused of human rights abuses. Nonetheless, his passion for the cause of Russia and Russians abroad was undeniable.

On 12 April 2014, Strelkov led his ragtag force into Ukraine, dodging both Russian and Ukrainian border guards. He opted to lead them to the town of Slovyansk, where anti-Kyiv protesters had already essentially taken control. There he took control of the local militia and together they were able to drive off an initial response by operators from the SBU, Ukraine's Security Service. Kyiv began mustering more formidable forces, but meanwhile the rebellion was spreading. In both Lugansk and Donetsk, armouries were captured and emptied and militias began to be formed. This was not coordinated, nor was it necessarily pro-Moscow, and the Kremlin was uncertain whether it actually wanted to be involved. After all, it had Crimea, the prize it had really desired.

Nonetheless, a sense grew in Moscow that this rising could not be allowed to fail – not least, to avoid nationalist protest at home – and also offered an opportunity. Some Kremlin figures believed that the anti-Kyiv protest in eastern Ukraine would naturally spread, but others looked instead at the arithmetic of power. As of March, the government could muster only perhaps 6,000 combat-ready troops from its entire army, and had to guard its borders and the Crimean isthmus. Surely, with just a little help, the rebellion could survive as long as needed to bring Kyiv to, as they saw it, its senses? At the time, one Russian professor with links to the Foreign Ministry told me, 'The Ukrainian junta has over-reached; but they must know they need Russian trade and friendship. Once they have come to their senses, we will be able to talk.'

Many in Moscow thought this way: they did not have any interest in annexing the Donbas. Rather, this was the shock treatment needed to get the new revolutionary government in Kyiv to 'come to its senses'. Everyone inside the system I talked to in Moscow at the time assured me it was just a matter of six months: by summer, Kyiv would have realized it could not break away from Moscow and all would be calm again. Of course, it turned out that they were wrong.

A WAR OF IRREGULARS

They misunderstood the nature of this crisis, assuming that the wider eastern Ukrainian, Russian-speaking population's genuine concerns about the new government would make them actively support the rebellion. For most, that was a step too far. They also misunderstood the degree to which ordinary Ukrainians, including many from that very same Russian-speaking community, would be willing to take up arms to defend their nation's sovereignty.

Government forces were indeed few and often badly equipped and unmotivated. Even relatively elite units were often unwilling to engage with rebels; in one distinctly embarrassing case, paratroopers from the 25th Airborne Brigade let rebels seize five BMD airborne infantry fighting vehicles (IFVs) and a Nona self-propelled mortar without a fight, while commanders of another of their columns meekly surrendered their rifles when faced with 'a crowd of men drinking beer and women yelling taunts and insults'.[2] In another instance, observed by a foreign journalist, Interior Ministry troops openly sold rebels guns and ammunition in return for home-brew and slabs of salo, cured pork fat.

However, much of the heavy lifting in the first months of the war was borne by pro-government militias. Some were akin to local self-defence volunteers, like the loyalists of the Donbas Battalion. Others were virtually the private armies of powerful Ukrainian oligarchs who bankrolled them, like Dnipro-1, a battalion founded by Ihor Kolomoisky, the billionaire whom Kyiv had appointed Governor of Dnipropetrovsk Region. Some of the more controversial came from political movements, like the neo-Nazis who formed the Azov Regiment. They turned out to be some of the more effective fighters of the initial stages of the war, but have also been dogged by allegations of war crimes and white supremacism (that led to the US Congress formally stipulating that military aid being sent to Ukraine could not go to Azov).

Arrayed against them was an equally varied mix of separatist militias, some made up of locals, others of mercenaries and volunteers from Russia, often with encouragement, weapons and guidance from Moscow. Many were also defectors from the government side: by summer of 2015, according to Ukraine's Chief Military Prosecutor, 5,000 police and 3,000 soldiers had joined the rebels. There was no standardization in size, origins or structure of these units, which ranged from relatively effective ones such as Mikhail 'Givi' Tolstykh's Somalia Battalion (reportedly so named because its fighters were 'as brave as Somalis') and Arsen 'Motorola' Pavlov's Sparta Battalion to grandiosely named but typically smaller militias such as the Russian Orthodox Army (drawn largely from Ukrainian Cossacks) and the splendidly named Hooligan Battalion. Rostov-on-Don, capital of Russia's Rostov region and an important port city and road and rail hub, became the logistical base for Moscow's undeclared war. Not only does it house arsenals from which materiel was dispatched over the border to support the rebels, but the GRU maintained a significant presence here. Potential volunteers and mercenaries for the militias were screened, armed and mustered in the city.

This was a messy, dirty conflict, with both sides being credibly accused of human rights abuses, in part often because of a lack of a clear chain of command. Indeed, although rebel 'People's Republics' would be formed, with Strelkov assembling a coalition of militias as the so-called South-East Army, these were shaky structures from the first. Their political leaders were often amateurish opportunists, and Strelkov was never able to monopolize the militias, because many local strongmen and warlords wanted to retain their autonomy. Indeed, some of these forces were little more than bandit gangs, more interested in plunder and extortion than any cause.

In May, the leaders of the self-proclaimed Donetsk People's Republic (DNR: *Donetskaya Narodnaya Respublika*) and Lugansk People's Republic (LNR: *Luganskaya Narodnaya Respublika*) announced their independence from Ukraine and that they were forming a confederation known as *Novorossiya* – 'New Russia' – with Strelkov as their defence minister. This never came to anything, though: Moscow was not going to underwrite and bankroll some new nation. The idea as far as the Kremlin was concerned was to force Kyiv to accept the Donbas back as part of a political deal that kept Ukraine divided and deferential to Russia's interests. Indeed, Strelkov would be dismissed in August, returning to Russia, where he became a vocal critic of Putin and the government, regarding it as inconsistent and weak in its defence of Russian interests and nationals abroad.

Ukraine, 2014–20

DNR/LNR control today
● DNR/LNR-controlled city
○ Formerly DNR/LNR-controlled city
● Other Ukraine-controlled city

Minsk II Ceasefire Lines
– – – DNR/LNR (19 Sept 2014 front line)
·········· Ukraine (15 Feb 2015 front line)

RUSSIA

KHARKHIV

LUHANSK

Severodonetsk

Sloviansk

Kramatorsk

Artemivsk

Pervomaisk

Alchevsk   Lugansk

Krasnoarmiisk

Horlivka   Debaltseve   **Lugansk People's Republic (LNR)**

Avdiivka

Krasny Luch

Makiyivka   Snizhne   Antratsyt

DONETSK   Donetsk   Torez

Donetsk People's Republic (DNR)

ZAPORIZHIA

Novoazovsk

Mariupol

Sea of Azov

N

0 ____ 25 miles
0 ____ 25km

BELARUS   RUSSIA

POLAND   Kyiv   Kharkiv

Lviv   Dnipropetrovsk   Lugansk

TRANSNISTRIA   Donetsk

MOLDOVA   Kherson   *Sea of Azov*

Odessa

ROMANIA   CRIMEA   *Kerch Strait*

BULGARIA   *Black Sea*

DNIPROPETROVSK

He was a ruthless and relatively competent commander, but he was not only politically inconvenient; he had become toxic for his role in the shooting down of Malaysia Airlines Flight 17. On 17 July 2014, MH17 was on a scheduled run from Amsterdam to Kuala Lumpur. While flying over eastern Ukraine, it was hit by a missile and crashed, killing all 283 passengers and 15 crew on board. Although Moscow has advanced numerous alternative explanations, a detailed inquiry by a Dutch-led Joint Investigation Team concluded that it was shot down by a *Buk* M1 SA-11 SAM fired from separatist-controlled territory in Ukraine. The system in question appears to have been one of several originally fielded by Russia's 53rd Anti-Aircraft Rocket Brigade, which was supplied to the rebels, likely with crews. Judging by a subsequently deleted social media post from Strelkov ('In the region of Torez, an AN-26 plane has been shot down, somewhere near the "Progress" mine. We warned them – not to fly "in our sky." Here is video-proof of yet another "bird fall."'), the rebels thought the target was a Ukrainian An-26 transport plane. The presence of heavy weapons systems such as the *Buk* demonstrates how quickly Moscow moved to support the rebels, and the provision of SAMs in particular helps explain why Ukraine has not been able to rely on its air assets much. However, there is no evidence that Russian military commanders were involved in the launch decision, also underlining the relative autonomy of their proxy warlords.

THE 'NORTHERN WIND'

On 1 May, Kyiv reintroduced conscription, as it prepared first to isolate and then to reconquer the rebel-held regions. Small-scale offensives were launched on towns under DNR control including Slovyansk, Mariupol and Kramatorsk. After repeated attacks, and heavy artillery barrages, Strelkov and his forces retreated from Slovyansk on 5 July, falling back to Kramatorsk. This seemed to trigger a general collapse in rebel unity and morale, and Kramatorsk and Artemivsk fell shortly thereafter, followed by Mariupol. Meanwhile, rebels and government forces were fighting over Donetsk International Airport, a short drive from the DNR's headquarters.

Up to this point, Moscow had been trying to limit its involvement. It was willing to let volunteers from Russia go to join the rebels, and was trickling in some heavier weapons such as shoulder-fired SAMs and then heavier air defence systems to counter the government's airpower advantage (though Kyiv was using it less after the loss of several helicopters and aircraft) and a limited number of tanks and howitzers. There was even one militia unit, the *Vostok* Battalion, which appears to have been raised by the GU from Chechen and Abkhazian veterans of the war in Chechnya and sent to Donetsk precisely as both to stiffen the rebel forces and, if necessary, act as Moscow's instrument there. Other Russian volunteers joining command positions with the LNR and DNR forces were probably 'volunteers', military officers sent to try to reverse the rebel retreat.

It didn't work. By August, the rebel-held areas were shrinking steadily. Above all, government forces seemed close to regaining control over the border with Russia, which would allow them to throttle off the supply of fighters, weapons and ammunition, as well as driving a wedge between the DNR and the LNR. This would mark the end of the rebels, and already there were hints that some of their leaders were seeking either to flee to Russia or make their own deals with Kyiv. Moscow's choice was to escalate or withdraw. It chose to escalate, abandoning any hope that deniable proxies with minimal assistance could hold their own against an increasingly confident alliance of government troops and militias. The Kremlin might not have started this rebellion, but having decided to try to co-opt it, it wasn't willing to let it be defeated.

On 7 August, government mechanized and airborne forces, supported by several militia battalions, launched an attempt to take back Ilovaisk, a railway junction east of Donetsk, which had been in rebel hands since April. At first, they were able to push back the DNR forces, and by 18 August they had fought their way to the centre of the city. It now seemed just a matter of mopping up. However, on 24 August a sudden counter-attack caught them by surprise, and saw the government forces encircled within the city when some 4,000 Russian regular troops, including both paratroopers and T-72B3 tanks of the 6th Tank Brigade, crossed the border in support of the rebels.

The 92nd Mechanized Brigade launched an attack to break through to the other government forces in Ilovaisk, but was hit by heavy and accurate artillery fire and then assaulted by Russian paratroopers, forcing it to retreat. Over a few days, the tactical situation had completely changed, and the encircled troops began trying to negotiate their way out. In what was an implicit acknowledgement of Russia's role, on 29 August Putin himself announced that a 'humanitarian corridor' ought to be opened to allow them to leave, and DNR prime minister Alexander Zakharchenko hurriedly agreed, even though the government forces would be expected to leave their armoured vehicles and heavy weapons behind.

When some 1,600 remaining government troops did begin to withdraw, disputes emerged over the route of the retreat and their determination to retain their armoured vehicles. Whether or not this was a deliberate ploy to justify breaking the ceasefire, it led to small-scale clashes that triggered Russian artillery bombardments. The discipline of the Ukrainians broke, and several hundred were taken prisoner. By 1 September, Ilovaisk was back in rebel hands, more than 350 government troops and militia were dead, and a new stage of the war had begun as the so-called 'Northern Wind' – direct intervention by Moscow – was blowing.

THE FIXING OF THE CONFLICT

In August 2014, the Russians deployed an estimated 3,500–6,500 troops into Ukraine, growing to a peak of some 10,000 by the end of the year. There had already been small detachments from the 2nd and 10th *Spetsnaz* Brigades, the 106th Guards Airborne Division and the 45th Guards Airborne *Spetsnaz* Regiment. Then, elements of the 9th and 18th Motor Rifle Brigades were deployed to prepare the ground. The first wave of regular combat forces saw the introduction of Battalion Tactical Groups (BTGs) drawn from fully ten manoeuvre units: the 17th, 18th, 21st and 33rd Motor Rifle Brigades, the 31st Guards Air Assault Brigade, the 2nd *Spetsnaz* Brigade, the 104th and 247th Air-Assault Regiments and the 137th and 331st Airborne Regiments. At this point, the age of so-called 'hybrid war', one in which disinformation, deniable political operations and other non-kinetic means are at least as important as the actual fighting on the battlefield, was virtually over. Instead this was looking much more like a conventional, even if undeclared, war in which both sides fielded mixes of regular forces and militias in sporadic, but brutal conflict.

The government forces had been able to win victories against the poorly disciplined and uncoordinated rebel militias, but the Ukrainians had no illusions about their ability to resist Russian forces. With Moscow's more overt entry into the war, Kyiv was forced to agree to the Minsk Protocol peace deal in September, although the ceasefire this was meant to bring proved pretty illusory. Sporadic clashes continued, followed by the much more serious Second Battle of Donetsk Airport as DNR troops fought to dislodge government troops from their last foothold in the city. It took almost four months of fighting – during which time the defenders gained the popular nickname 'cyborgs' for their seemingly inhuman tenacity – but by the end of January 2015, it was in rebel hands.

With direct Russian assistance, the rebels were able to make advances. A particular example was the strategically vital city of Debaltseve. Located between the territories held by the DNR and LNR, it was also a key road and rail hub on the way to Artemivsk and Slovyansk. The rebels had seized it in April 2014, only for it to be recaptured by Kyiv's troops in July. As a result, it was at the heart of a pocket of government-held territory wedged between the two rebel regions. In January 2015, in tough winter conditions and under a heavy artillery barrage, the rebels launched an offensive to capture the city. Government forces resisted, and in the ensuing artillery duel, soldiers and civilians alike were killed in significant numbers. As rebel forces encircled Debaltseve, ceasefires brokered by outside forces came to nothing. Attempts by Kyiv to relieve the 6,000 government troops in this 'kettle' were largely aborted by the volume of artillery fire being delivered, and it soon became clear that much of this was thanks to a Russian force drawn from the 8th and 18th Guards Motor Rifle Brigades and the 232nd Rocket Artillery Brigade, while the 25th *Spetsnaz* Regiment provided both assault troops and artillery spotters. A BTG based on the 136th Guards Motor Rifle Brigade was also leading the efforts to close the road corridor into the city, suffering sufficient losses that it had to be replaced with another from the 27th Guards Motor Rifle Brigade and the 217th Guards Airborne Regiment (from the 98th Guards Airborne Division). Ukrainian forces were eventually forced to withdraw under heavy fire on 18 February, leaving behind a shattered city but also a testimony to the scale of Russian involvement and the degree to which they could tip the balance.

Meanwhile, the Minsk Protocol having patently failed, negotiators were working on a new iteration, imaginatively named Minsk II. This was agreed on 12 February 2015, and proved no more successful. It envisaged an immediate ceasefire, elections in the rebel-held areas, their reintegration into Ukraine with a special status granting them considerable autonomy, and their return to government control. Any ceasefires were at best patchy and temporary, the elections held by the rebel authorities were deemed illegitimate by Kyiv, the law on special status passed by the Ukrainian parliament was damned as inadequate by the rebels, and the DNR and LNR remained resolutely in rebellion.

Instead, since 2015 the dynamic was largely one of consolidation: the conflict had not been fixed in the sense of being resolved, so much as fixed as in frozen in time. The government made considerable progress in rebuilding its military, and as of 2022 had over a quarter of a million men and women under arms. The pro-government militias were incorporated into a new National Guard and although some, especially those associated with ultranationalist movements, were still often wilful, in the main the patriotism evident in the volunteer units of 2014 was successfully harnessed.

STALEMATE

On the other hand, a new pattern had been established. To erstwhile Ukrainian president Petro Poroshenko's government, this was an 'Anti-Terrorist Operation' (ATO). To the Kremlin, this was not a war at all; only in December 2015 did Putin finally admit that there were Russians in the Donbas 'resolving various issues' but even then, he denied they were combat forces.[3] After all, when it could, Moscow continued to rely on its proxy militias, albeit increasingly under Russian officers. However, despite efforts to build them into a serious conventional army, they were often undisciplined or simply outgunned. Whenever government forces looked as if they were likely to make serious gains, though, the Russians surged in their battalion tactical groups to turn the tide.

In the first years of the conflict, the front lines ebbed and flowed and towns such as Debaltseve would exchange hands several times. As government forces became more competent and confident, the rebels' ability to make gains diminished. Indeed, 2016 was the first year in which Kyiv lost no ground. In January 2017, the rebels launched an offensive against the government-held town of Avdiivka that was reminiscent of the full-on warfare of 2014, with mass artillery bombardments and close ground engagements. The government forces held the line, though, and in 2018, Kyiv adopted new language, calling the rebel areas 'temporarily occupied territories' and replacing the term ATO with 'Joint Forces Operation'.

What may sound like an essentially meaningless bit of wordplay did have significance, as it also coincided with a more assertive line from the government forces. By 2017, they were episodically nudging their positions forward, deeper into the so-called 'grey zone', the no-man's land along the line of contact. They realized that this could not be converted into a serious attempt to roll back the rebel lines, though, without triggering a Russian response. Conversely, while Moscow continued to support the rebels, maintained large contingents ready to intervene, and deployed a range of other assets, including army and FSB sniper teams, it knew that breaking the stalemate would require a major and overt military escalation, with all the political costs that would entail. So the pattern was one of on-off ceasefires, trench warfare, sporadic local fighting, mutual sniping and shelling, and equally mutual recrimination, until 2022 when Putin decided that it was time to break the stalemate.

16

Lessons of the Donbas War

It was 2020, and I was sitting in on a briefing about Operation *Orbital*, Britain's capacity-building mission in Ukraine. Since 2015, it had provided training in a whole range of basic military skills, from leadership and planning to bomb disposal and field medicine. This being a modern Western military there was, of course, an entirely superfluous PowerPoint presentation (though the Americans are still kings of the slide deck), with lots of facts, figures and nice maps. Afterwards, though, one of the presenters, an infantry captain, was keen to emphasize that it was not a one-way street: 'Let's be honest, we can also learn from the Ukrainians, too. No one else has the same experience in fighting a modern, peer rival in conventional war.' He paused. 'I've seen action in Iraq and Afghanistan; I've been under fire. But I've never faced a tank.'

For all the attention paid to so-called 'grey zone' or 'hybrid' operations in Ukraine – the cyber-attacks and electronic mischief-making, the propaganda and subversion, the economic and political pressure – the 2015–22 Donbas War was largely a conventional one, in which sniper attacks or artillery exchanges periodically gave way to open battles using the full panoply of modern warfare. No wonder that Western armies whose recent experience had largely been in dusty counter-insurgency wars against scattered irregulars, were eager to tap the Ukrainians' experience. At the same time, it provided the Russians an opportunity to test theories and learn lessons in a conflict longer than the brief Georgian campaign and less specific than Syria.

After all, though the Russians never made quite such a dramatic shift to 'small wars' as the West, implicit within the 'New Look' reforms had been the notion that all conceivable future operations would be limited interventions in post-Soviet Eurasia. Their architect, Gen. Makarov, had been explicit, in a speech to the Academy of Military Sciences, saying that 'it is important to understand that the combat zone is not far to the west or to the east, it is along the borders of the Russian Federation, in the CIS countries.'[1] Such conflicts would put a premium on the speed with which force groupings could be mobilized, but not sheer mass. The war in the Donbas, though, and the consequent worsening of relations with the West, once again reminded the High Command and the Kremlin of the risk of larger conflicts. This led to the partial return of the division, for example. More broadly, the war demonstrated a number of specific Russian strengths and weaknesses.

COMMAND AND CONTROL IN A PROXY WAR IS HARD

Alexander Mozgovoi was a native son of Lugansk who found his passion and his passing in the rebellion. Up until then, he had been a senior sergeant in the Ukrainian military and then a cook in St Petersburg, but he had returned home at the start of 2014, and when the rebellion began, discovered new talents as warlord. He formed a militia group called the *Prizrak* ('Ghost') Battalion, and although at first he nominally pledged allegiance to Strelkov, Mozgovoi kept *Prizrak* separate from the Army of the South-East and even LNR People's Militia command structures. It acquired a reputation as brutal but effective, such that it even attracted volunteers from abroad, most of whom went into its largely Francophone Continental Unit, and Unit 404, a detachment of foreign Communist fighters also known as the Biryukov-Markov Unit.

It is fair to say that Mozgovoi, having finally become a 'someone', was not willing to share the limelight or bend the knee. He regularly clashed with other militia commanders, in at least one case even drawing a gun on one of his notional allies. He also took to considering himself a law unto himself. In October 2014, he even held a kangaroo court at which a suspect was executed for alleged rape on the basis of a show of hands from the audience. Just as Kyiv moved as quickly as it could to bind the volunteer units into its National Guard, by 2015 so too was Moscow trying to forge a more unified command structure within the 1st (Donetsk) and 2nd (Lugansk) Corps. Mozgovoi was unwilling to accept subordination, so at first the LNR authorities and the Russians tried to put pressure on him by limiting the supplies of food and ammunition sent to *Prizrak*. In response, he upped the ante, formally setting up his own political party, *Narodnoye Vozrozhdeniye* (National Renewal), by application to Kyiv.

Two weeks later, on 23 May 2015, Mozgovoi was returning to his base of operations at Alchevsk after a meeting in Lugansk. He was accompanied by his press spokeswoman and six bodyguards, travelling in three cars. The bodyguards were heavily armed, as there had been an attempt on his life a couple of months before. They didn't have a chance to use them, though. Six Russian-built MON-50 directional mines had been secreted along a stretch of the road outside the village of Mykhailivka, linked together by command wire. As Mozgovoi's motorcade passed them, unseen ambushers detonated the mines, each of which blasted 540 steel balls towards their target. Mozgovoi, his driver and two bodyguards were killed instantly. The attackers then raked the cars with AKM assault rifles and RPK machine guns, finishing off the rest, before disappearing into the night.

The LNR authorities immediately blamed the attack on Ukrainian special forces, as did the new commander of *Prizrak*, but Mozgovoi's closest allies claimed that he was assassinated by Russian *Spetsnaz*. After all, while Kyiv would shed few tears for Mozgovoi, there is little evidence that it had the kind of ninjas who could infiltrate rebel-held areas, carry out such a precise assassination (which required knowledge of his movements) and exfiltrate, all without leaving a trace. Besides, there had been something of a pattern of misfortunes facing militia commanders who found themselves in opposition either to the local leaderships or to Moscow. As well as Mozgovoi, controversial commanders Alexander 'Batman' Bednov and Pavel 'Batya' Dremov met their ends in 2015, and in 2016, 'Motorola' Pavlov met the same fate. In most cases, they were killed by bombs, booby traps or ambushes. Most shocking was the murder of Alexander Zakharchenko, who headed the DNR from August 2014 until his death in August 2018.

While the official line is always that they were killed by Kyiv's agents, in not a single case was any evidence in support of this found.

Instead, suspicion has fallen on Russian special forces or mercenaries from the Wagner Group (see Chapters 18 and 26) or, in a few cases, organized crime rivals, such as the figures behind the gunning down of Yevgeny Zhilin, commander of the *Oplot* Brigade, in a Moscow restaurant in 2016. In 2016, former LNR prime minister Gennady Tsyplakov seemingly hanged himself in prison after being accused of trying to stage a coup against Igor Plotnitsky, at the time head of the LNR.

In essence, Moscow has had to accept that irregular proxy forces may be relatively cheap but that you get what you pay for: while they may be individually brave and sometimes effective on the battlefield, much of the time they are thuggish opportunists who are unimpressive in battle and undisciplined off it. As discussed in Chapter 26, the best way of understanding modern Russian thinking on operations below the threshold of full-scale war is not as 'grey zone' or 'hybrid', but 'political war', the use of every means at a state's disposal, overt and covert, short of direct warfare to accomplish its political ends. This certainly seems to have been the Kremlin's approach in the early, more confused phase of the Donbas conflict, until it became clear that a random collection of thugs, nationalists, opportunists, Cossacks and idealists could not stand against the government forces, and Moscow had to step up or step out.

Without formal means of enforcing discipline and removing commanders, the Russians turned to bloodily informal ones. At first, they tried setting up their own militia groups such as the *Vostok* Battalion, and then using the Wagner Group mercenaries. They also tried to control more powerful systems. When Moscow reluctantly sent six TOS-1 Solntsepyok thermobaric launchers to the DNR, for example, it ensured not just that the crews were its own people, but that it had to grant authorization to release the rockets for use. By 2019, though, while the majority of the soldiers in the 1st and 2nd Corps were locals, supported by a smattering of Cossacks and other Russian volunteers, the higher command structure was overwhelmingly made up of regular Russian officers assigned to their positions, even if hiding behind fake names or callsigns. According to Kyiv, for example, Col. Gen. Andrei Serdyukov, who went on to command the VDV paratrooper corps, was in 2015 in overall control of operations in the Donbas, with the callsign 'Sedov'. They are backed and commanded through the conventional military hierarchy. The 8th Guards Army, which was reformed in 2017, is based south of Rostov-on-Don, at Novorossiisk. Although the 20th Guards Army at Voronezh to the north certainly also played a role, the 8th appears to have been made the operational hub for deployments into the Donbas, even as it posed the main conventional threat to Ukraine.

INFORMATION WARFARE IS A POWERFUL FORCE MULTIPLIER

On the other hand, the Russians have a keen awareness of how political operations can support kinetic action and how information and communications systems are not only crucial force multipliers of the future, but they are also battlegrounds. Avdiivka is an industrial city on the northern approaches to Donetsk, which had first been captured by rebels, then retaken by government forces in July 2014. Promzona, the so-called 'Industrial Zone' in the east of the city, had been delineated as a neutral zone because of its proximity to the M04 highway out of Donetsk, but in March 2016, government forces began establishing positions there, posing an implied threat to the route. Sporadic local clashes continued through the year, but in January 2017 they escalated to full-scale combat. Each side accused the other of having initiated hostilities, but the actual trigger seems to have been the government's decision to build up a position called Almaz-2 which could cut the road.

In response, the rebels began shelling the city, creating a humanitarian crisis as its remaining 17,000 or so inhabitants found themselves with no or limited heat or power in the height of winter. Over the next few days, rebel forces launched repeated offensives against Avdiivka's defenders, largely troops from the 72nd Mechanized Brigade, but despite several times being able to break through their lines, they were never able to concentrate enough forces to exploit these local successes. This was despite a serious attack from the rebel-held village of Spartak just south of Avdiivka, in which an armoured column looped round the city limits to engage from the north-west, trying to take the strategically important Avdiivka Coke and Chemical Plant. By 4 February, though, the fighting was starting to die down, as a local ceasefire was agreed, and the next day, heat and electricity supplies were restored to the long-suffering residents.

This was some of the most bitter fighting since 2014–15, and demonstrated just how far the Ukrainian army had come in rebuilding its fighting form. One of the striking innovations of this particular battle, though, was that in the midst of battle, Ukrainian soldiers' mobile phones began pinging with a series of disconcerting text messages. 'Nobody needs your kids to become orphans.' 'Your body will be found when the snow melts.' 'You're just meat to your commanders.' Some even seemed to come from the numbers of neighbouring soldiers' phones.

Such fake messages had been encountered before in the war, but never in such density and with so many appearing to be sent by soldiers' comrades. It seems to have been thanks to a Russian RB-341V Leer-3 electronic warfare system, a truck-based piece of advanced technology that can deploy a cell site simulator on a drone. Lofted near the battlefield, it can hijack up to 6,000 phone connections at once over a 6-kilometre-wide area. Whereas in other situations it was used to locate mobile phones so that the Russians could direct artillery fire accurately on Ukrainian positions, in Avdiivka, it was used to try to demoralize them, and since then, the information operations deployed have become more advanced and imaginative.

IMPLAUSIBLE DENIABILITY HAS ITS PLACE

When MH17 was shot down over the Donbas in 2014, Moscow's narrative control machine went into overdrive. Crash investigators were sent to the area to police the wreckage as far as they could, removing evidence of a Russian-built missile, while its overt and covert media outlets began spinning alternative explanations for the crash of varying degrees of implausibility. These ranged from that it was shot down by a Ukrainian Su-25, even though this is actually a ground-attack aircraft, to, most extraordinarily, that the people on the plane were already dead, part of an elaborate provocation staged by the CIA to blacken Russia's reputation.

Beyond that, despite the reams of reports on Russian men and materiel in the Donbas, open source investigations geolocating images to specific locations there, even the incautious selfies Russian soldiers posted on their social media pages with street signs and landmarks in the background, Moscow claimed to have no direct role in the war.

In part, this was to wrong-foot and bamboozle the West. However, while there are some who would still believe Putin over their own press and leaders, in the main this is a narrative that has long since lost any credence. Even back in 2015, when Foreign Minister Sergei Lavrov tried to spin the official line in front of an audience of officials and experts at the Munich Security Conference, he was met with derisive laughter. In the main, the continued deception, just like the dependence on proxies and mercenaries, reflected rather the Kremlin's attempt to conceal the true nature and scale of the war from its own people.

A substantial proportion of Russia's soldiers are conscripts, which posed some particular political and operational challenges for Moscow. By law, conscripts may not serve in military operations abroad, except when war has formally been declared, unless they volunteer. Even if they do choose to do so, they are serving just 12 months in service, and after their basic and unit training, they are typically only considered truly useful for three or at most four months of their term. Furthermore, there was – rightly – considerable discomfort in the Kremlin about the potential backlash from ordinary Russians, if conscripts began to die in a war that officially wasn't being fought. Hence the use of battalion tactical groups which could be assembled from *kontraktniki* in one or more brigades, a practice which may have become standard for projecting force but which to a considerable degree started as an expedient in the Donbas. This was not without significant cost. To generate the estimated 42,000 troops rotated through or near the Donbas in 2014, for example, meant drawing on some 117 combat and combat-support units.

The war also, though, consolidated a Russian commitment to ensuring that it control the narratives around any wars it fights as far as it can. It failed to do so in the First Chechen War and paid the price, so made sure that it could present the 2008 Georgian War purely as a response to Tbilisi's 'aggression'. However, the Donbas was the first long-term foreign war it tried to manage in this way.

DRONES ARE THE NEXT BIG THING

On 11 July 2014, two Ukrainian mechanized brigades, the 24th and 72nd, along with a battalion of the 79th Airmobile Brigade and Border

Troops, mustered outside the town of Zenopillya in southern Lugansk region, prior to launching an attack on rebel forces to their north. What they did not know, though, was that the Russians had tracked their movements by satellite and electronic means, and had massed artillery at Rovenky on their own side of the border – but just 15 kilometres away. Shortly after 0400 hours, two Russian *Orlan*-10 drones buzzed the government positions, sending back detailed targeting information, and the Ukrainians' communications began to be jammed. Russian 122mm Tornado-G rocket systems (rather more advanced than the dated BM-21s issued to the rebels) started firing well-aimed salvos, 40 in all, that in a matter of minutes had turned the encampment into an inferno of shrapnel and fire. Thirty-seven soldiers were killed, over a hundred wounded, and trucks and armoured vehicles, including T-64 tanks, were left burnt-out across the field. The 1st Battalion of the elite 79th Brigade was so badly mauled that it had to be reconstituted, and both the 24th and 72nd were soon pulled out of the line, considered no longer combat-ready. Even in the age of 'hybrid war', artillery remains the last argument of kings. It was a case study in the power of concentrated firepower, when accurately targeted – and also the use of drones to allow that targeting.

Their use of drones was been particularly noteworthy in the Donbas, as the Russians made strides to catch up with Western practice. As well as the *Orlan* ('Eagle'), they used the *Granat*-1 and -2, the *Forpost*, the *Eleron* 3SV, the *Zastava* and the hand-launched ZALA-421–08 for observation and fire control. This helped make up for the Russians' decision not to use their considerable superiority in airpower, both to preserve a modicum of deniability but also because it was certain that they would suffer losses in the process.

As well as using drones, the Russians also appreciated the need to combat them. Ukraine had relatively few, but the Organization for Security and Cooperation in Europe (OSCE), which tried, often vainly, to monitor breaches of the Minsk Accords and the many short-term ceasefires, found the quadcopter drones it used shot down, or rendered useless by jamming: by April 2021, more than half of its flights were experiencing signal interference. Ukraine's drones faced the same problems. Russia's R-330Zh *Zhitel* system can jam the GPS satellite navigation many rely on, while some reports have suggested they have trialled the *Pishchal* handheld jamming 'rifle' there, too.

THERE WAS NO QUICK END TO THE WAR

In 2017, Ukrainian Chief of the General Staff Gen. Viktor Muzhenko suggested he could retake the Donbas in as little as ten days – albeit at the cost of 3,000 military dead and another 7,000–9,000 wounded, along with more than 10,000 civilian deaths.[2] Whether or not he was advocating this – and, as will be discussed later, even then there were those in Kyiv who did talk of reconquering the Donbas by force some day – Moscow retained escalation dominance. There were too many ways they could surge more forces into the region or strike against Ukraine from other directions.

In order to try to make the best of this stalemate, in 2017–18, the Ukrainians adopted tactics based on making small, incremental advances into the 'grey zone' of no-man's land along the line of contact, to occupy more defensible positions or ones with better fields of view, and in the process nudge the effective border forward. They could hardly have 'salami sliced' their way to victory, but it demonstrated that they were still committed to restoring their control over the contested regions, eventually.

After all, rather than inducing Kyiv to capitulate, the intervention into the Donbas generated an unprecedented sense of national identity: when *Cyborgs: Heroes Never Die*, a film about the Second Battle of Donetsk Airport, was released in 2017, it immediately became a local blockbuster. Meanwhile, Moscow was having to subsidize the unrecognized pseudo-states of the Donbas as well as defend them, in a conflict that was neither acknowledged nor at all popular at home.

This was a human tragedy. As of the end of 2021, its toll was estimated at more than 14,000 dead, and nearly 2 million internally displaced.[3] The urbanized and industrialized Donbas region once held nearly 15% of Ukraine's population and generated an equal share of its gross domestic product, but the economies of the DNR and LNR had all but collapsed. According to Ukraine's National Security and Defence Council, it was costing Moscow $3 billion a year to subsidize them, at least as much as its military operations. Even those parts of the region not controlled by the rebels suffered from economic dislocation thanks to a 420-kilometre-long front line cut through it and the presence of populations of refugees. Kyiv was able to leverage its status as a victim of Russian aggression to win more support from the West, but nonetheless had to spend heavily on national defence: 5.95% of GDP in 2022. The aim was to make Ukraine a tough enough enemy not lightly to be challenged. Perhaps that prospect was looking too real to Putin, though. In 2021, Russia began massing unprecedented forces around Ukraine, and after almost a year of escalating rhetoric, these were unleashed on Ukraine, in the all-out war that had been looming for almost eight years.

17

Syria, 2015– (1): The Unexpected Intervention

Blink, and you could have missed it. When US president Barack Obama met Putin for a photo opportunity in the margins of the United Nations General Assembly in September 2015, it was one of the shortest ever: just 13.5 seconds and the chilliest and most perfunctory of handshakes. So it may seem surprising that a hawkish Russian professor and pundit, of the sort who regularly consults for the government or writes op-ed pieces in the press about the coming decline of the 'American empire', would have a framed photo of it in his office. Asked about it, his dour face broke into a wicked grin: 'That was a meeting Obama didn't want to have, but we made him. We showed him that Russia could not be ignored.'

There were a number of reasons why Russian forces intervened in the vicious and bloody Syrian Civil War that year, but that certainly was one. At the time, Washington was trying diplomatically to isolate Moscow as punishment for its Ukrainian adventure. In response, the Kremlin was determined to inject itself into a conflict which mattered to the Americans to make it clear that they could not avoid having to engage with Russia and consider its interests – and an awkward photo opportunity was just an especially delicious example of this. The irony is that the more unhappy Obama and his team were, the more satisfied were the Russians, as it underlined the extent to which this was something forced upon them by necessity – and initially by just 50 aircraft.

A LONG, BLOODY WAR

Syria has been in turmoil since 2011 when demonstrations against President Bashar al-Assad's authoritarian regime, part of that year's wider Arab Spring wave of protests, were suppressed with extravagant brutality. Violence on both sides escalated, and a coordinated series of risings in major towns led the regime to unleash the army into the cities: by the end of May, an estimated thousand civilians and 150 members of the security forces were dead. The regime's heavy-handed tactics failed to quell the protests but instead served to exacerbate the crisis: peaceful protest soon turned into armed insurrection, and mass defections from the military led to the formation of the Free Syrian Army (FSA) rebel movement and in due course other groups, including the Kurdish–Arab Syrian Democratic Forces (SDF), the Islamic State of Iraq and the Levant and a range of other jihadist groups linked to Al-Qaeda.

By mid-2012, the FSA was receiving considerable support from the United States, and lesser amounts from the United Kingdom and France. With the rise of Islamic State, combating this force became as much of a priority for Washington as fighting Damascus, so by fits and starts US involvement grew, backing both the Kurds and the FSA against them. By 2016, US Special Forces were covertly being deployed in Syria both to fight and to train, but in 2017 the American role became more obvious when government forces used chemical weapons against the rebel town of Khan Shaykhun, killing at least 89 civilians and injuring more than 540. In response, the US Navy destroyers USS *Ross* and USS *Porter* fired 59 Tomahawk missiles at the government airbase in Shayrat, from which the chemical attack had been launched. However, Turkey was arguably an even more active participant in the war, having from the first supported and, along with Saudi Arabia and Qatar, armed the FSA – in Ankara's case as much as anything else to use it to put pressure on the Kurds. Given Turkey's long-running struggle against its own Kurds, it inevitably saw the SDF as a threat.

Russia, a long-time ally and military supplier of Syria's, had been more restrained in its earlier support for al-Assad. It had supplied weapons – largely on a cash basis – and technical help, especially with the country's air defence system. By 2014, shipments carried out by Black Sea Fleet vessels were so regular, with seven ships making ten round trips every year, that this was being dubbed the 'Syrian Express'. In addition, it had offered credits and financial help, but Russia's main role had been in providing a degree of political cover, not least at the United Nations. It had also tried repeatedly, if with no success, to broker some kind of accord between Damascus and some rebel groups. Until September 2015, though, arguably the most concrete assistance for the regime was coming from Iran and the Lebanese Hezbollah movement. Tehran provided not just political and financial assistance, but also Iranian Revolutionary Guard Corps trainers and specialists and, at least as important, money and logistical assistance for Hezbollah militia units to fight in support of Damascus.

By mid-2015, the al-Assad regime was in a precarious state, despite this help. Most of the country was in the hands of the various rebel groups, and even parts of Damascus were essentially no-go areas for government forces while Damascus International Airport was under regular bombardment. The regime had lost most of the country's oil fields, and was running out of money to pay its remaining forces. There was a very real fear that the whole regime could suddenly collapse, one more setback triggering a cascade of desertions and defections that would acquire its own momentum. Gerasimov later framed the situation starkly:

> If we had not intervened in Syria, what would have happened? Look, in 2015 just over 10% of the territory remained under government control. A month or two more, by the end of 2015, and Syria would have been completely under ISIS [Islamic State].[1]

A FRIEND IN NEED

Stumbling into this mess might have seemed a quixotic move at best, a stupid one at worse. After all, not only had Russia never intervened at scale into any conflict away from its own borders (and there were serious questions about its capacity to sustain any such commitment), but it seemed to be joining the losing side. From Moscow's point of view, though, there were some good reasons to get involved. There was, of course, the wider desire to force the West to realize that Russia could cause it problems in theatres far from its usual playground, so long as it was trying to isolate and marginalize it. Its support for the FSA and other elements became seen as yet another example of a Western strategy of toppling leaders not in its pocket through proxies and finally decisive military action.

To many in Moscow, this was Libya all over again. There, too, protests against the regime of capricious and authoritarian Muammar Gaddafi escalated into civil war. NATO airstrikes helped ensure that the rebels won, with Gaddafi himself being summarily executed in October 2011. There was a strong belief in the Kremlin that the West had effectively conned then-president Medvedev by convincing him not to veto a UN resolution approving airstrikes as a last resort to protect civilians and then using that as the justification to hammer Gaddafi's forces. There was also a suspicion that this was a blueprint for a new Western way of 'hybrid war', stirring up unrest and then using that to topple regimes of which it disapproved, which often seemed to be ones with good relations with Russia. To the Kremlin, that deception needed to be avenged, and this approach defeated in the future.

Beyond that, there was also a more specific desire to intervene to protect an ally – one of Russia's very few, after all. If Moscow was not willing to help, Damascus would have no alternative but to become wholly dependent on Tehran, the only other power willing to support it. Iran, after all, is perhaps best characterized as a 'frenemy' for Russia: Tehran and Moscow often have certain interests in common, especially when it comes to pushing back US influence from the Middle East, but they are also competitors for regional influence.

Finally, there was a sense that they could: the Russian military had long contacts with their Syrian counterparts and had been watching the war closely, and their assessment was that a light footprint intervention, relying mainly on airpower, could turn the tide. Furthermore, the distance between Syria and Russia, while a logistical challenge, ironically also made the adventure a little safer a bet. Moscow was determined to keep its commitment very limited, and one that could easily also be withdrawn. Unlike the Soviet invasion of Afghanistan or later involvement in Ukraine and other post-Soviet states, the chance of direct blowback was limited. To put it very bluntly, if Syria nonetheless fell into murderous anarchy, it was safely far from Russia's borders.

On the other hand, there was a fear – genuine, if perhaps a little over-stated for public consumption, to make the war more meaningful to a sceptical Russian public – that if Damascus fell, it would be to radical Islamists, and that this would hearten terrorists closer to home. Again, to quote Gerasimov:

> [Had Damascus fallen] ISIS would have continued to gather momentum and would have spread to adjacent countries. We would have had to confront that force on our own territory. They would be operating in the Caucasus, Central Asia, and [Russia's] Volga region.[2]

HEADING TO HMEYMIM

In July, Bashar al-Assad had formally requested military assistance, and on 26 August an agreement was signed that granted Moscow free use of the Basel al-Assad airbase, which the Russians call Hmeymim, some 50 kilometres north of Russia's very modest naval facility of Tartus which, at the time, was scarcely much more than a couple of piers and some warehouses. In Russian parlance, it was not even a base, but a mere Material-Technical Support Point. However, by then preparations were already at an advanced stage, and the actual decision had probably been made at the start of the month. As usual, there are no definitive accounts of how the decision to intervene was made. As with Crimea, Putin convened a small circle of his trusted allies, apparently Presidential Administration head Ivanov, Security Council Secretary Patrushev, and Defence Minister Shoigu. In 2014, over Crimea, Shoigu had been uncomfortable with a military adventure, but this time he seems to have been much more bullish, not least because Gerasimov was reassuring him that the military could handle it.

There was a clear appreciation from the first within the General Staff that the intervention was going to require a serious effort to address issues relating to command and control, not so much because it was being fought far from the Motherland but because this was such a messy conflict. After all, there was an army in disarray, multiple government forces (including the Syrian Arab Army, the elite Republican Guard and other paramilitaries), and Iranian- and Hezbollah-backed and dominated and pro-government militias. Thus, this saw the inauguration of the new National Defence Management

Centre (NTsUO: *Natsionalny Tsentr Upravleniya Oboronoi*), described in Chapter 29, which had become fully operational at the end of 2014. A Combat Management Group (GBU: *Gruppa Boyevovo Upravleniya*) was set up within the NTsUO, to provide overall direction and support for the battlefield commander who would operate out of Hmeymim. The first commander of what would be the Group of Forces in Syria (GVS: *Gruppirovka Voisk v Sirii*) was to be Col. Gen. Alexander Dvornikov, the chief of staff of the Central Military District, a man already with a reputation for imagination and flexibility.

By the middle of September, aircraft were flying to Syria, through the airspace of Iran and Iraq (with their permission), such that by 30 September, when the Russian parliament rubber-stamped a request for them to be used in combat operations, there were 33 aircraft in-theatre: 12 Su-24M2 bombers, 12 Su-25SM/UB ground attack aircraft, four Su-34 bombers, and four S-30SM heavy multi-role fighters, along with one reconnaissance aircraft, an Il-20M. There was also a helicopter wing of 12 Mi-24P gunships and five Mi-8AMTSh transports. The Russian bases were protected by Naval Infantry from the 810th Brigade, supported by a company of T-90A tanks, along with a battery of S-300V4 long-range SAMs, which was later supplemented with another to extend the air-defence umbrella across eastern Syria.

Over time, the contingent would wax and wane in line with the needs of the campaign. After Turkey shot down a Su-24 in November, for example, it would acquire four advanced Su-35 air superiority fighters, four more Su-34s and Mi-35 gunships. As it became clear that the Syrian troops would also need more than just air support, artillery units were also brought in, along with *Spetsnaz*, especially from the KSSO Special Operations Command, for target designation and other missions. In addition, the network of Russian advisors within the Syrian command structure – often they were actually leading units as much as anything else – steadily expanded.

At the time, there had been a real question amongst Western observers as to whether Russia could truly sustain such an operation. I recall one Washington-based pundit predicting that by the end of the year, 'planes will be breaking down due to poor maintenance, which probably won't make a great difference as they'll already have run out of precision munitions, or even fuel'. Once, he no doubt would have been right, but the Russian military was in a very different place compared with, say,

2008. Aircraft were rotated or properly maintained, and the supplies kept coming. There was a constraint on the number of landing ships available for the 'Syrian Express', but the Russians simply bought bulk cargo ships from Turkey to supplement this sea lift capacity. Meanwhile, Il-76 transports and a few of the mammoth An-124 airlifters kept up an airbridge for resupply. In 2018 alone, for example, 1,608,000 tons of supplies and equipment were brought in via 342 supply trips by sea and 2,278 by air.

HMEYMIN'S HAMMER

The VKS forces deployed to Syria lost no time in making their presence felt on the battlefield. Within a few hours of the final parliamentary approval, they had started launching airstrikes. That first day saw 20 sorties, hitting both FSA and Islamic State positions, followed by more the next few days that concentrated on Islamic State forces and command centres. This wave of airstrikes – typically around 30 sorties a day in the first week of operations – was coordinated with an offensive by Syrian forces against the Islamic State-held town of Al-Qaryatayn in the contested province of Homs. The Russians also extended their operations to Raqqa, the unofficial capital of Islamic State in Syria. On 8 October, after the strike by naval *Kalibr* missiles, for the next couple of days, the tempo of air attacks increased to over 60 sorties every 24 hours, hammering the rebels with everything from unguided rockets to KAB-500KR precision-guided bombs, which reportedly killed more than 200 Islamic State fighters, including two of their commanders in one strike. The aim was clear, to provide a devastating and convincing demonstration that the Russians had arrived and meant business: to hearten their Syrian allies, demoralize the rebels, and warn off the West.

Over time, the Russians would not only cycle a majority of their aircrews through Syria, but they also deployed a wide range of aircraft, from the later Su-57 stealth fighter (two of which spent two days in Syria in February 2018 for combat trials) to a Tu-214R intelligence-gathering platform. At peak, from mid-2016 to late 2017, the GVS air contingent comprised up to 44 jets, increasingly more modern Su-34s and Su-35s, along with helicopters, transports and reconnaissance aircraft. In addition, though, the Russians used the campaign to further their growing fascination with the use of drones. Rather than use them to launch attacks themselves, as is often Western practice, their use is to locate enemy forces to allow artillery and air fires to be directed against them, often to devastating effect. The Russians have largely been using the *Orlan*-10, which beams real-time video back to its operators. This even allowed the Russians quickly to locate the surviving crewman from the Su-24 shot down by the Turks in November, so that a rapid response team of marines could rescue him before he was killed or captured by rebels.

As well as airpower, the GVS deployed substantial amounts of artillery, often with Syrian crews under Russian officers. At different times, the full range of systems have been used, from massive TOS-1A Solntsepyok thermobaric rocket launchers and 152mm Msta-B howitzers to the ubiquitous 120mm Grad multiple-launch rocket systems. They also used *Iskander* (SS-26) short-range ballistic missiles to hit high-value targets, including rebel command posts and arms and ammunition dumps. They were periodically supplemented by long-range strikes by ship- and submarine-launched *Kalibr* (SS-N-27/SS-N-30A) cruise missiles which were as much about testing and showcasing the system as prosecuting the war, starting with a 26-missile volley from a frigate and three corvettes of the Caspian Flotilla on 7 October 2015, hitting both FSA and Islamic State targets. In November 2016, even one of the *Bastion*-P coastal defence missile systems based at Tartus, presumably to deter any Western interference with the 'Syrian Express', launched two supersonic *Oniks* missiles against inland rebel ammunition stores.

However, it soon became clear that the Russians could not simply rely on long-range firepower. The Syrian military was, in 2015–17, just too weak to operate on its own. Although any major Ground Forces commitment was out of the question, there did need to be something there beyond advisors to provide certain technical capabilities (especially spotting for artillery and airstrikes and electronic warfare), a stiffening of the Syrian army's backbone and an assault force for tougher operations, especially taking defended cities.

TURNING THE TIDE

This was – and as of writing, remains – a confused and confusing war, one in which multiple rebel movements combine and divide and

are as often fighting each other as the government. Charting the full
ebb and flow between the Russian intervention and mid-2022 would
legitimately fill a book in its own right. While the next chapter will drill
down into some specific battles to illustrate wider lessons of the war to
date, the broad trajectory is as follows.

After Moscow's intervention, 2015 and 2016 saw escalating Russian
involvement, starting with airstrikes and moving into the deployment
of limited ground assets, especially special forces and Wagner Group
mercenaries, alongside Iranian and Hezbollah elements. In November
2015, in response to its bombing of a Russian civilian airliner flying
from Sharm El Sheikh in Egypt to St Petersburg – which killed all 224
passengers and crew on board – the Russians turned their attention on
Islamic State. As well as their forces at Hmeymim, they used Tu-160
and Tu-95MS strategic bombers flying out of Russian airfields to launch
long-range cruise missiles and smaller Tu-22M3s to drop conventional
bombs. As well as obvious military targets, they focused on Islamic
State oil production, refining and transport facilities, and managed to
deliver a devastating blow to the group's economy. Nonetheless, this
was a brief, if devastating campaign, and soon enough the Russians
turned back to the so-called 'moderate rebel' factions – which tended to
mean US-backed – posing the most immediate threat to the regime. By
the end of 2016, the regime was looking much more stable politically,
not least because it had retaken much territory, including the key city of
Aleppo, which fell after a long and brutal offensive in which government
forces allegedly used chemical weapons. Meanwhile, Turkey had begun
to launch offensives against Kurdish forces inside Syria, essentially
staking out territory along the border and in the north-western corner
of the country and controlling them through Sunni Arab rebel forces,
often of jihadist bent.

The overall situation was still complex, not least because many areas
under government control were enclaves within regions either held by
rebels or where there was no effective control. In 2017, then, the focus
shifted to connecting some of these enclaves to project Assad's power
more strongly into the countryside. Damascus itself was still one such
enclave, with suburbs to its south and north-east held by rebels since
2013, but by mid-2018, these too had been retaken.

Meanwhile, the Kurdish SDF, with US support, was pushing Islamic
State back, and in October 2017 had taken their capital, Raqqa. At

the same time, Russian and government forces had been fighting a campaign to push Islamic State from the central desert and drive them out of Deir ez-Zor on the Euphrates River, the largest city in eastern Syria, which was accomplished by November. Having once briefly looked as if their advance was unstoppable, then, Islamic State had been pushed back to only one-twentieth of its former holdings and were essentially beaten in Syria.

Rebels were being driven out of Ghouta, east of Damascus, and an offensive launched in south-western Syria, which saw FSA-held Daraa, birthplace of the original uprising, fall in July 2017. As more and more cities were returned to government control, the former provincial capital of Idlib in the north-west of the country became a renewed bone of contention. It had long been a rebel stronghold, and although government forces had retaken it in 2012, they had been driven out in 2015 by the 'Army of Conquest', led by the al-Nusra Front. To an extent, Idlib had been a useful safety valve, a safe haven for refugees and rebels whom Damascus could allow to flee there to clear them from elsewhere. As it looked as if this might change, Turkey – fearing the influx of millions of refugees if it fell – began making belligerent noises, while Damascus seemed ready to call Ankara's bluff. Russia was not ready to risk having to fight Turkey and so in September 2018, it brokered a deconfliction deal that effectively imposed a rough-and-ready stalemate on the area. This suited the Russians well enough for now, but it hinted at potential problems in the future.

At the end of 2018, US president Donald Trump announced that as Islamic State had been defeated, all American forces would be withdrawn from Syria. He partly walked back the decision under pressure from his officials, but from then it was clear that Washington was no longer a committed player in the war. In October 2019, most remaining US troops pulled out ahead of a major Turkish offensive against Kurdish-led SDF areas, abandoning them to their fate. The Americans had been providing top cover for the SDF and so, looking to the lesser of two evils, the SDF struck a deal with the Russians: they allowed Syrian and Russian forces into their territory in return for protection from Ankara.

While the Turks were prosecuting their war against the SDF, the Russians and Syrians continued to mop up remaining FSA holdouts. A series of offensives in the second half of 2019 saw them drive further into northern regions, and the humanitarian crisis there reached

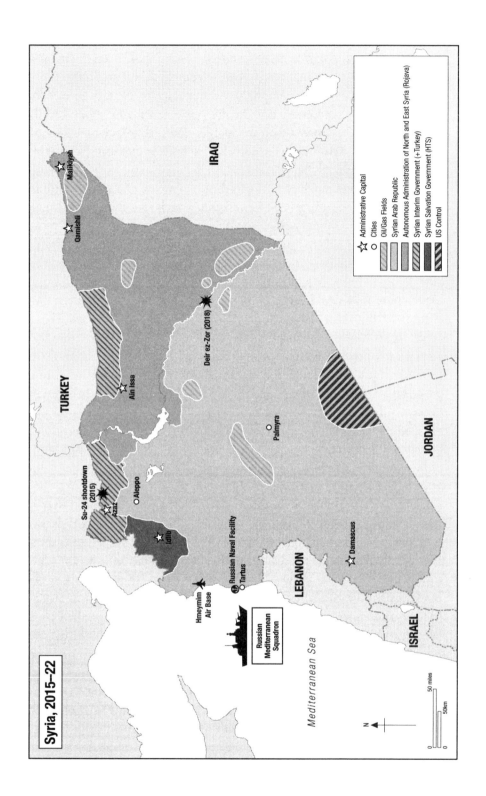

Syria, 2015–22

Administrative Capital
Cities
Oil/Gas Fields
Syrian Arab Republic
Autonomous Administration of North and East Syria (Rojava)
Syrian Interim Government (+Turkey)
Syrian Salvation Government (HTS)
US Control

TURKEY

IRAQ

JORDAN

LEBANON

ISRAEL

Mediterranean Sea

Malikiyah
Qamishli
Ain Issa
Deir ez-Zor (2018)
Su-24 shootdown (2015)
Azaz
Aleppo
Idlib
Palmyra
Damascus
Russian Naval Facility
Tartus
Hmeymim Air Base
Russian Mediterranean Squadron

N

50 miles
50km

such a pitch that Ankara again came to fear a flood of more refugees. Meanwhile, the Idlib agreement had collapsed, as Syrian forces – with Russian backing – had again tried to take the city, while Turkey had failed to fulfil its commitments to disarm and demobilize jihadi groups in the region. Once more, the risk of a Russo-Turkish clash seemed to be growing, but again both sides were ultimately more keen to talk than fight. After weeks of fighting between their proxies, in March 2020, they agreed a new ceasefire that saw joint patrols and the creation of a security corridor along the key M4 motorway, which connects the government-held cities of Aleppo and Latakia.

VICTORY OF SORTS

Since then, and as of early 2022, a new status quo has largely held. Damascus controls most of the cities and about two-thirds of the country, up from less than a third in 2014. There have been attempts to create a pretence of normality, including a predictably rigged election in 2021 that saw Assad re-elected, but the country is in ruins. Various peace talks – UN-brokered ones in Geneva, the Russian-backed 'Astana Process' – have come to nothing. Over 12 million Syrians – around half the pre-war population – are refugees: 5.5 million abroad, 6.7 million internally displaced.

Nonetheless, from the perspective of Moscow – and Assad – the intervention has been a success. The regime is looking more like a working state again. Its armed forces still bear the scars of past defeats, but have regained much of their capacity and morale. Islamic State is essentially beaten in this particular battlespace, Turkey confined to the north, and the United States withdrawn. Although Iran is still a significant partner, and its Hezbollah proxies continue to play a role, Russia is the unquestioned main patron of the regime. With that, it has acquired a renewed stake in the Middle East and also the eastern Mediterranean, and even managed to maintain its relations with Israel, even while it bombed Russia's allies, and one of its own aircraft got caught in the crossfire. After all, Damascus's alliance of necessity with Iran and Hezbollah inevitably saw it caught up in the wider conflict between Tehran and Jerusalem. Moscow, by contrast, was eager not to get involved – indeed, it may even have been quite happy to see the Israelis, with whom the Russians had good relations, giving the Iranians a hard time. Periodically, the Israelis would launch airstrikes on Iranian and Hezbollah forces, having first notified the Russians. They, in turn, would switch off their advanced air defence systems and pointedly sit the engagement out. On 17 September 2018, a Russian Il-20M 'Coot-A' electronic intelligence aircraft was over the eastern Mediterranean, returning to Hmeymim, when four Israeli F-16s launched an attack on targets in Latakia. The Syrians engaged them with their 1960s-vintage S-200 (SA-5) SAMs and one hit the Il-20M, downing it and killing all 15 of its crew. Despite suggestions that the Israelis were using it as cover, the truth seems to be that the Syrians were either firing semi-blind because of Israeli jamming or that the identification friend or foe (IFF) systems which should have identified the spyplane as a friend were not working. Israel issued an apology, and Putin dismissed the shoot-down as the result of 'a chain of tragic accidental circumstances'[3] – but the Russians did then supply the Syrians with more modern S-300s that were not only more effective but also more likely not to lead to similar blunders in the future.

Moscow had proven that it could project power far from its borders. Its aircraft turned the tide of the war. Tartus, once little more than a naval corner shop, was built up with expanded maintenance and repair facilities and even a floating dock, and Russian warships became an increasingly common sight in the region. At least as important, though, were the lessons of the war for the Russians, and to those we now turn.

18

Syria, 2015– (2): Lessons of the Syrian Campaign

Even more than Chechnya or the Donbas, the Syrian War was a learning opportunity for the Russians.[1] Many soldiers served a three to four-month tour there, including most senior Ground Forces commanders and more than half of brigade- or regiment-level commanders, while the majority of the VKS's pilots have, as of the start of 2022, at least some genuine combat experience in its skies. The war has allowed the Russians to test and refine tactics and, especially, their command and control systems, as well as posing new challenges for their logistical chains. They have showcased new weapons like the *Kalibr* cruise missile and been able to experiment with how they use others, from precision-guided munitions to drones. Much of this has fed into the wider evolution of the modern Russian military, discussed in later chapters. However, certain engagements illustrate certain very specific lessons of the campaign.

AIRPOWER IS NOT (USUALLY) ENOUGH

In May 2015, Islamic State had captured the historic and strategic city of Palmyra in what had been its largest offensive in Syria to date, imposing a bloody reign of terror that saw scores of supposed government sympathizers executed in the main square. In July, Syrian forces tried to recapture it, but were driven back. Col. Gen. Alexander Dvornikov, the first commander of the GVS, wanted to test the forces at his disposal before turning to the more significant target of Aleppo; he was also shortly due to return to Russia and it may be that he wanted a headline victory to his credit. Either way, the decision was made to take back Palmyra.

The initial plan had been for the offensive to be launched by Syrian forces, supported by Russian airpower. Palmyra was a hard target, though, with more than 2,000 Islamic State defenders, behind a ring of trenches and strongpoints. Although the Central Command in Damascus was apparently bullish, Dvornikov's own commanders were much less confident that most Syrian forces, with the exception of some elite forces such as the Republican Guard's Marine Regiment and Air Force Intelligence's Tiger Forces, had the stomach for close-quarters urban battle. They were also unconvinced that Syrian scouts were yet able to provide the kind of accurate and timely targeting information that would really make their air attacks count.

To this end, the Russians quietly committed the deniable 'pseudo-mercenary' force known as the Wagner Group to provide a reserve of shock troops for the assault, while teams of special forces operators from KSSO would act as forward air and artillery observers. Although their role was downplayed at the time, not least to save Damascus's blushes, several officers involved in the Syrian operations have since confirmed that they were crucial in tipping the balance; as one put it, 'It often wasn't about firepower but determination – they held the line when a small retreat could have triggered a rout.'

The operation began on 9 March 2016 with rocket and artillery barrages and extensive airstrikes: 15–20 sorties on each of the first few days. After three days to soften up the defenders, the Syrians began to attack strongpoints on three sides of the city, as well as heights which commanded it. They did not move quickly, but they did manage to take their objectives, helped by the confusion created when a Russian rocket hit the headquarters of Khalil Mohameed, Islamic State's 'emir' of the city, killing him and several of his staff. So far, though, the Syrians had been able to rely on concentrating strength of numbers on isolated targets; as they approached Palmyra itself, there would be no more easy victories. On 17 March, though, a sudden sandstorm gave Islamic State an opportunity to counter-attack, and although it was beaten back, this seems to have shaken the morale of the government troops. Syrian Marines and veteran Hezbollah militia were rushed to the front line, but at this point Dvornikov decided not only to deploy Wagner but to order the KSSO teams closer to the city to try to target any further attacks. His fear, according to someone who was on his staff at the time, was that another sally might trigger a Syrian rout. He also stepped up the tempo of air attacks, with up to 25 sorties a day.

The methodical pace continued – Dvornikov simply did not feel he could rely on the Syrians for anything more daring. The airstrikes were having a significant impact on Islamic State, especially thanks to the KSSO spotters who were having to put themselves in harm's way. One, for example, was 25-year-old KSSO operator Senior Lt. Alexander Prokhorenko. On 17 March, he was separated from the rest of his team when he encountered some Islamic State fighters retreating from their failed counter-attack. Pinned down and surrounded, there seemed no hope for him, so as his last fire order, he called down an airstrike on his own position, ensuring that they too would share his fate. He was posthumously awarded the Hero of Russia.

Nonetheless, at this stage all Russia's artillery and bombers could do was disrupt – the battle would be won or lost on the ground. Meanwhile, more reinforcements for the government side arrived: militias of the National Defence Force and Iranian-supported Shi'ites. This campaign had to end in victory, if it was to help the Syrian forces begin to regain their confidence, and Dvornikov and the Central Command were willing to throw in whatever it took.

By 24 March, the attackers were just outside the city and that evening they started pushing their way in. The offensive degenerated into a series of attacks on heavily defended strategic objectives, such as Palmyra Prison and the Semiramis Hotel, and here Wagner's veterans were often crucial in forcing the attack. Fighting was fierce, and as neither Damascus nor Moscow wanted to be accused of risking the historic ruins to the west of the city, artillery and air support was largely limited to other neighbourhoods. By the 27th, the city was back in government hands, bar some final mopping up. It was badly damaged, and Islamic State left hundreds of landmines that Russian and Syrian engineers would take over a month to clear.

Symbolically, on 5 May, the Mariinsky Theatre Orchestra and virtuoso cellist (and old friend of Putin's) Sergei Roldugin performed a concert, at the Roman amphitheatre of Palmyra, dedicated to Prokhorenko's memory. Although Islamic State would briefly recapture the city again

in December 2016, only to lose it the next year. The government victory
in March at Palmyra had demonstrated to the Russians that they could
not rely entirely on arm's length 'non-contact' firepower so long as their
allies could not be trusted to exploit this advantage on the ground. On
the other hand, though, it confirmed their belief that relatively small
numbers of the right men at the right place can have a disproportionate
impact. More than 7,000 soldiers had been deployed to the attack,
of whom Wagner seem to have provided possibly as few as 300, but
their presence at the front in the assault helped maintain the necessary
momentum to take the city.

Likewise, fewer than a hundred *Spetsnaz* were present there, some as
snipers, most as forward air and artillery controllers. Nonetheless, they
allowed the Russian airstrikes to be much more precise and effective
than they would otherwise have been, and for them to be launched
safely closer to the precious ruins of Palmyra. In short, although there
was already a general understanding in both Moscow and Hmeymim
that airpower alone cannot win such a war, as one Russian officer put
it in 2017, 'This battle helped quickly to demonstrate to some of the
more extreme proponents of "non-contact warfare" the limitations of
the approach.' Ironically, in his opinion, both the Ground Forces and
the Aerospace Forces quickly generated their own spin: the groundhogs
used it to underline their continued centrality, while the pilots could
excuse any mistakes they made by blaming insufficient targeting
assistance from them.

MERCENARIES HAVE THEIR PLACE, BUT NEED TO KNOW IT

On 7 February 2018, a force of some 500 Syrian troops from the
so-called 'ISIS Hunters' unit of the 5th Corps, Iranian-trained militias
and Wagner Group mercenaries approached an SDF post near the
town of Khasham, on the Euphrates route towards Deir ez-Zor, which
the SDF had captured from Islamic State the year before. They crossed
the river and began shelling the post. However, the Americans had a
significant presence here and close ties with the local SDF. Indeed,
there were US Special Forces operators at that post. Of course, US
reconnaissance had seen this force assemble and begin moving days
before, and as it neared Khasham, they used their deconfliction line

to Hmeymim, as well as turning to their GVS liaison officer in Deir ez-Zor itself, to ask what was going on. Were these Russian forces? Nothing to do with us, was the reply. So the Americans felt free to make something of a display of the firepower at their disposal. In response to its attack, the force was targeted by everything from B-52 bombers and F-15E Strike Eagle jets to rocket artillery and missiles fired from AH-64 gunships. The attack was shattered in four hours of hell, suffering more than 200 casualties, including perhaps a couple of dozen Wagner mercenaries. One SDF soldier was injured in the initial attack, and no Americans were hurt.

Was this a Russian blunder? Was the command in Hmeymim simply too embarrassed to admit Wagner's presence? Actually, what seems to have happened is that while in 2015 and 2016, the GVS needed the mercenaries, in 2017 it decided their job was done. The Syrian military was in better shape, and the over-paid and all-too-cocky mercenaries – who might be being paid twice or even three times as much as the regular soldiers and posted to the GVS, and were not shy about saying so – were no longer needed.

At peak, Wagner had maintained a force of some 2,500 mercenaries in Syria, in four battalion-strength, three-company line units, a tank company with T-72s, an artillery battalion, a reconnaissance company, and support elements. This was expensive to maintain, and by 2017, payments from the Defence Ministry had stopped or at least begun to taper off (accounts vary). But the Kremlin wanted Wagner to be maintained, in case it was needed somewhere else, and Yevgeny Prigozhin, the businessman charged with this duty, thus looked to make cuts and find new opportunities. By all accounts, from early 2017, the quality of Wagner's new hires and replacement kit began to decline, as they could no longer afford to pay so well. More importantly, in January 2018, a deal was struck between Syria's Energy Ministry and EvroPolis, another of Prigozhin's companies, that meant that the latter would get a quarter of all the oil and gas revenues from areas Wagner retook for the government. And Deir ez-Zor has both oil and gas. This was war as business, as Prigozhin tried to balance the books.[2]

This was nothing to do with the GVS, which seemed only too happy to let the Americans teach the overweening mercenaries a lesson. After Deir ez-Zor, although Wagner would later crop up in a range of other conflicts, from Libya to Venezuela, its role in Syria shrank dramatically. The Russian military had learned that private military companies could be valuable instruments for both deniable operations and quick boosts to capacity, and would in fact go on to create their own. However, they also came to realize how important it was to avoid the danger of, shall we say, the tail Wagnering the dog: the mercenaries need to know who's boss.

BRUTALITY CAN WORK, BUT HEARTS AND MINDS MATTER, TOO

Since 2013, Aleppo, Syria's largest city, had been effectively divided, with loyalists holding the west of the city, the FSA the east. Having defused any immediate threat from Islamic State, in July 2016 the stalemate was broken when government forces managed to encircle the rebel-held parts of the city, cutting their supply lines. After weathering several serious but unsuccessful counter-attacks, in November they launched their own major offensive on the rebel positions, forcing them to evacuate the city the next month.

Taking Eastern Aleppo was a brutal exercise in pragmatic modern siegecraft. Supply routes were cut, and humanitarian assistance to the 300,000-strong civilian population in the rebel-held neighbourhoods blocked. It was no easy task, to be sure, but by September, government forces had closed their grip. Despite another rebel counter-offensive, government forces were able slowly to push them back, and by the end of October they were in control of about half of Eastern Aleppo.

They were able to do this in part because of a massive and sustained bombing campaign that mixed targeted and indiscriminate raids. Russian VKS forces were more precise, but the strong suspicion is that they deliberately targeted not just military objectives but also aid stations and hospitals, to make life in besieged Aleppo unendurable. The Syrians were even more brutal. As well as a couple of reported uses of chlorine gas – banned under international law – they made widespread use of 'barrel bombs', crude improvised munitions that were little more than oil drums or the like, stuffed with explosive and metal fragments. Rolled out of helicopters, they were the dumbest of bombs, but also the most vicious, with the largest packed with almost a tonne of TNT and shrapnel. These were terror weapons; with no real attempt to aim them at military targets, they hit homes and shops, mosques and hospitals, schools and shelters. At peak, Aleppo was being hit by as many as 1,500 a month. Indeed, on 19 September 2016, Syrian helicopters hit a UN/Red Crescent aid convoy heading to Aleppo as well as a clinic in a rebel-held town near Aleppo with a combination of barrel bombs and rockets. More often, though, they were simply dumped out of helicopters in the vicinity of strategic objectives, on the principle that while most would not hit their target, they would still hit *something*, spreading terror and carnage behind the rebel lines. As a survivor recounted, Aleppo became a 'circle of hell', whose 'streets are filled with blood'.[3]

By mid-December, most of the city was either in government hands or essentially no one's, with the exception of Sheikh Maqsood neighbourhood, a predominantly Kurdish district controlled by its own People's Protection Units (YPG). While technically connected to the wider rebel FSA, in practice the Kurds had stuck to defending their own territory and at times had fought both the government and rebels. In any case, at this point, the aim of the Russian and Syrian forces was simply to expel the rest of the rebels, and those civilians deemed to be potentially their sympathizers. After a couple of false starts, interspersed with periods of intense bombardment, 'humanitarian corridors' were established that allowed both fighters and civilians to leave, mainly to the rebellious Idlib Province, where a spectrum of guerrilla forces from the FSA to jihadists were still in contention. By 22 December 2016, the evacuation was over and Damascus was claiming to have complete control over the city – or at least what was left of it, strewn with the remains of the estimated 31,000 men, women and children who died in this four-year siege.

Aleppo had needed to be taken, and taken as quickly as possible, hence the ruthless tactics employed. However, the Russians also demonstrated an awareness that in a complex civil war like Syria's, hearts and minds operations were also vital. They provided food parcels and demined civilian neighbourhoods (indeed, they quickly set up aid and medical stations in Aleppo), and brought order to areas which had been terrorized by bandits and jihadists. Engineers were deployed to conduct mine clearance missions (and from 2017, train Syrian sappers at new training centres established in Aleppo and Homs), as well as bridge rivers, clear roads and generally assist the mobility of the Syrian and allied forces. Furthermore, as the areas under government control expanded, the need for troops able to carry out rear-area security, humanitarian and deconfliction missions increased, especially as ceasefires began to be brokered on various fronts.

Since December 2016, this has become a primary mission of a sizeable contingent of the Russian Military Police (VP: *Voyennaya Politsiya*), a force that only became fully operational in 2014. With their distinctive red berets and brassards, they have become the official face of the GVS on the ground, and by 2020, a majority of the entire Military Police force had rotated through Syria. Furthermore, to increase their ability to find common ground with the locals, two special VP battalions were established in 2016, each of some 600 men recruited from the predominantly Muslim regions of Tatarstan and the North Caucasus. Indeed, according to unconfirmed reports, at least one battalion may actually have been *Kadyrovtsy*, the personal forces of Chechen autocrat Ramzan Kadyrov. Technically members of the National Guard, they were, it is claimed, transferred temporarily to the VP as part of Kadyrov's 'penance' for having ordered or sanctioned the murder of prominent opposition figure – and relentless Kadyrov critic – Boris Nemtsov in Moscow in February 2015. Nonetheless, in their own way they do demonstrate a growing sophistication in Russian 'hearts and minds' operations.

FRENEMIES CAN FIND THEMSELVES IN BATTLE

On 24 November 2015, two Russian Su-24M bombers were returning to Hmeymim after a sortie against rebels in northern Syria. As had become usual for Russian pilots on this run, they were cutting briefly into Turkish airspace, over a small piece of land that protruded into northern Syria. Two Turkish F-16s, which had deliberately been patrolling at low altitude, engaged them, 17 seconds after they crossed the border. An AIM-120 AMRAAM missile hit one bomber. Both of the aircrew ejected: the pilot was gunned down by Syrian Turkmen Brigade fighters while still descending on his parachute, the weapon officer was recovered in a search and rescue mission conducted under fire by Naval Infantry in two Mi-8AMTSh helicopters, but one marine was also killed in the operation.

Turkish strongman Recep Tayyip Erdoğan had clearly been irked by the repeated incursions, however brief, especially as they were bombing

Turkish-backed rebels, which is why this aerial ambush had been laid. A visibly furious Putin placed sanctions on Turkish goods, but Erdoğan in many ways out-Putined Putin and refused to back down. In due course, the Russians quietly relented. After all, despite their divergent interests in Syria, one of the most interesting relationships Russia has developed in recent years is with Turkey, a NATO member, but one that feels itself something of a neglected outsider, especially as the European Union is clearly reluctant to make it a member. (A common observation among Turks is that the Europeans are 'happy for Turks to fight for them, happy for Turks to work for them, but not happy to let Turks join them'.)

Erdoğan has clear ambitions for a sphere of influence in the Balkans and the Middle East, which makes Turkey a regional rival for Russia, something that really came to the fore during the 2020 Nagorno–Karabakh War (see Chapter 28). Yet it also means that Ankara and Moscow share certain common interests and above all something of a common approach to geopolitics. As a former Russian official put it to me, 'with the Turks, we don't always agree, but we can always talk to them'.

Turkey had backed its 'own' rebel forces from at least 2013, suborning elements of the FSA such as the Syrian Turkmen Brigade, especially because it was wary of the ethnic Kurds of north-eastern Syria, who make up about 10% of the country's total population. The concern was that if they were too successful in establishing their own militias and de facto nation, they would be allies and an inspiration to Turkey's own unruly Kurds. As a result, Ankara was hostile not just to Damascus but also to the broadly based Syrian Democratic Forces, not least because the YPG were their single most effective SDF element. As well as Islamic State, the SDF was often in contention with Turkish-backed rebel groups, and so there was sometimes a complex 'enemy of my enemy is my friend' relationship between Moscow and Damascus and the SDF – and between Ankara and Islamic State.

Likewise, Ankara and Moscow managed to hammer out some kind of an understanding when the earlier de-escalation agreement over Idlib was broken in December 2019, when Syrian and Russian aircraft launched Operation *Dawn of Idlib 2*, a major bombing campaign on what was one of the last remaining rebel-held areas. The Turks were already unhappy about the upsurge in refugees crossing their border, but in February 2020, 33 Turkish soldiers were killed when a Syrian airstrike hit one of their border military posts. In response, Turkey's Operation *Spring Shield* saw artillery bombardments and air and drone strikes launched against government forces. Reportedly, more than 300 government and Hezbollah troops were killed and several Syrian planes downed; Turkey lost more than 40 men and four drones. The danger was that Russia would be sucked in, but instead Presidents Erdoğan and Putin met in Moscow and concluded another and more serious de-escalation agreement that saw joint Russian and Turkish patrols monitoring a ceasefire.

In a way, one could expect two similarly ambitious and aggressive autocrats to be able to reach pragmatic deals. For Moscow, though, at least as striking was the way that, as one Russian Foreign Ministry staffer put it, 'we learned Americans can be sensible, too'. By sensible, he meant pragmatic. Given that one of the drivers behind the intervention had been to challenge Washington's efforts diplomatically to isolate it, it is hardly surprising that Russia and the US often found themselves at loggerheads. Nonetheless, however contradictory their goals – in 2016, President Obama warned that 'the Assad regime cannot slaughter its way to legitimacy'[4] – both countries were very careful to avoid direct engagement. After the brutal attack on Aleppo, for example, Washington abandoned talks about sharing intelligence against Islamic State, but they maintained official and unofficial lines of communication with the Russians to avoid accidental clashes. In 2017, as US-backed forces pushed against Islamic State east of the Euphrates, and Russian-backed forces moved in from the west, Washington and Moscow developed strong deconfliction arrangements. The one seeming failure of this process, the Deir ez-Zor incident discussed above, was not actually a failure at all: it is not that the Russians were not involved, it was that they washed their hands of Wagner.

A NICE LITTLE WAR IS GOOD FOR BUSINESS

Syria has provided a showcase for the latest Russian weapons, no doubt in part with an eye to sales. Igor Kozhin, presidential assistant for military-technical cooperation, linked increased interest in Russian weapons to the conflict, noting that 'countries of the Middle East want to buy our weapons, which have proven their effectiveness' in Syria.[5]

Admittedly, not every would-be exercise in showmanship worked. When the aircraft carrier *Kuznetsov* was sent to fly the flag and hammer the rebels, it did so, but also lost two of its planes: a MiG-29K that fell into the sea when it ran out of fuel, and a Su-33 which crashed when the arresting cable meant to slow it on landing failed. While repairs were made, the air wing had to transfer to Hmeymin.

However, it has been rather more useful for the professional soldiers. Although the practical impact of four-month in-country tours of duty should not be overstated just as, in the words of security scholar Pavel Baev, 'a return flight to [Hmeymin] cannot make the Su-57 a combat-tested fighter',[6] it has had a value in blooding the officer corps, weeding out some who proved unable to cope in genuine action, and creating a greater sense of esprit de corps. The most able have been able to rise faster, new approaches to command and control have been tested, and above all, Russia's capacity to wage a successful intervention war in a complex battlespace far from its own borders has been demonstrated. This all stands as testament to the successful reform of all the arms of service, as will be considered in the following chapters.

PART FOUR
Rearming Russia

19

Rumble for Ruble

The question from the auditorium was the usual one: 'How can Russia, with a defence budget close to the United Kingdom's, afford to field a million-man army?' This was at an event at the Royal Military Academy Sandhurst, but I've fielded variations on the same question at locales from Naval Station Norfolk in Virginia to the Führungsakademie der Bundeswehr in Hamburg. And it seems an entirely fair question. According to the official projections in 2019 (before COVID-19 upended everyone's spending plans), Russia would be allocating 3.1 trillion rubles (which converts to some $47.7 billion) in 2020, 3.24 trillion rubles ($50 billion) in 2021, and 3.3 trillion rubles ($51.3 billion) in 2022. All told, that would mean the National Defence line in the state budget would be equivalent to 2.4% of GDP in 2020, 2.7% in 2021, and 2.6% in 2022.[1]

So far, so moderate. According to Treasury figures, British defence spending in 2019–20 was £54.5 billion, or around $72.5 billion, which would make it more than half as much again as Russia's.[2] Yet Russia maintains armed forces which are not quite a million strong – closer to 900,000 – which nonetheless dwarf the United Kingdom's 153,000 active personnel. What is more, they have modernized on a massive scale, doing everything from deploying the new *Borei*-class nuclear missile submarine to finally replacing the venerable and under-powered 1950s-vintage Makarov standard service pistol. Never mind 'bang for buck', how does Russia get so much rumble for its ruble?

WHEN COMPARISONS FAIL

This is a classic case where straightforward comparisons simply don't work. In practical terms, the real level of Russian military expenditure is equivalent to perhaps three or even four times its paper value. First of all, much military-related expenditure is actually buried in other budget line items, from education to science and technology. This is easy to note, hard accurately to quantify. The national 'Ready for Labour and Defence' programme, a Soviet-era initiative designed not just to improve national health but also to ensure draftees join the military fit for service, was revived in 2007, and is paid for by the Sports Ministry. Much military research and development is conducted under the auspices of projects funded through civilian budgets. Certain troop movements by train are in effect covered by budget subventions to RZhD, the national rail operator. In times of war, the heavily armed Interior Troops of the National Guard would be fully integrated into the warfighting command. Yet technically it is just an internal security force, for all that its operators have already been deployed to Syria, so it falls under a different budget line. And so it goes: when the state is so committed to its mission of national defence – even if 'defence' may entail projecting power far from its borders – then even without the desire to mislead outsiders, military roles are threaded into so many aspects of government activity.

Much more serious is the impact of a crudely mechanical conversion of the ruble at market rates. For a start, historically, the ruble has often been a volatile currency (I can remember trips when a pound would buy me 65 rubles at the start of my visit, and over a hundred when I left), and the comparisons often suffer from when in the cycles of rising and falling market value they are made. More to the point, Russia is essentially self-sufficient in military terms. Everything from the research and development for its new systems to the procurement of kit, even buying food for its soldiers and fuel for its vehicles, is done domestically – using the ruble, not the dollar, pound or euro. Thus, a much better measure is what is called Purchasing Power Parity (PPP) exchange rates, which factor in the differences in costs between countries. This helps explain, for example, why Russians are willing to join the armed forces on a professional basis. These so-called *kontraktniki* earn 62,000 rubles per month, which as of writing would be around £700 – vastly less than the £1,700 or so at which a British private's salary starts. However, the average cost of living in Russia is around £450 a month (almost two-thirds that *kontraktnik*'s salary), compared with £1,250 in the United Kingdom (almost three-quarters the private's). So while the Russian soldier looks much worse off, in relative terms, he is doing at least as well as his British counterpart.

Obviously, national economics are somewhat more complex, but the basic principle holds true. Indeed, if anything the Kremlin has even further advantages, such as its capacity to be more ruthless with its defence industries if it chooses, to constrain their profits, and its continued use of cheap conscripts. All told, when compared on the basis of PPP, Russian military spending is actually holding quite steady at around £110–130 billion ($150–180 billion) annually, or two to two-and-a-half times the United Kingdom's defence budget, and that only applies to the official figures. Factor in the hidden spending, and it could be more like £145 billion ($200 billion).[3] On this basis, Russia has consistently remained the fourth largest military spender in the world, behind only the United States, China and India. (The same issue of trying to assess real expenditure by market-rate exchange comparisons leads to a serious under-estimate of Chinese rearmament, something of which we should all be aware.)

Every year sees the government issue its State Defence Order (GOZ: *Gosudarstvenny Oboronny Zakaz*), a budgeted plan for procurement within the multi-year State Armament Plan (GPV: *Gosudarstvennaya Programma Vooruzheniya*), the result of painful and often acrimonious wrangles between the arms of service, the Defence and the Finance Ministries, and lobbyists for various regions and industries, presided over by the powerful Security Council Secretariat. Equally, each year sees recriminations and excuses for failures to meet targets or standards. Admittedly, this is hardly unique to Russia, but it does highlight the limitations of the system: even having the money and the political will is not always enough to get the results the Kremlin wants.

After all, the money is generally there. The defence budget has been pretty constant, with occasional peaks reflecting the need to clear debts to the arms industries more than real rises, and the Kremlin is clearly aware of the need to avoid the kind of runaway military spending that ended up bankrupting the Soviet Union (although in fairness, its cumbersome, corrupt and creaking planned economy was heading towards eventual collapse regardless). In any case, the bulk of the procurement scheduled under Putin's modernization programme, needed to drag the armed forces into the 21st century, has been completed. Although, as discussed below, it is likely to be slower and harder to finish the job, nonetheless progress has been impressive.

'LET US STARVE, BUT LET US EXPORT'

You don't often get management consultants quoting late 19th-century finance ministers, but when I visited an arms export fair in 2012, one did work into his speech a line from Minister Ivan Vyshnegradsky. In 1891, he infamously declared, 'Let us starve, but let us export', in the name of modernizing Russia's industries, even as famine raged in the countryside. Things were obviously in no way as serious then, but the contemporary parallel being drawn was the way that the Russian armed forces were 'starving' – something of an exaggeration, it had to be said – because the arms companies were so keen to export. In other words, export orders that earned foreign currency were jumping the queue, leaving domestic ones delayed.

Of course, this is hardly surprising given the tight margins the state forces on arms companies when they sell local, and much R&D and plant modernization capital has been on the back of exports. The Russians have three advantages – they have a lot of good products, a lot of cheap products, and in the main they will sell (almost) anything to (almost) anyone – which they have exploited to the fullest. Thus, as of 2021, they remained second only to the United States in their share of global arms exports. According to the Stockholm International Peace Research Institute, in the period 2016–20, they accounted for 20% of the total, by value (the United States was at 37%), almost equivalent to the next four largest (France, United Kingdom, Germany, China) combined.[4]

It is all the more impressive that it has done so, considering the state of Russia's defence-industrial base. Putin has, from his first year as president, put serious resources and political capital into reforming his military, and turning it from being a cut-down version of the Red Army to a modern, capable force that is able to project power even away from Russia's borders. Yet it has done so under some distinctive handicaps.

Since 2014, for example, it has had to cope with the loss of access to Ukraine's defence industries (which used to produce several crucial components, not least the gas turbine engines originally intended for Russia's new frigates) and also some Western technologies. These are essentially technical challenges, and Russia's industries have largely been able to make up for these absences, albeit at a cost in time and money. Consider, for example, the case of Project 22350, a crucial design meant to replace Soviet-era *Neustrashimy-* and *Krivak*-class frigates. The intention was that they would be fitted with combined-diesel-and-gas engines (CODAG), marine engines made by Ukraine's Zorya-Mashproekt enterprise. The first, the *Admiral Gorshkov*, did indeed receive them before the conflict, and was commissioned in 2018. However, then the problems started. The second in what is planned to be at least 15 ships, the *Admiral Kasatonov*, was then fitted with combined gas turbine and gas turbine engines instead, and only in 2018 was Russia's United Engine Corporation able to deliver the first of two M55R CODAG engines to the Severnaya Verf shipyard in St Petersburg for the third ship, the *Admiral Golovko*. The fourth, the *Admiral Isakov*, only got its engines in 2021. To be fair, it seems almost impossible to find a major military construction project anywhere in the world that goes to schedule these days, but although there were also the inevitable teething problems with the ships' systems, the delay in commissioning these relatively small workhorses does, as will be discussed later, raise doubts about any plans to build larger ships up to and including aircraft carriers.

THE METAL-EATERS

In any case, rather more important are the structural weaknesses of the sector that former Soviet leader Nikita Khrushchev called the 'metal-eaters'. There was an old joke that the Soviet Union did not *have* a military-industrial complex – it *was* a military-industrial complex. The 'metal-eaters' had inordinate power and almost every aspect of the economy was channelled towards military production and power, whether the way that every truck and lorry had its so-called *avtokolomka* designation so that it could be mobilized in time of war, to the way the defence companies got first pick of raw materials and components. It is hard to see the same kind of dominance now. More generally known as the *oboronka*, after *oborona*, the Russian word for defence, the sector directly employs more than 2.5 million people, one in five of all Russian manufacturing jobs. Although there are some bright sparks of efficiency and innovation, they are in the main infamous for their Soviet-era habits of inflexibility, corruption and close ties with the state. Not only do they depend on the government for sales, and the state-owned Rosoboronexport agency for overseas business, but many are wholly or partially owned by Rostec, Russian Technologies, whose cumbersome full name is the State Corporation for Assistance to the Development, Production and Export of Advanced Technology Industrial Product Rostec. As the name suggests, this is a state-owned holding conglomerate that invests in strategically important companies, especially in the high-technology and defence sectors. Big beasts such as Uralvagonzavod (which builds the T-80 and T-14 tank, along with lines such as railway rolling stock), the United Aircraft Corporation (which includes such marques as MiG, Sukhoi and Tupolev), Russian Helicopters and Kalashnikov are all part of the Rostec stable – and its Chief Executive Officer is Sergei Chemezov, a former KGB officer who worked alongside Putin in East Germany in the 1980s and is still very much one of his inner circle.

No wonder, then, that the Kremlin is able to squeeze the 'metal-eaters' hard, demanding that they accept what it is willing to pay them. Sales, whether exports or for domestic use, have tended to be on the basis of low prices. A T-80 tank may be less capable than an American M1A1 but it also costs about half as much, and while the stealthy US F-22 Raptor may be much more capable than the Russians' Su-35 Flanker-E, they have a unit cost of $150 million to $85 million, respectively. The trouble with selling cheap(er) kit is that it leaves much less of a margin for research and development, though, which is fantastically expensive these days. So they depend on state assistance, as well as state sales, and the government often pays partially or late, and demands new kit that stretches companies' research projects to and beyond the limits. But they can hardly say no.

The result has been growing debt, as plants are paid late or partially by the state and have to take out loans to cover the shortfall. In 2016, the government paid off debts worth 800 billion rubles ($10.5

billion) and a further 200 billion ($2.6 billion) the next year. Then, in 2020, another 750 billion rubles ($9.8 billion) of debt was covered or restructured. Even so, Deputy Prime Minister for the Defence Sector Yuri Borisov admitted at the end of that year that the total debt stood at 3 trillion rubles ($39.5 billion).[5] Some of these companies are spending about one-tenth of their debt each year just in servicing it, paying interest on loans that likely will never be repaid. Indeed, it has been suggested that more than one in ten of all defence-industrial enterprises are nearing bankruptcy, only being kept afloat by new loans or periodic government debt forgiveness. So the state saves on the one hand – but then has to pay for it with the other.

This inefficient model likewise manages also to hinder further development. Delays getting the new Su-57 stealth jet in service, for example, in part resulted from the difficulty that manufacturing company KnAAZ, the Komsomolsk-on-Amur Aircraft Plant, had in getting all the necessary components. The price they had to pay for them (as suppliers sought to cover some of their debts) ended up being paid by the military, just so they could get their plane.[6] It has also compounded problems with coming up with genuinely new designs, rather than evolutions of Soviet-era ones. This does not mean that the latter are not often excellent systems. The air force, for example, is significantly more effective thanks to its new Su-30 and Su-35 fighters and Su-34 fighter-bombers, regardless of whether they are all based on the Su-27 Flanker, an airframe that first flew in 1977 and entered service in 1985. Likewise, the T-72B3 and T-90 are modernized versions of older tanks, but have proven capable for all that. Much slower and less clearly successful have been the programmes to produce and field truly new systems, whether the T-14 Armata tank (the initial plan was to buy 2,300 by 2020; instead, the first 100 are expected to be delivered in 2022), the fifth-generation Su-57 multi-role fighter (originally 52 would be in service by 2020, and another 150–160 by 2025; only one non-test aircraft was in service by the end of 2021) or the fourth-generation *Lada*-class diesel-electric submarine (four to six were meant to be launched by 2015; as of 2022, only the prototype is operational).

Part of the problem is also the usual Kremlin fascination with gigantism, with having a few, politically controllable megacorporations dominating the sector. In the 2000s, a defence sector which, in fairness, did need serious rationalization, was largely consolidated into fewer than 20 such national champions. They had flashy logos and snappy adverts, but at heart they were often still very Soviet in their ways of doing business, hierarchical and bureaucratic. But this was no longer the planned Soviet economy, and they struggled to operate in an environment in which their suppliers of tools and components could charge whatever the market could bear. Back in Soviet times, for example, TVs sold to regular customers had a terrible reputation for reliability, in part because the factories which produced cathode-ray tubes were required by law to send their best products to defence plants for radar sets. Civilian factories got the rest. Now, if the defence companies want components – and if they have special requirements – they have to pay for them.

BUYER BEWARE

Instead of being able to produce the best kit or source the best components, they often have to rely on politics. After all, they often actually have more political muscle than the generals. It is hardly unknown in the West for procurement decisions to be decided based on which factory or shipyard is in which constituency, or the scale of a manufacturer's lobbying budget. It is at least as true in Russia. Indeed, this goes back to Soviet times, and often meant that the military ended up fielding parallel lines of weapons – like the T-64 and T-72 tanks or the T-80 and T-90 – whether it wanted to or not. Today, similar duplication is also rife. When the military announced the Typhoon design competition for a new, heavy mine-resistant armoured personal carrier, both the Ural and Kamaz corporations put forward their own versions. And both models, designed to achieve exactly the same purpose, are now in service.

A particularly good example may be the much-hyped new T-14 Armata tank. Back in 2015, on the fringes of a particularly dull military colloquium in Moscow (at which both Russian participants duly expressed their mutual desire for cooperation and friendship with the West, for all that they were already at daggers drawn over Ukraine), I got the chance to share a drink with some officers from the Kantemir Division. More formally the 4th Guards Kantemirovskaya Order of Lenin Red Banner Tank Division named for Yuri Andropov, this is one of the elite 'palace guard' units based around Moscow. In 2009 it had briefly been converted to a brigade, but earlier in 2015 had been reconstituted as a full division, something about which they were all relieved.

The conversation, inevitably, turned to tanks. The 4th was equipped with the T-80U, but that year it was announced that they were going to be one of the first to receive some of the 2,000 T-14 tanks the Defence Ministry was going to buy from Uralvagonzavod. The T-14 is the first truly new-generation Russian tank, a supposed marvel of modern electronics, with an unmanned turret mounting a fully automated, high-power 125mm 2A82-1M gun, and an armoured capsule within the main hull for the three crew. How excited were they about this? The conversation followed what I found to be the familiar trajectory when a nosy Brit starts asking these kinds of questions. First, the official line: that this was an honour, that the Armata was the most advanced tank of its kind, that it was a mark of the prowess of Russia's military technology. But after a while, a more nuanced perspective emerged. Was it just too expensive? Was it needed? Above all, was it just too advanced, potentially too finicky for the real battlefield?

Although to an extent this is a carry-over from the days of the Second World War, when rugged but simple Soviet vehicles often were fixed in battle with all kinds of field expedients and the expertise a driver might have gained repairing a collective farm's combine harvester, there is nonetheless some truth to the proposition that Soviet vehicles were quick to break down, but also quick to get moving again. What about the T-14 Armata, with all its fancy, solid-state electronics? The fear was that when it suffered anything more serious than a thrown track or a jammed gun, all that could be done was trundle it back to a specialized repair depot. It was, they concluded, not so much the tank the army needed, but the tank Uralvagonzavod wanted to sell them.

While the T-14 looks impressive on paper, Uralvagonzavod is a major employer, and in 2011, when Putin was facing angry protests against his re-election, a foreman from the tank production plant at Nizhny Tagil offered to come to Moscow 'with the guys' to deal with them. It became something of a media sensation, not least as it played to the Kremlin's efforts to portray the protesters as middle-class elitists, out of touch with 'real Russia'. The foreman, Igor Kholmanskikh, was later made a presidential representative, and Uralvagonzavod got the Armata contract. Putin knows to reward loyalty.

Those Kantemir officers may have had a point. Although they were meant to have received their T-14s by 2018, as of writing – mid-2022 – they are still fielding T-80Us. As well as running late the project is also coming in over-budget: the price tag for the new tanks has gone up from 250 million to 450 million rubles (£2.5–4.4 million) per unit. Partly as a result, as mentioned previously, the order has shrunk from 2,300 by 2020, to 100 by the end of 2022. And shortly after that colloquium, in the rehearsals for the annual Victory Day parade, one of the eight T-14s being shown off for the first time broke down in full view of the cameras. An attempt to tow it failed, but then it was able, after some 15 minutes of frantic tinkering, to drive off under its own steam. The announcer tried to pass it off as part of a planned test, but no one was fooled.

MODERNIZING THE MILITARY

For all that, the system works, in its own way. As of 2021, according to the Defence Ministry, 71% of all ships, submarines and aircraft, 85% of helicopters, 79% of artillery pieces, 82% of armoured vehicles and 100% of ground missile systems were officially rated as 'modern'. The service break-down was 85% of Ground Forces kit, 80% for the air force, and 85% for the navy.[7] One could quibble as to quite what this means – much of the 'modern' kit is simply updated versions of Soviet-era designs – but it nonetheless represents an impressive response to the crisis which had gripped the Russian military.

After all, most armed forces renovate themselves all the time, constantly repairing, modernizing and only then replacing equipment that, in such circumstances, can continue to be serviceable for decades. The American F-15 fighter entered service in 1976, but thanks to rolling upgrades is still going strong. By the later 1980s, though, the Soviet R&D complex was in crisis as the money dried up and Gorbachev looked to disarmament. The 1990s saw next to no serious procurement or modernization programmes, nor even the funds or the interest in basic upkeep. Even when Putin came to power in 2000, the initial focus had to be on personnel. The result was more years of neglect, such that in 2008, when mighty Russia took on tiny Georgia, more than a quarter of all the armoured vehicles deployed simply broke down before they even reached the battlefield.

So much of the older kit was simply beyond practical or economic repair or refurbishment, that no wonder modernization became such a priority for successive defence ministers. It meant not just the difference between the leading-edge and the still-serviceable, but it often meant the gaping gap between the usable and the unusable. Of course, there are weapons which have rather longer lifespans. Although the AK-74 rifle, introduced in – predictably enough – 1974, is scheduled for replacement by the AK-12, in practice it will remain in use for years to come. That is no great drawback, though, as the later AK-74M (issued from 1991) is still a perfectly effective weapon. However, the advances in everything from precision munitions to targeting and sensor systems meant that replacing the most venerable and vulnerable kit had to be a priority – and to a large extent, the Russians have accomplished this. As will be explored in the following chapters, thanks to deep reforms on the level of organization, doctrine and equipment, Gerasimov's proud boast that 'the Armed Forces are now arriving at a fundamentally new level of combat readiness' did not seem that misplaced – until, that is, his military was tested in a true, full-scale war in Ukraine.[8]

20

Armiya Rossii

Surreal though it may sound, near enough opposite the US embassy on Moscow's Novinsky Boulevard, part of the busy Garden Ring road, is a shop selling high-end fashion – branded *Armiya Rossii*, or 'Army of Russia'. Part of Voyentorg, the military's official clothing and food supplier, it sells camouflage leggings and t-shirts emblazoned with Defence Minister Sergei Shoigu, nicely packaged versions of standard field rations, and even denim jackets with 'Team Putin' patches, and all at quite a price. This is part of Shoigu's attempt to rebrand the military and a soldierly career as something chic and desirable, but is also striking that it is called 'Army of Russia', not 'Russian Military' or the like. For all the dependence on nuclear deterrence or the new capabilities of the Aerospace Forces, Russia has always been essentially a land power, and the Ground Forces remain the undisputed heart of its military. The Royal Navy may be the 'Senior Service' in the United Kingdom, because it pre-dates any real standing army (which essentially began with Oliver Cromwell in the 17th century). However, Russia's standing army dates back to Ivan the Terrible's *Streltsy* (Musketeers) of the mid-16th century, more than a century before it acquired a navy in Peter the Great's reforms of 1696.

Russia's Ground Forces (SV: *Sukhoputnye Voiska*) have their own banner, with crossed golden swords and flaming grenade on a red background, their own professional holiday (31 May, marking the formation of the *Streltsy*), their own patron saint (Alexander Nevsky, who famously defeated the Teutonic Knights in the 13th century), and their own motto: *Vpered pekhota!*, 'Forward the Infantry!' They are also the largest arm of service in the Russian military, numbering some 280,000 officers, men and (some) women as of the start of 2022.

Formally, they are all subordinated to the SV Main Command, but this is essentially an administrative element of the Defence Ministry, responsible for training, tactics and organizational management, with real operational command running from the General Staff through Military Districts (or Joint Strategic Commands in time of war). Indeed, in 1997, the SV Main Command was actually abolished and replaced with the Defence Ministry's Main Directorate of Ground Forces, Directorate of Missile Forces and Artillery, Directorate of Military Air Defence and Directorate of Army Aviation. This proved an unhelpful reform, blurring the lines between the role of the ministry and the military command structures, and so in 2001, Putin decreed the recreation of the SV Main Command. As of writing, the Ground Forces commander-in-chief is Gen. Oleg Salyukov, a career tank officer, but at 66 he is nearing the age at which he would be expected to surrender the position to a successor.

THE BATTALION TACTICAL GROUP

Although, as will be discussed further below, the division is making a limited come-back, in the main the army is still primarily structured around the smaller brigade, one of the key innovations of the 'New Look' brought in by Serdyukov and Makarov. The brigade, though, is still a relatively large formation and most will typically be staffed with a mix of *kontraktniki* and conscripts, the latter of whom cannot by law be required to serve outside Russia's borders except in time of war. As a result, even before the Donbas conflict made the need for such units necessary, the Ground Forces had begun to establish the means to create composite Battalion Tactical Groups (BTGs), modular forces typically drawn from all-volunteer elements in existing brigades. At first, in the Donbas, these often had to be based on soldiers from more than one parent brigade, posing some interoperability challenges as soldiers not used to fighting together adjusted to their new structures. The need to rotate them through the Donbas to replenish casualties, resupply, and allow soldiers necessary rest and recreation, did at first also mean that maintaining the supply of such units was something of a headache for the personnel and

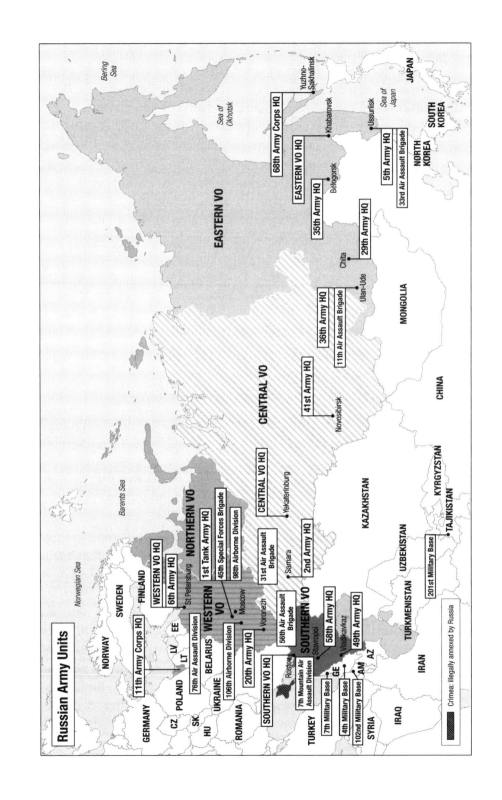

Russian Army Units

NORWAY
SWEDEN
FINLAND
GERMANY
CZ
SK
POLAND
HU
BELARUS
UKRAINE
ROMANIA
LT
LV
EE
TURKEY
SYRIA
IRAQ
IRAN
GE
AM
AZ
TURKMENISTAN
UZBEKISTAN
KAZAKHSTAN
KYRGYZSTAN
TAJIKISTAN
CHINA
MONGOLIA
JAPAN
SOUTH KOREA
NORTH KOREA

Bering Sea
Sea of Okhotsk
Sea of Japan
Norwegian Sea
Barents Sea

NORTHERN VO
WESTERN VO
CENTRAL VO
EASTERN VO
SOUTHERN VO

WESTERN VO HQ
6th Army HQ
1st Tank Army HQ
45th Special Forces Brigade
98th Airborne Division
31st Air Assault Brigade
CENTRAL VO HQ
2nd Army HQ
41st Army HQ
36th Army HQ
11th Air Assault Brigade
29th Army HQ
35th Army HQ
EASTERN VO HQ
68th Army Corps HQ
5th Army HQ
33rd Air Assault Brigade
11th Army Corps HQ
76th Air Assault Division
106th Airborne Division
20th Army HQ
56th Air Assault Brigade
SOUTHERN VO HQ
7th Mountain Air Assault Division
58th Army HQ
49th Army HQ
7th Military Base
4th Military Base
102nd Military Base
201st Military Base

St Petersburg
Moscow
Voronezh
Yekaterinburg
Samara
Rostov
Stavropol
Vladikavkaz
Novosibirsk
Ulan-Ude
Chita
Belogorsk
Khabarovsk
Ussuriisk
Yuzhno-Sakhalinsk

Crimea: illegally annexed by Russia

logistical planners, pulling in troops from all across Russia. However, it did mean that the Russians could deploy meaningfully sized field forces drawn wholly from professionals. Soon it became possible for almost every brigade to be able to generate its own BTGs, and as already noted, the BTG will generally take a lion's share of its support elements. This becomes a powerful way of quickly generating deployable forces drawn from *kontraktniki* in a peacetime army but, as became clear with the invasion of Ukraine, it means only one or two battalions from each brigade can actually be fielded – and that only by cannibalizing the rest of the force.

The details of BTGs vary, their structure reflecting both operational needs and available personnel, but in general they are mechanized battalions of up to 900 officers and men, with two to four tank or mechanized companies and attached artillery, reconnaissance, engineer, electronic warfare and rear support platoons. For example, a BTG generated by the 58th Army's 19th Motor Rifle Brigade from Vladikavkaz in North Ossetia included a mechanized company in BMP-3 infantry combat vehicles, another in BTR-82As, a tank company with T-90s, a battery of Msta-S SPGs (Self-Propelled Guns), a battery of Tornado-G MLRS (Multiple-Launch Rocket Systems), a drone company and an oversized sniper platoon from another brigade. This is lighter than many other BTGs, but reflects the upland terrain in which it operates. BTGs' actual structure and level of manning thus vary wildly: in the invasion of Ukraine, some only had 250 men. The result is a fairly self-sufficient ground combat unit with disproportionate fire and rear support, in some ways a scaled-down version of the brigades which are the basic building block of the Russian army.

THE RETURN OF THE DIVISION

The shift to a brigade structure under Serdyukov was essentially predicated on the notion that the only wars Russia was really likely to have to fight were going to be smaller-scale wars of intervention abroad – essentially much like the thinking that shaped most NATO armies in the post-Cold War era. Under Shoigu, with the eruption of undeclared war in Ukraine and the worsening of relations with the West, the Russian military also began to contemplate the possibility of full-scale war against a peer or near-peer adversary on or close to its borders.

What that requires are not only heavy forces, but also higher-order structures that can incorporate battalions from other Military Districts and command and supply them in the field. The concern was that managing what might be dozens of new brigades and BTGs transferred from elsewhere in Russia would overwhelm an army or VO commander. Thus, at the same time that light, high-mobility forces were being created, so too did divisions make a partial come-back. When Shoigu started the process by restoring the elite and prestigious Taman and Kantemir Divisions, he was not only playing to the generals, but he was also marking the start of this process. As of the end of 2021, Russia had restored nine Ground Forces divisions: eight mechanized and one tank. In addition, in 2014 the 1st Guards Tank Army was reactivated. These larger formations are disproportionately based in the west of the country, especially around Ukraine, with none in the Central VO.

ARMY DIVISIONS, 2021

Western VO

1st Guards Tank Army
2nd Motor Rifle Division
4th Tank Division
20th Guards Combined Arms Army
3rd Motor Rifle Division
144th Motor Rifle Division

Southern VO

20th Guards Combined Arms Army
3rd Motor Rifle Division
144th Motor Rifle Division
58th Combined Arms Army
19th Motor Rifle Division
42nd Motor Rifle Division

Eastern VO

5th Guards Combined Arms Army
127th Motor Rifle Division
68th Combined Arms Army
18th Machine Gun Artillery Division

In part, this change of step reflects an evolution of military thinking and lessons from Russia's operations in the Donbas. There, the army depended on assembling ad hoc battalion tactical groups from the all-volunteer elements of brigades across the country. This often created serious interoperability problems, as soldiers who had not trained together were thrown directly into battle. While they were generally able to win individual engagements against Ukrainian forces, due not least to greater firepower and a technological edge, they were often unable to exploit these victories effectively. These re-formed divisions will therefore be used not just as rapid response defensive elements but also as the core of combined-arms formations able to deliver shattering blows quickly, in a reprise of the Soviets' own take on blitzkrieg.

It is not that Russia is abandoning the brigade. Rather, it is going to field a mix of brigades and divisions, with the former more oriented towards projecting power in 'small wars', divisions in larger ones. Furthermore, these divisions range in size, from the equivalent of the old Russian four-regiment structure down to smaller, two- or three-regiment ones that are in some ways more like bulked-out brigades, albeit with greater redundancy in their command capacity and support units. Most divisions will thus have anything from 6,000 to 7,000 personnel (compared with around 13,000 and 10,000 in the old Soviet motor rifle and tank divisions, respectively).

It is easier to announce the creation of a division and award it its own flag than actually bring it to full operational status, though. Back in November 2014, for example, it was announced that a motor rifle division was going to be re-established at Yelnya, east of Smolensk, to use the base of what was once the 144th Motor Rifle Division, a unit withdrawn from East Germany in the early 1990s and then disbanded in 1998. In July 2015, it was announced that it would be stood up within two years, on the basis of an existing brigade, which turned out to be the 28th Independent Motor Rifle Brigade from Yekaterinburg. In practice, while the 144th Motor Rifle Division was indeed operational by the end of 2017, instead of the original four manoeuvre regiments it was meant to have, three motor rifle and one tank, even as of 2020, it had just three, still being short a motor rifle regiment. Finding troops, reshuffling commands and relocating forces all takes time.

HEAVY METAL

Arguably, two classes of equipment truly epitomize the Russian military: the tank and the artillery. Western and especially European armies have tended to run down their stocks of tanks, seeing little use for them in the kind of dusty counter-insurgency conflicts that they believed would be their usual challenge in the coming years. On the other hand, tanks remain crucial to Russia's high-tempo and aggressive approach to warfighting. The T-72, designed in the 1960s and first fielded in 1970, remains a mainstay, progressive upgrades meaning that the 2,000 or so T-72B3 versions currently in use are still very creditable assets on the modern battlefield. The later T-80 has had a more chequered history, but like the T-90/T-90M – itself a modernized T-72 – will remain in service for the foreseeable future because of the delays and downsizing of the T-14 Armata project.

Historically, artillery has been Russia's 'god of war', and while all armies rely primarily on long-range firepower – the role of the other manoeuvre forces is often to find and fix the enemy long enough for the artillery to break them – the Russians still field a lot of it. For example, while a typical Russian battalion tactical group will have two or three batteries with a mix of 122mm and 152mm self-propelled guns and rocket artillery, as well as several platoons of mortars, a standard US battalion has just a mortar platoon. This is not a wholly fair comparison – the BTG is a specialized force that takes up the lion's share of the support elements of the brigade that generates it, and the US model is to concentrate artillery at higher levels of command, to support the regiments in the field. However, even looking at the brigade level, a full-strength Russian mechanized brigade will typically include two artillery battalions and a rocket battalion, to its US counterpart's single artillery battalion.

This all gives some sense of the priority the Russians give to having lots of artillery in play, and explains why (beyond lobbying for better guns of his own) US Chairman of the Joint Chiefs of Staff Gen. Mark Milley, while still Army Chief of Staff, told a Senate Armed Services Committee hearing that when matched up against the Russians, 'we don't like it, we don't want it, but yes, technically [we are] outranged, outgunned on the ground.'[1] That point about being outranged is also important: the US's standard M109 152mm self-propelled gun has a range of 21 kilometres, or 30 kilometres with a rocket-assisted shell. The Russians' new 2S35 Koalitsiya-SV, already coming into service, has a reported – though unconfirmed – range of 40 kilometres, or 80 kilometres with a rocket-assisted round. Russia's heavy multiple-launch rocket systems can also hit targets 90 kilometres away, and they also field the *Iskander* (SS-26) ballistic missile with a 500-kilometre range, which can be fitted with a range of conventional warheads, including cluster munitions, a thermobaric fuel-air explosive and even an electromagnetic pulse device that can burn out electrical systems in its blast radius. Range isn't everything: everything from rate of fire and accuracy to reliability and survivability all count. Nonetheless, this is an area where the Russians have a clear strength.

SPECIALIZED FORCES FOR SPECIALIZED OPERATIONS

The adoption of the brigade structure also gave the SV Main Command greater scope for experimenting with specialized formations adapted to particular combat environments. The Chechen wars had led to a resurgence of units trained and equipped especially for mountain warfare, and there had long been a particular emphasis on cold-weather operations for units in the High North of the Arctic. However, this became much more formal and extensive as Putin began to consider the prospect of operations in new combat theatres.

The last Soviet specialized unit, the 68th Independent Motor Rifle Brigade (Mountain), was disbanded in 1991, and the absence of such forces was a clear problem during the Chechen wars. As a result, in 2004, Putin announced the creation of two special mountain brigades in the Northern Caucasus, made up of *kontraktniki*. The Defence Ministry originally promised that they would be operational in 2005, but it took until the end of 2007 for the 33rd and 344th Independent Motor Rifle Brigades to be ready, based in Botlikh in Dagestan (later, Maikop) and Zelenchukskaya in Karachaevo-Cherkessia, respectively. Each has a strength of around 2,000 troops, although questions continue to be raised about whether they truly have the skills and physical conditioning for the mission.

Beyond that, Russia has long relied on its ability to fight in cold-weather conditions as both a defensive and offensive asset, but as

Moscow increasingly looks to the High North as a strategic theatre, it is forming and equipping forces to match. To a considerable extent this is the responsibility of the air forces and the navy. New military facilities are also established, such as the innovative *Arkticheski Trilistnik* ('Arctic Trefoil') on the island of Alexandra Land, part of the Franz Josef Land archipelago, Russia's most northern base. As a result, there is a perceived need for ground forces able to operate in extreme polar environments. The 200th Brigade, headquartered at Pechenga, and the 80th Independent Brigade at Alakurtti are designated Arctic units, with specially modified equipment – and also a revival of low-tech solutions such as sleds pulled by either dogs or reindeer, especially useful for covert reconnaissance and raiding given their relative silence. Of course, it is not simply or even mainly a matter of kit. These forces train in the unforgiving High North environments increasingly frequently and realistically.

Back in the 1920s, the Soviet struggle against the *Basmachi*, the rebels of Central Asia, was often led by the Red Cavalry. Today, experiences in Syria have encouraged the Russians to experiment with light mechanized forces, a modern counterpart. In 2009, the 56th Independent Airborne Assault Brigade had tried mounting elements in UAZ-31512 'Hunter' jeeps, but although they demonstrated the potential value of 'super-light' mechanized forces, the vehicles were just too small to be practical, unable to accommodate heavy weapons and adequate supplies, so they were first re-equipped with GAZ-66 trucks, then returned to conventional APCs. However, in 2016, the Russians supplied the Syrian Arab army with armed UAZ Patriot pickup trucks intended as highly mobile convoy escorts and also as a counter to the numerous armed 'technicals' – improvised armed trucks, often based on the ubiquitous Toyota Land Cruisers and Hiluxes – fielded by the various rebel groups. This sparked a wider interest in such vehicles, and in 2017 it was decided that one of the 30th Motor Rifle Brigade's four battalions would be equipped with UAZ Patriots. The 30th Motor Rifle Brigade is based at Samara in central Russia, hardly desert territory, but a region of steppes, forests and mountains. Given that the UAZ Patriot can reach speeds of 150 kilometres per hour and is much more fuel efficient than heavier, armoured APCs, the idea appears to be to test the notion that such a force could provide highly mobile raid and reaction forces in a range of difficult environments, from deserts to woodland, where the larger BTR-80s of the rest of the brigade would have trouble or be forced to move more slowly.

LOGISTICS

For all this, the old saw that 'amateurs talk about tactics, but professionals study logistics' is perfectly true, and historically the Russians have tended to put more effort into 'teeth' than 'tail'. This should not be taken as an absolute, as they and their Soviet predecessors absolutely could and would put much effort into preparation. However, just as their tanks and ships were optimized for speed and firepower more than comfort and survivability, in the past especially, they gave less priority to looking after their soldiers and anticipated more breakdowns and equipment failures.

This was changing even in late Soviet times, as the High Command came to appreciate that modern war puts demands on soldiers that had to be addressed, and also that experienced combatants were too valuable to waste. The war in Afghanistan saw an unparalleled military-medical apparatus in place, from the *Bissektrisa* ('Bisector') Mi-8MB casevac air ambulance that would lift casualties off the battlefield, to the dedicated An-12 and Il-18 medical transport flights that would take serious cases back to the Soviet Union and the military hospital in Tashkent. In the 1990s, much of this practical experience was not so much lost as unable to be applied: one army doctor who had served in Afghanistan and then Chechnya described to me having to use converted fanbelts looted from a car repair shop as tourniquets in the latter conflict, simply because they had no official supplies. However, as soon as the money was available, the lessons learned were readdressed, especially as the new emphasis on higher-skilled soldiers and recruiting and retaining volunteers also demanded a more solicitous approach to the ranks.

More broadly, though, logistics is still an Achilles heel of the Russian forces, and it doesn't help that Putin, with his relatively minimal military experience, still seems more impressed by 'teeth' than 'tail', creating no political pressure to address the latter. In the Donbas in 2014–22 – admittedly, where sometimes the need to retain a little implausible deniability did limit operations – high-intensity BTG operations would sometimes peter out after a few days simply because supplies, especially ammunition, were being consumed that much more quickly than they could be replenished. After all, one consequence of having brigades and BTGs with so much more artillery and air defence capability than their Western counterparts is that they also have greater supply needs – yet their 'tails' are not equally large. Certainly, once full-scale operations in Ukraine began in 2022, the logistical challenges of sustaining major combat operations became very clear.

Each army is meant to have its own material-technical support brigade, but not all do – or else it is largely there only on paper. Instead, major operations would still be very dependent on the railway network, hence why Russia's military also has Railway Troops, ten specialized brigades tasked with building, repairing, securing and maintaining track and facilities (the actual rolling stock is the responsibility of RZhD and the country's other train companies). Even so, Russia uses a wider gauge track than is the norm in Western Europe: it is only to be found in Finland, eastern Slovakia and short stretches in Poland and Hungary. This would have extremely serious implications in the case of any hypothetical Russian invasions outside the former USSR where it remains the norm. Supplies moving from 1,520mm 'Russian Gauge' to the more common 1,435mm 'Stephenson Gauge' would have to be cross-loaded to new wagons or else be on ones which can adjust their wheels. Locomotives cannot do this, though, so new engines would be needed either way. In any case, this would add extra time and complexity into the supply process – at a time when these narrow ribbons of steel would presumably be prime targets for artillery, air attacks and partisans. The Railway Troops may know their trade, but having constantly to repair the lines would slow things even further.

Away from railheads, and when the trains are not running, the Russians would have to rely on trucks, and here, even if they conscript vehicles and drivers from the commercial sector, it is doubtful that they have enough to sustain major operations. One credible estimate is that they simply could not sustain high-tempo operations more than 150 kilometres from their supply dumps, which in turn are difficult and time-consuming to establish deep into hostile territory. To give a specific example:

Although each army is different, there are usually 56 to 90 multiple launch rocket system launchers in an army. Replenishing each launcher takes up the entire bed of the truck. If the combined arms army fired a single volley, it would require 56 to 90 trucks just to replenish rocket ammunition. That is about a half of a dry cargo truck force in the material-technical support brigade just to replace one volley of rockets.[2]

What's more, that is just the army's rockets, not considering its six to nine artillery battalions, and all the mortars, tank guns, anti-air and anti-tank missiles, grenades and bullets it would expend; and all the fuel; and food and water. In other words, the Russian army probably could not launch and maintain full-scale combat operations far from its borders and its rail network.

CAPABILITIES

How does all this translate into genuine capacity to project force outside Russia's borders? A 2020 report from the US thinktank RAND posited a series of notional scenarios, from an escalation to conventional warfighting in Ukraine, all the way to a stability operation to protect the government in Venezuela, on the other side of the world.[3] For each, they considered the stresses placed on the Russian military in assembling the forces, moving them to their theatre of operations, whether by land, sea or air, and then sustaining them. With the exception of the Ukrainian scenario – which the authors themselves considered an unpredictable outlier – only one would *not* trigger 'excess stress' on one or other of the variables. This one posited a rising Islamic State insurgency in neighbouring Tajikistan and the deployment, with the local government's approval, of a battalion of *Spetsnaz* and six regular BTGs plus supporting elements. Even so, this would put moderate stress on Russia's airlift capacity; as we will be discussing in the next chapter, this is a distinct limiting factor on any rapid or distant deployment.

All the other five scenarios, from sending a relief force to Syria to clashing with China over Kazakhstan, put excessive strain on some aspect of Russia's rail, airlift or sealift capabilities, while the latter also exceeded the predicted capacity to raise the contingent (18 manoeuvre battalions, only one-tenth of total forces) in the timeframe needed. After all, even movements by rail within Russia and its immediate neighbourhood require huge logistical efforts. The transport of a single division demands between 1,950 and 2,600 wagons, for example, which could mean up to 50 whole trains.

The conclusion is that Russia's Ground Forces are powerful in theatres close to their western and south-western military infrastructure – as the Georgians and Ukrainians know to their cost – but not in a position globally to project and above all maintain large forces, and even on its southern and eastern borders, it will often struggle to move fast. This is not to denigrate the Russian military. It has very real capabilities, especially when used as intended, and this provides Moscow with a whole suite of strategic options, from credible 'heavy metal diplomacy'[4] – coercive diplomacy – all the way through to kinetic operations, as will be discussed below.

Yet this is not the Red Army, and thoughts of it crashing through Western Europe to the Channel or even of a quick push along the Baltic coast, simply are not borne out by the technical details of force structure, logistics and lift. Indeed, the way the 2022 Ukrainian invasion quickly bogged down was evidence both of the challenges of logistics and of the catastrophic degree to which Putin and his commanders had failed properly to consider them. Assessments such as the RAND's are essentially all based on structural and physical capacities – numbers of tanks, volume of fuel pipelines, range of transport aircraft. They cannot account for all the intangibles of training, morale, discipline and command. As will be discussed later – and as has been very evident in Ukraine – on these indices, progress had clearly been much less impressive than Shoigu's PR machine had led everyone, even Putin, to believe.

21

The Sky is Russia's!

It must have been hard for the airmen. As Russia took its nationalist turn, gung-ho action movies began to be churned out – some pretty good, some atrociously bad – showing heroic engineers or infantry, sailors or *Spetsnaz*. The Air Forces hadn't really had their chance at a blockbuster. They played a minimal, supporting role in Crimea; they were conspicuously absent from the skies over the Donbas; and carpet-bombing Chechen cities, full of civilians who were Russian citizens, after all, somehow lacked glamour. Syria changed all that, and a big release for 2021 was *Nebo* ('Sky'), loosely based on the shooting down of a Su-24M bomber by Turkish fighters in 2015. Of course, this time, it's made clear who the good guys are, and both the aircrew of the downed plane are saved. It's perhaps a little too Slavically soulful to be considered Russia's answer to *Top Gun*, but it is slick and pyrotechnic and, thanks to the Defence Ministry's active support (part of it was actually shot in Syria), uses genuine aircraft and locations to good effect. There's even a Shoigu-alike, who growls that 'we don't abandon our people'.

After a decade of decline, followed by a decade in some ways in the shadows, the late Putin era and especially the Syrian intervention has provided the Russian Aerospace Forces (VKS: *Vozdushno-Kosmicheskiye Sily*) with a chance to, well, spread their wings. Some 90% of all ground attack, bomber, interceptor and transport flight crews have now served at least one tour in Syria, and some flew 150–200 sorties there, equivalent to the total annual flying time for many Western counterparts.[1]

Meanwhile, about three-quarters of the air fleet is considered to be modern or modernized.

ALWAYS IN TRANSITION

Russia has had an air force since 1912; the Imperial Air Force played a role in the First World War, and was succeeded by the Workers' and Peasants' Red Air Fleet in 1918, later the Air Force of the Red Army. Much of what was by then the Military Air Forces (VVS: *Voyenno-Vozdushniye Sily*) was shattered on the first days of the German invasion in 1941, often destroyed on the ground thanks to Stalin's wilful refusal to believe his own spies and generals about the imminence of war. Rebuilt at speed during that apocalyptic confrontation, it continued its regular re-invention, and through the Cold War years developed and expanded. By 1980, it was the largest such force in the world, with around 10,000 aircraft of all types, within three distinct elements: the strategic bombers of Long-Range Aviation (DA: *Dalnaya Aviatsiya*), the interceptors and ground attack aircraft of Frontal Aviation (FA: *Frontovaya Aviatsiya*), and Military Transport Aviation (VTA: *Voyenno-Transportnaya Aviatsiya*).

Beyond that, there was – and still is – also a separate Naval Aviation (AV-MF: *Aviatsiya Voyenno-Morskovo Flota*). Meanwhile, having been first a division of the artillery and then, in 1941, the Main Directorate of Air Defence of the Red Army, after the Great Patriotic War, in 1954, it became a full arm of service, the Air Defence Forces (PVO: *Protivovozdushnoi Oborony*), divided into the Anti-Aircraft Missile Forces, Fighter Aviation and Radio Engineering Troops.

When the Soviet Union was dissolved, Russia retained the same structure and the lion's share of Soviet air assets: some 65% of personnel and 40% of aircraft. Nonetheless, air forces are especially vulnerable to periods of inaction and inattention: pilots who do not fly enough hours see their skills degrade; airframes not subject to regular maintenance become unflyable or unsafe; air fleets not modernized become quickly obsolescent. The 1990s were thus especially hard on the VVS and the PVO. By 1995, Frontal Aviation had shrunk from over 5,000 warplanes to fewer than half that, for example, of which two-thirds were already deemed close to obsolete. A similar pattern obtained across the other air forces.

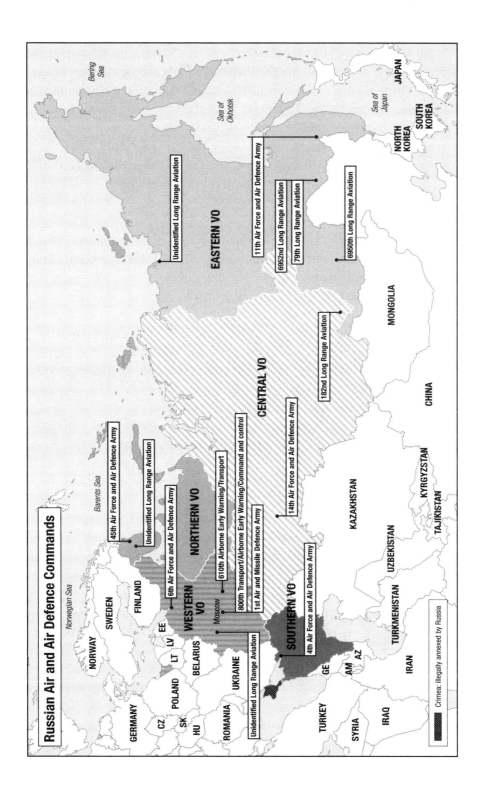

Russian Air and Air Defence Commands

EASTERN VO

- Unidentified Long Range Aviation
- 11th Air Force and Air Defence Army
- 6952nd Long Range Aviation
- 79th Long Range Aviation
- 6950th Long Range Aviation

CENTRAL VO

- 14th Air Force and Air Defence Army
- 182nd Long Range Aviation

WESTERN VO

- 45th Air Force and Air Defence Army
- Unidentified Long Range Aviation
- 6th Air Force and Air Defence Army
- 610th Airborne Early Warning/Transport
- 800th Transport/Airborne Early Warning/Command and control
- 1st Air and Missile Defence Army

NORTHERN VO

SOUTHERN VO

- 4th Air Force and Air Defence Army
- Unidentified Long Range Aviation

Crimea: illegally annexed by Russia

Bering Sea

Sea of Okhotsk

Sea of Japan

JAPAN

NORTH KOREA

SOUTH KOREA

MONGOLIA

CHINA

KAZAKHSTAN

KYRGYZSTAN

TAJIKISTAN

UZBEKISTAN

TURKMENISTAN

IRAN

GE
AM
AZ

TURKEY

SYRIA

IRAQ

ROMANIA

UKRAINE

BELARUS

POLAND

GERMANY

CZ
SK
HU

LT
LV
EE

Moscow

FINLAND

SWEDEN

NORWAY

Barents Sea

Norwegian Sea

In 1998, the PVO were rolled into the VVS, while certain aspects of the strategic defence of the Motherland fell to the new Space Forces, established in 2001. These, in turn, became the basis of the Aerospace Defence Forces (VVKO: *Voiska Vozdushno-Kosmicheskoye Oborony*), formed as a distinct arm of service in 2011. The game of musical chairs was not yet over, though, and in 2015 they merged with the VVS to form the new, all-inclusive Aerospace Forces, which includes everything from helicopter gunships to anti-ballistic missile systems.

THE AEROSPACE FORCES

The VKS has now around 148,000 personnel, of whom around three-quarters are professionals. As of the start of 2021, the VKS operated some 1,709 fixed-wing combat aircraft and some 1,500 helicopters. These included 380 Su-27 and 267 MiG-29 fighters, 131 MiG-31 interceptors, and the first five new advanced MiG-35 fighter-bombers. There were also 274 Su-24 and 125 Su-34 bombers, and 193 Su-25 ground attack jets. Long-Range Aviation also fielded 16 Tu-160, 42 Tu-95, and 66 Tu-22M bombers. To these can be added 91 aircraft in Naval Aviation: 22 MiG-29s, 43 Su-27/33s, 22 Su-24s, and four Su-25s. There are also transport aircraft and reconnaissance and command platforms, including the 16 Beriev A-50 airborne early warning and control aircraft of the 144th Airborne Early Warning Regiment, with their distinctive massive radar rotodome atop the fuselage. Then there are more than 650 helicopters in the operational air fleet, although this is out of a nominal total fleet of more than 850. The expectation is that the share that is fully operational will steadily rise, not least as Soviet legacy helicopters are formally scrapped or mothballed as new models are brought into service.

This is a substantial air fleet, second only to that of the United States, although it is still dependent on Soviet-era airframes. While some of these have proven amenable to extensive modernization, attempts to create wholly new designs, such as the Su-57 stealth fighter, represent, as already noted, quite a challenge. Nonetheless, Moscow is serious about building up its air forces both to defend the Motherland and also to support its Ground Forces in both defence and offence. It is a mark of the new emphasis on the vertical integration of forces that while, as of writing, commander-in-chief of the VKS Gen. Sergei Surovikin may wear air force blues, until 2017, he was a Ground Forces officer. He rose in the ranks of the mechanized infantry, fighting in Afghanistan, Tajikistan and the Second Chechen War (where he was wounded in action) and in 2017 commanded the Russian contingent in Syria. He has a reputation not just as a tough and uncompromising soldier – in 2004, one of his subordinates shot himself in Surovikin's office following a bad review – but also a problem-solver able to come up with creative solutions. He spent a tour in charge of the General Staff's Main Operations Directorate, often the mark of a high-flier tipped for the top, and had already demonstrated his innovative capacities in 2012, when he was tasked with forming the new Military Police. His career has not been without controversies, but he has so far been able to survive them, whether the seven months he spent in custody after the 1991 August Coup (three men died during clashes when Surovikin was leading a battalion of troops loyal to the plotters) or when, in 1995, he was convicted of having stolen and sold a service weapon (the charge was later quashed). Nonetheless, he is regarded as perhaps best combining the decisiveness and future-oriented thinking Russia's military needs, and his unprecedented second tour heading forces in Syria in 2019 was another signal that this is a man to watch – possibly even a future Chief of the General Staff.

The Air Forces and the Air and Missile Defence Forces (PVO-PRO: *Voiska Protivovozdushnoy i Protivoraketnoy Oborony*) are largely divided into four tactical Air and Air Defence Armies, one for each main military district: the 6th for the West, 4th for the South, 14th for the Central and 11th for the East. These field mixes of interceptors, tactical bombers, reconnaissance aircraft and ground-to-air missile systems. The 6th Air and Air Defence Army, for example, is based in St Petersburg and includes the 105th Guards Composite Aviation Division with three squadrons of interceptors, one of fighter-bombers and one of reconnaissance aircraft, the 2nd and 32nd Air Defence Divisions with seven regiments of SAMs, and also naval assets based in the Kaliningrad exclave: the 4th Independent Naval Aviation Attack Regiment, the 689th Guards Naval Aviation Fighter Regiment and the 44th Air Defence Division. All told, that accounts for 12 squadrons of combat aircraft, nine SAM regiments and five radio-technical regiments. It also has three regiments of helicopters and one of transport aircraft. Admittedly, the Western VO is a priority theatre, and is in any case supplemented by the special 1st Air Defence and Missile Defence Army, responsible for Moscow. This has two divisions (nine regiments) of SAMs and the 9th Anti-Ballistic Missile Defence Division. This last maintains the Don-2N battle management phased array radar site at Sofrino, north-east of the capital, and five launch sites with a total of 68 53T6 (ABM-3) short-range interceptor missiles. Given that they try to defeat incoming missiles by themselves detonating a 10-kiloton thermonuclear warhead in the stratosphere above Moscow, they are very much a last resort. Nonetheless, even if the Western VO is especially well provisioned (though the 6th does labour under one of the duller mottos: 'Securely guarding Russia's North-Western Sky'), this gives a sense of the kind of range of assets within one of these formations.

Long-Range Aviation remains separate, flying some 60 veteran TU-95MS Bear long-range turboprops, 50 smaller supersonic Tu-22M3 Blinders and 17 of the newer Tu-160M2 'Blackjack' swing-wing bombers. Although subordinated to the commander-in-chief of the VKS and also used for conventional fire missions, all playing a role in the Syrian campaign for example, they are part of Russia's nuclear triad, and thus DA is discussed below in Chapter 25 along with the Space Troops, which likewise are subordinated not to the VOs but to Aerospace Command in Moscow.

DEFENCE OF THE MOTHERLAND

Some Western (especially US) strategic planners have become increasingly alarmed about what they call a growing problem of Russian A2/AD, standing for 'Anti-Access and Area Denial'. The central notion is that, with a combination of long-range anti-shipping and anti-air missiles, the Russians could counter Western freedom of manoeuvre and its technological and mobility edge. As with so many of these 'new way of war' scares, it is both overblown and also a misunderstanding of Russian doctrine. As Michael Kofman put it:

> Russian 'A2/AD capabilities' have also become woefully overhyped, often depicted as some kind of defensive bubbles or no-go zones on a two-dimensional map. Illustrations of Russian air defense range

rings or missile rings, popularized by media, have at times reduced Russia military analysis to the study of angry looking red circles on a map.[2]

To be sure, Moscow has developed quite extensive anti-shipping and, especially, anti-air capabilities. However, the idea that it would sit safely in any such bubble misunderstands both the impenetrability even of modern, integrated air defence systems (some attacks will get through) and also the Russian style of war (which relies on its capacity actively to degrade the enemy and counter-attack).

Instead, Moscow's particular concern is the threat of a Massed Missile-Aviation Strike (MRAU: *Massirovany Raketno-Aviatsionny Udar*), that NATO would use its numerical strength and technological edge in the air to begin a conflict with a devastating blow intended to shatter Russian command and control structures, degrade its manoeuvre forces and generally try to win any war at first blow. This too may be overhyped: for every Western concern that the Russians have some new conceptual approach that gives them some fearsome edge, so too the Russians tend to over-estimate the capacities of Western military technologies. In any case, this has brought a greater urgency to the air defence mission of the VKS, and it is significant that the most recent iterations of the massive Zapad military exercises that are held every four years in western Russia and Belarus have begun with a simulated 'blue' MRAU that the 'red' defenders must resist, defeat or, in the worst cases, weather, before moving onto the counter-attack.

Ground Forces units have their own integral air defence elements, while PVO-PRO forces are not a battlefield but a strategic asset, deploying both interceptors and ground-based S-350, S-400 and S-500 long-range missile systems, supplemented by short-range systems such as the *Pantsir*-S1 (SA-22), a mobile vehicle mounting its own radar as well as two 30mm guns and 12 missiles. In the initial MRAU, their role is to ensure that the command structures that can muster and coordinate battlefield forces survive long enough to turn the conflict to their own advantage, especially as the enemy begins to run low not just on missiles, aircraft and pilots, but also on the information assets needed to launch its strikes, from communications networks to radars.

To this end, there is a sustained campaign to modernize Russia's fighter fleet. The mainstay will be agile Su-30SM2 and Su-35S fighters, developments of the combat-proven Su-27 Flanker airframe, supplemented by lighter MiG-35s, although there seems less enthusiasm for this modernized version of the MiG-29 Fulcrum, and the current order appears as much as anything to keep the Mikoyan-Gurevich design bureau in business. Eventually, the Su-57 stealth fighter is coming into service, with 76 on order, although no clear sense as to whether the target of deploying a full regiment of 24 of them by 2025 will be met.

FIST OF THE MOTHERLAND

While recognizing the threat from Western aerial assets, the Russians have also placed much effort into developing their own attack capabilities. To a considerable degree, their way of thinking about the use of these forces is rooted in Soviet thinking. The notion of Deep Battle, pioneered by Marshal Mikhail Tukhachevsky in the 1920s, saw the path to victory as not just on the front line, but by shattering and disrupting the enemy's forces throughout the depth of the battlefield, essentially seeking to overwhelm their capacity to coordinate and respond and break their lines of command and supply. This helps explain, for example, the Soviets' enthusiasm for paratroopers able to land well behind the line of contact. This was originally something to be achieved primarily through major ground attacks deep into enemy territory, but by the 1970s another innovative military thinker, Marshal Nikolai Ogarkov, was looking at how long-range missiles, precision munitions and airstrikes could be used to supplement the corps-sized Operational Manoeuvre Group on the ground.

The Soviets lacked the capacity to build adequate quality and quantities of precision munitions for this truly to take root (to an extent, Russia still does), and instead relied on copious amounts of tactical airpower and artillery. However, the sight of the way Allied technology provided such a decisive edge during the 1991 *Desert Storm* campaign in Iraq made it clear how important this would be. Through the 1990s, Russian military theoreticians wrote about the power of long-range 'non-contact warfare', but the armed forces lacked the funds and leadership to do much about it. Since then, the Russians have made strides to catch up, and while much of this is about long-range systems such as the *Iskander* tactical missile or the Kh-101 air-launched cruise missile, it also speaks to the continued importance of battlefield airpower.

The VKS's battlefield close air support capabilities are especially well represented by the dated, but still effective Su-25 jet and also a wide range of helicopter types. The Su-25 *Grach* (Rook) has been in service since 1981, and despite various upgrades is showing its age. Nonetheless it is a tough and hard-hitting aircraft, a fitting descendant of the legendary Il-2 *Sturmovik* of Second World War fame. Although there was talk of its being replaced with a new ground attack jet, in practice for the moment it is helicopters which are picking up any slack. The old bruiser is the Mi-24/35 'Hind' flying tank, a gunship and assault troop carrier. However, the main ground attack role is now played by nimbler, dedicated attack helicopters: the Mi-24 Havok and the Ka-50/52, with its distinctive two contra-rotating coaxial rotors.

The strategic bombers will be discussed later, but in the medium-range bomber fleet, the old Soviet-era standard, the Su-24 Fencer, is slowly being replaced by the Su-34 Fullback, an all-weather supersonic fighter-bomber developed on the basis of the Su-27 fighter. It demonstrated its capabilities over Syria, with dramatically better avionics than the Su-24 and the capacity to carry 8 tonnes of bombs, rockets and missiles. The Su-24 will remain in service for some time to come, though, and in a neat workaround, given Russia's continued shortage of precision-guided munitions and the systems necessary to use them effectively, it has been fitted with the new SVP-24 aiming system that accounts for speed, altitude, wind and the like to allow it to drop cheap 'dumb' bombs almost with the accuracy of pricy 'smart' ones.

HEAVY LIFT

They may not be as exciting as high-flying interceptors, rocket-laden ground attackers and battlefield-scouring bombers, but the 225 or so transport aircraft of the VTA are not only essential to strategic mobility across this huge country, but they have also proven crucial to Moscow's wider power projection. At peak, they were flying 2,000 tonnes a day in materiel to Syria.[3] Furthermore, in January 2022, the president of Kazakhstan requested the intervention of a peacekeeping contingent from the CSTO (the Collective Security Treaty Organization, Moscow's attempt to create a Eurasian NATO analogue) in the face of widespread protests that he rather unconvincingly claimed were mobilized by foreign terrorists. That Russian paratroopers were on their way in hours attests not only to their readiness, but also that of the VTA. Indeed, Russian transport aircraft also ferried the small Belarusian and Armenian contingents taking part in the deployment.

Until 2009 known as the 61st Air Army of the Supreme Command, the VTA has also incorporated strategic transport assets formerly within the Navy and Strategic Missile Forces, and it maintains a fleet based on four types of aircraft. The An-26 is a twin-engine turboprop tactical transport that can carry 40 people or just under 6 tonnes. The larger, four-engine An-12 can carry 100 paratroopers or 20 tonnes of cargo and acquired an infamous reputation in the Soviet–Afghan War as the 'Black Tulip' that also brought home the bodies of dead soldiers. The Il-76 is the standard heavy lifter, a rugged long-range jet able to carry 126 fully equipped paratroopers, 145 troops or 50 tonnes of cargo, albeit it is still dwarfed by the ten or so operational wide-bodied An-124 'Ruslan' aircraft in service, each of which can carry 880 soldiers or 120 tonnes.

Nonetheless, the VTA, like every one of Russia's air forces, is also showing the strain. That figure of 225 aircraft relates to those still flying – there are perhaps another hundred still on the books but not flight-worthy and probably being cannibalized for spare parts. There are maybe 90 Il-76s still operational, 40 An-26s, and 56 An-12s, as well as a last three dated An-22 turboprop heavy lifters. Indeed, much of the VTA fleet is getting old, and keeping them running is tough, especially as the Antonovs were built originally in Ukraine, so getting new components is a particular challenge now. Furthermore, the Il-76 workhorse is ill-suited to serious power projection. Whereas the An-124 can even carry three battle tanks in its cavernous hold, anything larger than the paratroopers' deliberately low-profile vehicles needs to be dismantled to fit in an Il-76. Although a new Il-112V is meant to replace the increasingly dated An-26 as the standard light transport, the first prototype crashed in August 2021 and the project's status is unclear. But while a modernized Il-76MD-90A began to be brought into service from 2018, though it may be a little longer-ranged and a little more efficient, it is no bigger. The VTA will have to lean heavily on those few An-124s in case of any serious future operations away from Russia and its railways.

DRONES

Russia may have come late to realizing the full capacities of the drone, but it is now a convinced fan, with more than 500, ranging from small scouts to missile-armed unmanned combat aerial vehicles (UCAVs). Its own early examples were of indifferent quality, to say the least, but having observed how Georgia used Israeli Hermes 450s in 2008, Moscow opted instead to buy Israeli. First, in 2009, it bought 14 Bird-Eye 400, I-View Mk 150 and Searcher Mk II drones, and the next year, it concluded a $400 million contract to licence-produce the Bird-Eye 400 and Searcher Mk II as the *Zastava* and *Forpost*, respectively (both, confusingly, translate as 'Outpost'). It used this to galvanize its own domestic production. Since then, drones have directed artillery fire onto Ukrainian forces in the Donbas, tracked rebel supply caravans in Syria and featured regularly in the over-excited broadcasts of the military's own *Zvezda* ('Star') TV channel. Once, in 2021, three successive episodes of *Voyennaya Priyomka* ('Military Acceptance' – probably better translated as 'Military Grade') I watched had segments exalting the capabilities of Russia's new drones.

Following the brief 2020 Azerbaijan–Armenian War, in which much was made of the Azeris' use of Turkish-made Bayraktar TB-2 drones to hammer Moscow-supplied Armenian forces (albeit ones without the kind of integrated air defence system that would screen Russian troops), there was a clear attempt to demonstrate a similar or greater capacity. It is not just about showing off Russia's own drones, such as the *Forpost* and *Orlan*-10 scouts and the *Inokhodets-RU* ('Pacer') and Orion UCAVs, able to drop bombs or launch missiles at a target. It is also about new capabilities. Most recently, an Orion was shown shooting down another drone with an air-to-air missile, opening up a new age of drone dogfights.

All that said, the Russians are still playing catch-up, not least because of shortages and deficiencies in some of the electronic and avionic systems. Their long-range strategic reconnaissance drone, the Altius, is really Moscow's answer to the American RQ-4 Global Hawk, for example. Whereas the RQ-4 has been in use since 2001, though, the Altius is, as of writing, only just about to go into service. Likewise, while the new Sukhoi S-70 *Okhotnik* ('Hunter'), a heavy stealth UCAV, looks impressive in theory, it is still in the prototype phase. This is in part because of that perennial problem for all such projects, new capabilities and features such as a new, stealthier flat engine nozzle being added in the process. The idea is that it will be able to be networked with Su-57s or operate independently, but it is no more clear when it will be ready than Sukhoi's manned stealth fighter-bombers.

22

Contesting the Sea

The *Admiral Kuznetsov* is the largest ship in the Russian navy, its only aircraft carrier, and a powerful combat unit that, as well as an air wing of 18 Su-33 Flanker-D air superiority fighters, six MiG-29K Fulcrum-D multi-role jets and a mix of Kamov Ka-27 and Ka-31 helicopters, mounts 12 P-700 *Granit* (SS-N-19) long-range anti-shipping cruise missiles. It seems to be the unluckiest ship in the Russian navy, too.

It was commissioned in Soviet times but only became operational in 1995. Even its name is a guide to the changing politics of the era. First it was to be called the *Riga*, after the capital of what was then the Latvian Soviet Socialist Republic, then, after his death, the *Leonid Brezhnev*, after the late Soviet leader. Brezhnev's corrupt and conservative ways faced increasing criticism in the Gorbachev years, so instead it was decided to name it the *Tbilisi*, for the Georgian capital. As the collapse of the USSR became increasingly plausible, it seemed to be tempting fate to name it after a city potentially soon not to be under Moscow's control, so in 1990, the ship was renamed *Admiral Flota Sovetskovo Soyuza N.G. Kuznetsov*, after Admiral of the Fleet Nikolai Kuznetsov, the well-regarded People's Commissar for the Navy through the Second World War.

The *Kuznetsov* has the characteristically aggressive lines of a Soviet warship, and was designed for a different mission than US supercarriers. Instead of 'blue water' power projection around the world, it was largely conceived to provide air support for the defence of the Motherland's waters – and to sink NATO counterparts. However, its track record has been rather less impressive. Time and again, it has broken down or suffered serious malfunctions, from engine failures to broken evaporators, such that on deployment it is always accompanied by a tug, just in case. It doesn't help its image that its steam turbines burn the heavy, low-quality fuel oil known as *mazut*, which often gives off a dense black smoke, making it look in trouble even when steaming at speed.

Two years after it had joined the fleet, the *Kuznetsov* ended up back at dock for major repairs, and since then it has been in and out of shipyards, albeit in some cases simply for upgrades. In 2016–17, it participated in the Syrian War, and its aircraft reportedly carried out 420 combat missions, hitting 1,252 hostile targets. On the other hand, as noted previously, it also lost two planes from its air wing from accidents and for a while they were actually flying out of Hmeymim. In 2017, though, it sailed back to the Northern Fleet headquarters at Severomorsk. It was due further maintenance and modernization, but the problem for the Russians was that it had been built in the Mykolaiv shipyards on Ukraine's Black Sea coast, and with Moscow and Kyiv in a state of undeclared war, it could hardly go back there. Russia lacked dry dock facilities that were really adequate to the task, and the best they could offer was the PD-50 floating dry dock at Roslyakovo, near Murmansk.

On 30 October 2018, though, PD-50 suddenly sank, as the *Kuznetsov* was leaving it. One of the dock's cranes smashed onto and through the carrier's flight deck. In 2019, work began on joining two dry-land docks to create one that could accommodate its 305-metre length. Then in December of that year, a serious fire broke out on the ship while it was being worked on: two people died and yet more damage was done that would need to be repaired. Further accidents, mishaps and acts of God permitting, it is scheduled to be operational again by the end of 2023, with new avionics, power plant and, potentially, missiles. One suspects that a lot of admirals and naval engineers are crossing their fingers most fervently.

On one level, the story of *Kuznetsov*'s (mis)adventures could be taken as proof that the Russian navy is a paper tiger (or perhaps water-soluble orca), a force with ambitions that far outreach its capabilities. There is some truth in that, although, in fairness, everyone's ships suffer breakdowns and need regular upgrades, even if not always with the

Kuznetsov's striking frequency. However, one can also read much into its distinctive design and role, as well as the way that Moscow persists in repairing it, despite some suggestions that it would be better to cut the navy's losses and decommission it or put it up for sale. After all, this is what happened to its planned sister ship, the *Varyag*, whose hull the Ukrainians ended up selling to China, who commissioned it as the *Liaoning*. Rather, in its own way, the *Kuznetsov* saga illustrates Russia's particular vision for its navy, one rooted in geography, history and current ambitions.

NEVER A NAVAL POWER

As befits a country that for most of its history had no warm-water ports, and instead sprawls across a substantial swathe of Eurasia, Russia has never really been a serious naval power. In the 17th century, Peter the Great was the first tsar seriously to make this priority, both because Russia was increasingly a Baltic and Black Sea power, and also because of his own fascination with boats. This was, in part, a vanity project, and with his death in 1725, it was becalmed until the mid-18th century, not least due to growing rivalries with the Ottoman Empire. Under the legendary Adm. Fyodor Ushakov, who became known even amongst the Turks with respect as 'Ushak Pasha' and who never lost any of the 43 engagements he commanded as admiral, the power and prestige of the Imperial Russian Navy certainly rose. (Ushakov, incidentally, was in 2001 canonized by the Russian Orthodox Church and declared the patron saint of the strategic bomber fleet.)

By the beginning of the 19th century, the Imperial Navy had its Baltic and Black Sea Fleets, and the Caspian, White Sea, and Okhotsk Flotillas. Its navigators were circumnavigating the globe. However, just as the 1853–56 Crimean War highlighted the backwardness of the Russian army compared with its British and French counterparts, the same was true of the navy. It made no serious attempt to contest at sea, and sailors instead were pressed into service as infantry. After that, attempts were made to modernize, but they would always be limited by a lack of funds and technology – but also by the very real question of just how great a priority should the navy be given, compared with the army?

In essence, Russia's navy was bound to be an essentially regional, not global one, its main missions being the defence of the coast and the projection of power into seas immediately abutting onto the Motherland. This would carry through into the Soviet era, with naval personnel again often being pressed into a role as infantry in the desperate early days of the Great Patriotic War. Indeed, the very first order to fire on attacking German aircraft came from Black Sea Fleet chief of staff R. Adm. Yeliseyev. After the war, with the USSR's new status as a global superpower, renewed efforts would be made to expand the reach of the Red Navy, but this would again always be a secondary mission.

It was telling, after all, that the first priority was to build a submarine fleet – the aim was to deny access to Soviet waters and then to disrupt enemy naval operations and supply lines, rather than anything else. The forceful and thoughtful Adm. Sergei Gorshkov, commander-in-chief of the navy for most of the post-war era (1956–85), was a consistent advocate of an expanded surface as well as submarine fleet, and a 'blue water', ocean-going one at that. Soviet leader Nikita Khrushchev was often opposed to what he considered these grandiose and expensive designs, though, and the 1960s actually saw cuts. Nonetheless, Gorshkov was insistent and under Khrushchev's successor, Leonid Brezhnev, his plans coincided with the Kremlin's growing desire to project Soviet power around the world – and specifically to contest the US Navy for control of the oceans. Of course, this was never a viable proposition given the disproportion of the Soviet and US economies and the continued pre-eminence of land power in Moscow's calculus, but nonetheless, by Gorshkov's retirement in 1985, the Soviet fleet was at its peak, with more than 1,500 vessels ranging up to the nuclear-powered *Kirov*-class battlecruisers and *Akula*-class ('Shark') ballistic missile submarines, both the largest vessels of their class in the world.

RUSTED, REBUILT

Of course, the late 1980s and 1990s saw massive contractions and decay as a result of disuse and neglect. A particular issue, which would come back to haunt both Moscow and Kyiv in 2014, was what to do with the Black Sea Fleet (ChF: *Chyornomorsky Flot*). After all, the division of most of the Soviet navy in 1992 was relatively straightforward.

The agreement was that forces would devolve to the new nation on whose soil they were based (there was an exception made over nuclear assets, covered below), but with the Baltic States already independent, most of the fleet had sailed to Russian ports. The exception was the Black Sea Fleet, one of the most important, which was headquartered at Sevastopol, on the Crimean peninsula. Most of its sailors, though, wanted to be Russian – and Moscow itself was not willing to give up the lion's share of the fleet to a Ukraine that, to be blunt, could hardly afford to maintain it. Furthermore, losing all the ChF's Crimean stations would leave Russia with almost no assets in the Black Sea. Tensions within the fleet between those who professed loyalty to Moscow and those willing to join the new Ukrainian navy grew, and in a precursor of later events this began to trigger pro-Russian nationalists in Crimea.

After protracted negotiations, with the brief and uncomfortable establishment of a joint fleet (albeit under a Russian admiral), in 1997 a proper partition was agreed which saw the bulk of the ChF pass to Moscow, which also took out a lease on port facilities and ancillary land on Crimea. Originally, this was just until 2017, then extended until 2042, with options for further extensions. Nonetheless, this was always something of an uncomfortable stopgap. Ukrainian nationalists, not unreasonably, were unhappy with the thought of foreign bases on their territory. The Russians, equally with merit, were uncomfortable with having to depend on the goodwill of a government with which their relations were not always good. Arguably, the seeds of 2014 were sown in 1997 – and even 1991.

In any case, the Putin era has been one of reconstruction – up to a point. The navy was clearly not an early priority for him, for all that his father had originally served as a Soviet submariner. Indeed, in the 2000s, most of the budget allocation for naval shipbuilding was directed to shoring up Russia's nuclear capability, being spent on developing the *Borei*-class submarine and the R-30 *Bulava* ('Mace') submarine-launched ballistic missile. In the next decade, a greater share of the procurement budget went to the navy: 25% of the total, compared with 15% for the Ground Forces. While this undoubtedly had a major impact on the industry, building ships takes time, especially when the industry itself has been in the doldrums for years. It was not until the later years of the decade that it really began to be felt, and issues such

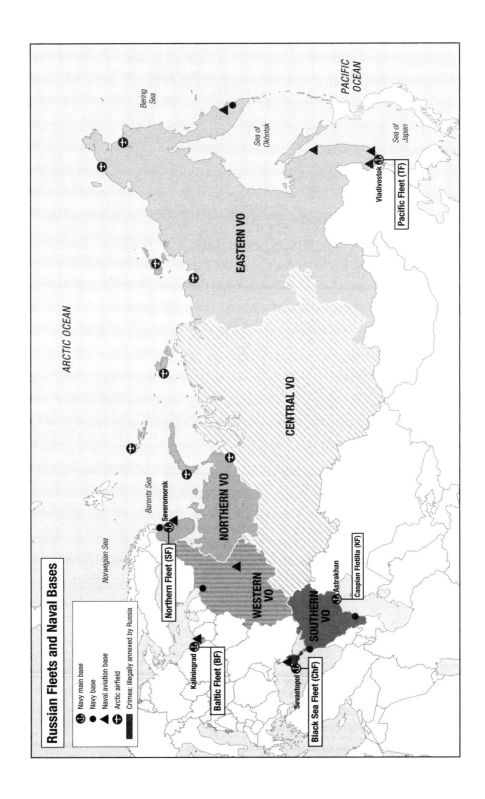

Russian Fleets and Naval Bases

Legend:
- Navy main base
- Navy base
- Naval aviation base
- Arctic airfield
- Crimea: illegally annexed by Russia

ARCTIC OCEAN

PACIFIC OCEAN

Bering Sea

Sea of Okhotsk

Sea of Japan

Barents Sea

Norwegian Sea

EASTERN VO

CENTRAL VO

NORTHERN VO

WESTERN VO

SOUTHERN VO

Vladivostok

Pacific Fleet (TF)

Severomorsk

Northern Fleet (SF)

Astrakhan

Caspian Flotilla (KF)

Kaliningrad

Baltic Fleet (BF)

Sevastopol

Black Sea Fleet (ChF)

as the loss of Ukrainian-made gas turbine engines also slowed progress on larger designs.

The 2011–20 State Armament Programme had planned for 54 ships and 24 submarines to be delivered by 2020. In fact, it only managed fewer than half that, and production skewed towards smaller vessels. In fairness, that was also in part because the lead vessels of several whole new designs were being built, which tends to take longer than their subsequent reproduction, but nonetheless this ambitious programme is lagging. The Kremlin is also wary of excessively grandiose plans by the admirals. In 2012, for example, Adm. Viktor Chirkov, then navy commander-in-chief, outlined his goals out to 2050, including not just one, but a series of full-deck aircraft carriers to be the core of ocean-going task forces. As of writing, this is an idea the leadership is firmly sitting on.

ORGANIZATION

The navy is divided into four fleets and a flotilla subordinated to appropriate Military Districts, and the Northern Fleet, which in 2014 was made a Joint Strategic Command in its own right to reflect the growing importance of the High North.

The **Baltic Fleet** (BF: *Baltiisky Flot*), headquartered in the Kaliningrad exclave, is part of the Western Military District. It is also the smallest of the fleets, perhaps reflecting the fact that it would be hard pressed to operate especially confidently in the Baltic in a time of war. This has also determined the nature of its reconstruction, which has focused on smaller corvettes and missile boats, including the new semi-stealthy *Karakurt* class, which is just 67 metres long yet nonetheless mounts tubes for eight *Kalibr* or *Oniks* supersonic anti-shipping missiles, as well as a launch cradle for an *Orlan*-10 drone. On the other hand, given that Kaliningrad has increasingly been built up as a forward base for the Russian military, it is unsurprising that the BF also has a powerful air and coastal defence component. The former is based around a division of S-400 SAMs and the 34th Mixed Naval Aviation Division with both interceptors as well as attack aircraft. The latter includes an anti-shipping missile brigade with Bal and *Bastion* systems, the 336th Independent Naval Infantry Brigade, and a Naval *Spetsnaz* unit, while Kaliningrad is also home to the 11th Army Corps, with the 18th Guards Motor Rifle

Division, the 7th Independent Guards Motor Rifle Regiment and two brigades of artillery.

The **Black Sea Fleet** (ChF: *Chyornomorsky Flot*), still headquartered in Sevastopol in Crimea, is part of the Southern Military District and tasked with projecting power into not simply the Black Sea but also the Mediterranean, to which end since 2013 it has also included the Permanent Operational Formation of the Russian Navy in the Mediterranean Sea which, presumably to everyone's relief, is generally known simply as the Mediterranean Squadron. This is primarily made up of ChF vessels, but also regularly includes ones from others, both to lighten the burden on the one fleet and also to give the others a chance to gain further experience. Originally including up to 15 ships – at least six combatants and the rest support vessels – it has fluctuated in size from ten to 20, with the Syrian conflict providing a particular impetus towards expansion and a base in the increasingly significant facility at Tarsus on the Syrian coast. The ChF has seen more than its share of action, having sent ships to the Abkhazian coast and landed troops during the 2008 Georgian War, played a key role in the 2014 annexation of Crimea, supported the Syrian intervention and engaged in the 2022 Ukrainian war, even seeing its flagship, the missile cruiser *Moskva*, sunk in action.

Also subordinated to the Southern VO is the separate **Caspian Flotilla** (KF: *Kaspiiskaya Flotilya*). Although relatively small, with nine corvettes and 15 gunboats and minesweepers, it is nonetheless the most powerful naval formation in the Caspian Sea, whose waters Russia shares with Azerbaijan, Iran, Kazakhstan and Turkmenistan, and its corvettes have even launched *Kalibr* missiles all the way to Syria. Two divisions of anti-shipping missiles are likewise enough essentially to control the sea at will. As part of a general upgrade of the flotilla, in 2020 its headquarters was moved from Astrakhan to Kaspiisk and its Naval Infantry regiment has received new T-72B3 tanks.

The **Pacific Fleet** (TF: *Tikhoökeansky Flot*), with its headquarters in Vladivostok, is part of the Eastern Military District. In the 1990s, it suffered the hardest from a lack of resources and attention, as it seemed to have least strategic significance at the time. Until the 2010s it was scarcely able to operate as a fleet. Since then, it has received a number of new vessels – ironically, the very scale of the previous neglect has meant that it is now one of the most modern formations, as many of its older vessels simply could not be updated. It is, though, still relatively reliant on smaller vessels. Its largest vessel is the flagship *Varyag*, a *Slava*-class missile cruiser, and it has just a single destroyer and three frigates, but fully 16 corvettes and 32 missile boats, patrol ships and minesweepers, along with landing and support ships. The TF also fields four nuclear-powered ballistic missile submarines, five other nuclear-powered submarines, and eight diesel submarines. Given the size of its area of operation, as well as the specific need to patrol the waters around Kamchatka and the disputed Kuril Islands, the TF was also one of the first to use drones for maritime reconnaissance, flying from its Yelizovo base on Kamchatka.

The **Northern Fleet** (SF: *Severny Flot*), as mentioned, is the core component of the Northern Military District. Headquartered in Severomorsk on the Barents Sea, it also has land and air components (the 14th Army Corps and the 45th Air Force and Air Defence Army) as it is responsible for the Murmansk and Arkhangelsk Regions, as well as the Komi Republic and the Nenets Autonomous District. Nonetheless, its primary missions are to support Russia's nuclear missile submarine fleet in the northern waters – keeping foreign hunter-killer submarines away from its own ballistic missile submarine 'bastions' – and more broadly securing the icy but thawing seas along the country's northern borders.

The SF is also called on disproportionately for flag-flying missions, not least because it has three of Russia's relatively few nuclear-powered surface ships, best able to mount long-range missions: the *Kirov*-class battlecruisers *Pyotr Velikiy* ('Peter the Great') and *Admiral Nakhimov* and the carrier *Kuznetsov*. The real striking power of the SF is in its underwater contingent. These number fully 28 boats in four submarine divisions (the 11th, 18th, 24th and 31st), and another eight under construction. Of these, nine are nuclear-powered strategic missile submarines, including *Dmitry Donskoi*, the lead ship in the massive *Akula* ('Shark') class (known as Typhoon class to NATO), which was also a testbed for new RSM-56 *Bulava* ('Mace') ballistic missiles. Four more are nuclear-powered cruise missile submarines, ten nuclear-powered hunter-killers and five quiet but shorter-ranged diesel attack submarines. Together, they represent a powerful strike force, although it is worth noting that many of the missile boats are getting dated and will soon need to be replaced.

BUT WHAT'S IT FOR?

However, for all these new vessels and increased activity, it is still important to recognize the limits of even today's Russian navy. After all, its official missions are, in order of priority:

- To deter the use or threat of military force against Russia;
- To assert national sovereignty into internal and territorial waters, as well as Russia's rights to its exclusive economic zone and freedom of the high seas;
- To ensure the safety of maritime economic activity in the World Ocean;
- To maintain a naval presence in the World Ocean through flying the flag and demonstrating its military capabilities;
- To participate in military, peacekeeping and humanitarian actions carried out by the global community that meet the interests of the state.

This is a strikingly – and explicitly – defensive set of roles. While, of course, Russia's 'offensively defensive' security posture means that aggressive operations could be launched in the name of deterrence or the protection of the Motherland, the language makes it clear that even the new Russian navy is not intended or able to play the kind of role assumed by the US Navy. It is not going to become a serious 'blue-water' force capable of contesting the World Ocean. It lacks the global network of naval bases that would require: it only has Tartus in Syria, at present, and while it has docking and refuelling rights at other ports, it is questionable whether they would be upheld in time of war. Beyond that, it also lacks the modern, long-range warships able to mount credible stand-alone task forces.

Indeed, in a full-scale conflict, it is more likely that the navy, at least its surface combatants, would be bottled up by the NATO threat and forced to huddle under the protection of land-based missiles and aircraft. I remember once hearing a Russian naval officer serving as a defence attaché abroad mournfully admit that 'unless we had air superiority, the Italian navy' – which, in fairness, is quite large and proficient – 'could deny us the Mediterranean'. At best, they can hope to close certain maritime chokepoints such as the three Danish Straits connecting the Baltic with the North Sea, and keep NATO – primarily, US – forces away from Russia's coastline. This is not least because within the whole concern about the threat of the MRAU, the Massed Missile-Aviation Strike, there is a particular worry about sea-based land attack missiles such as the doughty American Tomahawk. Nightmare scenarios include volleys launched from US submarines, as well as fleets that are both protected by missile defences and staying well away from Russia's integrated air and surface defences, hitting civil and military infrastructure with impunity.

This helps explain some of the Russians' priorities. They have a massive arsenal of mines, for example, well suited to trying to deny stretches of sea to an overconfident enemy. Long-range supersonic and even hypersonic missiles that have a chance of sinking high-value ships, and which at the very least may encourage the enemy to stand clear. Submarines, some of which are well crewed and advanced, and which again are not just a direct threat to enemy shipping, but whose very *potential* presence influences their planning and movement.

Instead, under Putin Russia has been building what is informally classified as a 'green-water' navy. It is not just a 'brown-water' one confined to its shallow littoral waters, but dreams of a 'blue-water' fleet able to project power across the oceans are unrealistic. Instead, it can command its coastal waters, and operate in nearby open seas, but neither that far, nor necessarily that confidently. They may take part in multi-national anti-piracy operations off the Horn of Africa, fly the flag across the Pacific and Atlantic and posture as a global sea power, but this is one domain in which the Russians make no bones about being unable to compete with NATO.

23

Power Projection: Blue and Black Berets

It certainly used to be the case that 2 August was the day a lot of Russian police got to pocket a lot of overtime. It probably still is. That day is *Dyen Vozdushno-Desantnykh Voisk*, or Day of the Airborne Troops, and whether you're in Palace Square in St Petersburg, Gorky Park in Moscow or squares and war memorials all across Russia (and in many post-Soviet states, for that matter), you'll see knots and clusters of serving and above all former paratroopers, in their sky-blue berets and blue-and-white striped *telnyashka* vests, chatting, singing, splashing about in public fountains, reminiscing and, of course, drinking. A chance to honour the brave, mourn the fallen and race around town in cars mounting blue and green flags and sometimes even fake turrets.

It can be a pretty rumbunctious affair, ending up in brawls with the OMON riot police, but it has become rather more sedate in recent years, not least as the state has come to recognize and thus co-opt it. You'll as likely now see wives and girlfriends there, often also in matching *telnyashki*; you can even buy suitably striped romper suits for babies and matching coats for dogs. Watermelons have, for some unfathomable reason, become something of a fixture, often handed out for free by local authorities. Nothing helps make boisterously tipsy, muscle-bound ex-paras look less intimidating than seeing them all cradle oversized fruit.

Russia has days for all kinds of professions and arms of military service and these are meaningful things, not just marketing gimmicks dreamed up to sell banal greetings cards. Even so, one does not see train drivers (1 August) sporting in public fountains, social workers (8 June) picking fights with riot police, or tax inspectors (21 November) expecting free fruit. Indeed, there are special days for every element of the military, from submariners (19 March) to radio-electrical warfare operators (15 April). But Paratroopers' Day is distinctive, not just as an expression of Russia's cult of hypermasculinity, something only deepened by Putin's bare-chested politics of sovereignty and nationalism, nor simply because of paras' macho clannishness and esprit de corps, but also increasingly through a sense that they – and the other power projection forces able to operate sometimes far beyond the country's borders – are the real expression of great power status.[1]

When Putin came to power, after all, the priority was holding on to what Russia had and defending the Motherland, whether from Chechen insurgents or some threat beyond the border. Although nuclear weapons were the ultimate guarantor, they are too crude, too dangerous an instrument for anything but the most existential threat, and so reforming the conventional military was crucial. Increasingly, though, Putin became more ambitious: it was not simply a matter of holding the borders but being able to assert and defend Russia's interests beyond them. From the 2008 Georgian War and anti-piracy operations off the Horn of Africa beginning that same year, to the seizure of Crimea and intervention into the Donbas in 2014, the Syrian deployment of 2015 and the 2022 Ukrainian invasion, Moscow has steadily been more willing to project its power abroad.

To establish Russia's status as both a global power and also the regional hegemon and security guarantor in most of post-Soviet Eurasia, it maintains substantial intervention forces: the Air Assault Troops (VDV: *Vozdushno-Desantniye Voiska*), the Naval Infantry (MP: *Morskaya Pyekhota*), and the *Spetsnaz* special forces (as well as a growing establishment of shadowy and ambiguous semi-private semi-state Private Military Companies). As the best-equipped and most professional units within the military, mainly staffed by volunteer soldiers, they represent the cutting edge of Russia's military. Once, they were often pressed into service – and grotesquely misused – as light infantry in Chechnya and elsewhere, simply because their training and fighting spirit made them the only units which could be relied upon. Now that the rest of the Ground Forces are increasingly competent, they can be used for the missions for which they are intended: power projection, rapid response and behind-the-lines mayhem.

'NOBODY BUT US!'

Nikto kromye nas, 'nobody but us', is the slogan of the VDV, and a fittingly bombastic one for a service which can claim to be one of the very first of its kind. The Soviets were pioneers of parachute warfare. Whereas Germany's *Fallschirmjäger* were only founded in 1936 and the British Parachute Regiment in 1940, the Soviets staged their first experimental jumps in 1930, established a company-strength Aviation Motorized Landing Detachment the following year, and by 1932 had a full airborne brigade. Their operations may have been relatively crude – at first they had to climb out onto a plane's wings to jump – but they fitted well into the aggressive style of 'deep warfare' pioneered by military thinkers such as Marshal Mikhail Tukhachevsky. The idea was that airborne units would strike far beyond the enemy's front line, to cut their supply lines, attack their headquarters, and spread chaos and dismay.

This mission continued into the post-war era, when the VDV became the Kremlin's political enforcers abroad. They led the way in Operation *Whirlwind*, the suppression of the anti-Soviet 1956 revolution in Hungary and Operation *Danube*, the invasion of Czechoslovakia in 1968 to end the liberal Prague Spring. They played a crucial role not just in the initial invasion of Afghanistan in 1979, but in the whole ten-year war. Of the 65 Soviet servicemen made Heroes of the Soviet Union for their conduct in Afghanistan, over one-third came from the VDV.

In the 1990s, although Defence Minister Grachyov was one of their own, they again were forced to shoulder a disproportionate burden in the First Chechen War and deployments into the Balkans. They also suffered cuts, even though ex-paratrooper and briefly Security Council secretary Alexander Lebed almost came to the point of mutiny as a result. During Gen. Igor Rodionov's brief tenure as defence minister, when he was trying to rationalize the services and was proposing a reorganization that would in effect subordinate the paratroopers to the Ground Forces, Lebed furiously rolled up to the VDV Main Staff headquarters and denounced the plans as 'tantamount to criminal' and vowed to block them. The VDV officers present stood up and chanted 'Glory to the army! Glory to Russia!' and for a while there was a serious fear Lebed might actually try to use his standing with the military as the basis for a coup.[2] As it was, he was quickly outmanoeuvred and soon thereafter dismissed, but it was a stark reminder of the paratroopers' prickly esprit de corps. In any case, Rodionov didn't last long either, and while the paratroopers suffered some reductions, they remained effectively autonomous.

They have prospered under Putin, despite successive reorganizations that have seen divisions such as the 104th Guards Airborne Assault Division downscaled to brigades and then re-formed again, back to divisional strength. There has, after all, been a deep ambiguity to the role of the so-called 'winged infantry' as an arm of service in its own right. Historically, VDV divisions were envisaged as strategic forces at the disposal of the General Staff, while regiment- or brigade-strength air assault units were operational forces supporting Military District commands. However, this was really geared for mass, conventional war. Besides, not only is the notion of the mass paratrooper drop controversial, the Military Transport Aviation (VTA: *Voyenno-Transportnaya Aviatsiya*) lacks the capacity to deliver more than – at best – two regiments of paratroopers at once. It would take the entire VTA fleet two and a half full sorties to lift a whole division. Meanwhile, the need to keep them capable of parachute or at least helicopter insertion means they need a whole suite of specialized equipment, from the BMD family of air-droppable light armoured fighting vehicles to their own, lighter version of the standard body armour.

In 2009–10, Defence Minister Serdyukov and Chief of the General Staff Makarov were reportedly contemplating abolishing the VDV as a separate combat arm altogether and transferring all their existing assets to the army. They were saved not just because Serdyukov and Makarov had other, more pressing priorities, but also because this was a time when the Kremlin was looking to a newly assertive foreign policy, for which it needed a national power projection reserve for intervention in regional or distant conflicts. This has proven prophetic: they were at the forefront of the seizure of Crimea in 2014, played a role in the Donbas conflict that followed, and in 2021 provided the lion's share of the international peacekeeping force deployed into Kazakhstan, which was itself led by the VDV commander-in-chief, Col. Gen. Serdyukov. The expectation is that they will continue to be busy.

Serdyukov – no relation to the former defence minister – has proven not just a tough and demanding field commander, but a capable advocate of the VDV's interests and its future role. As one former subordinate put it, 'he sweats blue' – in reference to the paratroopers' distinctive blue berets and badges. He was a paratrooper from the first, enlisted as an officer cadet and graduated from the Ryazan Higher Airborne Command School in 1983. He was quickly put in charge of a reconnaissance platoon, suggesting that his instructors thought he had particular initiative and determination. They were right. He rose steadily through the ranks, and distinguished himself during the First Chechen War, and in 1999, in the composite VDV battalion assigned to the multi-national peacekeeping force in Yugoslavia that made the 'Pristina Dash' to seize Kosovo's airport ahead of NATO troops. In 2002, Serdyukov briefly side-stepped into the Ground Forces, commanding a brigade in the Second Chechen War, before taking command of the 106th Guards Airborne Division in 2004. He then had higher command positions in the 5th Combined Arms Army and then as chief of staff of the whole Southern VO, playing a significant role in the annexation of Crimea, and then reportedly commanding Russian forces in the Donbas under the codename 'Sedov'.

In 2016, he was appointed commander-in-chief of the VDV. In 2017, though, Serdyukov was involved in a traffic accident that left him with severe head injuries and a fracture of the spine. With characteristic determination, he returned to active duties and although his planned stint as commander of the Russian contingent in Syria was delayed, he went on to serve a six-month tour there in 2019, for which he was made a Hero of the Russian Federation. As a participant in every major declared and undeclared Russian military operation since 1991, he has not only a wealth of practical experience but also great authority within the VDV and the officer corps as a whole.

BY PARACHUTE, PLANE OR TRACK

So the VDV was saved and is actually being revamped and, according to plans, expanded. It remains a strategic asset, and although one brigade is attached to each Military District, in practice command is usually exerted through the VDV headquarters in Moscow. They also work closely with military intelligence; this has been especially evident since 2014 in the Donbas, where elements of all the divisions have been identified as present by Ukrainian government sources. It is being used as the basis for new airmobile forces, but it is certainly not abandoning the parachute. Indeed, the Russians remain unusual in their commitment to large-scale drops. In the *Vostok*-2018 exercises in the Russian Far East, for example, a whole battalion with 50 vehicles was dropped by day from some 25 Il-76MD heavy transport aircraft, while the more recent Zapad-2021 exercise in western Russian and Belarus saw the first battalion-strength night drop in post-Soviet times. Around 600 soldiers and 30 BMD-2K-AU and BMD-4M airborne IFVs from the 76th Division's 234th Regiment were dropped in the rear of the simulated enemy, moving out to seize an airfield to allow heavier reinforcements to be flown in more conventionally.

Unsupported paratrooper forces – even mechanized ones – are relatively fragile when deployed without such prompt support, though, and such operations are likely to be rare in today's SAM-dense battlefield. Instead, the VDV is increasingly being configured as a multi-platform intervention force, capable of insertion by helicopter, by aircraft, or on the ground, and able to conduct strategic missions ranging from special operations – significantly, since 1992 they have had their own commando unit, the 45th Guards Independent Reconnaissance Brigade (a regiment since 2015) – through to major offensives. In essence, the notion is that the VDV will be able to generate power projection forces for interventions without having to rely on support from the Ground Forces. As one paratrooper officer told me in 2019, 'the VDV is going to be Russia's equivalent to the US Marine Corps – a separate little army, ready to be deployed wherever it is needed.' To be sure, this was a loose parallel and delivered with more than a little bravado: even though the VDV is meant to be expanding to a planned 60,000, there is no way it will rival the 180,000-strong USMC, let alone acquire the same air and sea capabilities.

However, it does speak to Putin's broad ambitions. The VDV is amongst the first in line for new kit, from the AK-12 rifle to the BMD-4M. They are acquiring new high-mobility vehicles, from *Sarmat*-2 buggies and AM-1 quadbikes to the heavier 4x4 Typhoon-VDV personnel carrier.[3] Indeed, little speaks more to the importance Moscow places on the VDV than the range of specialist vehicles designed for them, including the BMD-4M *Sadovnitsa* ('Gardener'). This is a personnel carrier that bristles with enough weapons also to be considered a pocket tank, even though it is too lightly armoured to fare well against the real thing. Like the VDV itself, it is light, fast, hard-hitting, and can be air-dropped by parachute, even with its crew inside (which is reportedly either terrifying or exhilarating, to taste) – yet is also very vulnerable if it gets caught in regular combat. Considering that the VDV is meant in the future not just to take ground but also hold it, it is also reacquiring proper tanks: T-72B3s. These will not be dropped by air, but instead deployed overland or flown to airfields to support VDV deployments.

Meanwhile, airmobile units which will be moved by helicopter are to be formed in all VDV brigades and divisions, as it acquires its own dedicated aviation brigade of four helicopter squadrons, rather than having to depend on external assets. This will field 12 massive Mi-26T2 heavy lifters, 24 Mi-8AMTSh assault transports and 12 Mi-35M day/night gunships.

In 2016, the VDV comprised 45,000 paratroopers in four divisions, four brigades and one special forces brigade. The plan is that by 2025, there will be 60,000 of them, in five divisions, two brigades and one special forces brigade. The new division, presumably the 104th Guards Air Assault Division, would be formed on the basis of the 31st Independent Guards Air Assault Brigade at Ulyanovsk, thus reviving a formation dissolved in the 1990s. Of course, all these plans will depend on the resources, not just money to buy the equipment, but also men (and women – the VDV is increasingly recruiting them, albeit not for front-line combat missions) to fill these new posts. The paratroopers are currently 70% *kontraktnik*, and Gen. Serdyukov has expressed a desire to bring this to 80%, if not higher. However, there is a lack of suitably fit and willing volunteers, and so long as he is determined also to maintain standards amongst his blue berets, it is unclear if he can hit these targets in the foreseeable future, at a time when all the other arms of service are also competing for professionals.

VDV ORDER OF BATTLE (PROJECTED FOR 2025)

38th Guards Command Brigade	Medvezhye Ozera, Moscow Region
7th Guards Air Assault Division	Novorossiisk
58th Guards Air Assault Regiment	Feodosia
108th Guards Air Assault Regiment	Novorossiisk
247th Guards Air Assault Regiment	Stavropol
1141st Guards Artillery Regiment	Anapa
76th Guards Air Assault Division	Pskov
104th Guards Air Assault Regiment	Cherekha
234th Guards Air Assault Regiment	Pskov
237th Guards Air Assault Regiment	Pskov
1140th Guards Artillery Regiment	Pskov
98th Guards Air Assault Division	Ivanovo
217th Guards Air Assault Regiment	Ivanovo
331st Guards Air Assault Regiment	Kostroma
1065th Guards Artillery Regiment	Vesely Kut
104th Guards Air Assault Division	Ulyanovsk
N/A	
106th Guards Air Assault Division	Tula
51st Guards Air Assault Regiment	Tula
137th Guards Air Assault Regiment	Ryazan
1182nd Guards Artillery Regiment	Naro-Fominsk
11th Independent Guards Air Assault Brigade	Ulan-Ude
83rd Independent Air Assault Brigade	Ussuriisk

THE BLACK BERETS

Back at the end of the 1980s, I remember meeting a so-called *morpekh*, a contraction of *Morskaya Pyekhota* (MP), or Naval Infantry. He had served in Afghanistan: so desperate had the Soviet High Command been to send soldiers who were better motivated, trained and conditioned than the average conscript, that they raided the MP of every fleet for people to send to this landlocked country. He had hair-raising tales of the time his unit was sent to man an 'eagle's nest' – a mountaintop observation post – that was hit by rebel mortars or snipers every day for a month, or of the stress of convoy escort work along the Salang Highway, never knowing if there was an ambush or a mine round the next corner. Nonetheless, he was still upbeat about his time in service, and had a wide range of comrades-in-arms around the country with whom he still kept in touch. 'All sorts: other marines, army, a bunch of engineers, some border guards, even a couple of helicopter pilots.' 'Paratroopers?' I incautiously asked. His face darkened at the thought that he might be friends with 'those fucking *chestolyubtsy*' – 'glory hounds' is probably the best translation. His main beef seemed to be that while the paras were expected to fight hard, they were also treated specially, while the MP were treated just like any other soldiers.

'BLACK DEVILS'

After all, Russia does have another main intervention force: the 'black beret' marines of the Naval Infantry. They date back to the 18th century, but as important as their past glories are their 20th-century exploits. Many sailors were enthusiastic supporters of the Bolsheviks in the 1917 Revolution, and during the Civil War that followed, the 1st Naval Expeditionary Rifle Division played a part in many of the victories of the Red Guard (later, Red Army), especially against the 'Whites' under Gen. Pyotr Wrangel in Ukraine. After the end of the Civil War, most marine units were disbanded. In July 1939, though, the 1st Independent Special Rifle Brigade was formed within the Baltic Fleet, later becoming the 1st Special Marine Brigade. Additional units were formed during the Great Patriotic War, as sailors were turned into infantry in the desperate struggle to hold back the Axis advance: in all, ten divisions and brigades, ten regiments and 34 battalions with a total strength of more than 120,000 were raised, many from fleet reservists who had no ships to go to. Many proved tenacious fighters, earning themselves the nickname the 'Black Devils' from their German counterparts.

After the end of the war, the marines were again disbanded – the Red Navy was not an immediate priority and it was essentially a coastal defence force at that stage. However, as Soviet capacities grew, and ambitions with them, their value became again appreciated. In 1963, a first Naval Infantry regiment was stood up, again in the Baltic Fleet, with more to follow. Like the VDV, the MP had largely been used simply as infantry in the Second World War, but they had also pioneered special operations, and as the post-war Soviet navy began to operate further afield they acquired new roles. However, the Soviet Union – like Russia today – was never an especially convincing 'blue water' maritime power, and the MP lacked the same opportunities as the VDV to refine their tradecraft and make their name during the Cold War.

They remain somewhat in the shadow of the paratroopers, who are at once more numerous, more prestigious and more readily deployed in the kind of interventions with which Russia is now asserting itself. (And whose distinctive blue-striped *telnyashka* vest, marines will still grumble, was copied from their own black-striped one.) It may be unfair to suggest that the MP as a whole have something of a chip on their collective shoulder about the prestige of the VDV, but at least the Crimean operation and then the Syrian intervention both served to demonstrate their capacities. Their previous commander-in-chief, Lt. Gen. Alexander Kolpachenko, a former paratrooper and Afghan War veteran himself, fought to have them gain the same level of recognition. His successor, Lt. Gen. Viktor Astapov, another transfer from the VDV, has reaped the benefits. In 2021, the MP acquired a new flag and emblem, with a flaming gold grenade and fouled anchor on a black and red cross on a white field.

While this may sound trivial, it reflects a growing status for the MP which, while still part of the Coastal Troops and coming, in turn, under the Naval Main Staff, are closer to being treated as an arm of service in their own right. More to the point, with the new flag also came new money, as part of a further re-equipment that includes replacement tanks and APCs and new-generation landing ships. The only MP division that survived into the 2000s, only to be downsized into a brigade in 2009 – the Pacific Fleet's 55th Division – isn't coming back any time soon, but the effective strength of the brigades is certainly growing. Just as the VDV are expanding, so too may the MP, sooner than later.

'WHERE WE ARE, THERE IS VICTORY!'

Tam gdye my, tam – pobeda!, 'Where we are, there is victory!' goes their slogan, and since the collapse of the USSR, they have been far more active than at any time since the Great Patriotic War. They served in Chechnya, in both wars, and seized the southern Abkhaz port of Ochamchire in 2008. They served in anti-pirate patrols off Somalia from 2008, although not without controversy. Russia's reputation for what could at best be described as a no-nonsense approach to policing was given something of a boost by the conduct of its navy and MP when, in May 2010, the destroyer *Marshal Shaposhnikov* responded when Somali pirates boarded the MV *Moscow University*, a Liberian-flagged Russian tanker, forcing the crew to barricade themselves below decks. Supported by an armed Ka-27 helicopter, which returned fire when shot at by the pirates, killing one, a marine boarding party in small boats intercepted the tanker, overpowered the pirates and freed the crew. The marines then disarmed the surviving ten pirates and set them adrift some 300 nautical miles (560 kilometres) off the coast, in an inflatable boat with provisions but no navigation equipment. Although their fate is still unknown, it is generally assumed that they perished at sea.

Since then, the MP took the lead in the seizure of Crimea in 2014 and played a part in the subsequent operations in Donbas, including the 2022 invasion. They were also deployed to Syria in 2015 in support of Russia's air campaign to prevent the collapse of the Assad regime. Indeed, one of Russia's relatively few acknowledged casualties is a marine who died during the operation to rescue the two flight crewmen of the Su-24 shot down by Turkish fighters in 2015.

In total, there are just under 13,000 marines. Reflecting their status, they wear army-style combat dress, but black naval parade uniforms, and privates are called *matros*, 'seaman'. However, the organization of the bulk of the MP is along Ground Forces lines. Each fleet has at least one brigade, which varies in size, but will typically have two to four infantry battalions, a tank battalion and a reconnaissance battalion, a sniper company, and support elements, now including a drone company. Many also have a dedicated air-assault battalion trained for parachute insertion.

NAVAL INFANTRY ORDER OF BATTLE

Baltic Fleet
     336th Independent Guards Brigade   Baltiysk

Black Sea Fleet
     810th Independent Guards Brigade   Sevastopol
     382nd Independent Battalion   Temriuk

Caspian Flotilla
     177th Regiment   Kaspiisk

Northern Fleet
     61st Independent Brigade   Sputnik

Pacific Fleet
     155th Independent Brigade   Vladivostok
     40th Independent Regiment   Petropavlovsk-Kamchatka

UNDERWATER SENTINELS

The MP, being part of the wider Coastal Forces of the Navy, also include highly specialized anti-saboteur teams with the rather indigestible name Independent Special Designation Detachments to Combat Submarine Subversive Forces and Means (OSpN PDSS: *Otryad Spetsialnovo Naznacheniya Borby s Podvodnymi Diversionnymi Silami i Sredstvami*). These are the counterparts to the Naval *Spetsnaz* combat divers discussed in the following chapter, troops trained rather to defeat enemy efforts to sabotage vessels and coastal installations. They are largely recruited from within existing Naval Infantry, selected on the basis of their hardiness, diving and swimming skills and emotional stability.

There are 12 OSpN PDSS companies, which vary greatly in size, depending on the perceived local threat. The Black Sea Fleet, for example, clearly fears Ukrainian (or Western) sabotage at its Sevastopol base, so its 102nd OSpN PDSS is the largest of all, with two platoons of combat swimmers, a platoon of divers (also trained in explosive ordnance disposal) and a radio-electronic platoon (responsible for detecting and jamming enemy communications and detonation signals), for a total strength of 120 men. Others can be as small as just 30 men. They are armed with both conventional small arms and Russia's distinctive array of underwater weapons including the SPP-1 four-barrel flechette pistol and the DP-64 Nepryadva 'anti-sabotage grenade launcher', a double-barrelled weapon that typically is loaded with one pyrotechnic round to show an enemy's location – it floats to the surface and burns with a bright red flare – and one high-explosive round for a rather more forceful response. Just as it is said that a liar more often assumes he is being lied to, it says something that the Russians have such elaborate provisions to resist sabotage, of the sort that is a speciality for their *Spetsnaz*.

24

The *Spetsnaz*

Most countries' special forces emphasize physical fitness, determination and aggression.[1] Russia's *Spetsnaz* are certainly no exception, although apparently they are not necessarily quite as dedicated to overt displays of machismo as the VDV, for whom any open day seems incomplete without paratroopers breaking wooden beams with their heads or throwing a sharpened *sapyorka* – the Russians' distinctive short-handled entrenching tool – while leaping through a ring of fire. As one *Spetsnaz* veteran once told me, 'precision and silence beats strength and courage, any day'. When he was asked why he seemed to be disparaging courage, he paused, and said that the *Spetsnaz* were more concerned with determination: 'courage is the willingness to die trying to reach the objective; determination is the will to find a way to get there, without dying.'

Much is written and claimed about the *Spetsnaz*. Rather less is known for sure, despite what is now quite an industry in Russian-language books on them, from memoirs to survival skills guides. Apart from the fact that much is historical, and some purely fantastical, it often misses the point about quite who the *Spetsnaz* are and, more to the point, what they are meant to do.

The mythology around the *Spetsnaz* is thus as often misleading as it is extensive. In the West, much of this dates back to the writings of the Soviet defector Vladimir Rezun, who wrote a series of supposed exposés under the pseudonym 'Viktor Suvorov'. When it came to the *Spetsnaz*, which he portrayed as an implacable and uniformly lethal threat to NATO, he was full of engaging detail: they tested their unarmed combat skills on convicted criminals, whom they would kill; they had boots with reversed tread so their footprints would appear to lead the wrong way; they used a knife with a powerful spring that would shoot its blade at an enemy. Much has since been debunked as either not quite right (they did, for example, sometimes use the NRS-2 'shooting scout knife', which didn't launch its blade, but did incorporate a single-shot gun in the hilt) or downright wrong, but nonetheless, the image of the remorseless Soviet Terminators proved to have an awful appeal.

SPECIAL PEOPLE, FOR SPECIAL TASKS

The evolution of Russia's special forces has been shaped by an emphasis on mass war and the primacy of strategy coming from the top of the system over individual prowess by the men at the base. Their name is a contraction of *Spetsialnoye Naznacheniya*, 'of special designation' or 'of special purpose'. This is quite a significant detail: they are not 'special forces' as such in the Western sense, which places the emphasis on the 'specialness' of the operators themselves. Instead, what is distinctive is the special *role* which is assigned to these troops. After all, until recently, many or even most *Spetsnaz* have been conscripts, and while 'more special' than regular soldiers, even paratroopers and the like, they can hardly be considered in the same elevated terms as the Western elite forces with which they were often misleadingly compared, such as Britain's SAS or America's Seals and Green Berets.

A further source of confusion is the way all sorts of other units are also formally or informally known as *Spetsnaz*, from the genuinely elite anti-terrorist commandos of the FSB's Special Designation Centre (TsSN: *Tsentr Spetsialnovo Naznacheniya*) to the not-quite-so-formidable rapid response units of the Federal Forestry Agency. Of the more serious, the Foreign Intelligence Service's *Zaslon* ('Screen') is primarily tasked with protecting VIPs and diplomatic facilities in high-risk environments, but also with covert operations overseas. Then there are forces that overlap much more closely with the military *Spetsnaz*. The National Guard Interior Troops *Spetsnaz* include the Moscow-based 33rd Special Purpose Detachment '*Peresvet*' as well as a series of local Special Rapid Response Detachments (SOBR: *Spetsialny Otryad Bystrovo Reagirovaniya*) that largely provide armed response to the police, but were, like the Interior Troops, also deployed in Chechnya and Ukraine. In Syria, we know operators from the FSB's TsSN were deployed because four men killed by a mine during an ambush near Latakia in February 2020 turned out to be from its Directorates S (its main counter-terrorist unit) and K (responsible for operations in the North Caucasus). They had been scouting a potential meeting area for Turkish and Syrian military leaders. Operators from the National Guard and *Zaslon* have also served in Syria, while in February 2020, the Ukrainian government released video footage of TsSN operators in the Donbas.

The main role of the *Spetsnaz* is as scouts and saboteurs, though, deployed for battlefield reconnaissance and also behind-the-lines operations against enemy chains of command and lines of supply and, in particular, NATO tactical nuclear weapons. After all, the modern *Spetsnaz* are really products of the Cold War, (re)created in 1957 within the GRU as battalion-strength units able to range behind NATO lines to locate and, ideally, destroy weapons such as the Matador intermediate-range ballistic missile. The Matador had a maximum range of 700 miles, but as new systems were introduced, the *Spetsnaz* mission grew, and so did the distance they were expected to penetrate into Europe. In 1962 the five battalions became six brigades, and in 1968 they began to acquire their own specialized training facilities.

As Moscow's imperial ambitions became more expansive, it also needed forces able to project power globally and also surgically respond to troubles within the existing 'empire'. *Spetsnaz* trained elite forces in Cuba, protected Soviet shipping from South African saboteurs in Angola and played crucial roles in the suppression of the rising against the puppet regime in Hungary in 1956 and the liberal 'Prague Spring' in 1968. In Afghanistan in 1979, they not only led the initial coup de main that removed existing leader Hafizullah Amin and installed a new regime, but they then raided rebel supply caravans, hunted US-supplied Stinger SAMs, guarded visiting VIPs, and sometimes simply ended up pressed into service as infantry.[2] Even so, being better than most of the Soviet army's miserable and recalcitrant conscript forces did not make most of them truly special, special forces. It was precisely a need for such elite operators that forced the Soviets to start standing up ad hoc units drawn from KGB sabotage specialists (who formed *Zenit*, the unit that led the mission to assassinate Amin), and then increasingly create informal elements within the *Spetsnaz* comprising only professional NCOs and officers who could be tasked with especially difficult missions.

This was again the case in the 1990s, when the *Spetsnaz* were once more (mis)used as infantry in Chechnya. For some missions, scratch teams of professional soldiers were created for particular operations. Nonetheless, it was getting harder to recruit and retain good soldiers. While some units managed to retain a degree of their old esprit de corps, others responded to the years of low wages, broken promises and corrupt hierarchies with a slide into criminality and indiscipline, as journalist Dmitry Kholodov discovered to his cost when he investigated claims that they were moonlighting in the mafia (see Chapter 3). They bounced back relatively quickly under Putin, though, and have also benefited especially from the new drive to recruit *kontraktniki*. As of 2020, only some 20% were conscripts, and not only is this proportion continuing to decline, but those draftees are absolutely the pick of the crop, typically young athletes and graduates of school-age military skills training programmes (and fully half enlist as volunteers at the end of their compulsory term).

TIP OF THE SPEAR

The *Spetsnaz* traditionally filled a gap between regular military reconnaissance forces and the intelligence-gathering assets and units of the intelligence and security agencies. Their sabotage mission, though, has expanded in the modern world of 'active measures' and 'political warfare', and they have acquired a much wider role as the Kremlin's politico-military instrument of choice. The Kremlin sees in the *Spetsnaz* a flexible (and even sometimes deniable) weapon, which it can use as easily to fight guerrillas here as to support an insurgency there, the tip of the spear in its new adventures. They fought in Georgia; in Crimea, they led the operation; in the Donbas they provided crucial special capacities to the insurgents; in Syria, they likewise helped ensure Russian airpower hit its targets. In the scrappy, messy security environment of the 21st century, a hundred well-trained *Spetsnaz* can prove more usable and effective than a whole armoured brigade.

There are some 17,000 *Spetsnaz* and they thus fill a role similar to, if more covert than, those of the VDV and MP (and it is worth remembering that the paratroopers have their own *Spetsnaz* unit, the 45th Guards Independent Order of Kutuzov, Order of Alexander Nevsky Special Purpose Brigade). This is still not a force that as a whole could be considered 'Tier One' special forces, and they are perhaps best understood as spearhead expeditionary light infantry, roughly analogous to the US 75th Ranger Regiment, the British 16th Air Assault Brigade or the French Foreign Legion, although admittedly a new Special Operations Forces Command (KSSO: *Komandovaniye Sil Spetsialnalnykh Operatsii*) was established in 2012, which must be considered comparable to other 'best of the best'.

Precisely for this reason, they have been a bone of contention in the kind of inter-service rivalry that has been a particular problem for the Russians. After the 2008 Georgian War, the GRU was politically weak, having been blamed (largely unfairly) for the lacklustre Russian performance. Thus in 2011, the army made a successful takeover bid, and on 24 October 2010 – the very day when the *Spetsnaz* were celebrating their 60th anniversary – Ground Forces Deputy Chief of Staff for Reconnaissance Col. Vladimir Mardusin announced that the *Spetsnaz* were being transferred from being a strategic asset of the GRU (or GU as it had become) and instead would be subordinated to the Military Districts. The idea was that the GU should concentrate on spying and the *Spetsnaz* would be battlefield assets. However, the spooks were not going to take this lying down, and when the ailing former GU head was succeeded at the start of 2011 by the much more vigorous and politically savvy Lt. Gen. Igor Sergun, they began lobbying for the old status quo. Meanwhile, the GU fought a bureaucratic rear-guard action, nominally transferring the *Spetsnaz* to the Ground Forces but in practice delaying the move on all kinds of practical and procedural grounds. The appointment of Shoigu and Gerasimov proved decisive, as both saw the need for these forces as strategic-level assets able to be used in political-military operations. In 2013, they were formally returned to the GU (if they had ever really left).

PUTIN'S *SPETSNAZ*

The *Spetsnaz* comprise seven regular brigades of various sizes, in total constituting perhaps 19 battalion-size units called Independent Special Designation Detachments (OOSN: *Otdelny Otryad Spetsialnovo Naznacheniya*), each with around 500 personnel. The relatively small 22nd Brigade has just two OOSN, the 173rd and the 411th, for example, while the large 14th Brigade – which is responsible for the whole Eastern VO – has fully four, the 282nd, 294th, 306th and 314th. Each OOSN is divided into a command and staff company and three company-strength units of some 140 personnel, each in turn divided into four 14-man units, a command team, and extensive support elements including medical and technical personnel. The four Independent *Spetsnaz* Naval

Reconnaissance Points (OMRPSN: *Otdelny Morskoy Razvedyvatelny Punkt Spetsialnovo Naznacheniya*), the marine equivalent of the brigades, require greater technical support because they deploy in anything from light boats to underwater sleds and are instead built around three, slightly larger companies (again, with four 14-man teams of operators), the first optimized for land missions, the second for coastal reconnaissance, the third 'combat divers' especially configured for mining enemy vessels and installations underwater.

These brigades are responsible to the GU's Fifth, or Operational Reconnaissance Directorate, although in the field they are subordinated to operational commanders. Beyond that, there are three other separate *Spetsnaz* elements. One, the 100th Independent Brigade, is often used as a testbed for new ideas and equipment. Two others were created in 2011–12 as part of the security preparations for the Sochi Winter Olympics in south-western Russia: the 25th Independent Regiment, especially trained and equipped for operations in the turbulent North Caucasus, and the 346th Brigade, a truly elite force closer to an OOSN in size, which ended up becoming the main operational element of a new special forces command.

SPETSNAZ

Special Operations Forces Command (KSSO)
   346th Brigade (Kubinka-2)
Army *Spetsnaz*
   2nd Brigade (Pskov)
   3rd Guards Brigade (Tolyatti)
   10th Brigade (Molkino)
   14th Brigade (Ussuriisk)
   16th Brigade (Moscow)
   22nd Guards Brigade (Stepnoi)
   24th Brigade (Irkutsk)
   100th Brigade (Mozdok)
   25th Independent Regiment (Stavropol)
VDV
   45th Guards Independent Special Designation Brigade (Kubinka-2)
Navy
   42nd Naval Reconnaissance Special Designation Point (Vladivostok; Pacific Fleet)
   420th Naval Reconnaissance Special Designation Point (Severomorsk; Northern Fleet)
   431st Naval Reconnaissance Special Designation Point (Sevastopol; Black Sea Fleet)
   561st Naval Reconnaissance Special Designation Point (Kaliningrad; Baltic Fleet)

Recruits are generally expected to be at least 160 centimetres tall, and weigh around 75–80 kilograms, fit and healthy with good eyesight, hearing and balance. However, the main criteria are tested through a series of gruelling ordeals, including a 30-kilometre forced march carrying a 30-kilogram load. Naval *Spetsnaz*, who face particular demands, must also prove that they can swim through a narrow space simulating a torpedo tube, as well as demonstrate their nerves by diving underwater, removing their mask such that water fills the helmet, then replacing the mask and bleeding out the water from the helmet through a special valve before returning to the surface. So stressful is this that potential recruits get two tries before failing.

While they may not be as obsessed with physical prowess as the VDV, the *Spetsnaz* nonetheless maintain an arduous fitness regime, with the usual route marches in full kit and exercise sessions leavened with regular hand-to-hand combat sessions. In particular, they train in *Sambo*, a distinctive Russian martial art whose name is a contraction of *Samozashchita Bez Oruzhiya*, 'self-defence without weapons', but which in its combat form has developed into something akin to a mixed martial art, in which the fighters can use not just hands and feet but weapons or indeed anything that comes to hand. Of course, they also train with an extensive range of weapons, including at least some familiarity with those used by potential enemies, such as the American M-16 rifle family.

As well as getting first access to new weapons and kit, the *Spetsnaz* also have increased freedom both to customize their equipment and outfit and also to experiment with new ideas and vehicles. They are typically deployed in regular army-issue APCs and IFVs, although they are also increasingly using UAZ Patriot jeeps and other light vehicles. For example, they have been enthusiastic adopters of quadbikes and buggies, and an unconfirmed but persistent rumour is that they are seeking individual combat platforms described by one source as an 'all-terrain Segway'.

Spetsnaz are not all parachute-trained, though about one-third are, and every OOSN has at least one fully airdroppable company. They do all receive training in operating from helicopters, though, including rappelling from hovering ones on ropes. As Naval *Spetsnaz* are expected not only to carry out the same missions as their land-based comrades, including spotting for naval artillery bombardments and scouting or sabotaging enemy coastal installations, but also to conduct landing and naval mining operations, they also receive additional training for such missions.

THE SPECIAL OPERATIONS COMMAND

As the *Spetsnaz* became more professionalized, and also as the demands likely to be put on them became increasingly specialized, moves were finally made to establish a proper special forces command as part of the Serdyukov/Makarov 'New Look' programme. The GRU had long had a training base called *Senezh* (named for the nearby lake, although often simply known by its military post box number, V/ch or Unit 92154) at Solnechnogorsk, north-west of Moscow. In 2009, it was decided that this was going to become the base for a new special forces unit which – as this was a time when the agency was in the doghouse – would no longer be subordinated to the GRU, but directly to the General Staff. The first commander charged with setting up the unit was Maj. Gen. Igor Medoyev, who was soon replaced by Lt. Gen. Alexander Miroshnichenko. Tellingly, both of them were veterans of the rival FSB's *Alfa* anti-terrorist commando force.

The idea was that *Senezh* would become the base of a new Special Operations Forces Command (KSSO: *Komanda Sil Spetsialnovo Naznacheniya*) built around an OOSN outside the regular brigade structure and dedicated air assets. Its missions would range from counter-terrorist operations in peacetime – especially with an eye to the forthcoming 2014 Winter Olympics in Sochi – to sabotage and assassination in war. When Shoigu and Gerasimov assumed control of the military, there were some concerns as to whether the KSSO project would continue, or whether the role of FSB veterans meant that the force would be transferred to them. They need not have worried. In March 2013, Gerasimov made a point of using a meeting with foreign military attaches to signal an acceleration of the project meant to build on the best practices of other nations.[3]

By the end of the year, the KSSO had been stood up, on the basis of the 346th Brigade, deliberately kept under-strength (just one and a half OOSNs, in effect) to allow it to be manned purely with the very best of the *Spetsnaz*'s contract soldiers. *Senezh* became more of an operational command centre, and the KSSO acquired additional training facilities at Kubinka-2, west of Moscow, where the VDV's 45th Brigade is also based. The KSSO has priority claim to a squadron of Il-76 heavy-lift transport aircraft, and also a mixed helicopter attack and transport squadron at Torzhok airbase, many of whose pilots are actually instructors at the 344th Army Aviation Combat Training Centre when not flying missions for the KSSO.

Their first operational use was in Crimea, and since then they have appeared in the Donbas, Syria and Ukraine. They have also expanded from their original strength of around 500 to 2,000–2,500, although this includes trainers and support personnel, and maybe 1,000 are actual operators. The command unit (Unit 99450) is based at *Senezh*, then there are three operational detachments (Units 01355, 43292, 92154) largely operating out of Kubinka-2 and a further naval one based at Sevastopol (Unit 00317) under the auspices of the 561st Emergency Rescue Centre. Each comprises 200–300 operators. The KSSO is still a strategic asset under the direct subordination of the General Staff rather than the GU, but it nonetheless shares with the regular *Spetsnaz* an orientation towards both battlefield operations and military-political 'active measures'. Some KSSO operators, for example, have transferred to the GU's Unit 29155, its dedicated assassination and subversion force. This connection – which mirrors the way the other intelligence agencies have their own special force units, the Special Designation Centre for the FSB and the rather smaller *Zaslon* ('Screen') unit for the SVR – emphasizes their role as also a covert subversion and sabotage force. Although analogies can be misleading, this would suggest they are in some ways comparable to the US Army's Intelligence Support Activity, the CIA Special Operations Group or the British Special Air Service's E Squadron. The KSSO is undoubtedly intended for a key role in the shadowy 'grey zone' wars of the future.

25

The Nuclear Backstop

In March 2018, just before he stood – again – for re-election, Putin was delivering his annual state of the nation address. This timing might explain why at the end of an event usually marked by a mix of dubious pledges and a soporific barrage of facts and figures, came a burst of ultra-patriotic and techno-militarist bombast. To a series of (sometimes slightly tacky) video presentations, he began to enumerate six new weapons systems, which became known as the 'magic six'.[1] Some were already off the drawing board, like the *Avangard* hypersonic glide vehicle, a nuclear warhead that can dodge and kink as it approaches its target to avoid missile defences as 'it heads to its target like a meteorite, like a fireball'. There was the air-launched hypersonic Kh-47M2 *Kinzhal* ('Dagger') missile, able to travel 2,000 kilometres and manoeuvre at more than ten times the speed of sound, with a nuclear or conventional warhead. There was the *Peresvet* anti-missile and anti-air laser system, mounted on a truck or a railcar. There was the Poseidon unmanned nuclear submarine, essentially an underwater drone, armed with a 'dirty' nuclear bomb that could wipe out a carrier battle group or blast and irradiate a port. There was the *Burevestnik* ('Petrel') nuclear-powered cruise missile that could fly around the world, albeit trailing a plume of radioactive exhaust that while, in Putin's words, it 'is invincible against all existing and prospective missile defence and anti-air systems', probably ensures it will never actually see service.

Then, on track to make its first test flight in a few years, there was the SS-28 *Sarmat* super-heavy inter-continental ballistic missile (ICBM), armed with up to 15 independently targeted nuclear warheads, *Avangards*, and decoys. As Putin was boasting about its capabilities, the animated footage showed missiles being launched from the Russian steppe, arcing round the world, and then unloading a volley of nuclear warheads onto what looked very much like Florida. Indeed, it almost looked as if they were directly targeting then-President Donald Trump's Mar-a-Lago resort.

This could just be coincidence – footage showing a strike on Florida had been aired years before. But it could well not have been, and certainly generated a storm of comment in the West, and in a way, this was the point about Putin's defiant performance. Russia's strategic arsenal is not only the final backstop of national defence, but it is also meant to be a showcase of the country's technological and industrial prowess, and also something that ensures that it is unquestionably a global power, whose concerns and interests must be taken seriously. 'No one has managed to restrain Russia,' he said. As Putin concluded, in the past, 'nobody really wanted to talk to us …, and nobody wanted to listen to us. So listen to us now.'

POST-SOVIET ARMAGEDDON

Russia inherited a full nuclear triad – ground-, sea- and air-launched missiles – from the USSR. The Soviets had a world-destroying yet ageing arsenal of some 40,000 or more individual warheads, from tactical missiles up to the latest RT-2PM *Topol* (SS-25) truck-based ICBM. Proliferation was a serious concern even before the actual end of the Soviet Union (the military had already for perhaps a year been quietly moving tactical weapons and some command systems back to Russian soil), and Belarus, Kazakhstan and Ukraine, the only three other republics on which there were nuclear weapons left, were all keen or at least willing to see them go. After all, maintaining a working nuclear capability is extremely expensive in terms of maintenance, security and proper targeting and command systems. Besides, the West was willing to pay well to encourage them to divest themselves of these errant nuclear weapons.

In July 1991, Mikhail Gorbachev had signed the Strategic Arms Reduction Treaty (START) with the United States, which envisaged both sides cutting their long-range arsenals to no more than 6,000 warheads carried by no more than 1,600 bombers and ICBMs. In May 1992, an addendum known as the Lisbon Protocol bound Russia, Belarus, Kazakhstan and Ukraine to honouring the USSR's commitments, with a view to the latter three giving up their nuclear weapons to Russia, which undertook to decommission those that exceeded the START limits. In both Belarus and Ukraine, there was resistance, with some calling for the retention of a minimal nuclear deterrent capability, but ultimately neither could realistically afford to maintain one, and in any case Moscow retained the electronic codes needed to launch or arm them.

Both were instead willing to be compensated economically and politically in return. The 1994 Budapest Memorandum on Security Assurances saw Belarus, Kazakhstan and Ukraine receive assurances as to their territorial integrity and political sovereignty, guaranteed by the United States, the United Kingdom and, ironically enough in light of later developments, the Russian Federation. By the end of 1996, all Soviet nuclear weapons were in Russian hands.

Through the course of the 1990s, the United States and – not least thanks to US assistance in the form of money and expertise – Russia achieved the safe decommissioning of their stocks in excess of the START limits. The nightmare scenarios of 'loose nukes' and the proliferation of expertise never came true (see Chapter 3), even if they did make good fodder for thrillers and action films. START came to its formal end in December 2009, although both Russia and the United States agreed to keep observing its terms while a new treaty was hammered out. One of the key sticking points was the US determination to base anti-missile systems in Central Europe, ostensibly (if implausibly) to target not Russian but incoming Iranian launches. President Medvedev threatened, in what would become a recurring gambit, to place *Iskander* tactical missiles – which can deliver a conventional or nuclear warhead – in the exclave of Kaliningrad in response. Nonetheless, negotiations did lead to the imaginatively named New START agreement, which reduced the ceiling for deployed strategic nuclear warheads to 1,550 (although in practice it can be fudged a few hundred higher because a bomber only counts as carrying one warhead even though it may carry several). Furthermore, it limits the total number of strategic bombers and land and sea launchers to 800. Signed in Prague in 2010, it came into force in 2011 and, having been extended in 2021 – even during a period of daggers-drawn political tension, neither Moscow nor Washington wants to tempt fate – it will remain in place until 2026. Nonetheless, even in 2009, the Russians were making one thing clear: they might end up with fewer nuclear weapons, but they were willing to spend what it took to make sure they had better ones.

RAIL, ROAD AND TUBE

Land-based missiles can often be big, but they are inherently vulnerable compared with deep-swimming submarines and high-lofting bombers. To this end, Russia has a mix of platforms, putting missiles in armoured silos in the ground and also heavy transporters that can trundle to new launch stations by road. They even used to have ICBMs mounted on special rail carriages until they were decommissioned under the terms of the START II nuclear arms reduction treaty signed by Russia and the USA in 1993, although a replacement, the BZhRK *Barguzin*, is currently under design. These are all the responsibility of the Strategic Rocket Forces (RVSN: *Raketniye Voiska Strategicheskovo Naznacheniya*), a separate arm of service some 60,000 strong, directly subordinated to the General Staff. From its command centre in a deep bunker under the closed township of Vlasikha, north-west of Moscow, it controls a reported 320 missiles that can deliver up to 1,181 warheads.

THE STRATEGIC ROCKET FORCES

Central Command Post RVSN – Unit 95501 (Vlasikha)

27th Guards Rocket Army (Vladimir)
> 7th Guards Rocket Division (Ozerny)
> 14th Rocket Division (Yoshkar-Ola)
> 28th Guards Rocket Division (Kozelsk)
> 54th Guards Rocket Division (Krasny Sosenki)
> 60th Rocket Division (Svetly)

31st Rocket Army (Orenburg)
> 8th Rocket Division (Pervomaisky)
> 13th Rocket Division (Yasny)
> 42nd Rocket Division (Svobodny)

33rd Guards Rocket Army (Omsk)
> 29th Guards Rocket Division (Irkutsk)
> 35th Rocket Division (Sibirsky)

39th Guards Rocket Division (Gvardeisky)
62nd Rocket Division (Solnechny)

Missile Ranges and Cosmodromes
Kapustin-Yar
Sary Shagan (Kazakhstan)
Yasny Cosmodrome

The bulk are heavy RS-24 *Yars* (SS-27 Mod 2) ICBMs, which can carry up to four separate warheads, multiple independently targetable re-entry vehicles (MIRVs), of either 500- or 150-kiloton yield. There are 149 of these: 14 in silos at Kozelsk in west-central European Russia, and 135 road-based ones. Then there are 60 silo-based and 18 road-mobile RT-2PM2 *Topol*-M (SS-27) missiles, relatively accurate and carrying a single 800-kiloton warhead, 45 of the older RT-2PM *Topol* road-based missile, and 46 remaining R-36M (SS-18) ICBMs with up to ten MIRVs, although scheduled to be replaced by the new *Sarmat*. Some reports suggest the RVSN still have two RS-18A (SS-19) ICBMs in the 13th Rocket Division, although these are likely only being used to test the *Avangard*.

Russia no longer has any land-based intermediate-range ballistic missiles (IRBMs), defined as those with a range of 3,000–5,500 kilometres, or medium-range ones (MRBMs), with a range of 1,000–3,000 kilometres, following the terms of the 1987 Intermediate-Range Nuclear Forces (INF) treaty. The United States withdrew from the treaty in 2018–19, alleging that Russia had tested missiles that violated its terms, something Moscow denies – while counter-claiming that Washington's decision to deploy missile defence systems in Europe was in itself a breach. Either way, at present, Russia does not deploy any such land-based missiles, but as is discussed below, it may in the future, with an eye not to established old rival NATO, but the potential one coming over the horizon: China.

These are all protected by the specialist troops of the 12th Main Directorate of the Defence Ministry (12 GU MO). It is an elite and secretive organization, which controls not just the guard units of RVSN nuclear bases, but also the Special Tactical Groups tasked with moving warheads around the country and protecting road-based missiles. Its soldiers do not have their own special insignia (they usually wear artillery patches) and are instructed not to tell even their own families what they do. They do have distinctive vehicles in support of their role, though, like the Taifun-M Anti-Sabotage Combat Vehicle, with an extensive electro-optical sensor suite, a listening device meant to allow a trained operator to distinguish the steps of a person from those of an animal, and even a small *Eleron-3SV* drone.

UNDER THE WAVES

By contrast, Russia's submarine-based nuclear force is part of the navy, albeit with its own special command and communications structures and strict criteria for recruitment. Apart from tradition, the rationale is that the missile boats need to be protected by hunter-killers and surface vessels, to prevent their being tracked and sunk before they could launch, so they need to be able to work in tight coordination with the rest of their respective fleet. After all, the key advantage of the strategic submarine fleet is as a retaliatory and thus deterrent force: an enemy might feel confident of being able to take out land-based missiles, even the bomber fleet, but would be unlikely to be able to destroy all the submarines hiding deep under the oceans or Arctic pack ice, leaving them open to a devastating counter-strike.

At present, the Russians have ten nuclear-powered missile submarines, seven in the Northern Fleet and three in the Pacific, able to carry a total of 144 missiles armed with up to 656 warheads in theory, although in practice the deployed number is fewer, to comply with the New START limits. From hardened submarine pens at Gadzhiyevo on the icy Kola peninsula, the Northern Fleet deploys six *Delfin*-class (Delta IV) boats – although one, the *Yekaterinburg*, is being decommissioned in 2022 – and two of the new *Borei* class. The *Delfin* ('Dolphin') class is a sound design that carries R-29RMU2.1 Lainer (modernized versions of the SS-N-23A) missiles with up to four 500-kiloton or 12 smaller 100-kiloton warheads each. The new *Borei* is a larger, faster, yet stealthier boat. It can carry 16 RSM-56 *Bulava* ('Mace') (SS-N-32) missiles, each of which can deliver six to ten 100–150-kiloton MIRVs. Admittedly, its development has been a protracted and sometimes troublesome process involving a considerable number of often-embarrassing failures, including the failed tests that led to the 2009 'Norwegian Spiral Anomaly', a blue beam of light that tapered into a grey spiral that could be seen all across northern Norway and Sweden. The Pacific Fleet's 25th Submarine Division based at Krasheninnikov Bay hosts a single older *Kalmar*-class (Delta III) submarine dating back to 1980, with 16 R-29R (SS-N-18) missiles, as well as three *Borei*-class boats.

STRATEGIC AVIATION

In yet a further variation on a theme, Long-Range Aviation (DA: *Dalnaya Aviatsiya*) is a separate command, but within the Aerospace Forces. It fields perhaps 66 flightworthy strategic bombers, although many of the older Tu-95MS airframes appear to be nearing the end of their operational lifespans, especially given Moscow's recent habit of yanking NATO's chain by sending them roaming close to (and occasionally briefly into) European airspace, forcing a ritual scrambling of fighter jets to escort them away. (It is a pretty pointless and mutually expensive dance: it is not as though the bombers would opportunistically start a war if they were not intercepted.)

The DA fields two operational divisions and various support units including tanker squadrons and mixed aviation regiments used primarily to shuttle personnel and spares between bases. All told it has 16 Tu-160 (Blackjack) supersonic bombers (seven in the newer Tu-160M configuration) and 48 Tu-95MS (Bear-H) turboprops. In addition, it fields 52 Tu-22M3 (Backfire-C) bombers, but these are essentially strike bombers, able to carry tactical nuclear weapons but generally armed with conventional bombs or missiles, and thus they are not considered strategic forces.

LONG-RANGE AVIATION

Long-Range Aviation Command (Unit 44402) (Moscow)
63rd Mitavsky Independent Communication Centre (Smolensk)
22nd Guards Heavy Bomber Aviation Division (Engels)
    121st Guards Heavy Bomber Aviation Regiment (Engels): 7 Tu-160M, 9 Tu-160
    184th Heavy Bomber Aviation Regiment (Engels): 18 Tu-95MS
    52nd Guards Heavy Bomber Aviation Regiment (Shaikovka): 23 Tu-22M3
    203rd Independent Guards Aviation Tanker Aircraft Regiment (Ryazan):
        12 Il-78M, 6 Il-78
    40th Mixed Aviation Regiment (Vysoky): 2 An-12, 3 Mi-26, 8 Mi-8MT

326th Heavy Bomber Aviation Division (Ukrainka)
    79th Heavy Bomber Aviation Regiment (Ukrainka): 14 Tu-95MS
    182nd Guards Heavy Bomber Aviation Regiment (Ukrainka): 16 Tu-95MS
    200th Guards Heavy Bomber Aviation Regiment (Sredny): 15 Tu-22M3
    444th Heavy Bomber Aviation Regiment (Sredny): 14 Tu-22M3
    181st Independent Mixed Aviation Regiment (Sredny): 2 An-12, 3 An-30,
       2 An-26

43rd Guards Centre for Combat Application and Retraining of Long-Range Aviation
  Flight Personnel (Ryazan)
    49th Instructor Heavy Bomber Aviation Regiment (Ryazan): 6 Tu-95MS, 6
      Tu-22M3, 1 Il-78, 1 Tu-134AK, 2 Mi-8MT
    27th Mixed Aviation Regiment (Tambov): 2 An-12, 8 An-26, 10
      Tu-134UBL

The massive Tu-95MS is a beast with a wingspan that could almost accommodate four London buses, overshadowed only by the mighty American B-52 Stratofortress. Still being built as late as 1991, it nonetheless is a design dating back to the early 1950s, known for the distinctive deafening drone generated by the way that the tips of its four contra-rotating, double-propellor turboprops actually break the sound barrier. In some ways, though, its age is of little bearing, as it is essentially simply a platform for long-range cruise missiles. It can carry six Kh-55, Kh-101 or Kh-102s in an internal drum magazine (and some can carry up to ten more under their wings, albeit at significant cost to range and performance). The Kh-101 and -102 are stealthy, modernized versions of the Kh-55, the former with a conventional warhead, the latter with a nuclear one and a range of 4,500 kilometres. Given that the Tu-95MS has a combat radius of 7,500 kilometres, if unhindered, a plane from the 184th Heavy Bomber Aviation Regiment based at Engels in southern Russia could hit Washington DC with ease.

The elegant (but also massive) Tu-160 is a supersonic swing-wing jet, similar to but this time larger than the comparable American B-1B. It can carry 12 Kh-55, Kh-101 or Kh-102 cruise missiles in two internal drums. Despite entering service in 1987, it saw its very first combat action only over Syria, launching conventionally armed Kh-555 and Kh-101 missiles against Islamic State targets. After a hiatus, a modernized version is now being built.

THE NUCLEAR BACKSTOP 305

SPACE FORCES

Having a global nuclear strike capacity requires not just weapons and platforms, but the command, control and communications networks to be able to guide and direct them. Detecting and with luck defeating an enemy's attacks also requires an extensive infrastructure, and all this is largely the responsibility of the Space Forces (KV: *Kosmicheskiye Voiska*), since 2015 another branch of the Aerospace Forces. The KV is responsible for military space launches, operating Russia's military satellite constellations, and detecting space-based threats, from incoming ballistic missiles to debris which might hit a satellite.

Its main operational element is the 15th Special Designation Aerospace Army, headquartered in the closed city of Krasnoznamensk, south-west of Moscow. The closed city – technically the Closed Administrative-Territorial Entity (ZATO: *Zakrytoye Administrativno-Territorialnoye Obrazovaniye*) – is a holdover from Soviet times, the sites of especially sensitive military bases, defence industries, research centres or the like. Once, many did not even appear on official maps or have their own names, simply being designated by the nearest major centre, although the remaining 38 are publicly known and named. Ozyorsk, where the Mayak Chemical Plant produces plutonium, for example, used simply to be Chelyabinsk-40, while Snezhinsk, home of the Zababakhin All-Russian Scientific Research Institute of Technical Physics, which develops nuclear weapons designs, used to be Chelyabinsk-70. The headquarters of the RVSN at Vlasikha, for example, and the bases of most of its divisions are ZATOs. Some of these, like Krasnoznamensk, are fenced and guarded, and access requires a special pass. Even in those that are more open, the police can stop anyone who looks as if they do not belong and demand to see their documents.

The 15th Army commands the G. S. Titov Main Testing Centre that, despite its name, also controls unmanned space craft, the 820th Main Missile Attack Warning Centre that constantly monitors the input from ten land-based early warning radars as well as satellites to spot potential launches, and the 821st Main Space Situation Reconnaissance Centre, which tracks and scans orbital space. The KV also maintains its own spaceport, the Plesetsk Cosmodrome in the northern Arkhangelsk Region. In orbit, Russia has a large range of satellites, including early warning, communications and optical and electronic spy platforms, as well as the constellation supporting GLONASS, Russia's equivalent of the GPS navigation system. The KV is therefore also crucial not just for Russia's offensive nuclear capabilities, but also for its limited anti-ballistic missile system.

MODERNIZATION AND MAGIC

As Putin's 2018 speech demonstrated, he is keen to position Russia as a leading-edge military power, even if some of the projects look of questionable practicality. The *Peresvet* laser system, for example, is much-touted – and reportedly was even field-tested in Syria – yet there is a suspicious dearth of the kind of video footage one might have expected. Defence expert Igor Korotchenko rather acidly noted that it might perhaps work against drones, but only 'when there is no fog, no sandstorm, no rain; that is, in ideal conditions'.[2] It is perhaps fitting that it was named *Peresvet*, as the result of a national competition, after a medieval warrior-monk and champion in the fateful battle of Kulikovo against the Mongol-Tatars – and who quite likely never really existed. There is a great deal of modern mythology, too.

However, there is a good deal of less unpredictable but certainly significant modernization under way. Pavel Baev of the Peace Research Institute Oslo sees this as a process 'driven by the interplay between the bureaucratic and arms-parading traits in the military-strategic culture' – in other words, spending driven by both departmental self-interest and the Kremlin's desire for theatre – yet which nonetheless has also influenced real strategic thinking.[3] To put it bluntly, the generals realized that if so much of the defence budget was anyway going to have to be spent on nuclear forces, they ought not to waste it and so come up with ways to use these new weapons. (Even though Putin's fixation on his six 'magic weapons' did seriously distort the original planning assumptions of the 2027 State Armaments Programme.)

Thus, the *Borei*-class submarine programme continues, with the goal of producing 14 to replace the *Delfins* and final *Kalmar*, and while the fixation with penetrating essentially non-existent American anti-missile defences may be driven by a desire to win cheap political points, the *Sarmat* missile does meet a need. As for the Poseidon nuclear drone submarine, it is essentially another doomsday weapon as much as anything else, one that does not just provide a capacity but does so with a degree of theatricality.

WHY NUKES MATTER SO MUCH

Indeed, that may speak to part of the reason for Putin's focus on the strategic forces. They have a practical role, to be sure, as the final guarantor of national security – and also a protection against being, in effect, faced with nuclear blackmail. It was quite striking when, during a long conversation that I once held with a Russian defence scholar of quite nationalist views, he off-handedly raised a theoretical situation in which a country without adequate nuclear capabilities could be forced under threat of seeing one of its cities blasted, to demilitarize, even surrender part of its territories, regardless of the strength of its conventional forces. This seemed to me a ludicrously unlikely situation, not least as the aggressor would find itself an international pariah, but the matter-of-fact way he advanced it, and his surprise when I challenged it, spoke volumes about the kind of thinking held at least within his circle. And, it is worth noting, he on-and-off consulted for the Presidential Administration. Worried discussions in Ukraine and the West about whether Putin might resort to nuclear weapons to break a stalemate on the ground obviously reflect this kind of debate in Moscow.

In part, after all, Russia's nuclear arsenal is a political instrument. It continues to explain Moscow's position on the roster of permanent members of the United Nations Security Council; it forces the only superpower left (for now), the United States, to engage with it; it grants a certain status as a serious global player. Yet it is not just that – if so, why spend so much on it, given that much smaller nuclear forces would have a similar effect?

Moscow remains committed to seeing such weapons as a defensive asset, although one that can be used for more than just retaliating against a nuclear attack. Instead, Russian doctrine also envisages their use in case of an 'existential threat' to the Motherland, even if that were conventional. The implication is that this threat could come from NATO, and certainly exercises such as Zapad regularly wargame scenarios where 'blue' forces from the West are engaged in offensive operations. However, while we can never underestimate the paranoias and resentments of Putin and his inner circle, many veterans of the

Soviet security apparatus, and all gripped with the trauma of the loss of empire, at least for the military professionals there seems an understanding that while NATO may not be the purely defensive force claimed – they look at Kosovo, Libya, Iraq and Afghanistan – it is not for the foreseeable future going to be in any position to launch an invasion of Russia. Instead, the inference must be that the only serious potential such threat in the future would have to come from China, today's much-touted ally yet, as discussed in Chapter 28, a growing worry for Russian strategic planners.

PART FIVE

The Future

26

Political Warfare

Beware the snappy turn of phrase, as it may come back to haunt you. In 2013, Gen. Gerasimov delivered a lecture at a military conference that was then published in the rather niche *Voyenno-Promyshlenny Kuryer*, the *Military-Industrial Courier*.[1] This was no big deal; the Chief of the General Staff delivers a speech there every year, and it is probably drafted by someone in his office, anyway. But it made some interesting points, and so I published a translation by Robert Coulson of the Radio Free Europe/Radio Liberty news agency on my blog, *In Moscow's Shadows*, along with my own thoughts and annotations. In order to liven it up, I gave the post the tongue-in-cheek title 'The "Gerasimov Doctrine" and Russian Non-Linear War'.[2]

Big mistake. I had unleashed a monster. Although in the text I explicitly stated that it wasn't a doctrine and wasn't even necessarily Gerasimov's thinking, the title, with its deliberate nod to blockbuster films and thick airport paperbacks, acquired a life of its own, quoted everywhere and even making its way into Western politicians' speeches and military manuals. The problem was that this was at the time of the Crimean annexation and Donbas conflict, and people were primed to believe Russia had some masterful 'new way of war'. The real irony was that Gerasimov had been talking precisely about what he considered to be the West's 'new way of war', one in which 'wars are no longer declared and, having begun, proceed according to an unfamiliar template' which starts with 'military means of a concealed character, including informational attacks and special forces operations' such that 'a perfectly thriving state can, in a matter of months and even days, be transformed into an arena of fierce armed conflict, become a victim of foreign intervention, and sink into a web of chaos, humanitarian catastrophe, and civil war'. In the West, this was seen as Russia's blueprint for the Donbas, but Gerasimov was talking about the Arab Spring risings, the Syrian Civil War and even the 'coloured revolutions' of other post-Soviet states, which he presented as being instigated by the West.[3]

THE RISE OF THE SPOOKS

War has been changing; new technologies have created greater opportunities for information operations, economic interdependence has made sanctions more significant, and the price of conflict, in terms of both money and political risk, has skyrocketed. Although the Kremlin's assumptions that its allies and clients are toppled thanks to CIA plots (and in fairness they still tend to assume that Britain also plays some sinister and subtle role) may largely be as fanciful as the 'Gerasimov Doctrine', this new context is undeniable. Furthermore Russia, as a relatively weaker power than the United States, let alone the collective West, has had all the more reason to adopt 'guerrilla geopolitics', to use unconventional means to try to move conflict into domains where it feels it has more of an advantage.

A growing interest in using non-military means such as subversion and disinformation to supplement actual combat operations also reflects the growing power of Russia's intelligence and security services. Vladimir Putin, of course, was an officer of the Soviet KGB and briefly directed the Federal Security Service, the FSB, 1998–99. Many of his closest allies and advisers also have a background in the security agencies. The closest thing to a national security adviser in the Russian system is the secretary of the Security Council, and since 2008 that has been Nikolai Patrushev, a career KGB security officer who succeeded Putin as director of the FSB. Patrushev is on record as saying that he believes the United States 'would very much like Russia not to exist at all as a country',[4] and has not only pushed for a confrontational line with the West but also ensures Putin gets much of his picture of the outside world from the intelligence agencies.

THE INTELLIGENCE AND SECURITY SERVICES

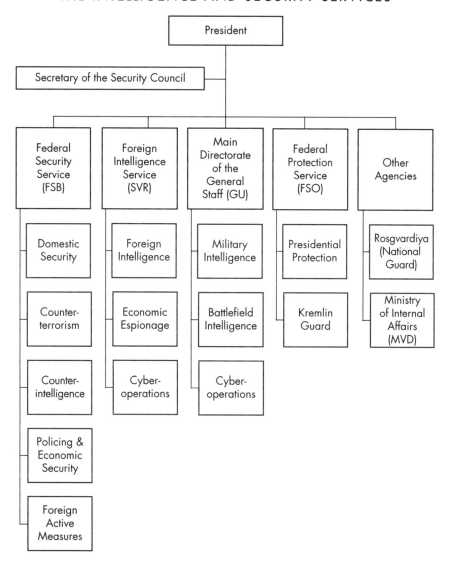

After all, at the start of his working day, before anything else, Putin receives three briefing books. One is from the Foreign Intelligence Service (SVR: *Sluzhba Vneshnei Razvedky*), on foreign events. One is on the domestic situation, from the FSB. One, compiled by the Federal Protection Service (FSO: *Federalnaya Sluzhba Okhrany*) keeps him up to date on what is happening within his own elite. More than once I have heard grumbles from Russian diplomats that Putin puts more weight on the assessments coming from the spooks than his own foreign minister. The security agencies have almost unparalleled access to 'the Body' as Putin is known by his own staff. The directors of the SVR and FSB have weekly one-to-one meetings (the GU head's findings are instead relayed through Shoigu), and it is generally known that the Security Council secretariat – which tends to manage the security-related flow of reports and papers to Putin's desk – gives priority to those documents coming from the agencies.

Their budgets have proven even more secure than the Defence Ministry's, and as the confrontation with the West has deepened, they have become more, not less, central to Kremlin thinking and policy. After all, unlike Western agencies, their role has never just been essentially to gather actionable information. Instead, they are wartime agencies, there not just to gather intelligence but to draw their own conclusions, lobby the government on policy, and carry out direct actions. As a service focusing on human intelligence collection with a growing cyber-espionage capacity, for example, the SVR is often broadly compared with the CIA or SIS (MI6). However, the better parallels for Russia's agencies are with such warfighting Second World War institutions as the US Office of Strategic Services (OSS) and Britain's Special Operations Executive (SOE), established in 1940 with the specific mandate to 'set Europe ablaze'.

Few elements better demonstrate the warfighting mentality of Russia's intelligence agencies than the GU's Unit 29155. Since its formation as *Registrupr* in 1918, Russian military intelligence has had its units tasked with assassination and sabotage, so-called 'wet work' (because it gets bloody ...), but Unit 29155 was stood up around 2009–10. It has been associated with a range of operations. Its members placed explosives in weapons being sold to Ukraine at the Vrbětice arms depot in the Czech Republic in 2014 and then attempted to poison the Bulgarian arms dealer responsible in 2015. They were reportedly involved in an attempted coup in Montenegro in 2016 and the assassination attempt against GRU officer turned MI6 asset Sergei Skripal with Novichok nerve agent in Salisbury in the United Kingdom in 2018. The unit is believed to number only around 20 operators involved in overseas missions, mainly drawn from the *Spetsnaz*, as well as some 200 support staff, although it is able to call on assistance from other arms of the GU and it is based at the 161st Special Purpose Specialist Training

Centre in eastern Moscow. Assessments of Unit 29155's operators tend towards extremes, presenting them as either Russian superspies or else murderous incompetents, given that many of their operations have led to the deaths of innocent victims and subsequent revelations of Russia's hand. However, the truth is that they are neither, and their relatively high profile reflects both their aggressive mission and also the GU's own culture, where bad publicity and disclosure are less important than pressing on towards the target, a partial success being better than none.

HYBRID, AMBIGUOUS, NON-LINEAR, POLITICAL

Powerful, aggressive and with an institutional bias towards covert and political operations, the intelligence agencies have also helped shaped Russian notions of modern war. All kinds of labels have been used to try to encapsulate them, and most have fallen short. 'Hybrid war' because they blend military and non-military means, but in reality, what war does not? 'Ambiguous war' because of their covert tactics and habit of skirting the hazy threshold between war and not-war (is a cyber-attack whose ultimate source cannot be 100% proven an act of war?), but often the Russians are anything but ambiguous. 'Non-linear war' because of their tendency towards asymmetric means and goals, but again, they are often distinctly linear, too.

Part of the reason for this problem is that there are really two schools of thought at work in Moscow. For the soldiers, new forms of 'non-kinetic' warfare – subverting the enemy's morale, chain of command, cohesion and effectiveness – are simply force multipliers, applied especially in the phase before the shooting starts. This is in effect what in the West are often called 'shaping operations', establishing the conditions for successful military action. On the other hand the civilian national security establishment from Patrushev down appears also to see such operations not simply as a prelude to war, but as a possible alternative, a way to impose Russia's will without necessarily resorting to dangerous and expensive combat. If anything, this seems closest to the notion of 'political war' outlined by veteran American scholar-diplomat George Kennan in 1948 as:

> the logical application of Clausewitz's doctrine in time of peace. In broadest definition, political warfare is the employment of all the means at a nation's command, short of war, to achieve its national

objectives. Such operations are both overt and covert. They range from such overt actions as political alliances, economic measures ... and 'white' propaganda to such covert operations as clandestine support of 'friendly' foreign elements, 'black' psychological warfare and even encouragement of underground resistance in hostile states.[5]

As will be outlined in the next chapter, while the spooks practise political war, Russia's soldiers still first and foremost train, equip, exercise and plan for essentially conventional military conflicts, from local interventions all the way to full-scale peer-to-peer war. The intelligence services and a wide range of other political war instrumentalities, from the state foreign-language media to covert political operatives, will continue to wage a campaign of subversion, but that is really for another book.[6] However, this does mean that they have a particularly strong awareness of the opportunities in employing non-kinetic means in conflict and, given the technological lead the West continues to enjoy in most sectors, of the value in finding countermeasures to these capabilities.

OUTSOURCED WARFIGHTERS

The intelligence agencies employ all kinds of outsourced assets. These range from gangsters coerced or hired to generate funds or carry out assassinations (the man who shot dead Chechen Georgian anti-Russian fighter Zelimkhan Khangoshvili in the middle of Berlin in 2019, for example, turned out to be a contract killer engaged by the FSB) to businesspeople encouraged to support pro-Kremlin politicians abroad. Often, subversion can do what military power cannot. However, a particular example of this fusion of business, warfare and geopolitics is the Kremlin's increasing use of mercenaries – or rather a strange, very Russian kind of blend of soldier of fortune and deniable operative.

The most (in)famous example is Wagner, a unit that began in the Donbas, served in Syria, and has then cropped up in a wide range of other conflicts, increasingly in Africa. Its greatest virtue as far as the Kremlin is concerned is deniability – not so much with the West, although it does keep them guessing about the scale of Russian interest or commitment to any conflict, but with the Russian people themselves. The Crimean annexation notwithstanding, foreign wars are not popular with the population. Syria, for example, was sold by the government to the people as an arm's-length technowar, in which Russia's involvement was strictly in aircraft high in the sky or artillery positions far back from the front lines. Yet there was, in 2015–16 at least, an evident need for competent ground troops to spearhead assaults and stiffen the Syrians' spines. Sending regular troops was unacceptable, as once substantial numbers of soldiers started coming home as 'Cargo 200s', as combat deaths are known, then the public mood was likely to turn quickly and for the worse.

So the answer was Wagner. Back in 2013, Moscow had experimented with the use of mercenaries in Syria, setting up the Slavonic Corps, a Hong Kong-registered front company to advertise for veterans willing to guard Syrian energy facilities for what was, by Russian standards, a princely $5,000 a month. By October of that year, there were some 267 contractors in Syria, divided into two companies. The deployment ended up as a farce. The promise of advanced equipment came to nothing, and they ended up issued not the T-72s they had expected, but busses fitted with improvised metal plating. On their way to the Deir ez-Zor oil refineries, they were even hit by a Syrian helicopter, which crashed while flying low over the convoy. On arrival, instead of guard duties, they were ordered to reinforce the Syrian army garrison, but came under attack by a much larger force of Islamist rebels. They retreated, covered by a fortuitous storm. They were lucky to lose no men – six were wounded – but less lucky when, on returning to Russia in disgrace, they were arrested because under Russian law it is illegal to fight as a mercenary. Even though the government had been behind the formation of the Slavonic Corps, it wanted nothing to do with these failures.

The Wagner Group, though, was rather different. It emerged in the Donbas war, a unit of relatively competent professional soldiers commanded by former *Spetsnaz* Lt. Col. Dmitry Utkin, taking its name from his own callsign, Wagner. Utkin had been part of the Slavonic Corps, but escaped any punishment and turned up in Lugansk in 2014. In 2015, though, it pivoted to Syria. The force was constituted more clearly as a commercial entity, apparently registered in Argentina to get round Russia's laws and according to the US, British and EU authorities, is part of the Concord Group of businesses owned and run by Yevgeny Prigozhin, a man known as 'Putin's chef' not because he is known for his cuisine but rather because his firms have a range of government catering contracts. As a man whose wealth depends on the Kremlin, Prigozhin has emerged as one of the government's deniable proxies, doing whatever is needed, from setting up social media 'troll farms' to managing mercenaries.

Wagner acquired a base on the grounds of the 10th *Spetsnaz* Brigade's training ranges at Molkino, and the funds to recruit some of the best recently serving soldiers from the special forces, paratroopers and marines. In October 2015, it was being ferried to Syria in naval ships. Wagner allowed Moscow to introduce elite soldiers without the need for formal recognition of their role. When one of these mercenaries fell in battle, there was no official statement, no military funeral. It was just a 'private contractor' technically working for Damascus. Admittedly, in December 2016, Utkin was personally presented with the Order of Courage by Putin.

The Deir ez-Zor fiasco described in Chapter 18 essentially ended Wagner's primacy in Syria, but since then its members have cropped up in a number of other deployments. In 2017, they began training government troops and guarded gold mines in Sudan. In 2018, they deployed to the Central African Republic, filling a gap left by France after it withdrew its forces from the country in 2016, where they got involved in its brutal civil war, as well as Madagascar and Libya. In 2019, they briefly deployed to Venezuela to protect Russian business facilities. In 2019–20, they fought in Mozambique's Cabo Delgado but withdrew after some reverses and growing tensions with the Mozambiquan military, but in 2021 they switched to Mali, again to support the government after the draw-down of French troops which had previously been helping in the struggle against Islamists.

Is this an example of Russian state adventurism under a thin veil of denial? Or private enterprise as Prigozhin monetizes his military force? It is either and both. Russia is a hybrid state, in which the boundaries between public and private are very permeable, and Wagner seems to operate in both realms. In Syria, it began as an arm of the military, then once disowned turned into a 'proper' mercenary organization driven by the search for profit. Although in its later adventures it obviously never would have gone against the Kremlin's wishes, only in Libya and Venezuela does it seem to have been working specifically at the government's behest. Elsewhere, its members are soldiers for hire – often for a share in local gold or other industries – but with the proviso that at any point the Kremlin could task or take them over. With new private military companies also appearing, with names such as *Shchit* ('Shield') and *Patriot*, generally close to the Defence Ministry, this kind of hybrid mercenary organization is likely to be a feature in the future, too.

INFORMATION WARFARE

In 2017, Shoigu announced that specialized Information Operations Troops (VIO: *Voiska Informatsionnykh Operatsii*) had been stood up.[7] Many interpreted this to mean cyber-attackers and the like, but they also or mainly turned out to be specialists in propaganda and psychological warfare. In Syria, they have sometimes used traditional methods such as dropping leaflets or broadcasting messages through loudspeakers, but they also have the capacity to use electronic interception to get their messages across, such as the aforementioned case of Ukrainian soldiers being sent disconcerting messages by cellphone (see Chapter 16).

This merges into a wider area of particular Russian interest at present: jamming or spoofing Western communications, targeting and navigation signals (and locating their sources, to give the artillery something to shoot at). Given the degree to which Western soldiers rely on GPS for navigation, advanced communications to coordinate their fires, and drones to scout and strike, this should not come as a surprise. As the commander of Russian's electronic warfare (EW) forces put it, these capabilities are 'asymmetric measures that negate the benefits of an adversary's highly sophisticated systems and means of armed combat'.[8] In practice, though, Russia's capabilities operate against enemies both conventional and irregular. As rebels in Syria turned to weaponized commercial drones to attack Hmeymim, for example, the Russians deployed not just anti-air but also EW assets. In January 2018, 13 rebel drones were used to try to swarm the defences: six were taken down simply by EW systems. At the other end of the technological spectrum, the GPS systems used by cruise missiles are also apparently vulnerable, with an unknown number of US Tomahawks launched on Syria as punishment for a chemical weapons attack in 2017 – the Russians say 36, but this is disputed and hard to credit – brought down by a Russian Krasukha-4 EW system at Hmeymim, more than 100 kilometres away. Now, every manoeuvre brigade has its own EW company, and every major formation on land, sea and air has EW assets, and each Military District has its own dedicated EW brigade (two for the Western VO).

Given that anyone looking on their smartphone map while close to the Kremlin tends to find it telling them they are actually at Vnukovo airport, some 25 kilometres to the south-west, it is hardly surprising that the Russian military have likewise elevated the spoofing of GPS and other navigation signals to a fine art. Sometimes this is to decoy or foil drones or missiles, but it also used for propaganda purposes. When the British destroyer HMS *Defender* and Dutch frigate HNLMS *Evertsen* were in the Black Sea in June 2021, for example, Russia spoofed maritime Automatic Identification System signals to show them steaming straight for the Sevastopol naval base in an apparent act of aggression, even while live webcams showed them both docked in Odessa.

In many ways this is a simple extension of a traditional Russian strength in *maskirovka*, which is broadly translated as deception, disguise or sometimes simply camouflage. Obviously the Russians, like all other militaries, use camouflage on uniforms, vehicles and installations alike, and are also trying to catch up in the realm of stealth technologies. However, this is conceived much more broadly, and also involves the extensive use of deception, misdirection and subterfuge. The most infamous recent example is obviously the way the 'little green men' took Crimea, while Moscow denied any involvement, and the use of deniable proxies where appropriate, from the militias of the Donbas to the growing use of mercenaries. These are often less effective on the battlefield, but not only provide a degree of political cover but leave outsiders guessing as to their real role and goals. However, *maskirovka* is built into every aspect of Russian military art, from the battlefield to national strategy. The force which invaded Ukraine in 2022, after all, had been assembling for the best part of a year, but despite Western intelligence reports of Putin's intent, there was still widespread uncertainty as to whether the Kremlin was mounting a massive and painstakingly realistic bluff. This is the essence of strategic deception.

27

New Generation Warfare

In some 30 years of interacting with soldiers – Soviet, Russian, NATO, whoever – it has often struck me that they tend to be practical and realistic. If called to fight, they will do so, at whatever cost to themselves, but they rarely display the gung-ho jocularity or belligerent eagerness towards their trade one sometimes encounters from civilian politicians who have never served or fought. Some years back, I was talking to a couple of Russian captains, one a helicopter pilot and the other an infantryman. Once we had got past their inevitable wariness at talking to a Westerner, it became clear that they were at once reverential and dismissive towards Putin.

They absolutely considered him a strong and capable national leader, the man who had saved Russia from oblivion and irrelevance. But they were less comfortable with his image as a man of action. Yes, at university Putin did compulsory military training as a reserve officer, in the artillery, but this was pretty perfunctory, and as soon as he joined the KGB he stopped having to do his reserve refresher training. They didn't appreciate all the photo opportunities of Putin sitting in a cockpit or driving a tank, they weren't convinced he understood the realities of their world, and they were unsure that he, the commander-in-chief, truly understood warfare, or even Russia's own Military Doctrine.

In a colourful metaphor, one said, 'I wouldn't want a virgin telling me what to do on my wedding night.'

This certainly proved prescient considering how the invasion of Ukraine unfolded, as discussed in the penultimate chapter, and the degree to which military imperatives were hijacked by Putin's own instincts. Russia has, after all, a very intellectual and deliberate approach to its military art, and the military is definitely, in today's jargon, a 'learning organization'. As a result, its military thought is complex and evolving.[1] Indeed, Russia's Military Doctrine envisages six different types of war or conflict, each with its own characteristics. Military danger and then military threat are essentially challenges still in potential form, which could still be averted or neutralized by diplomatic as well as military means. Then there is an armed conflict, a limited clash between either states or rivals in a civil war. A local war is one fought over specific military-political objectives and confined to the warring states. Once it involves more than two nations, then it becomes a regional war, while a large-scale war is one fought between coalitions of states or global powers, with 'radical military-political objectives' and which thus demands the 'mobilization of all physical resources available and the moral strength of the participating states'.[2]

SMALL WARS

The Russian notion of the small war is not simply measured in terms of number of troops involved or size of the country. Rather, it is about lower-level military dangers and threats that may be able to be dealt with by deterrence, coercion, surgical strikes and the use of proxies. Even the amorphous 'armed conflict' and some local wars still represent smaller-scale operations. Syria provided a first real test of how the Russians would respond in such circumstances with what they call 'a strategy of limited actions', avoiding escalation and keeping the use of force and Moscow's footprint to the minimum possible or necessary. In Gerasimov's words:

> The most important conditions for the implementation of this strategy are gaining and maintaining information superiority, anticipating the readiness of command and control systems and comprehensive support, as well as the covert deployment of the necessary [force] grouping.[3]

Ideally, threats will be dealt with through diplomatic moves, even of the more coercive kind, with forces mobilized and potential offensive scenarios openly rehearsed in the context of snap exercises as a threat. If forces must be deployed, then what is called a Combat Management Group (GBU: *Gruppa Boyevovo Upravleniya*) will be stood up within the new National Defence Management Centre (NTsUO: *Natsionalny Tsentr Upravleniya Oboronoi*). When the NTsUO was opened in 2014, it was rightly hailed as a major step forward in Russian command and control. Buried in the basement of the Defence Ministry building on Frunze Embankment, it employs more than a thousand military and civilian personnel supporting 24/7 operation, using one of the most powerful military supercomputers in the world. Commanders in the Centre can watch cyber-attacks unfold in representative form, or streaming video from a soldier on the battlefield. The NTsUO is not only a command hub, although it has both a main situation room and a suite of smaller ones to deal with potential and less pressing developments; it is also a fusion centre bringing together data and analysis from not just military and intelligence sources, but across the government. It can also coordinate operations with the police, National Guard and other agencies, in keeping with the eclectic challenges of multi-domain 'New Generation Warfare'.

The GBUs formed within the Centre are mission specific, in place for as long as a crisis may last, whether a few days or – as in Syria – already seven years. Led by officers from the General Staff's Main Operations Directorate, it will draw on other NTsUO staff and whoever may be needed from other military services or even outside structures. The GBU which coordinated the 2022 deployment to Kazakhstan, for example, was heavy on paratrooper officers, as the VDV provided the troops, but also included liaison officers from both the Foreign Intelligence Service and the Foreign Ministry. It is at least believed within the Main Operations Directorate that even the choice of room assigned may give a sense of the likely scale and priority of the mission. The seven main halls of the NTsUO are named after famous Russian commanders but there are many other, perfectly functional but rather less impressive rooms and suites. The word is that if a GBU is assigned sole access to one of the more extensive and highly sought-after situation rooms or suites, then the High Command expects it to be a serious mission, compared with those forced to book rooms competitively.

Either way, a GBU is not an operational command structure. Rather, its main role is to set up the necessary task force for any mission and then set strategy, monitor progress and ensure the commanders on the ground have what they need to do their job, 'collecting and assessing situation data, analysing the decisions taken by the command of the grouping and planning further actions'.[4] The actual operational command for anything less than a full national effort will be vested in either a Military District (Joint Operational Command) or an army headquarters for crises within or adjacent to national borders or a Command Post of a Group of Forces (KPGV: *Komandny Punkt Gruppirovki Voisk*) for overseas deployments. The (officially denied) Donbas deployment to Ukraine up until the invasion, for example, was managed through the Southern VO, with its 8th Army handling operational supervision, while the Syrian contingent is an obvious example of a KPGV.

LIMITED DEPLOYMENTS

Sometimes, military deployments are purely for political missions. In January 2022, for instance, the Central Asian country of Kazakhstan erupted in violent unrest, as rising fuel prices sparked long-simmering discontent at corruption and the 33-year rule of *Elbasy*, or 'Father of the Nation' Nursultan Nazarbayev. This seems to have been the opportunity for a palace coup against Nazarbayev by his own hand-picked proxy, President Kassym-Jomart Tokayev. Kazakhstan is a member of the Russian-led Collective Security Treaty Organization and appealed for assistance. Given that the CSTO's charter only envisages support in cases of external aggression, Tokayev claimed on the flimsiest of evidence that the protests were being whipped up by foreign Islamist radicals. It is not as though he really needed extra support: Kazakhstan has over 100,000 troops and almost 50,000 security personnel. Rather, he needed a signal of Moscow's approval for his ousting the 81-year-old Nazarbayev to help swing the loyalty of the elite – including the police and army generals – to his side.

Moscow agreed, and, in an impressive demonstration of its capacity to deploy forces rapidly, within 24 hours almost 2,000 paratroopers from the 98th Division and 45th *Spetsnaz* Brigade were being airlifted to Kazakhstan. There they were supplemented by smaller contingents from fellow CSTO member states Armenia, Belarus, Kyrgyzstan and Tajikistan, who were also flown in by the Russian VTA (although this took the lion's share of its heavy lifters, especially the An-124s). The contingent didn't have to fire a shot, and was withdrawn a week later, but it performed its wider political task, Nazarbayev 'voluntarily stood down' from his position as head of the powerful Security Council, Tokayev consolidated his position, and Moscow had demonstrated that for its allies, it was still willing and able to provide security assistance at a moment's notice.

At other times, the notion of 'limited actions' will involve using proxies for the heavy lifting, with Russian forces supplying strategy, command and control, and whatever specific military capabilities needed to supplement the proxies. The Donbas and Syrian conflicts are, in their own ways, examples of this approach. In both cases, Moscow sought to limit its direct involvement, but instead exerted overall command at the strategic level. The proxies – militias in the Donbas, mercenaries, militias and government forces in Syria – are often of indifferent quality, but they are also, from Moscow's perspective, cheap and politically expedient. In the Donbas, the Russians provided a backstop that limited Kyiv's capacity to use its military overmatch to crush the rebels, as well as heavy weapons and intelligence support. In Syria, it is largely airpower and also small contingents of Military Police able to insert themselves as more neutral forces to secure ceasefires and deconfliction lines.

BIG WARS

When it comes to regional or large-scale wars, or even the more serious local wars, we actually have a pretty good idea of how the Russians would intend to fight them. After all, they have discussed them in countless technical articles, wargamed them in large-scale exercises, and encoded their thinking in the decisions made about force placement, training and procurement. The exercises, of course, are always framed in defensive terms, but even then, Russian military thinkers work on an essentially offensive basis. From the Russians' fighting retreat that saw Napoleon reach Moscow in 1812 to the initial response to the Germans' Operation *Barbarossa* invasion in 1941, they have often had to rely on defensive depth, but that is not their intent or expectation in today's world of long-range firepower and rapid deployment. Indeed, if necessary and possible, the aim would be to get the first blow, possibly as the enemy is mobilizing. In Gerasimov's words, 'The basis of our response is an active defence strategy, which, given the defensive nature of the Russian Military Doctrine, provides for a set of measures to proactively neutralize threats to the security of the state.'[5]

These do not necessarily mean full-scale military operations, but could be diplomatic initiatives, intimidatory manoeuvres or surgical strikes intended to signal resolve or degrade capability. This will be part of a pre-conflict period that will also see non-military means employed to try to weaken the enemy, such as subversion and psychological warfare. Assuming that fails, though, the working assumption if fighting the West, as already mentioned, is that at first the Russians will face a massive missile and air offensive, which NATO will be relying upon so heavily to damage and disrupt them that it will be decisive. Russia's goal, then, would be to pre-empt, suppress and endure this, so that US hopes of a quick victory are dashed and it can seize and maintain the initiative.

That means strategic operations that, in turn, inflict strategic-level consequences on the enemy, degrading their capacity and will to continue fighting. Whether the aim is to manage escalation or bring the war to a close, it will always be an essentially political process, prosecuted by military means. To this end, the Russian High Command has adapted the old Soviet notion of 'deep battle' to the modern world, and whether it is in a particular maritime theatre, or near orbit, or the electromagnetic spectrum, the aim is through coordinated operations to break the enemy's ability to operate as a whole, not just in that particular territory or domain.

What does this actually mean, though? On the ground, the Russians believe that much warfare will be 'non-contact', with units often having little direct sight of their enemy. Instead, artillery will prove decisive (as, especially to the Russians, it always has). 'Reconnaissance-strike' and 'reconnaissance-fire' complexes of integrated intelligence, surveillance, and reconnaissance assets and automated command and control systems will dominate the battlefield, as various sensors, from drones to scouts, rapidly and accurately direct devastating precision-guided weapons on a target in the former case, massed artillery or rocket fire in the latter. The Russians, after all, have a lot of heavy guns and multiple rocket launchers; to quote Les Grau and Charles Bartles, 'the Russian Army is an artillery army with a lot of tanks'.[6] Furthermore, this artillery is mobile, so as well as being the main weapon with which to break enemy units, it at once denies the enemy freedom of manoeuvre – since it creates spaces in which it would be dangerous to move – and in the process enables the Russians'.

This would not be a war of massed Second World War-style formations and clear front lines, but a fluid and fast-moving battlefield (whether on ground, air, sea or space) which is not so much about seizing terrain as about disorganizing and neutralizing the enemy, while preserving one's own forces. After all, Russia's planners do not assume they will have overwhelming numerical strength, and in any case, Western precision-guided munitions are still likely to be more numerous and more accurate, so they pose a serious threat to the Russians. Operation *Desert Storm* may be 30 years ago, but it still presents a painful case study of how a seemingly powerful and competent mechanized force can be chewed through by a technologically more advanced enemy if it does not understand the nature of modern war. To this end, 'offensive' operations need not necessarily mean counter-attacking onto an enemy's territory, so much as using attacks to degrade their capacity to fight. Meanwhile, the invisible battlefields of the electromagnetic spectrum and cyber-space will be, in their own way, as viciously contested as the physical domains.

ESCALATION, DE-ESCALATION AND LESSER APOCALYPSES

Russia may suspect it has a greater will to continue fighting than NATO, but it cannot count on that, and also works on the assumption that it cannot win a war of attrition with an alliance with more people, more soldiers and larger economies. If undermining Western will and unity beforehand, if demonstrating that it cannot be knocked out quickly by an air and missile blitzkrieg, and if rapid and coordinated active defence do not quickly bring any major war to an end, what then? Inevitably, this is where the question of the nuclear forces comes squarely into centre stage.

There is a widespread myth that Moscow has an aggressive 'escalate to de-escalate' strategy whereby it would launch an attack, make some gains, and then initiate or threaten a limited nuclear strike to deter any counter-attack and effectively freeze the conflict at its point of advantage. There is no real basis to this belief; the Russians appear well aware of the dangers of initiating nuclear retaliation, and are very clear that they see nuclear weapons as essentially defensive tools.

That said, they do see scope for tactical nuclear weapons as tools for escalation management in a regional or large-scale war, where Russia's conventional forces are proving unequal to the task of bringing the conflict to a close or preventing enemy advances. However, with more long-range strike weapons like the *Kalibr* cruise missile, *Kinzhal* air-launched ballistic missile and *Iskander* missile being capable of delivering powerful conventional payloads, there is also the belief that their use, when combined with cyber-attacks and electronic warfare, could sufficiently disrupt an enemy's command and control and critical national infrastructure such as to have an equivalent effect without needing to turn to nuclear options.

As regards strategic nuclear forces, their role is to deter an enemy nuclear attack, deliver a second-strike retaliation if that fails, or only otherwise be used in case of an existential threat to the Motherland. That said, though, one wonders what would happen were Russia to find itself in a full-scale war not with NATO – a constellation of democratic states quite comfortable in their essential affluence – but with a future rising China, authoritarian and assertive. This is one of the frustrating topics on which I have never been able to get any Russian soldier who may know anything to talk. There is a contingency plan for war with China – this is only to be expected, as it is the role of military planners to have options ready for whatever (within reason) could face them. There is probably at least what in Western parlance is a CONPLAN, a concept plan, for alien invasion or Siberian secession, after all. Yet how, realistically, could Russia east of the Urals be defended conventionally, given that there are relatively few forces there, dependent on two railway lines – the Trans-Siberian and the Baikal-Amur Magistral – that could quickly and easily be closed? The suspicion must be that this would be a conflict that very quickly ticked up the escalation ladder, towards tactical and then strategic nuclear options.

28

The Challenges of the Future

Is a future war with China plausible, given that at present Vladimir Putin and Xi Jinping are hailing the friendship of their nations and their solidarity against America's alleged attempts to maintain its 'unipolar' hegemonic power in the world? For the moment, it seems not, but defence planners must think not of tomorrow or even the day after but in decades, not least given the time new weapons systems can take from concept to deployment, and the need to consider everything from demographic trends to leadership succession.

Back in 1991, I had been finalizing the research for my PhD thesis in Moscow, and rumours of coups were circulating throughout the city. As it was, I flew back to London on the Friday before the hard-liners' 'August Coup'. I still begrudge missing that, and wholly unreasonably feel Russia 'owes' me a coup. In any case, though, that very Monday, I had a long pre-arranged meeting with someone in the British Ministry of Defence, so at least I felt I was going to get the inside insight into what was happening. But when I asked, he looked sheepish: 'The communications intercepts haven't come in yet from Cheltenham' – home of GCHQ, the United Kingdom's electronic intelligence agency – 'so, we're watching CNN.'

It was at once heartening and depressing to find that, in the moment, even governments knew relatively little more than the rest of us. (Of course, soon enough they came to know much more.) It also highlighted the extent to which defence planners are squeezed between the Olympian realm of long-term geopolitical trends and the insistent tyranny of day-to-day developments. It is often said that Putin has played a weak hand well, and that Russia is in a strong position in the world. In many ways, that is true, but there are long-term social, political, economic and even demographic challenges the Kremlin must face. The potential risks along its own borders are also serious and arguably growing. What's more they are, as in 1991, often going to come from unexpected directions or in unexpected ways. In that context, the job of a Russian defence planner is certainly not an easy one, either.

THE WESTERN FLANK

These are not the happiest times for Ukraine, Belarus and Moldova, sandwiched between Russia and the West. All three nations are, in their own ways, feeling the weight of Moscow's aspirations towards great power status – and thus its belief that it needs buffer states and deserves a sphere of influence – yet also posing different challenges to Russia.

Under long-standing ruler Alexander Lukashenko, Belarus had long maintained its independence by playing Russia off against the West. Although since 1997 formally part of the Union State of Russia and Belarus, this meant almost nothing beyond some trade and visa coordination, and the presence of Russian air defence assets in Belarus: a radar station at Gantsevichy, the Vileyka naval communication centre, and the Baranovchi joint air force and air defence training centre. In August 2020, in response to blatant falsification of general election results, a massive wave of peaceful protests broke across the country. The security forces responded with violence, and as the West protested, Lukashenko was increasingly forced to turn to Putin for political, economic and military assistance. Although he is a wily operator and has maintained a degree of autonomy, Lukashenko is now essentially a Russian client, and one result is the growing Russian military presence in Belarus, including forces which were used to open a separate front against neighbouring Ukraine in 2022.

Nonetheless, this acquisition comes with its own challenges for Russia. While the protests have for the moment largely been contained, the regime has lost its legitimacy. Even some members of the security apparatus are unhappy with the situation. Others are still Lukashenko loyalists, though, and if Moscow should someday feel it needs to try to impose a less toxic and more malleable leader in his place, they may resist. Conversely, if protests explode again, potentially violent ones, then Moscow will presumably feel it has no alternative but to provide whatever assistance the regime needs to survive, up to and including troops, lest a new, pro-Western opposition take power, as it did in Ukraine.

As for Ukraine, it is hard not to see Putin's personal crusade to keep it within Russia's orbit as already lost. The Donbas adventure was an expensive mistake, and the Russian threat since 2014 drove Kyiv to reform its military with impressive speed and effectiveness. It also united once-disparate Ukrainian communities and brought more Western assistance. By 2022, it had built an army of just under 150,000 troops, many of whom were veterans with the kind of experience facing front-line Russian forces that no NATO counterparts could claim, even if much of their equipment is dated. As well as the 45,000-strong National Guard under the Interior Ministry, there was also a large reserve force that could be mobilized to form 150 Territorial Defence battalions. No wonder that hawks in Kyiv had been dreaming of some day being able to have their own 'Croatian' solution to Donbas, after the way Croatia first lost control of the self-declared 'Republic of Serbian Krajina' in 1992, in part because of Serbian involvement, but regrouped and in 1995 retook it. As it was, in February 2022 Putin decided on trying to impose his own military solution to the stalemate, apparently assuming that the government was as weak as it had been in 2014 and as easy to collapse. As will be discussed in the next chapter, he was painfully and dangerously wrong.

Finally, spare a thought for all-too-often overlooked Moldova, between Ukraine and Romania. Europe's poorest country, it not only has to endure the continued presence of the unrecognized but Moscow-backed pseudo-state of Transnistria on its eastern border, but also periodically faces pressure from Moscow, especially as it is dependent on Russian gas supplies. After the election in 2020 of Maia Sandu, a former World Bank economist who favours reform and closer alignment with the European Union, Russia turned to its 'energy weapon', cutting supplies by one-third and refusing to extend the existing contract. Although a new deal was struck, Moscow's determination to foil attempts by any countries in the region to move towards the EU continues to be an obvious driver for conflict – and in this case, a reason to continue to maintain a military presence in Transnistria as a lever in the future.

THE TURBULENT NORTH CAUCASUS ...

Not all challenges are outside Russia's borders. Chechnya is officially pacified – but only by accepting its virtual autonomy under an erratic and brutal leader who not only has territorial claims on neighbouring North Caucasus republics but also expects Moscow to pay for his personal army, his grandiose prestige projects, and his and his cronies' lavish lifestyle. (Kadyrov himself has a palace larger than the old Russian tsars' Winter Palace and a fleet of cars including one of the only 20 Lamborghini Reventons ever made.) Periodically, his many enemies in Moscow urge Putin that something must be done to clip his wings or even take him down, after the latest embarrassing story about him, but the president – to whom Kadyrov regularly pledges his personal loyalty – either doesn't want to act or feels he can't.

After all, there is a real fear that without Kadyrov, Chechnya may explode into violence again, and there is no appetite for a third Chechen war. Even under his heavy hand, there are still occasional acts of terror in Chechnya. Perhaps more serious is the threat that the Chechen elite could turn on itself, as various strongmen and warlords compete to take Kadyrov's place and control of the huge revenue streams from Moscow.

Victory of sorts in Chechnya did not wholly pacify the region, either. There is a continued sporadic problem with terrorism and insurgency across the North Caucasus, largely from jihadist groups which exploit the deep poverty of the local population, as well as anger at corrupt or unresponsive local administrations. Low-level violence is a constant issue, as is the danger that this will resurge as more organized insurgent or terrorist *jamaats* (Islamic militant groups). All this helps explain why Moscow has to continue to maintain an extensive military and security force presence in the region. The Southern Military District's 58th Army is based in Vladikavkaz in North Ossetia, and its many manoeuvre elements are the 19th Motor Rifle Division (Vladikavkaz), the 42nd Guards Motor Rifle Division (Khankala, Chechnya), the 136th Independent Motor Rifle Brigade (Buynaksk, Dagestan), and the 100th *Spetsnaz* Brigade (Mozdok, North Ossetia). Beyond that, the North Caucasus National Guards Troop District includes the 2nd Independent Interior Troops Special Designation Division in Krasnodar, along with a further seven Interior Troops brigades, five regiments, eight battalions, eight motorized police battalions and four special forces units. Until recent relocations around the Ukrainian border, this meant the North Caucasus had the greatest density of forces in the country.

... AND THE TURBULENT SOUTH CAUCASUS, TOO

Following the 2008 Georgian War, the South Caucasus appeared for a long time to be relatively quiescent from Moscow's perspective. Georgia was distinctly unhappy with the post-war status quo, but in practice could do nothing for fear of Russian overt or covert retaliation. In 2019, for example, following protests at the visit of a Russian politician, Moscow suspended direct flights between the countries, citing security concerns, and placed new regulatory burdens on imports of Georgian wine and mineral water – two staples of its trade.

Likewise, although relations between Armenia and Azerbaijan remained hostile, from Moscow's perspective this was no bad thing, giving it a certain leverage on both nations. When peaceful protests brought down the government of long-standing Armenian leader Serzh Sargsyan and opened the way to centrist new prime minister Nikol Pashinyan, Russia was neutral. Although it had worked perfectly well with Sargsyan, Pashinyan made it clear that although he planned reform in domestic policy, he would not change Armenia's orientation towards Russia.

However, in September 2020, the long-standing and bitter rivalry between Azerbaijan and Armenia, which has deeper and broader roots but has focused on the disputed territory of Nagorno-Karabakh, erupted again into war. Azerbaijan is a larger country, a richer country, and had been spending solidly on its military since the last war in 2016. Furthermore, it was backed by Turkey, which had not only sold it Bayraktar TB-2 strike drones but provided advisors and even mercenaries hired from Syria. Although the war only lasted until a ceasefire was implemented on 9 November, the Armenian forces were destroyed piecemeal by artillery (with drones spotting for them), loitering munitions (essentially kamikaze drones) and drone-fired missiles. Claims that it demonstrated that the drone was now king of the battlefield, though, were premature: Armenia had failed to prepare adequately, not least by failing to develop a proper integrated air defence system which allowed Azerbaijan's unmanned aircraft pretty much free rein.

This represented an unparalleled Turkish intrusion into what Moscow considers its sphere of influence, yet the Kremlin was unwilling to intervene on Armenia's side. It would have required a substantial military commitment, alienated Azerbaijan's leader Ilhan Aliev, and risked a direct confrontation with Turkey. Instead, it brokered a ceasefire that saw Azerbaijan consolidate its territorial gains, but a Russian peacekeeping force of some 2,000 soldiers, initially from the 31st Independent Guards Air Assault Brigade, and around as many Border Troops, was deployed to keep the warring sides apart in Nagorno-Karabakh and along an agreed transit corridor.

The Kremlin has long regarded the South Caucasus as part of its 'Near Abroad' sphere of influence. Not an empire as such, but a region in which it was hegemon. Its inability and seeming unwillingness to control this six-week war and its forced acceptance of Turkey now as an active local player is a game-changer. Aliev, in his speech welcoming the ceasefire, mentioned Putin but fulsomely thanked 'my dear brother Recep Tayyip Erdoğan'. What's more, in 2022, Turkish company Bayraktar, which supplied the TB-2 drones to Azerbaijan, announced that it was going to open a factory in Ukraine, which has also begun to buy them. At best, by inserting itself as peacekeeper, Moscow has recovered some lost relevance and authority in the South Caucasus, but at a cost.

That Moscow had to escalate its commitment to retain its position brings home the extent to which, on its southern flank, it is engaged in managing decline more than maintaining control. In a pattern reminiscent of the changing orientation in Central Asia – where Moscow retains the overt trappings of hegemony, while behind the scenes Beijing's economic power is increasingly dominant – so too in the South Caucasus, Russia is having to accept new players in what was once its unquestioned backyard.

CENTRAL ASIA: INSTABILITY AND JIHAD

Continuing round Russia's borders, post-Soviet Central Asia is still more solidly within Russia's effective sphere of influence, but even here there is both the risk of instability and the danger of growing rivalries. The experience of empire – tsarist and Soviet – is still very present, with all five nations to greater or lesser degrees being patchworks of ethnicities and linguistic groups within pretty arbitrary boundaries. Although most of the region's 75 million or so people are at least notionally Muslim, their governments are largely secular. There is a constant fear that Islam could be mobilized against them, and this, combined with the inevitable tensions generated by widespread poverty and corruption, has often led to risings from below – and heavy-handed rule from above.

With the exception of Kyrgyzstan, which has managed to hold on to a ramshackle kind of democracy despite periodic uprisings and waves of protest, the region is characterized by corrupt, personalistic authoritarianisms. As mentioned earlier, in Kazakhstan, President Tokayev has recently usurped the power of long-standing ruler Nursultan Nazarbayev (who had the capital city renamed in his own honour), and it will have to be seen whether he is able to consolidate this position. In Turkmenistan, President for Life Saparmurat Niyazov ruled with increasingly totalitarian whimsy (he renamed the month of April after his mother, and erected a massive gold statue of himself that rotated to face the sun) until his death in 2006. He was succeeded by his deputy, Gurbanguly Berdimukhamedov, who shows every sign of being a worthy successor, in that he banned black cars in the capital, Ashgabat, because it was 'unlucky' and has instead raised a golden statue of himself riding a horse. Uzbekistan, like Kazakhstan, was ruled by a relic of the Soviet era, Islam Karimov, until his death in 2016. His successor, Shavkat Mirziyoyev, has made some moves towards reform, but the country remains corrupt and unfree. Finally, under President Emomali Rahmon, Tajikistan remains perhaps the most unstable of the countries in the region, impoverished and vulnerable to both drug trafficking and jihadist influences from neighbouring Afghanistan.

This poses a particular problem for Moscow. Historically, after all, Russia's security apparatus has concentrated on Islamist militants from the North Caucasus, which had been the main source of serious terrorist attacks, including a mass hostage-taking at a theatre in Moscow in 2002 and suicide bombings on the Moscow metro in 2010 and Domodedovo airport in 2011. Many of these are loosely affiliated with either Islamic State or Al-Qaeda, but they have also faced serious suppression by the security forces. Increasingly, though, the Kremlin has started to be worried about the implications of jihadism in Central

Asia and its potential spread amongst Russia's estimated 400,000-plus Central Asian migrants and temporary workers (at least half of whom are unregistered). In 2017, for example, an ethnic Uzbek from Kyrgyzstan blew himself up on the St Petersburg metro, killing 14.

Moscow's claim to a degree of authority over the region is not entirely based on historical connections and its own pretensions. It remains a significant economic partner – Tajikistan is especially dependent on the remittances sent back by Tajiks who go to work in Russia – but above all is a security guarantor. On its western borders, Russia is generally regarded as a bully and an interloper, but in Central Asia, while there are the inevitable grumbles about high-handed Russians (though polls show them to be more popular than the Americans or the Chinese), Moscow is a welcome protector. When Afghanistan fell to the Taliban, Tajikistan appealed for more support, and Russia beefed up its 201st Base there, sending in more modernized T-72B3M tanks and S-300 SAMs, then staging joint exercises with the local military as a symbol of its commitment to Tajik security. At the same time, the parliament of Kyrgyzstan was ratifying an agreement that allowed Russia to deploy drones at its base in Kant, which began receiving *Orlan*-10s and also a general upgrade with new helicopters and air defences.

It was, after all, Moscow which acted as kingmaker in Kazakhstan, and the undignified and destabilizing US withdrawal from Afghanistan in August 2021 only seemed to support a widespread notion that the Russians are the only reliable security guarantors in the region. This has clear benefits for Moscow, granting it the kind of authority it feels a great power should be able to wield in its strategic neighbourhood. However, it also brings with it distinct potential challenges.

First of all, the instability of the region cannot be understated, riven as it is with ethnic, historical, clan and factional rivalries. The tragic irony is that brutal authoritarianisms tend to be secure, but if figures such as Tokayev and Mirziyoyev do seek meaningful reform, this is likely to generate instability, at least in the short term. Combined with the risk of jihadist spill-over from Afghanistan, whether in the form of actual physical incursions (as has happened in the past) or simply a spread in radical ideas, then Moscow might find its blank security cheques being cashed more often than it might like. (Although it would take an extraordinary threat to get Moscow back into Afghanistan.)

There is also a strong China dimension. Until now, China has been willing to let the Russians play the role of strategic hegemon and security guarantor, while it stuck to its economic agenda, making its own investments and above all developing its Belt and Road infrastructure projects meant to build a 'New Silk Road' connecting it to the economies of Europe, Africa and the Middle East. This means that it will also be expecting Moscow to live up to its promises, and if regional instability does begin to become a problem, Beijing will either be pressing the Russians to act or else perhaps – even more dangerously for regional stability – deciding to act itself.

China is, after all, becoming increasingly assertive on all fronts. It may feel it either has to protect its interests itself or even opt to use Central Asia as an opportunity to flex its muscles. It already has a small military base in Tajikistan, near the Afghan border, and in 2020 it agreed to fund a base for Tajikistan's Rapid Reaction Group – Interior Ministry special forces – in the remote Gorno-Badakhshan Autonomous Province. While initially it was said that no Chinese personnel would be stationed there, several observers have questioned this. After all, Dushanbe is having to tread carefully with Beijing. In 2011, it ratified a 1999 deal to cede China territories in the Pamir Mountains, to end a 130-year dispute. China formally relinquished claims to other territories, but in 2020 stories began to run in the press advocating reopening this issue. Moscow and Dushanbe protested and Beijing claimed it was just unofficial and unauthorized speculation, but given the extent to which the media is state-controlled, the fear remains that China could press its case again, if it ever wanted leverage with Tajikistan.

CHINA, THE GREAT FRENEMY

When China's latest anti-terrorism law included a clause allowing it to deploy its forces outside its borders, it was widely interpreted as a signal that Beijing may be looking to project its military influence abroad, and its more muscular recent moves over Taiwan and the South China Sea also suggest this. Central Asia may be where it begins to test out its new strengths in practice.

Western leaders are clearly worried by what they see as a burgeoning Sino-Russian 'DragonBear' military alliance. In October 2021, for example, NATO Secretary-General Jens Stoltenberg warned that 'China is coming closer to us', and criticized 'this whole idea that we either look to Russia, or to China ... Because it goes together.'[1] The notion is not simply that NATO has to operate in a single, global security environment, but also more specifically that China and Russia are cooperating and coordinating their actions. It is certainly the case that both Putin and Xi Jinping have been happy to talk up their united front, both because they share a common mistrust of the West and also because they know such language gets the West's attention.

However, in stark contrast to the notion that there is some lock-step Sino-Russian axis, I remember a conversation back in 2013 with a retired Russian military officer, who had been a planner in the General Staff's Main Operations Directorate. His opinion was stark: 'In 20 years' time, Russia will either have become an ally of the West of some sort, or else a vassal of China's.' He wasn't alone in holding that opinion then, and although quite what kind of ally Russia could be with the West in the current environment is hard to tease out, nor is he now.

There clearly is a growing rapprochement, driven by mutual suspicion and resentment of the West and common economic interests. Even there, though, the relationship is distinctly asymmetrical: Moscow needs Beijing more than the other way round, and as far as the Chinese are concerned, whatever oil, gas, weapons and the like they need from Russia, they can just buy. Even then, they are ruthlessly pragmatic: when they concluded a $400 billion gas deal in 2014, for example, the Chinese knew that Russia needed a deal for political and economic reasons and exploited this ruthlessly: as Putin himself ruefully admitted at the time, 'our Chinese friends are difficult, hard negotiators'.[2]

Consider also the *Vostok*-2018 (East-2018) military exercises. These were massive, officially involving in total 300,000 soldiers, 36,000 tanks and other vehicles, 80 ships and 1,000 aircraft, operating right across the eastern half of Russia. To put that into context, that's equivalent to about one-third of the entire Russian military (although that 300,000 figure was likely inflated), or double the British armed forces. This was also double the size of the previous iteration, *Vostok*-2014. However, most foreign attention was focused on the presence of a Chinese contingent in the exercises, with overheated media claims that this represented the start of a new military alliance.

Never mind that the Chinese force was of just 3,200 troops and 30 aircraft. Or that they were essentially excluded from the higher-level strategic command post elements of the exercise. Or that they were not involved in the naval portion – so they sent an uninvited *Dongdiao*-class spyship tagging along to watch. While, in a deliberate act of performative choreography, Putin and Xi Jinping were holding a summit in Vladivostok and pledging closer business and political cooperation, there was much less to this military cooperation than the headlines suggested.

To a large degree, this is a deliberate geopolitical gambit, an information operation, a bid by both countries to play up their relationship to worry the West and elevate their own stock. However, there are good reasons to believe that in the long term, things may well be rather less amicable. First of all, there are long-standing Chinese claims to swathes of territory in the Russian Far East, seized during periods of Russian imperial expansion. Although the last border disputes were formally resolved in 2008, wider questions about the 1858 Treaty of Aigun and 1860 Treaty of Peking, which transferred large areas to Russia, could always be reopened. The forces in the Russian Far East are hardly elite, though, and often relatively static. Along the more than 4,000-kilometre-long border with China, Moscow deploys essentially defensive units whose purpose is to be both a tripwire to detect and deter any incursions and also a delaying force, to buy time for reinforcements to be rushed to the scene.

The 18th Machine-Gun Artillery Division, for example, is the primary unit assigned to defence of the Kuril Islands, an archipelago stretching from Russia's Kamchatka peninsula to northern Japan. They were annexed at the end of the Second World War, and Japan still lays claim to the four southernmost islands, which includes Iturup and Kunashir, two of the three largest. Although this is essentially a political dispute, nonetheless it means that the security of the Kurils has disproportionate priority, even if it poses specific challenges. This is reflected in the composition of the division, which is headquartered on Iturup Island, but also has a base on Kunashir. It fields two machine gun artillery battalions, an anti-tank battalion, an anti-air missile-and-gun battalion, an anti-air missile battalion, a battery of multiple rocket launchers and, for mobile defence, a single motor-rifle battalion mounted in highly mobile MT-LB carriers and a company of T-72B tanks. Even with the addition of K-300P *Bastion*-P ground-to-sea missiles, the expectation is that the division could hold the islands for no more than four days in the unlikely event of a full-scale Japanese attack. The thinking is, though, that this would be long enough for them to be reinforced or the pressure lifted by diplomatic means or posing an alternative threat to Japan.

Likewise, the 69th Independent Screening Brigade (the Russian word *prikrytiya* could as easily be translated as 'covering' or more figuratively as 'fortification') is under the Eastern VO's 35th Army. Headquartered at Babstovo in the Jewish Autonomous Region, a village originally established as a fortified Cossack township on the Chinese border, it comprises three machine-gun battalions, a battalion each of 152mm 2S19 Msta-S self-propelled guns, anti-aircraft guns and anti-aircraft missiles, and its sole mobile element, a battalion of T-80BV tanks. There would be little it could do in case of a serious Chinese incursion beyond go down fighting.

In any case, China's rise inevitably distorts the relationship. One of the many reasons why the ultra-nationalist Liberal Democratic Party of Russia tends to do well in the Russian Far East is that there is a sense that Chinese investment is beginning to come with political as well as economic strings attached. There is also a growing concern within the security apparatus. The FSB, while cooperating with its Chinese counterparts, is becoming more vocal about Beijing's own spying, including cyber-espionage, and publicly trying cases that previously would have been dealt with quietly. What happens when Beijing decides to lean on Moscow to sell technology it would rather not, or grant China contracts it would prefer to assign elsewhere? The fear is not of some sudden and cataclysmic break, but of an accumulation of small irritants as an increasingly confident Beijing begins to treat Russia as the junior partner – what then?

The most immediate problem is what happens if either country finds itself at war with the West. Beijing has indicated that while it supports Moscow's wider concerns with NATO expansion and sympathizes with its position over Crimea, it is not planning to get involved in any conflict over Ukraine (not least, one suspects, because it is also increasingly investing in the country, which is its main supplier of corn). Indeed, it never even acknowledged the 2014 annexation of Crimea. It is unsurprising that, unofficially, Moscow has clearly been less than impressed with Beijing's response to its war in Ukraine. On the other hand, were China and the United States to clash over Taiwan, then Beijing might expect Moscow to provide at least political and intelligence support, if not something more substantial. This would leave the Kremlin in a difficult bind, and anything short of providing the Chinese what they want – which would inevitable only worsen relations with the West – would open up a new and serious rift along a 4,000-kilometre border with a powerful and rapidly arming neighbour. These are uncomfortable thoughts for Russian strategic planners.

29

Ukraine 2022: Putin's Last War?

I was in Kyiv back in 2018, speaking at an event on defence-industrial affairs and using that as an opportunity to hold some side-meetings with military and security types. At one point, I was buttonholed by a Ukrainian special forces officer, in his dress uniform, festooned with medals. He was about 15 centimetres taller than me, and 15 centimetres broader, and no doubt knew 15 different ways to kill me with his bare hands, so I wasn't going anywhere as he proceeded to harangue me as the nearest representative of the West. Why were we so negative, so defeatist? Didn't we realize that in due course Ukraine was going to take back what had been stolen from it, and drive the Russians out? Hadn't we seen what had happened in Croatia in 1995, when in less than four days the Croatians had retaken that fifth of their land that Serbians had occupied, after four years of preparation? That would be nothing to what Ukraine will do, very soon.

Honestly, I thought this was barking mad. More, that it was dangerous, that people like this commando risked picking a fight with a country that was distinctly more powerful than Serbia, and a leader who never forgets a slight and takes evident pleasure in revenge. I absolutely accepted Kyiv's claim to retaking the lands it had lost, but at the time, just couldn't see how it could seriously expect to achieve it by unilateral military action.

And in a way, I was right. Ukraine couldn't do it alone. It would need lots of help from the West, but also from one other person. In 2022, it became clear what Kyiv's secret weapon would be: Vladimir Putin.

DREAMING OF A 'SPECIAL MILITARY OPERATION'

In spring 2021, Russia began building up its forces along the Ukrainian border. Initially, the Western response was relatively relaxed, regarding it as 'heavy metal diplomacy',[1] an attempt to intimidate rather than a prelude to invasion. By winter, though, things were beginning to look less encouraging. Some 140,000 troops had been assembled. More to the point, the 'tail' elements to complement the 'teeth' and which would be required for any serious military intervention were also beginning to be deployed, from fuel bowsers to pontoon bridges. Citing intelligence reports, London and Washington began warning that war was a real possibility, even as most European governments still doubted Moscow would be so reckless.

After all, common sense dictated not invading. Putin was, in effect, winning a bloodless war at the time. The looming presence of Russian troops was scaring investors away from Ukraine, which had lost access to international financial markets. The Kerch Straits between Crimea and mainland Russia, where FSB Border Troops ships had intercepted and seized three Ukrainian navy boats back in November 2018, were also now the focus for undeclared economic warfare. In April 2021, the Russians began imposing a 'soft blockade' on the Azov Sea ports of Mariupol and Berdyansk, delaying and impounding commercial vessels heading through the straits to further tighten the screw on the Ukrainian economy.

Meanwhile, a stream of foreign dignitaries were heading to Moscow to see Putin and try to ease the tensions. All this was putting him just where he wanted to be, at the heart of the geopolitical world. Indeed, behind the scenes, some European governments were even urging Ukraine's President Volodymyr Zelensky to make some concessions to Putin, in the name of peace. In December, he issued demands for 'security guarantees' that would not only impose neutrality and vulnerability onto Ukraine but would also force NATO into making substantial concessions, virtually returning it to the situation before it expanded eastwards in 1997. These were ridiculously ambitious, and probably intended as the start of a haggling process: put crudely, Moscow's ruthlessly effective bargaining strategy is usually to ask for all of the other side's cake, and settle for eating half of it. Nonetheless, while the West rejected the demands in principle, already there were those quietly discussing how big a slice might be enough to satisfy Putin's hunger.

Putin was winning. Were he really the cunning master of three-dimensional geopolitical chess that so many once claimed, he would have milked the situation for all it was worth. Despite the – admittedly always slightly hedged – warnings from the United States and United Kingdom, there seemed no good reason why Putin would break with his usual cautious approach and break a winning streak. To be honest, I must confess that until the beginning of February 2022, I was putting the chance of war as no more than 30–40%.

The problem was that what looked like common sense to outsiders, clearly did not for Putin. For years, he has been living inside an information bubble that has been getting smaller and smaller. As discussed in Chapter 26, he increasingly relies on what he is told by Security Council secretary Nikolai Patrushev and his intelligence chiefs. They, in turn, have learned that to get the president's favour, they need to tell him what he wants to hear, not what he needs to hear.

We can only speculate on Putin's frame of mind during his pandemic lockdown, in an extraordinary biosecurity regime – likely because of underlying health issues, which different accounts have claimed is anything from Parkinson's to cancer – such that most people wanting to meet him had to spend two weeks in a guarded government facility, then pass through a corridor fogged with disinfectant and bathed in germ-killing ultraviolet rays. In his opulent isolation, he brooded on Ukraine and the future, even writing a strange, historically illiterate essay trying to prove that it was really part of Russia.[2] He fulminated that the country was going to become some military outpost for a hostile NATO, while cronies and tame security officers assured him that Ukrainians themselves were restive under an American-dominated government and would welcome liberation. He may even have felt that his personal clock was ticking faster than he had once assumed, that his health gave him less time in which to achieve his ultimate goal of placing himself in the pantheon of Russia's great, state-building heroes. Whatever the reason, he decided to act.

NOT THE GENERALS' WAR

The irony is that the same Western analysts who were sure Russia was indeed going to invade, were also sure that it would win, and win quickly. The consensus seemed to be that after two weeks, while there might well be continuing resistance by guerrillas, the Ukrainian military would be destroyed and the country essentially in Moscow's hands. It didn't quite work out like that.

In part, this was because of the skill and will of the Ukrainians themselves. For eight years, they had been anticipating something of the sort and they had been thinking, planning and training precisely how they could take on the Russians, with defence in depth by motivated Territorial Defence troops, while small, mobile groups of regulars targeted the invaders' lengthening supply lines, to deprive them of the food, fuel and ammunition they needed to fight. From plumbers to professors, Ukrainians took up arms, and President Zelensky, whom many nationalists had been writing off as a 'clown' and a 'lightweight', rose to the challenge with humour and aplomb, becoming a rallying point for his people and a powerful advocate for support in the West.

It is not in any way to diminish the Ukrainians' efforts, though, also to note just how strange the Russians' strategy seemed from the very first. As discussed in Chapter 27, there is a distinct process the military would typically adopt and a clear sense of how they would fight a serious land war, such as the invasion of a country with a population of over 44 million people and more than 200,000 soldiers (before national mobilization). A Combat Management Group (GBU: *Gruppa Boyevovo Upravleniya*) would be set up well ahead of time to coordinate preparations. A force ideally able to concentrate a three to one local military advantage over the defenders would be assembled under a single operational commander. The war would start with a Massed Missile-Aviation Strike (MRAU: *Massirovanny Raketno-Aviatsionny Udar*) to crater every Ukrainian runway, suppress its air defences, break its lines of communications and disrupt and demoralize its troops, combined with devastating cyberattacks. Then, a carefully coordinated combined-arms operation would roll across the border.

Yet what happened on 24 February? The preparatory bombardment was limited and half-hearted, and left Ukraine with an air force and air defence system which could and did contest the skies. It was followed by small-scale assaults, including a landing at Hostomel airport (also known as Antonov airport) outside Kyiv by some several hundred Russian paratroopers who secured the airport, despite heavy resistance. Even reinforced, though, they were soon surrounded and forced to retreat. Although the Russians would later retake the airport for a while, the whole operation seems to have been based on the bizarre assumption that the Ukrainians would scarcely mount any resistance and that a couple of companies of paratroopers could just drive into Kyiv and arrest the government.

There were myriad other signs that this was not war as the General Staff would wage it. There were, by various estimates, three, maybe even five, separate operational commanders in charge of different fronts in the first six weeks of the war. Without any mobilization, the Russians were fielding units at peacetime strengths, and in particular lacked adequate numbers of infantry, so the sight of unsupported tanks being picked off by Ukrainian ambushes became almost a cliché. There were nowhere near enough supplies for a protracted fight – and the GBU whose job it would be to make sure that this was addressed was apparently set up not months in advance, as it should have been under normal General Staff practice, but just a day before the invasion. When reinforcements or new supplies were brought to the warzone, the various field commanders vied for who would get them, with no clear sense of overall operational priorities.

A POLICE ACTION, NOT A WAR

It seems clear that the initial strategy was cooked up by Putin and his inner circle, none of whom had any real military experience, and all of whom believed – or did not dare contradict – his fundamental and fatally flawed assumption that the Ukrainians lacked the spirit to fight. He called the invasion a 'special military operation' rather than a war not just for reasons of spin but also because this was how he was thinking of it. More like a police action: arrest Zelensky and his 'neo-Nazi' government, impose a puppet regime, and spend a week or two putting down any small-scale holdouts and dispersing some protests. Perhaps the western part of the country, across the Dnepr River, would not be willing to accept the new order, but most of Ukraine, in his vision, would quickly fall.

With Belarus already essentially dependent on Russian support since its dictatorial leader Alexander Lukashenko brutally suppressed resistance to his regime, that would mean the three great people of what Putin sees as the 'Russian World' had been gathered back together. Admittedly, the Ukrainians and indeed the Belarusians see themselves rather differently, but to a Russian nationalist such as Putin, this looked like a fitting high-point for his career.

Although clearly toying with invasion for months, Putin appears only to have made the final decision very late. Indeed, many of the commanders themselves only learned that they were invading a few days in advance. Especially telling was an intercepted voice message between Chechen leader Ramzan Kadyrov and one of his cronies, Daniil Martynov, who was commanding the Chechen National Guard contingent there. Martynov was clearly in on the secret and he recounted with glee the consternation – and dismay – of his fellow commanders when they were gathered in the week before the invasion to be told ('with bulging eyes') what was about to happen.[3] They were right to be worried – many of those National Guard units would take serious losses when they were deployed to take on not Ukrainian protesters but front-line troops. As one later wrote angrily on a social media channel used by serving and former National Guard, 'we were just thrown into the meatgrinder as cannon-fodder'. His unit, OMON primarily trained for crowd control and small-scale urban operations, was deployed near Kharkiv in light trucks. It was targeted by Ukrainian 122mm artillery and then engaged at extreme range by Ukrainian tanks, when all they had were RPG-29 *Vampir* rocket launchers, whose 800-metre range simply couldn't reach their tormentors. No wonder he was angry – and there have been numerous such expressions of anger from soldiers and security troops alike.

FROM KYIV TO THE DONBAS

At first, the Russians were clearly expecting to make rapid advances on all fronts. From Russian and Belarusian soil, forces moved against Kyiv in the north. From the Donbas 'people's republics' and Russia, columns drove towards Ukraine's second city, Kharkiv in the north-east, as well as along the coast of the Azov Sea in the south-east. Their goals seemed to be to encircle the Ukrainians of the Joint Forces Operation, who were dug in along the Donbas front, and to connect with the battalions pouring in from Crimea, which were heading both east towards Mariupol and west, aiming to take the major port of Odessa. Meanwhile, naval forces blockaded the Black Sea coast and positioned themselves to support a potential assault on Odessa.

Instead of concentrating, they spread themselves too thin, in operations which were inadequately prepared and conducted by soldiers who had not been expecting to be at war. The drive on Kyiv stalled, with a 65-kilometre-long convoy of some 15,000 troops getting bogged down some 20 kilometres outside city limits, mired not just by Ukrainian hit-and-run attacks with Bayraktar TB2 drones and teams using powerful Javelin and NLAW anti-tank missiles supplied by the United States and Britain, respectively, but also by disorganization, breakdowns and a shortage of fuel. By mid-March, the convoy was dispersing, and it soon became clear that Moscow had abandoned its hope of taking the increasingly well-defended capital. By the end of the month, all Russian forces had departed the Kyiv region. As they withdrew, they left evidence of truly horrific atrocities they had visited on civilian populations, most notoriously in the town of Bucha, where it has been alleged that more than 400 were executed, including children.[4]

With the abandonment of the Kyiv salient, Russian forces consolidated in the east, apparently hoping at least to secure the Donbas region and the 'land bridge' to Crimea. Although the battle for Kharkiv was touch and go, by late May, the city seemed firmly back in government hands, and although the Russians have made gains in the Donetsk and Lugansk regions, dogged resistance has meant that progress has been slow. At best, the Russians are taking one step back for every two forward. By mid-May, their offensive was making slow but real progress, even if only of one or two kilometres per day, but it looked unlikely this could be sustained into the summer. Already by then, supplies of precision munitions seemed to be running low – the Russians had even pressed anti-shipping missiles into service for strikes against land targets – and despite desperate efforts to recruit new *kontraktniki*, not least offering conscripts substantial bonuses to volunteer at the end of their draft terms, they were having trouble replenishing units mauled in the fighting.

The only real progress had been in the south. While an early move towards Odessa had been foiled, forces from Crimea did manage quickly to take Kherson and the North Crimean Canal, reopening water supplies for the peninsula – blocked since 2014 – and moved east, meeting the forces from the Donbas at the port city of Mariupol. This became the site of an apocalyptic siege that left the city in ruins, and a relative handful of defenders left bunkered in the massive Azovstal Iron and

Steel Works, an industrial complex that was also built to be a nuclear shelter. They managed to hold out for weeks before finally having to surrender in May. Nonetheless, this did mean that Russia finally did get its 'Crimean Corridor' along the northern coast of the Azov Sea, connecting the peninsula to the Russian mainland.

On 8 April, it was announced that Col. Gen. Alexander Dvornikov, the commander of the Southern VO and the first head of the Syrian deployment, was being put in overall charge of the invasion (something which, by standard Russian practice, ought to have been done before the operation even started). Certainly, there was growing evidence that the generals were being given more scope to fight the war their way. Already by then, though, their forces were heavily depleted and exhausted, weapons were flowing into Ukraine from a West that was also launching an unprecedented economic war on Russia, and the invaders were still trying to fight along a 500-kilometre front against a force that, with mobilization, was by then numerically equal to or even greater than their own. Nonetheless, there was a clear sense of greater realism and professionalism on the ground, even if from a pretty low base. The war became increasingly one of artillery, an area in which the Russians continue to have the advantage – at least until enough Western guns and counter-battery systems can be deployed – and of slow, methodical progress rather than over-ambitious gambits.

Perhaps more crucially, the goal seemed to be to secure a defensible front line before the offensive 'culminated', in military jargon – in other words, ran out of steam. Then, Dvornikov's hope seemed to be that they could dig in and let the Ukrainians try to push them back, giving the Russians the advantage of being the defender. This seems as of writing a plausible strategy, if not guaranteed to succeed. Yet it was clearly worlds apart from Putin's original vision of taking all or most of Ukraine, and in a fortnight, at that, and was also a recipe for an inconclusive war that could drag on for a long time indeed.

HOW HUBRIS DESTROYED A MILITARY

Clearly, there were deep underlying flaws within the Russian military machine, from indiscipline and corruption to a continued neglect of basic maintenance. Under-strength units could not provide proper infantry support for tanks which were then vulnerable to Ukrainian missiles. Soldiers had clearly not been adequately trained for urban warfare and time and again fell prey to ambushes. Cheap Chinese tyres, apparently bought instead of heavy-duty military ones as part of a procurement scam, ripped and burst. Badly made or ageing bombs simply failed to explode on impact. Finding their field ration packs long out of date, soldiers resorted to looting homes and shops instead, something that encouraged a wider culture of banditry. The new Military Police, meant precisely to bring a degree of discipline and oversight to an army often lacking in both, have scarcely been seen, whether in preventing massacres at Bucha or in stopping the looting widespread amongst Russian forces.

However, the generals were not unaware of many of these fundamental problems and had created structures and strategies designed to offset them – but only when they had the time and authority to apply them. By forcing the generals to fight a powerful enemy without proper preparation, without adequate logistics, and to a strategy based on political prejudice rather than the facts on the ground, Putin ensured that none of these could be applied. Besides, the General Staff had presumed that any major land war such as this would be fought with forces bulked out with at least a partial mobilization not, as here, at peacetime strength.

It is impossible to overstate just how devastating the impact has been. Arguably, 20 years of high-spending military reform was wasted in 20 days. As of early June, although the exact figures are unclear, it was undeniable that the Russians had suffered more than 15,000 'Cargo 200s' – in other words, more men than the Soviets lost in ten years of fighting in Afghanistan. If the usual ratios of war apply, that suggests also at least 45,000 wounded. Many of these have been their best, too: the invasion was largely carried out by *kontraktniki*, and those from the VDV and *Spetsnaz*, at that. The army had also lost huge amounts of the most modern (and expensive) kit, including more than 800 tanks in two-and-a-half months of fighting, not least the latest T-90M *Proryv* ('Breakthrough'). It is worth noting that the fabled T-14 *Armata* had not yet been seen there – it was not just that there were still so few in service, but it may well also be that Moscow wanted to avoid the embarrassment of having any of them knocked out, too. Of the tanks lost, though, almost half were abandoned or captured, and the spectacle of Ukrainian farmers towing Russian tanks away with their tractors even became something of a meme of the war. Abandoned vehicles reflected the way morale and discipline had plummeted, with reported cases of desertion, open refusals to go to Ukraine, and covert resistance, with soldiers emptying their vehicles' fuel tanks to give them an excuse for not heading to the front.

In the air, an inexplicable failure to target Ukraine's air defences meant that the Russians were having to be cautious in their own use of their numerical superiority and were also still experiencing attacks from above themselves. In the first three months, they lost an estimated 200 aircraft. At sea, over-confidence meant that the *Moskva*, flagship of the Black Sea Fleet, was sunk by anti-shipping missiles in a particularly humiliating blow. Instead, the Russians had to rely on long-range missiles such as *Iskanders* and *Kalibrs* to punish and hammer Ukraine, especially the west of the country – there seemed a reluctance to send aircraft too close to NATO's borders – yet stocks of those already seemed to be running low. Thanks to Western sanctions affecting access to advanced electronics, it will be harder than ever to replace these precision-guided systems, which were meant to be the future of 'non-contact warfare'.

There is, admittedly, a Russian tradition of 'front-line generalling', but even so the degree to which generals had been forced out of their rear-area headquarters to get a sense of the situation on the ground or personally solve problems also left them vulnerable. Not least thanks to electronic interception – their new Era security communications system seems not to work in the absence of 3G and 4G signals, forcing them to use insecure means – the Ukrainians made something of a habit of killing Russian generals, with perhaps a dozen killed in three months. There were even rumours that Chief of the General Staff Gerasimov was wounded when he visited Izyum in the Kharviv region at the end of April to see the situation on the ground for himself.

DEADLOCK

As of writing, at the beginning of June, even if Putin acknowledges that this 'special military operation' is truly a war and orders a partial or full mobilization of his reserves, it seems hard to see him being able to take and hold all of the Donbas, let alone anything more. That move would be politically dangerous, generating an inevitable backlash at home in a population still being told that this is a limited conflict. Already, tens of thousands of Russians have been arrested for protesting against the war, and there has been a spate of firebombings of local draft offices. Furthermore, although in theory there are more than a million Russians on the reserve lists, the military would have serious trouble mustering, training, arming and deploying more than 100,000–150,000 men, and that would take some three months from any decision being made. Although they would largely be disgruntled, unfit, badly trained and poorly equipped – in May, 1960s-vintage T-62s were already being taken out of warehouses and sent to the war – there is no doubt that this many fresh troops would make a difference on the battlefield. However, they would also take heavy losses, and hence Putin continues, as of writing, to dither.

It is even possible that, as that Ukrainian special forces officer dreamed, Ukraine will be able militarily to take back its lost territories. Yet the Russian military's current problems with manpower stem from the fact that it is still fielding a peacetime army against a fully mobilized Ukraine. While Kyiv is essentially at full stretch, Moscow still has options as Russia has more than three times the population, and resources still untapped. Although it is difficult to regain momentum lost at the outset, it would be a mistake to write the Russians off too soon. It seems more likely that the result will be a long, ugly deadlock: neither side is strong enough to win, neither side weak enough to lose. Prediction is always dangerous, maybe even foolhardy, but assuming the Ukrainian will to fight continues (which seems certain) along with Western will to support Kyiv (which is more unclear, but appears in the main likely), then the real question is how long and at what cost will Moscow be willing to continue this futile and self-destructive campaign.

Putin may never be able to bring himself to admit defeat, lest that become his final, defining act as leader. He has tried to spin the failure of his initial plan as being the fault of NATO and reframed it in his 9 May Victory Day speech as a 'pre-emptive attack against aggression', a response to Western attempts to use Ukraine as a proxy force against Russia.[5] He is using it as an opportunity for a final crackdown on the last vestiges of opposition activism and independent media – even calling this 'special military operation' a 'war' could land someone in prison, conceivably for up to 15 years – and is looking for anything that can be presented as victories. The Donetsk People's Republic and Lugansk People's Republic may be annexed into Russia, and even South Ossetia and Abkhazia in Georgia. A new 'Kherson People's Republic' might be established in conquered southern Ukraine, and all this proclaimed as proof of Moscow's success and these subject regions' eagerness to join the embrace of the Motherland.

Yet apart from being internationally illegitimate, even these 'triumphs' will come with massive price tags. The more territory the Russians have to hold – in some cases against growing guerrilla resistance – the more demands on already-overstretched forces. Also, not only will these regions have to be incorporated into the Russian administrative system, but war-shattered cities will have to be rebuilt by a treasury already facing the costs of both war and sanctions. Although no one can really predict this with any accuracy, the Russian economy might shrink by as much as a quarter in 2022 alone, so whatever is spent on Mariupol or Kherson cannot be spent on Moscow or Kaliningrad, or in supporting Russians now facing unemployment, rising food prices and international isolation.

Having paralleled himself with historical figures such as Peter the Great, Putin risks actually looking more like Nicholas II, the last tsar, who thought the First World War was a chance to relegitimize himself and his regime, and found himself leading his country in a war it could not win. In the process he doomed himself and his dynasty. Maybe the tough decisions to end this war will end up having to be made by his successor, whoever and whenever that may be.

30

Conclusions: The Eurasian Sparta?

In 2016, Park Patriot was opened in Kubinka, west of Moscow, next to the country's main tank testing ground (where the finals of the Army Games discussed in Chapter 1 are held). Technically the Patriot Military Patriotic Park of Culture and Rest of the Armed Forces of the Russian Federation, this is 19 square kilometres of what has been called a 'military Disneyland'. It is a frankly amazing example of Sergei Shoigu's campaign to connect the armed forces to wider society. There are row upon row of tanks, aircraft and military vehicles of every kind, more than 600 of them, including ICBMs and a submarine. There is the Partisan Village, recreating the resistance of the Great Patriotic War. There is the Military Tactical Games Centre, where the whole family can don goggles and go play lasertag urban warfare – soon there will even be a replica of the Reichstag to storm, as if in Berlin in 1945. There are proper shooting ranges, tank and ship simulators, a canteen serving up military rations, huge displays devoted to the Syrian intervention and, since 2020, even the soaring Main Cathedral of the Armed Forces. Gold domes top khaki-coloured towers, and stained-glass mosaics in the vault recreate Red Army decorations and show angels looking down on Russian soldiers by a list of their feats, including 'bringing peace to Georgia' in 2008 and 'fighting against international terrorism' in Syria. The floor itself is metal, made of melted German weapons and tanks, trophies of the Great Patriotic War. I could go on.

Until Ukraine, it was easy to take Putin's Russia at face value, as a militarized society supporting a confident, hard-hitting global warfighter of a nation. There is the organized but undoubtedly popular ritual of Victory Day, cars sport 'To Berlin!' stickers, and half-way down the tourist-trap Arbat Street in Moscow is a huge mural, covering the whole side of a building, of Marshal Zhukov, hero of the Great Patriotic War. Earnest gaggles of *Yunarmiya* – 'Youth Army' – members, teenagers in tan uniforms and bright red berets, are a fixture at patriotic events. The Volunteer Society for Cooperation with the Army, Aviation, and Navy (DOSAAF: *Dobrovolnoye Obshchestvo Sodeistviya Armii, Aviatsii i Floty*), a revived hold-over from Soviet times, provides a wide range of courses and training deemed of value in military service for young men and women, from shooting to orienteering, parachute jumping to radio-electronics. Tens of thousands of young Russians thus enter the military already with some basic training. Even if you don't watch the Defence Ministry's own *Zvezda* TV station, there's a rich diet of war films, more modern tales of martial or espionage derring-do, news stories extolling new weapons or the latest exercises, and a distinctively Russian kind of evening geopolitical talk show that is closer to gladiatorial entertainment than serious analysis, shouty pundits competing to spin some more elaborately paranoid conspiracy theory about the West than the next.

Sometimes, though, volume is a product of inner insecurity, not confidence. Even before its lacklustre performance in Ukraine, one could seriously question whether Russia really was some new, 21st-century Sparta, and how far it was going to be able to assert a true and lasting claim to great power status on the back of its apparent military capabilities and its evident willingness to use them. If anything, the Kremlin let itself be seduced by all this theatre and not only over-rated its capacities when it came to Ukraine, but also failed to appreciate how far the old metrics of power – numbers of men, tanks and aircraft, how well they marched through Red Square – would mean less and less in a new age of precision munitions, space forces, 'mosaic war', quantum computing and artificial intelligence.

A NATION UNDER ARMS?

The war against Ukraine certainly demonstrated that there was an imbalance between the Kremlin's military ambitions and the peacetime forces it could readily muster. There is a line of argument that suggests this will only get worse and that Russia and its military will soon hit a serious demographic challenge – simply put, not enough young men. Even before the collapse of the USSR, Russia was going through a demographic crisis, with high death rates (especially due to poor healthcare and a serious alcohol problem), which only worsened in the 1990s, and although the situation has since improved, the impact will be lasting. A United Nations report, for example, found that while there would be a projected 14.25 million men aged 20–34 in Russia in 2020, that would have declined to 11.55 by 2025 and would continue to fall through to the 2030s, when it would again pick up. The implication is a 20% decrease in the number of eligible, conscript-age young men through the 2020s, even before COVID-19 hit. As if this were not enough of a headache, ethnic Russians have relatively fewer children, and a growing proportion of these young men come from the culturally Muslim south, the North Caucasus – the source also of the worst potential internal problems.

Given that the Kremlin is still committed both to maintaining armed forces of the current size – which requires conscription – and also to attracting and retaining *kontraktniki*, this raises all kinds of difficult policy dilemmas. Raise salaries further to make an army career more attractive? Possible, but expensive. Extend national service back to two years? That would make some military sense, but it would be politically very unpopular. There have been other initiatives, from recruiting more women (there are currently around 45,000 in the ranks, all volunteers), to moves to clean up the *voyenkomaty*, the draft boards, which used to be notoriously corrupt, allowing people to bribe their way out of service, but these only nibble at the corners of the problem.

This is, however, overblown. Draft-dodging has been falling (although the prospect of fighting in Ukraine may well send it back up), and although the military still struggles to get as many *kontraktniki* as it would like, in many ways it has done surprisingly well. (Besides, if Russia ever does annex the Donbas, there is another boost for the population.) Furthermore, the long-dilapidated reserve system which allows former conscripts and volunteers to be called back to arms – and ensures they have been getting regular training sessions to maintain at least some fighting form – has been the focus of considerable attention. By 2022, it was estimated that at least 100,000 reservists could be called up through the new National Army Combat Reserve (BARS: *Boyevoy Armeysky Rezerv Strany*) system, only set up the year before, which offers small stipends in return for participation. Even without a formal national mobilization, the BARS system has already been activated in spring 2022 to try to replenish the depleted battalion tactical groups in Ukraine, which will be a case study in its effectiveness, although tales of outright refusals to serve soon emerged.

THE MILITARY MYTH?

The willingness of young Russian men (and women) to serve depends on the willingness of the authorities to prosecute draft-dodgers, which they do, and on the salaries and benefits available to *kontraktniki*, but also on the degree to which they regard service in the armed forces as a valuable and honourable calling. In late Soviet times, this was a growing challenge, with those who could escape conscription by corruption or contacts doing so. The tales of horror and hardship filtering back from Afghanistan only exacerbated an existing aversion, as did increasing candour about indiscipline, abuse and bullying in the ranks.

Military service under Putin retained its dark corners and unnecessary hardships. That distinctively Russian form of violent and abusive hazing, *dedovshchina*, remains widely prevalent; according to the newspaper *Novaya Gazeta*, there were nearly 4,000 military court prosecutions in the period 2016–20.[1] There are also periodic cases of alcoholic indiscipline, like the soldier who, while drunk, thought he would borrow a BMP-2 infantry fighting vehicle to go and buy cigarettes. He managed to drive it into a ditch and so he returned to the training ground to liberate another BMP-2 in order to tow it out. However, he had neglected to power the first vehicle down properly, and so in the meantime, it caught fire. He ended up causing more than 1.8 million rubles in damage.[2]

There has been a campaign, especially under Shoigu, to burnish the reputation of the military and increase the appeal of military life. There are officially a quarter of a million in the *Yunarmiya* youth movement and more than 100,000 a year take part in some activity or another, from ceremonial guard duty at Great Patriotic War memorials to sports events. Even more striking has been the alliance between the Defence Ministry and the Russian Orthodox Church. As the Great

Patriotic War increasingly becomes an almost religious event, central to the new Russian state's identity, so too state, church and military have become intertwined. Some religious figures are uncomfortable with this, but Patriarch Kirill and the rest of the top hierarchy either genuinely support this alliance or accept it as politically unavoidable. Military chaplains were revived back in 2009 (not all Orthodox: there are also a few rabbis and imams), although the church drew the line at camouflage cassocks. Priests bless tanks and missiles, and while in 2020 Kirill instructed them not to consecrate nuclear weapons, *Borei*-class ballistic missile submarines do have a tiny chapel (and a small *banya*, or sauna, but that's another matter).

All this had an impact. Sergei Shoigu was consistently second only to Putin in public recognition and trust, and public attitudes towards the military as a whole definitely improved: as an institution, they polled second only to the presidency, above even the church.[3] However, Shoigu was popular and respected even before he became Defence Minister, and attitudes towards the military may have improved, but only from a frankly appalling low. Only 18.4% of Moscow students polled in 2020 believed that military service was a 'promising' field, a figure well below new technology (49.7%) and law (29%), but nonetheless in the middle of the range, above healthcare (12.8%), for example, and well above the arts (8.9%).[4] In any case, this was all before the invasion of Ukraine. Although the immediate response has been the predictable urge to rally round the flag, encouraged by strident state propaganda, as the realities of the war and news of the abuses carried out by Russian soldiers begin to become more widely known, it is likely the military's reputation will face the same kind of slump that its Soviet counterpart experienced after the war in Afghanistan. 'Cargo 200' casualties tend quickly to change the public mood.

THE SECURITY STATE?

Besides, respect for the military does not necessarily translate into support for the regime, let alone its militarized foreign policy. A growing mood of disenchantment and even active protest ever since Putin returned to the presidency in 2012, despite the temporary boost in his ratings following the annexation of Crimea, has led to a commensurate dependence on repression and the security apparatus. As well as a greater use of the FSB and the separate Investigative Committee (SK: *Sledstvenny Komitet*), both of which have increasingly sought to police not just what Russians do, but what they say and think, this has also resulted in an increased emphasis on paramilitary domestic security forces that could also play a role outside Russia's borders.

First and foremost, this means the National Guard, also called the *Rosgvardiya* as a contraction of its full name, the Federal Service of the Troops of the National Guard of the Russian Federation (FSVNG RF: *Federalnaya Sluzhba Voisk Natsionalnoi Gvardii Rossiiskoi Federatsii*). This is not a reserve military force like its American counterpart, but a militarized internal security and public order force. Although the idea of establishing such a force had been mooted in the 1990s and 2000s, it was only in 2016 that it was actually created. This was essentially a bureaucratic and political manoeuvre. Existing forces that until then had been subordinated to the Ministry of Internal Affairs (MVD: *Ministerstvo Vnutrennykh Del*) were transferred to an all-new agency, headed by Gen. Viktor Zolotov, the former head of Putin's personal protection detail and a loyalist with a reputation for brutal zeal. The forces which make up the *Rosgvardiya* are the Interior Troops, the OMON riot police and the police Special Rapid Response Detachments (SOBR: *Spetsialny Otryad Bystrovo Reagirovaniya*), as well as the state corporation FGUP Okhrana, the country's largest provider of private security. The reason for their resubordination to a new agency appears precisely to have been that the regular police who ran the MVD were increasingly disenchanted with playing the role of state stormtroopers. Putin wanted to be sure that if he did have to rely on mass repression, the relevant forces were in the hands of a man who would obey orders without question (or too much concern for the niceties of the law and constitution).

The Interior Troops (VV: *Vnutrenniye Voiska*) number around 170,000, of whom perhaps half are essentially static security personnel guarding everything from prisons to closed cities, but the other half, the so-called Operational Designation units, are mobile, light mechanized security forces. Most are organized into brigades or smaller elements, but the showcase force is the elite Moscow-based 1st Independent Operational Designation Division, still widely known as the 'Dzerzhinsky Division' since Soviet times. It has a strength of 15,000, with three mechanized regiments equipped with tanks and artillery, and the 604th Special Purpose Centre, a special forces unit formed in 2008 by combining two existing commando teams, *Vityaz* and *Rus*. Then, as well as the roughly 32,000 OMON riot police, there are also some 6,000 SOBR officers.

In Chechnya, the VV played a major part in both security and front-line roles, and in Syria it appears that many of the 'Military Police' present may actually be Interior Troops, drawn disproportionately from Chechnya and other North Caucasus nationalities. They are not trained or equipped for full-scale mechanized warfare of the sort they found themselves pitched into in Ukraine, though. They have suffered terrible losses there, and chatter on their social media fora suggests a growing anger at being used, as they put it, as 'cannon-fodder'. In one high-profile case, 12 National Guardsmen from Krasnodar flatly refused to go to Ukraine, and were sacked – and they then took their commanders to court. Who knows how many less public cases there are, how many officers are simply resigning rather than be fed into the meatgrinder? It may well prove to have been a political blunder for the Kremlin to allow its Praetorian Guard to be so alienated.

A WEAK HAND PLAYED WELL?

His tight personal control over the security apparatus is only one of the reasons for Putin's continued and seemingly incontestable grip on power, but an important one. For so long, the conventional truism was that he was 'playing a weak hand well'. Russia cannot even think of matching the United States in the old games of global status. US naval power, airpower, soft power and economic power may all be losing their hyperdominance, especially in the face of a rising China, but they are still well beyond Russia's capacity to match – trying to keep up bankrupted even the old Soviet Union. However, like good 'geopolitical guerrillas', the Russians instead sought to move the contest into new domains and develop new tools. This style of 'political war' may not have allowed Putin to define the new global order, but did give him disproportionate influence over his neighbourhood and forced the West to address the issues he wanted to discuss.

Yet Putin likely misunderstood how far this was not because of Russian strength but the product of a particular moment. In the late 2010s and early 2020s, there were transatlantic and intra-European tensions, the COVID crisis created new economic and social pressures, and the United States was still seeking to pivot to Asia. The invasion of Ukraine managed in one fell swoop to unite the West (at least for a while), galvanize NATO (and win it new members Sweden and Finland), remind Washington why Europe mattered, and undermine the freedom of manoeuvre on which Putin's 'political war' games relied.

Furthermore, while Russia had managed to gain a temporary advantage in some technologies such as hypersonic weapons, technological advantages tend to shrink as rivals catch up or new developments supersede them. Artificial intelligence, which could dramatically shorten the 'kill-chain' from spotting a target to destroying it, and manage much more complex drone swarms. Quantum computing, which could so outperform the regular kind that any encryption could be broken and any communications intercepted. Additive manufacturing systems that could 3d print ammunition and equipment wherever and whenever needed in the field. All kinds of science fictional breakthroughs await, and even before sanctions, it was hard to see Russia being able to catch up, let alone keep up. While it has come to value the drone, and is working on all kinds of new projects, from individual exoskeletons to allow soldiers to carry heavy loads at speed, to ground-based autonomous robots for front-line resupply, guard and combat duties, these do not represent the kind of fundamental breakthroughs that could again reshape war.

Besides, does it have the flexibility, redundancy and seamless command and control needed to respond to such potential future threats as 'mosaic warfare'? This is a warfighting approach being discussed in US military circles that seeks to overwhelm and disorganize the enemy by confronting it with a large, asymmetric and varied range of threats, all operating in their own distinctive way, like separate tiles in a mosaic. Instead of the most exquisitely capable systems, it puts the focus back on the small, the agile, the fluid, and the scalable: better many and innovative platforms that all have their own advantages. For every ridiculously expensive F-35 jet, for example, maybe the US will also deploy a half-dozen drones with different characteristics and weapons, creating a confusingly complex combat environment. Is the Russian High Command of the future up to this very different kind of warfighting, and comfortable with being the one on the receiving end of theoretical innovation?

Nor will Russia's armed forces be able to retain what appeared to be their advantage in Europe after Ukraine. They had benefited from Putin's commitment to spending heavily on rearmament and the High Command's refusal to lose sight of a focus on 'big wars'. With the war in Ukraine and consequent economic stagnation, it will not be able to spend in the same way, and the West has also rediscovered the 'big war'. Western leaderships had been reluctant to give up the 'peace dividend' brought by the end of the Cold War – as late as 2021, 19 of NATO's 29 members did not meet the common minimum level of defence spending, 2% of GDP – and military attention had shifted to 'small wars', intervention operations in the Middle East or Africa, where mobility, flexibility and hearts and minds operations were more important than mass, and where the enemy would not have airpower, armour or the rest of the panoply of a peer adversary.

That was beginning to change even before Ukraine, though. In 2011, for example, a cost-cutting Dutch army retired all its tanks. Later, it realized the mistake and made a deal with Germany that at least allowed it to form a squadron of 18 modern Leopard 2A7 tanks, with mixed Dutch and German crews. As for the UK, after some debate in which it looked as if it too might abandon the tank – far too heavy and temperamental for 'small wars', but invaluable in big ones – in 2021 it decided to upgrade 148 of its ageing Challenger 2 tanks to Challenger 3 standard. It is easy to say that this is too few, but nonetheless, the return in fashion of heavy metal was a sign of a changing attitude towards the kinds of threats NATO may face.

AFTER PUTIN?

Having in many ways pioneered the use of asymmetric and deniable forms of warfare to complement the regular, Russia faces a real question as to how far it can handle more unconventional threats itself. Ukraine is outfighting it in the information war, and even its internal security forces cannot stop a domestic campaign of anti-war subversion. The war means more and more casualties coming home, and although the Kremlin has now squeezed out the last independent journalistic outlets, it cannot hide these for ever, especially in an age of social media. It also means inflation, unemployment and shortages thanks to

Western sanctions. These two sources of grievance could combine in unpredictable and dangerous ways.

By the time this book comes out, Putin will be 70. Although constitutionally he can rule until 2036, when he would be 83, there are reasons to believe that he is getting tired of the position and its demands and, indeed, may be seriously ill. For that matter, his whole security elite is beginning to show its age. Security Council secretary Nikolai Patrushev will be 71, along with FSB director Alexander Bortnikov. Foreign Intelligence Service director Sergei Naryshkin will be 68. While both Shoigu and Gerasimov will be just 67, neither is looking especially comfortable as reverse after reverse happens in Ukraine.

One way or another, there will eventually be a political transition, and a new generation of political and military leaders will rise. While they will not necessarily be any less nationalistic, unlike their seniors they are not shaped by the trauma of the collapse of Soviet power and the dramatic reversal in their country's fortunes. They appear to be more pragmatic, less emotional in their attitudes towards the West, and more aware of the potential challenge of a rising China. They will also have had an object lesson in what happens if the Kremlin over-reaches and see less advantage in confrontation. Besides, even if Russia is not a real democracy, they will have to consider the views and tolerance of their public.

Since 2014, Putin has been pushing a legitimating narrative predicated on the need to force the rest of the world to accept Russia's status as a great power, whatever the cost in blood and treasure. However, polls conducted by the Levada Centre, the most respected independent public opinion company in Russia, found that when asked in 2021 what kind of country Russia should be, 66% said 'a country with a high standard of living, though not one of the strongest countries in the world'. Only 32% replied 'a great power that other countries respect and fear'. Furthermore, the proportion for whom quality of life is more important than national status has been growing ever since 2015.[5]

Of course, the immediate context of the Ukraine war has muddied the waters. Some feel they must defend their country. Others are afraid to say anything that might get them into trouble. Nonetheless, even as of writing in mid-2022, there is little sense of a genuine national will to sacrifice whatever it takes to build an empire on blood and bayonets. Putin may have believed he was founding a Eurasian Sparta, and he undoubtedly built a military machine able and willing to project his power in both Russia's strategic neighbourhood and beyond. Yet just as that machine foundered in 2022, beaten between the anvil of Ukrainian resistance and the hammer of his own hubris, he may find his dreams for Russia equally broken by reality. Will Russia be able to retain its expeditionary force in Syria? Will it remain the security guarantor of Central Asia? Will it be able to afford to replace all the equipment squandered in Ukraine? Will, in due course, the colonels and the generals, maybe even the spies and secret policemen, themselves turn against Putin, not so much because he sought to break Kyiv to his will, but because he did it so badly?

The story of Putin's presidency has been one of two halves. His first two presidential terms in the 2000s were strikingly successful, but so many of the gains made were wasted or embezzled away in the 2010s and beyond. So too with his military and security record. The Russian army was saved from collapse; Chechnya pacified, however ugly the means; and Moscow again became a power in global affairs. Had he been content with building a strong nation within its own borders rather than chasing fantasies of empire, Putin would likely have been remembered as a successful statebuilder. Instead, for years and perhaps decades, even under his eventual successor, Russia will still be recovering from the damage caused by his overreach. Its military, of course, but also its economy and its society will long bear the deep, painful scars of Putin's wars.

Notes

1 INTRODUCTION

1 Mark Galeotti, 'The International Army Games are Decadent and Depraved', *Foreign Policy*, 24 August 2018.
2 Mark Galeotti, *Kulikovo 1380: The Battle that Made Russia* (Osprey, 2019).
3 Todd Fisher, *The Napoleonic Wars (2)* (Osprey, 2001).
4 John Sweetman, *The Crimean War* (Osprey, 2001).
5 Geoffrey Jukes, *The Russo-Japanese War 1904–1905* (Osprey, 2002).
6 Mark Galeotti, *Storm-333. KGB and Spetsnaz Seize Kabul, Soviet–Afghan War 1979* (Osprey, 2021).
7 Gregory Fremont-Barnes, *The Soviet–Afghan War 1979–89* (Osprey, 2014).
8 Mark Galeotti, *Russia's Wars in Chechnya* (Osprey, 2014).
9 Mark Galeotti, *Armies of Russia's War in Ukraine* (Osprey, 2019).

2 BORN IN CHAOS

1 For studies of the end of the USSR, see Archie Brown, *The Human Factor: Gorbachev, Reagan, and Thatcher, and the End of the Cold War* (OUP, 2020); Mark Galeotti, *The Age of Anxiety* (Routledge, 1995); Serhii Plokhy, *The Last Empire: The Final Days of the Soviet Union* (Oneworld, 2015); Vladislav Zubok, *Collapse: The Fall of the Soviet Union* (Yale, 2021).
2 Yevgenia Albats, *The State Within a State* (1994), pp 276–77.
3 *Argumenty i fakty*, 5 May 2018.

3 A MILITARY IN CRISIS

1 *Moskovsky Komsomolets*, 20 June 1994.
2 *Moskovsky Komsomolets*, 16 October 2019.

3 Benjamin Lambeth, 'Russia's Wounded Military', *Foreign Affairs*, v. 74, no. 2 (1995).
4 Interfax, 7 September 1995.
5 *Trud*, 15 March 2001.
6 BBC, 18 October 1999.
7 Patriot, September 2007.

4 THE FIRST CHECHEN WAR

1 Parts of this chapter are adapted from the author's *Russia's Wars in Chechnya 1994–2009* (Osprey, 2014); for other good studies, see Arkady Babchenko, *One Soldier's War* (Grove, 2009); Dodge Billingsley, *Fangs of the Lone Wolf: Chechen Tactics in the Russian–Chechen Wars 1994–2009* (Helion, 2013); Anatol Lieven, *Chechnya: Tombstone of Russian Power* (Yale, 1998).
2 NTV, 11 August 1994.
3 *Svobodnaya Pressa*, 29 December 2009.
4 Yevgeny Fedosov, *Polveka v Aviatsii: zapiski akademika* (Drofa, 2004), p. 387.
5 Andrei Antipov, *Lev Rokhlin: Zhizn i smert generala* (Eksmo, 1998).

5 THE WARS OF RUSSIAN ASSERTION

1 Alexander Volkov, *Lev Rokhlin. Istoriya odnogo ubiistva* (Algorithm, 2012), p. 57.
2 Pavel Felgenhauer, 'Russian Military Reform: Ten Years of Failure', Proceedings of a Conference held at the Naval Postgraduate School on 26–27 March 1997.
3 'Presidential Address to the Federal Assembly', 25 April 2005.
4 *Japan Times*, 8 October 2001.
5 'NATO Expansion – The Budapest Blow Up 1994', US National Security Archive, 21 November 2021.
6 BBC, 9 March 2000.

6 PUTIN'S PRIORITIES

1 For studies of Putin, see Mark Galeotti, *We Need to Talk About Putin* (Ebury, 2020); Fiona Hill & Clifford Gaddy, *Mr. Putin: Operative in the Kremlin* (Brookings, 2015); Mikhail Zygar, *All the Kremlin's Men: Inside the Court of Vladimir Putin* (PublicAffairs, 2017).
2 'Vystuplenie na tseremonii vstupleniya v dolzhnost' Prezidenta Rossii', Kremlin.ru, 7 May 2000, http://kremlin.ru/events/president/transcripts/21399.

3 Interfax, 16 August 1999.
4 'Interview with David Frost', BBC, 5 March 2000.
5 *Putin, Russia and the West*, episode 1, BBC, 19 January 2012.
6 'Speech and the Following Discussion at the Munich Conference on Security Policy', Kremlin.ru, 10 February 2007.
7 *Kommersant-Vlast*, 20 October 2008.

7 THE SECOND CHECHEN WAR

1 This chapter draws on Mark Galeotti, *Russia's Wars in Chechnya 1994–2009* (Osprey, 2014).
2 RIA Novosti, 24 September 1999.
3 Lenta.ru, 4 June 2001.
4 Anna Politkovskaya, *A Small Corner of Hell: Dispatches from Chechnya* (University of Chicago Press, 2003).
5 'Address by President Vladimir Putin', Kremlin.ru, 4 September 2004.
6 Pavel Felgenhauer, 'Degradation of the Russian Military: General Anatoli Kvashnin', *Perspective*, v. 15, no. 1 (October–November 2005).
7 Perhaps the best study of the way the Russians learned the lessons of the war (and sometimes failed to) is RAND's *Russia's Chechen Wars 1994–2000: Lessons from Urban Combat* (2001).

8 IVANOV, THE INITIATOR

1 Condoleezza Rice, *No Higher Honour* (Simon & Schuster, 2012).
2 *Nezavisimaya Gazeta*, 26 March 2004.
3 Condoleezza Rice, *No Higher Honour* (Simon & Schuster, 2012).
4 BBC, 15 November 1999.
5 'Yozh v stanakh amerikantsev', *Regnum*, 19 October 2017.
6 *Lenta*, 13 July 2000.
7 *Kommersant-vlast*, 6 February 2007.
8 *Krasnaya Zvezda*, 12 February 2007.
9 'Russia Suspends Participation in CFE Treaty', *RFE/RL*, 12 December 2007.

9 SERDYUKOV, THE ENFORCER

1 NTV, 15 February 2007.
2 In the documentary *Poteryanny den: vsya pravda o Voine 08.08.08g* (2012).
3 *Kommersant*, 4 June 2008.
4 See Steven Zaloga, *T-90 Standard Tank* (Osprey, 2018).
5 Reuters, 16 December 2008.

10 GEORGIA, 2008 (1): TBILISI'S MOVE ...

1 Mtavari TV, 7 May 2021.
2 For good studies of the conflict, see Svante Cornell & S. Frederick Starr, *The Guns of August* (Routledge, 2009); Ruslan Pukhov (ed.), *The Tanks of August* (CAST, 2010).
3 *Kavkaz Uzel*, 2 May 2006.
4 *The Guardian*, 8 November 2007.
5 *Washington Post*, 8 August 2018.

11 GEORGIA, 2008 (2): ... MOSCOW'S COUNTER

1 RIA-Novosti, 12 August 2008.
2 Bloomberg, 12 August 2008.
3 *Gruzya Online*, 28 November 2008.
4 Reuters, 16 December 2008.
5 *Krasnaya Zvezda*, 1 August 2009.
6 *Moskovsky Komsomolets*, 28 August 2008.

13 SHOIGU, THE REBUILDER

1 *The Economist*, 7 November 2015.
2 Johan Norberg, *Training for War* (FOI, 2018).
3 Interfax, 14 January 2013.
4 The line is from 'Borodino' (1837), Lermontov's poem about this epic battle from Napoleon's 1812 invasion of Russia.
5 Interfax, 9 November 2012.
6 Interfax, 9 November 2012.
7 Rostec press release, 26 June 2019.
8 Kremlin.ru, 10 May 2011.
9 Mil.ru, 16 October 2014.

14 CRIMEA, 2014

1 This chapter draws on and develops text from Mark Galeotti, *Armies of Russia's War in Ukraine* (Osprey, 2019). Good studies of the annexation include Colby Howard & Ruslan Pukhov (eds), *Brothers Armed* (EastView, 2015) and Michael Kofman et al., *Lessons from Russia's Operations in Crimea and Eastern Ukraine* (RAND, 2017).
2 He was speaking in the documentary *The Path to the Motherland*, BBC, 9 March 2015.
3 *Sputnik*, 8 March 2014.
4 *Sputnik*, 23 December 2021.

15 DONBAS, 2014–

1 This chapter draws on and develops text from Mark Galeotti, *Armies of Russia's War in Ukraine* (Osprey, 2019). For good studies of this emerging conflict, see Anna Arutunyan, *Hybrid Warriors. Proxies, Freelancers and Moscow's Struggle for Ukraine* (Hurst, 2022) and David Marples (ed.), *The War in Ukraine's Donbas: Origins, Contexts, and the Future* (Central European University Press, 2022).

2 *New York Times*, 17 April 2014.

3 Kremlin.ru, 17 December 2015.

16 LESSONS OF THE DONBAS WAR

1 'Tezisy vystupleniya nachal'nika General'nogo shtaba Vooruzhennykh Sil Rossiiskoi Federatsii – pervogo zamestitelya Ministra oborony Rossiiskoi Federatsii generala armii N.E. Makarova', *Vestnik Akademii voennykh nauk*, Vol. 1, No. 26 (2009), p. 21.

2 *Ukrayinska Pravda*, 6 October 2017.

3 International Crisis Group, *Conflict in Ukraine's Donbas: A Visual Explainer* (2021), https://www.crisisgroup.org/content/conflict-ukraines-donbas-visual-explainer.

17 SYRIA, 2015– (1): THE UNEXPECTED INTERVENTION

1 *Komsomolskaya Pravda*, 26 December 2017.

2 *Komsomolskaya Pravda*, 26 December 2017.

3 *Times of Israel*, 18 September 2018.

18 SYRIA, 2015– (2): LESSONS OF THE SYRIAN CAMPAIGN

1 For useful analyses, see Mason Clark, *The Russian Military's Lessons Learned in Syria* (ISW, 2021); Robert Hamilton, Chris Miller & Aaron Stein (eds), *Russia's War in Syria* (FPRI, 2020).

2 For a good overview of the complex financial dealings, see 'Russian mercenary army financier made an oil deal with Syria just before clash with U.S. troops', *The Bell*, 21 February 2018, https://thebell.io/en/russian-mercenary-army-financier-made-oil-deal-syria-just-clash-u-s-troops/.

3 'The Circle of Hell: Barrel bombs in Aleppo, Syria', *Amnesty International*, 18 May 2020.

4 CNN, 16 December 2016.

5 *Kommersant*, 2 July 2018.

6 Pavel Baev, 'The Interplay of Bureaucratic, Warfighting, and Arms-Parading Traits in Russian Military-Strategic Culture', *Marshall Center Security Insights*, April 2019.

19 RUMBLE FOR RUBLE

1 TASS, 1 October 2019.
2 UK National Statistics, *MOD Departmental Resources 2020*, 10 December 2020.
3 Michael Kofman & Richard Connolly, 'Why Russian Military Expenditure is Much Higher than Commonly Understood (As Is China's)', *War On The Rocks*, 16 December 2019.
4 'Trends in International Arms Transfers, 2020', *SIPRI Fact Sheet*, March 2021.
5 Riafan.ru, 21 December 2020.
6 Alexander Golts, 'Skol'ko stoit khvastovsko Shoigu', Republic.ru, 19 July 2021.
7 'Osnashchenie sovremennymi obraztsami vooruzheniya, voennoi i spetsial'noi tekhniki', Mil.ru, n/d.
8 *Voyenno-Promyshlenny Kuryer*, 15 March 2017.

20 *ARMIYA ROSSII*

1 *Defense News*, 7 April 2016.
2 Alex Vershinin, 'Feeding the Bear: A Closer Look at Russian Army Logistics and the Fait Accompli', *War On The Rocks*, 23 November 2021.
3 Beth Connable, et al., *Russia's Limit of Advance* (RAND, 2020).
4 Mark Galeotti, 'Heavy Metal Diplomacy: Russia's Political Use of its Military in Europe Since 2014', *ECFR*, 19 December 2016.

21 THE SKY IS RUSSIA'S!

1 *Moskovsky Komsomolets*, 22 September 2019.
2 Michael Kofman, 'It's Time to Talk About A2/AD: Rethinking the Russian Military Challenge', *War On The Rocks*, 5 September 2019.
3 *Moskovsky Komsomolets*, 22 September 2019.

23 POWER PROJECTION: BLACK AND BLUE BERETS

1 See also David Campbell, *Soviet Airborne Forces 1930–91* (Osprey, 2020).
2 *Moskovsky Komsomolets*, 11 July 2021.
3 See Mark Galeotti, *Combat Vehicles of Russia's Special Forces: Spetsnaz, Airborne, Arctic and Interior Troops* (Osprey, 2020).

24 THE *SPETSNAZ*

1 This chapter draws on Mark Galeotti, *Spetsnaz: Russia's Special Forces* (Osprey, 2015).

2 See Mark Galeotti, *Storm-333: KGB and Spetsnaz Seize Kabul, Soviet–Afghan War 1979* (Osprey, 2021) and Gregory Fremont-Barnes, *The Soviet–Afghan War 1979–89* (Osprey, 2014).
3 RIA Novosti, 6 March 2013.

25 THE NUCLEAR BACKSTOP

1 This and following quotations are from 'Presidential Address to the Federal Assembly', 1 March 2018, Kremlin.ru.
2 RIA Novosti, 19 October 2018.
3 Pavel Baev, 'The Interplay of Bureaucratic, Warfighting, and Arms-Parading Traits in Russian Military-Strategic Culture', *George Marshall Center Strategic Insights,* April 2019.

26 POLITICAL WARFARE

1 'Tsennost Nauki v Predvidenii: Novyye vyzovy trebuyut pereosmyslit formy i sposoby vedeniya boyevykh deystviy', *Voyenno-Promyshlenny Kuryer*, no. 8 (2013).
2 'The "Gerasimov Doctrine" and Russian Non-Linear War', *In Moscow's Shadows*, 6 July 2014, https://inmoscowsshadows .wordpress.com/2014/07/06/the-gerasimov-doctrine-and-russian -non-linear-war/.
3 For other sources on the issues in this chapter, see Mark Galeotti, *Russian Political War* (Routledge, 2019); Oscar Jonsson, *The Russian Understanding of War: Blurring the Lines between War and Peace* (Georgetown, 2019); David Kilcullen, *The Dragon and the Snakes* (Hurst, 2020).
4 *Kommersant*, 22 June 2015.
5 George Kennan, 'The Inauguration of Organized Political Warfare', 4 May 1948, in State Department Office of History online collection, https://history.state.gov/historicaldocuments/frus1945-50Intel/d269.
6 Such as Mark Galeotti, *The Weaponisation of Everything* (Yale, 2022); Seth Jones, *Three Dangerous Men* (WW Norton, 2021); Carl Miller, *The Death of the Gods* (Windmill, 2019).
7 Interfax, 22 February 2018.
8 *Krasnaya Zvezda*, 14 April 2014.

27 NEW GENERATION WARFARE

1 For good studies, see Lester Grau & Charles Bartles, *The Russian Way of War* (FMSO, 2017); Michael Kofman et al., *Russian Military Strategy: Core Tenets and Operational Concepts* (CNA, 2021).

2 Russian *Military Doctrine* (2014), paragraph 8.
3 *Voyenno-Promyshlenny Kuryer*, 11 March 2019.
4 'Na forume 'Armiya-2017' obsudili itogi operatsii Vooruzhennykh Sil Rossii v Siriiskoi Arabskoi Respublike', Mil.ru, 25 August 2017.
5 *Krasnaya Zvezda*, 4 March 2019.
6 Lester W. Grau & Charles K. Bartles, 'The Russian Reconnaissance Fire Complex Comes of Age', *Oxford Changing Character of War Centre*, May 2018.

28 THE CHALLENGES OF THE FUTURE

1 *Financial Times*, 18 October 2021.
2 Reuters, 21 May 2014.

29 UKRAINE 2022: PUTIN'S LAST WAR?

1 See Mark Galeotti, 'Heavy Metal Diplomacy: Russia's Political Use of its Military in Europe since 2014', *ECFR Policy Brief*, 19 December 2016.
2 'On the Historical Unity of Russians and Ukrainians', Kremlin.ru, 12 July 2021.
3 BBC Russian, 26 February 2022.
4 This is, of course, challenged by the Russians, who claim everything from that it was the Ukrainians who committed killings as they retook the town to that the 'dead' were really actors. However, as international investigators dig through the scene, these claims are looking increasingly implausible. See, for example, 'Bucha Killings: Satellite Image of Bodies Site Contradicts Russian Claims', BBC, 11 April 2022; and 'Ukraine: Russian Forces' Trail of Death in Bucha', *Human Rights Watch*, 21 April 2022.
5 'Victory Parade on Red Square', 9 May 2022, Kremlin.ru.

30 CONCLUSIONS: THE EURASIAN SPARTA?

1 *Novaya Gazeta*, 12 October 2021.
2 RIA Novosti, 13 December 2013.
3 'Institutional Trust', *Levada*, 10 November 2016, https://www.levada.ru /en/2016/11/10/institutional-trust-2/.
4 Tatiana Litvinova, Olga Vershinina & Gennady Moskvitin, 'Social and Political Attitudes of Moscow Students on the Background of the All-Russia and Regional Youth Studies', *Social Sciences*, Vol. 9, No. 152 (2020).
5 'Kakoi dolzhna byt Rossiya v predstavlenii rossiyan', *Levada*, 9 October 2021, https://www.levada.ru/2021/09/10/kakoj-dolzhna-byt-rossiya-v -predstavlenii-rossiyan/.

Selected English-language Bibliography

Arutunyan, Anna, *Hybrid Warriors. Proxies, Freelancers and Moscow's Struggle for Ukraine* (Hurst, 2022)

Cooper, Tom, *Moscow's Game of Poker: Russian Military Intervention in Syria, 2015–2017* (Helion, 2018)

Fridman, Ofer (ed.), *Strategiya: The Foundations of the Russian Art of Strategy* (Hurst, 2021)

Galeotti, Mark, *Russian Security and Paramilitary Forces Since 1991* (Osprey, 2013)

Galeotti, Mark, *Russia's Wars in Chechnya 1994–2009* (Osprey, 2014)

Galeotti, Mark, *Spetsnaz. Russia's Special Forces* (Osprey, 2015)

Galeotti, Mark, *The Modern Russian Army, 1992–2016* (Osprey, 2017)

Galeotti, Mark, *Armies of Russia's War in Ukraine* (Osprey, 2019)

Hamilton, Robert, Chris Miller & Aaron Stein (eds), *Russia's War in Syria. Assessing Russian Military Capabilities and Lessons Learned* (FPRI, 2020)

Harvey, Neil, *The Modern Russian Navy*, 2nd edition (Neil Harvey, 2018)

Herd, Graeme, *Understanding Russian Strategic Behavior* (Routledge, 2022)

Herspring, Dale, *The Kremlin and the High Command: Presidential Impact on the Russian Military from Gorbachev to Putin* (University Press of Kansas, 2006)

Howard, Colby & Ruslan Pukhov (eds), *Brothers Armed. Military Aspects of the Crisis in Ukraine*, 2nd edition (EastView, 2015)

Jonsson, Oscar, *The Russian Understanding of War: Blurring the Lines between War and Peace* (Georgetown UP, 2019)

Kanet, Roger (ed.), *Routledge Handbook of Russian Security* (Routledge, 2021)

Kofman, Michael et al., *Lessons from Russia's Operations in Crimea and Eastern Ukraine* (RAND, 2017)

Kofman, Michael et al., *Russian Military Strategy: Core Tenets and Operational Concepts* (CNA, 2021)

McNab, Chris, *The Great Bear at War: The Russian and Soviet Army, 1917–Present* (Osprey, 2019)

Pukhov, Ruslan (ed.), *The Tanks of August* (CAST, 2010)

Renz, Bettina, *Russia's Military Revival* (Polity, 2017)

Sutyagin, Igor & Justin Bronk, *Russia's New Ground Forces* (Routledge, 2017)

Index